A Legal Assessment of the Efficacy of Consultation with Indigenous Peoples

Catarina Woyames Dreher

A Legal Assessment of the Efficacy of Consultation with Indigenous Peoples

The Case of Brazil

Springer

Catarina Woyames Dreher
Frankfurt am Main, Germany

ISBN 978-3-031-50538-6 ISBN 978-3-031-50539-3 (eBook)
https://doi.org/10.1007/978-3-031-50539-3

This Springer imprint is published by the registered company Springer Nature Switzerland AG
The registered company address is: Gewerbestrasse 11, 6330 Cham, Switzerland

Paper in this product is recyclable

Acknowledgments

This book would not have been possible without the guidance and support of a broad group of people. I would like to particularly thank Prof. Dr. Winfried Kluth, Prof. Dr. Dirk Hanschel, Prof. Dr. Gabriela Navarro, Dr. Mariana Monteiro de Matos and Dr. Alexandra Tomaselli. The study also benefitted immensely from the collaborative environment of the research center Society and Culture in Motion of Martin-Luther-Universität Halle-Wittenberg, and the center's funding for this research project is thankfully acknowledged. Furthermore, my gratitude also extends to Hon. Prof. Dr. Ulrich Widmaier, former Judge at the Federal Administrative Court in Germany, for awarding this manuscript the Human Rights Prize of the Faculty of Law of Martin-Luther-Universität Halle-Wittenberg.

I am moreover eternally grateful for the emotional and continuous support from my friends and family, notably my husband, Vincent, and my son, Theodoro.

Contents

Abbreviations

ADIP	American Declaration of Indigenous Peoples
AHRS	African Human Rights System
APIB	Brazilian Indigenous Peoples Association
BNDES	Brazilian Development Bank
CEACR	Committee of Experts on the Application of Conventions and Recommendations
CBD	Convention on Biological Diversity
CERD	Committee on the Elimination of Racial Discrimination
CESCR	Committee on Economic, Social and Cultural Rights
CNPI	Brazilian National Council for Indigenous Research
CONAMA	Brazilian Environmental Agency
COP	Conference of the Parties
EIA	Environmental Impact Study
FUNAI	Brazilian Indigenous Peoples Foundation
FPIC	Free, Prior and Informed Consent
IACHR	Inter-American Commission of Human Rights
IACtHR	Inter-American Court of Human Rights
IAHRS	Inter-American System of Human Rights
IBAMA	Brazilian Institute of the Environment and Renewable Natural Resources
IBGE	Brazilian Institute of Geography and Statistics
ICCPR	International Covenant on Civil and Political Rights
IIFB	International Indigenous Forum on Biodiversity
ILO	International Labour Organization
ILO No. 169	ILO Convention No. 169, Indigenous and Tribal Peoples Convention of 1989
INCRA	Brazilian National Institute for Agrarian Reform
IPP	Indigenous peoples' Protocols
MMA	Brazilian Ministry of Environment

MP	Brazilian Federal Prosecutor's Office
RIMA	Environmental Impact Statement
SESAI	Brazilian Special Department for Indigenous Health
OAS	Organization of American States
SPI	Brazilian Indigenous Protection Service
STF	Brazilian Supreme Court
STJ	Brazilian Superior Court
UNDRIP	United Nations Declaration of Rights of Indigenous Peoples of 2007
UNESCO	United Nations Educational, Scientific and Cultural Organization
UNPFII	United Nations Permanent Forum on Indigenous Issues
WGIP	Working Group on Indigenous Populations

List of Tables

Chapter 1
Introduction

1.1 Introduction

The legal contestation of projects of natural resource exploitation has experienced a significant increase in the Americas since the 1980s. This is due to a stark growth in the number of planned projects as well as an increased recourse to legal means of those affected by the projects. Although most of these conflicts are local, they are closely intertwined with transnational actors and developments. As exploitation projects are advancing, inhabitants of the affected areas, often indigenous peoples, seek ways to prevent or at least repair past violations of their rights and amend activities leading to the continued destruction of their lands. The implications hereof for indigenous peoples, as well as the role of transnational companies and states, transgress human rights violations and reveal contours of legal, political, and economic conflicts.[1]

In Brazil, the violation of human rights surrounds social and environmental issues based on the implementation of the title to territory of indigenous peoples, their cultural rights and their self-determination. The consolidation of the matter has gained visibility with the emerging framework of the requirement of consultation with indigenous peoples. The concept of consultation was first conceived in the Indigenous and Tribal Peoples Convention No. 169 of the International Labour Organization of 1989, as a procedural right of indigenous and tribal peoples, and later confirmed by the United Nations Declaration of Rights of Indigenous Peoples of 2007, which also introduced the additional aspect of consent as a substantive right that originates from self-determination.[2]

---

[1] See e.g. Doyle (2016), Rombouts (2014), and Garavito (2012).

[2] 'The consultation approach has become the strongest candidate to replace the integrationist approach, which dominated international and domestic law throughout the 20th century and which sought to solve the "indigenous problem" by assimilating indigenous peoples into the rest of society' Garavito (2012).

C. Woyames Dreher, *A Legal Assessment of the Efficacy of Consultation with Indigenous Peoples*, https://doi.org/10.1007/978-3-031-50539-3_1

This work intends to shed light on the legal aspects of consultation as it was first elaborated by the Indigenous and Tribal Peoples Convention No. 169, its consolidation, and by assessing the efficacy of the norm in the Brazilian state by taking into account the multi-dimensional perspective of self-determination and cultural rights. Within the framework of the commitments assumed by the Brazilian state through the ratification of international conventions and treaties, the absence of regulation does not exempt the state from the duty to act accordingly. As a matter of fact, Brazil ratified the Indigenous and Tribal Peoples Convention No. 169 in 2004 and the American Convention already in 1992, but it is far from full compliance with the requirement of consultation.

The analysis of consultation points to the troubled relationship between Brazil and indigenous peoples, marked by innumerous violent conflicts. In the international arena, the debate has not only advanced on consultation, but also on the broadened aspects that it should entail free, prior and informed consent (hereinafter, the FPIC), which shall lead to a mutual agreement among stakeholders and a possible veto for indigenous peoples in all matters that affect them.[3]

In the regional setting, the Inter-American System of Human Rights, through the jurisprudence of the Inter-American Court, expanded the interpretation of Article 21 of the American Convention on Human Rights of 1978, shaping the right to property to ensure consultation of traditional peoples. The right to consultation interpreted on the right to property however led to an insufficient protection regarding the advanced range of cases provided by the Inter-American Court; it also constituted a setback, as the decisions promoted a lower level of protection than as prescribed in international standards. For instance, the Inter-American Court has omitted international treaties, United Nations documents and especially the American Declaration on the Rights of Indigenous Peoples, which, since 2016, ensure the right to consent.[4]

Furthermore, when the Inter-American Court of Human Rights interpreted and applied international treaties on cases of consultation, the decisions encompassed the right to self-determination[5] and cultural rights in order to guarantee normative protection.[6] Thus, 'the unique relationship between indigenous peoples and land should be recognized and protected, shaping the nature and reach of human rights and principles'.[7] This form of interpretation understands that those rights are inseparable when implementing consultation in the region.

At the same time, groups representing indigenous peoples in Brazil took it on themselves to advocate for enforcement with the obligations, developing specific

---

[3] Schettini (2012).

[4] Pasqualucci (2009).

[5] 'In terms of strategic litigation within regional systems, human rights courts are bounded to their mandate, which is fixated in a binding treaty. Extrapolating this mandate could generate resistance from states through the advocacy of the application of the margin of appreciation principle. In this context, the construction of case law on land rights must be consistent, well justified and within the Court's mandate' Navarro (2021) and Follesdal (2017).

[6] Dannenmaier (2008).

[7] Navarro (2021), p. 61.

Protocols describing how consultation should be conducted.[8] At the core of consultation lies the question over the application of indigenous peoples' rights, and the presence of adequate policies and legislative measures to ensure the egalitarian participation of indigenous peoples in Brazil. Such rights have been established by the Federal Constitution of 1988, which derives its legitimacy from the guarantee of social and individual rights and the equality of people in a pluralist society.[9] The purpose of the indigenous peoples' Protocols is to ensure the necessary self-determination to articulate and provide space for deliberations subject to neither external nor internal pressures. In their own terms, the indigenous peoples thus attempted to ensure their claims were heard without coercion to artificially legitimize any natural resource or construction projects that were not in their best interest.

1.2 Conceptual Approach and Methodology

To crystallize this legal issue that can compromise the efficacy of consultation, this work seeks to delve further into the theoretical underpinnings of the legal aspects of the contemporary understanding of indigenous peoples' right to consultation as a way to strengthen the right in Brazil. The concept of dialogue in the strict sense is adopted for this study as a 'metaphor for analyzing forms of transnational interaction between judges in situations of constitutional pluralism, in which judges belong to a community of law and interpret common norms and there is no ultimate dispute resolution instance, but there are as many centers as jurisdictions involved'.[10] The main goal of the work is to foster a consistent application of consultation to improve the litigation system[11] in order to guarantee the efficacy of consultation with indigenous peoples.

Efficacy in this work is understood as the degree to which the Inter-American System of Human Rights is applied and enforced in the national legal system, taking into account the legal claims, the legislation and the indigenous peoples' Protocols.[12] It is thereby closely related to control of conventionality, which is defined as the requirement for ratifying states to interpret domestic law in accordance with an internationally agreed obligation. The work analyzes the control of conventionality as judges and state authorities must take past cases and advisory opinions into account, adjusting national norms to human rights standards in accordance with

[8] See e.g. Encuentro Nacional de Organizaciones Territoriales de Pueblos Originarios—ENOTPO Protocolo de Consulta Previa, Libre e Informada a Pueblos Originarios; Amin Lima da Silva and Mendes (2019) and Doyle et al. (2019).

[9] See e.g. (1988) Constitution of Brazil, Bourdieu and Nice (2013), Segato (2011), Duprat (2014), Cunha (2018), and Dallari (2017).

[10] Mera (2015).

[11] Navarro (2021).

[12] See e.g. Brownlie (1982) and Engstrom (2017).

the Inter-American System of Human Rights as well as extra-American developments.[13] Thus, international organs' contributions to the debate are also relevant and are taken into consideration.[14] This work considers that a norm is efficacious not only if observed by the legal system using the format of jurisprudence but also in case of the law-applying organs.[15] The research assesses legal claims, legislation and also examines in-depth the peculiar creation of the indigenous peoples' Protocols by the indigenous peoples themselves.[16]

As regards methodology and the research approach, the investigation draws on the analysis of literature, jurisprudence, international treaties, and official data, while also leveraging interdisciplinarity by considering studies of legal anthropology and sociology. Due to pandemic-related obstacles to conduct field work in-person, expert interviews that constituted an important part of the analysis were conducted online and by phone,[17] providing fresh and original insights to the analysis. Another relevant contribution of this research is the assessment of legislative and judicial documentation available only in the Spanish and Portuguese languages. These materials were translated into English by the author for the purpose of this analysis but may also constitute a general source for future comparative studies on the analysis of consultation with indigenous peoples and the field of international adjudication in general.

During the research process, the inquiry was narrowed down to examine the following overarching research question: What constitutes the efficacy of consultation with indigenous peoples in Brazil? In order to derive pointed responses, the main question was separated into three sub-questions: (1) Has Brazil applied consultation with indigenous peoples as required by the Inter-American Court of Human Rights? (2) Has the framework of international law contributed to the efficacy of consultation with indigenous peoples in Brazil? (3) Has the implementation of self-determination and cultural rights strengthened the efficacy of consultation with indigenous peoples in Brazil?

The questions were answered along the structure of the book, taking into consideration the theoretical and practical dimension of consultation, its limitations and potentials under the nascent international law for indigenous peoples.

---

[13] See e.g. Mac-Gregor (2015) and Carmelina Londoño-Lázaro and Carrillo-Santarelli (2019).

[14] See e.g. Gilbert (2006).

[15] See e.g. Kelsen (2005), Bobbio (2010), Alexy (2010), Burazin (2019), and Krieger (2000).

[16] Examples of Protocols, see: Wajãpi Indigenous Peoples (2014) Protocolo de Consulta e Consentimento Wajãpi; Munduruku (2014) Protocolo de Consulta Munduruku; Povo Juruna (2017) Protocolo de consulta Juruna (YudJá) da terra Indígena PaquIçamba da Volta grande do rIo XIngu.

[17] See e.g. Debenham (2007), Middha (2018), Braun et al. (2017), and Lupton (2020).

1.3 Structure of the Book

The second chapter sheds light on the genesis of the requirement of consultation, by addressing the control of conventionality, the evolving definitions under international law, the Inter-American System of Human Rights, the international treaties and the multilateral financial institutions, as all those are contributing to the consolidation of the legal concept. It also provides an outlook on the monograph and the methodological aspects that are considered. The conclusion of the chapter establishes the theoretical grounds for contemporary consultation, which is assessed in the third and fourth chapter when examining legal claims and legislative bills.

The fourth chapter analyzes the role that the Inter-American System of Human Rights plays in consolidating and implementing human rights in the region, by addressing the new criteria of interpretation related to international treaties and the advanced interpretation of Article 21 of the American Convention. The first part discusses how the question of the requirement of consultation has been a matter of concern for the Inter-American Commission of Human Rights from 1985 until 2010, listing some relevant cases: the case 7615, known as the *Yanomami v. Brazil*, for which the decision was taken on March 5 of 1985; the Report No. 75/02, Case 11.140, known as the *Mary and Carrie Dann v. the United States*, for which the decision was taken on September 27 of 1999; the Report No. 40/04, Case 12.053, known as the *Maya Indigenous Communities of Toledo District v. Belize*, for which the decision dates October 5 of 2004; and more recently, the Precautionary Measure 382/10, known as *Belo Monte v. Brazil*, of July 29 of 2011. The second part analyzes selected cases of the Inter-American Court of Human Rights including the case *Saramaka v. Suriname*, of 2007; the case *Kichwa de Sarayaku v. Ecuador*, of 2012; the case *Povos Kaliña e Lokono v. Suriname* of 2015; the case *Triunfo de la Cruz Garífuna Community and its members v. Honduras* of 2017; and the case *Indigenous Community de la Asociación Lhaka Honhat (nuestra tierra) v. Argentina* of 2020.

Henceforth, the results establish that consultation must be carried out in good faith, an adequate and accessible process and the need to conduct an environmental impact study. Bringing these three concepts together reveals the first attempts of establishing the legal framework for the requirement of consultation, in a way that shows how the application of consultation should be executed in states; however, it can also be observed that the cases do not yet include a better conceptualization of the right to consent.

The third chapter assesses the Brazilian judiciary and legislature. The cases in the chapter have been selected for assessing in detail the problems and juridical tensions underlying the guiding research questions. The cases chosen highlight frequent problems that indigenous peoples in Brazil experience related to the requirement of consultation in the specific context of natural resource exploitations, as they are translated into legal claims and possibilities to appeal. The cases include the *Taparajós* case; the *Volta Grande do Xingu* case; the *Polo Naval de Manaus* case; the case *Educação Escolar Indígena*; the case *Hidrelétrica São Luiz do Tapajós*; the case *Usina Hidrelétrica Teles Pires*; the case *Usina Hidrelétrica São Manuel*; the case *Polo Naval de Manaus*; the case *Parque Nacional of Superagui*, in Paraná; the case *Duplicação da estrada de Ferro Carajás*; the case *Linhão Manaus Boavista*, a case of resource exploitation of oil, gas and xisto in Acre; the case *Construção do porto no lago Maicá*; the attempt to change the regulation, which is an alteration in the Law No. 892 of 2013 regarding the indigenous teachers; the case *Belo Monte* and the case *Mineração Volta Grande do Xingu.*

The conclusion of the chapter highlights that due to resistance of the legislature and minimal oversight of the judiciary, stakeholders face few costs for not complying with the requirement of consultation. The efficacy of consultation moreover requires not only the affirmation of states' obligation under the Inter-American System of Human Rights but also to extra-American developments. In view of the numerous conflicts regarding indigenous peoples' human rights in Brazil and the persistent non-enforcement of the requirement of consultation, the conclusion points towards a mechanism developed by indigenous peoples themselves for increasing the efficacy of consultation, as discussed in the following chapter, the indigenous peoples' Protocols.

The fifth chapter is divided in two parts. The first part aims to comparatively examine indigenous peoples' practices in the application of consultation in Argentina, Bolivia, Chile, Colombia, Nicaragua, Paraguay as well as in a separate international system of human rights, the African Human Rights System. The analyses provide a comparative frame to assess the application and the protection of indigenous peoples' consultation rights in Brazil. The second part analyzes the contribution of the indigenous peoples' Protocols to the discussion on the application of consultation as means to realize self-determination and cultural rights. The Protocols are a response to the lack of enforcement by the state for applying the requirement of consultation. The assessment reviews the indigenous peoples' Protocols of Brazil and the indigenous peoples' Protocols of Paraguay. This dual investigation helps to better understand the legal nature of the Paraguayan national framework, the norms and legal system in which the Protocols are expressed; and by contrast, in Brazil, where the Protocols are not part of the *corpus legis*, but instead are being advocated by state judges. The indigenous peoples' Protocols reviewed include the *Wajãpi* Protocol and the *Juruna (Yudjá) da Terra Indígena Paquiçamba da Volta Grande do rio Xingu* indigenous peoples Protocol. The analyzed legislation features the Decree of the National Policy for Territorial and Environmental Management of Indigenous Lands and the Paraguayan Decree No. 1039 of 28th December 2018, which contains specifications regarding the procedures underlying indigenous peoples' Protocols.

The results of this chapter are key to a better comprehension of consultation, to understand how other states comply with the norm and ensure application, as well as to revisit the relevance of the indigenous peoples' Protocols. The implementation of self-determination and cultural rights as translated into consultation practices serves as a platform for the affirmation of consultation with indigenous peoples within the national normative framework providing the basis for the development of a strong corpus of specific measures to address injustices for indigenous peoples. More than that, the indigenous peoples' Protocols may be invoked to settle disputes, and to support and harmonize the extension of the internationally ordained right of the requirement of consultation as not only a procedural right but as a substantive right.

The sixth chapter analyzes the persistent legal uncertainty surrounding consultation and the different aspects of the definition provided by different actors diverging from the Inter-American System of Human Rights and the international normative framework; it also discusses the control of conventionality as a mandatory procedural step. The chapter provides overview tables as regards the judiciary and legislation under the Inter-American System of Human Rights as well as Brazil in order to comparatively assess original data on the implementation of consultation from 1985 to 2020. The current Brazilian economic and social policies, which to date do not guarantee the enforcement of the application of consultation with indigenous peoples, are also discussed based on this data. The results of this chapter suggest that the engagement of indigenous peoples in the process of the construction of the requirement of consultation should not became a tailor-made process. Self-determination and cultural rights are part of the transformative role through which consultation has the potential to achieve successful change within Brazil, as a multidimensional perspective of proactively reasserting the status of indigenous peoples in their own concepts and capacity to decide over their collective territorial rights.

The central theme of the analysis is then revisited in the conclusion and seventh chapter of the book, taking stock of the results of the study, the recommendations as well as avenues for future research. Work must continue to understand and assess the vivid process towards self-determination in which the indigenous peoples are embedded, a process that is still evolving and where consultation plays a central role.

References

Alexy R (2010) The argument from injustice: a reply to legal positivism, 1st paperback ed. Oxford University Press, Oxford

Amin Lima da Silva L, Mendes G (2019) Protocolo juruna de consulta prévia frente aos empreendimentos hidrelétrico e minerário na amazônia: caso belo monte e belo sun. Núcleo Antropol Direito Anais VI ENADIR-GT04

Bobbio N (2010) Teria Geral do Direito, 3rd edn. Martins Fontes, Brazil

Bourdieu P, Nice R (2013) Outline of a theory of practice. Cambridge University Press, Cambridge

Braun V, Clarke V, Gray D (eds) (2017) Collecting qualitative data: a practical guide to textual, media and virtual techniques, 1st edn. Cambridge University Press

Brownlie I (1982) The reality and efficacy of international law. Br Yearb Int Law 52:1–8. https://doi.org/10.1093/bybil/52.1.1

Burazin L (2019) The concept of law and efficacy. Encycl Philos Law Soc Philos

Carmelina Londoño-Lázaro M, Carrillo-Santarelli N (2019) The control of conventionality: developments in the case law of the Inter-American Court of Human Rights and its potential expanding effects in international human rights law. Max Planck Yearb U N Law Online 22: 319–346. https://doi.org/10.1163/18757413_022001013

Cunha MC (2018) Índios na Constitutição. Novos Estud CEBRAP 37

Dallari DA (2017) Índios e Direitos Agredidos. J Bras

Dannenmaier E (2008) Beyond indigenous property rights: exploring the emergence of a distinctive connection doctrine. Wash Univ Law Rev 86

Debenham M (2007) Epistolary interviews on-line: a novel addition to the researcher's Palette. Jisc TechDis

Doyle CM (2016) Indigenous peoples, title to territory, rights and resources - the transformative role of the free prior and informed consent. Routledge, New York

Doyle C, Rojas Garzón B, Weitzner V, Okamoto T (eds) (2019) Los protocolos de consentimiento libre, previo e informado como instrumentos de autonomía: Sentando las bases para interacciones basadas en los derechos, Institut für Ökologie und Aktions-Ethnologie (INFOE) e. V. Forest Peoples Programme, Köln

Duprat D (2014) A Convenção 169 da OIT e o Direito à Consulta Livre, Prévia e Informada. Cult Juríd 1

Engstrom P (2017) Reconceptualising the impact of the Inter-American Human Rights System/ Reconceitualizando o Impacto do Sistema Interamericano de Direitos Humanos. Rev Direito E Práxis 8. https://doi.org/10.12957/dep.2017.28027

Follesdal A (2017) Exporting the margin of appreciation: lessons for the Inter-American Court of Human Rights. Int J Const Law 15:359–371. https://doi.org/10.1093/icon/mox019

Garavito CR (2012). Etnicidad.gov: Los recursos naturales, los pueblos indígenas y derecho a la consulta previa en los campos minados. Centro de Estudos de Derecho, Justicia y Sociedad, Bogotá

Gilbert J (2006) Indigenous peoples' land rights under international law: from victims to actors. Transnational Publishers, Ardsley

Kelsen H (2005) Pure theory of law. Lawbook Exchange, Clark

Krieger H (2000) Das Effektivitätsprinzip im Völkerrecht. Duncker & Humblot, Berlin

Lupton D (2020) New resource: doing fieldwork in a pandemic

Mac-Gregor EF (2015) Conventionality control the new doctrine of the Inter-American Court of Human Rights. AJIL Unbound 109:93–99. https://doi.org/10.1017/S2398772300001240

Mera MEG (2015) Judicialização da discriminação estrutural contra povos indígenas e afrodescendentes na América Latina: conceptualização e tipologia de um diálogo interamericano/Juridicalization of structural discrimination against indigenous peoples and afro... Rev QUAESTIO IURIS 8. https://doi.org/10.12957/rqi.2015.16908

Middha B (2018) Everyday digital engagements: using food selfies on Facebook to explore eating practices. Commun Res Pract 4:291–306. https://doi.org/10.1080/22041451.2018.1476796

Navarro GCB (2021) Measuring the effectiveness of the Inter-American System of Human Rights: the case of indigenous territorial rights. Dissertation, Goethe-Universität Frankfurt, Frankfurt am Main

Pasqualucci JM (2009) International indigenous land rights: a critique of the jurisprudence of the Inter-American Court of Human Rights in light of the United Nations declaration on the rights of indigenous peoples. Wis Int Law J 27:51–89

Rombouts SJ (2014) Having a say: indigenous peoples, international law and free, prior and informed consent. Wolf Legal Publishers, Oisterwijk

Schettini A (2012) Por um Novo Paradigma de Proteção dos Direitos dos Povos Indígenas: uma Análise Crítica dos Parâmetros Estabelecidos pela Corte Interamericana de Direitos Humanos. SUR - Int J Hum Rights 63

Segato RL (2011) Que cada pueblo teja los hilos de su historia. El pluralismo jurídico en diálogo didáctico con legisladores. In: Chenaut V, Gómez M, Ortiz H et al (eds) Justicia y diversidad en América Latina: pueblos indígenas ante la globalización, Primera edición. FLACSO Ecuador; CIESAS, Quito, Ecuador: México, D.F

Chapter 2
The Legal Framework of Consultation with Indigenous Peoples

2.1 Introduction

As one result of contemporary globalization, disputes over indigenous peoples' territory against the background of the exploitation of natural resources now involve a multiplicity of national and international actors.[1] In the past three decades, the conflicts have intensified engulfing transnational corporations, states, non-governmental organizations, multilateral financial organizations, and transnational financial entities. The conflicts reveal contours of legal, political, and economic aspects that transgress human rights violations.

In this environment, mainly due to the resistance and activism of indigenous peoples,[2] their demands for rights 'have been progressively inserted into the international order, gaining legitimacy within the United Nations and regional systems of human rights protection, among other international institutions'.[3] This inclusion of indigenous rights in the international human rights agenda has initiated and enriched the debate on territory rights, self-determination, cultural rights, development, and more recently, the debate on consultation, strengthening the indigenous peoples' struggle to engage with the modern Western paradigm of legal analyses.[4]

---

[1] Although this is not the focus of the work, there are scholars that connect the economic system to the conflicts: 'It is precisely these lands where indigenous peoples who have been displaced from their ancestral territories have historically settled and where the most acute conflicts over prior consultation take place today' (. . .) 'In what follows, I call these territories and the spheres of social interaction within them "social minefields"' See Garavito (2012); also Harvey (2005) and Bourdieu and Nice (2013). On the general effects of globalization on national systems and parliaments see e.g. Kluth (2013).

[2] See e.g. Puig (2010), Clavero (2005), and Lupien (2020).

[3] Charters et al. (2010).

[4] See e.g. Santos (1998), Anaya (2004), and Clavero (2008).

C. Woyames Dreher, *A Legal Assessment of the Efficacy of Consultation with Indigenous Peoples*, https://doi.org/10.1007/978-3-031-50539-3_2

2.2 The Legal Basis

The concept of consultation was first conceived in the Indigenous and Tribal Peoples Convention No. 169 of the International Labour Organization of 1989 (hereinafter, the ILO Convention No. 169 or ILO No. 169), followed by the United Nations Declaration of Rights of Indigenous Peoples in 2007 (hereinafter, the UNDRIP).[5] The present study addresses the legal aspects of consultation as the core mechanism for the implementation of indigenous peoples' rights in context of its efficacy in the administrative bodies and the legislature in Brazil. As a matter of fact, however Brazil, one of the 17 countries that ratified the ILO Convention No. 169, in 2004 and the American Convention, in 1992, is far from compliant with the provisions of consultation.

It is key to a deeper analysis of consultation to establish that the judiciary of Brazil interprets the human rights standards in accordance with the Federal Constitution and international treaties, providing to indigenous peoples the most comprehensive protection as entailed in the jurisprudential understanding of the supra-legality of human rights. The Brazilian judiciary also recognizes indigenous peoples' rights and their application as a collective right. Therefore, the highest Court in Brazil, the Brazilian Supreme Court (hereinafter, in Portuguese, the STF) and also the Federal Courts have contributed to the leading interpretation, albeit the decisions are non-binding to future legal claims. In that sense, the high number of legal claims and legislative norms have reaffirmed the necessity of complying with international standards to harmonize the process.

Besides the non-binding character of the STF decisions, the application of consultation faces another obstacle, which are the remnants of the past military dictatorship. The legal appeals, the Suspension of Injunctions and the Anticipated Trusteeship can be taken exclusively by the state authority and are responsible for the backlash on the application of consultation. The legal instruments are known because they authorize the resource exploitation in indigenous peoples' territories by political motives 'transforming badly planned projects into faits accomplis'.[6]

Contrary to the few advancements achieved by the judiciary, the members of the Brazilian legislature are indeed far from compliant with the prerequisites of consultation in their congressional activities. Together with a set of other countries' national judiciaries and legislatures, Brazil also fails to comply with the adequate jurisprudence and legislation regarding consultation with indigenous peoples, as there is no clarity of interpretation nor legal guidance.

Relevant to the discussion one must note that within the framework of the commitments assumed by the Brazilian state through the ratification of international

[5] 'Thus, the consultation approach has become the strongest candidate to replace the integrationist approach, which dominated international and domestic law throughout the 20th century and which sought to solve the "indigenous problem" by assimilating indigenous peoples into the rest of society', 50, *translated by author.*

[6] RCA (2016).

conventions and treaties—the Inter-American Court of Human Rights (hereinafter, the IACtHR) and the Vienna Convention of Law of Treaties (hereinafter, the Vienna Convention)—the absence of regulation does not exempt the state from the duty to act accordingly to the treaty, in this case, consultation.

The analysis of the efficacy of consultation points to the troubled relationship between Brazil and the indigenous peoples, marked by innumerous violent conflicts. At the core of consultation lies the question over the implementation of indigenous peoples' rights, and the presence of adequate policies and administrative and legislative measures to ensure the egalitarian participation of indigenous peoples in Brazil; as established by the Federal Constitution of 1988, which derives its legitimacy from the guarantee of social and individual rights and the equality of people in a pluralist society.[7]

Some attempts for the application of consultation date back to the year of 2012, when the Brazilian government designed an initiative to introduce consultation in the legal system. Through the Inter-ministerial Working Group (in Portuguese, *Grupo de Trabalho Interministerial*), there was the beginning of a discussion towards the needed proceedings and legal parameters for fulfilling the requirement of consultation, however, 2 years later the deliberations were discontinued. This untimely end of the legislative debate on the subject had a negative impact on the efficacy of the requirement of consultation with traditional communities in Brazil, including indigenous peoples.

By contrast, in the international arena, the debate advanced not only on the efficacy of consultation, but also on the aspects that it should entail free, prior and informed consent, which shall lead to a mutual agreement among stakeholders and a possible veto for indigenous peoples. Moreover, in the regional setting, the Inter-American System of Human Rights (hereinafter, the IAHRS) expanded the interpretation of Article 21 of the American Convention shaping the right to property to ensure that consultation in all projects of resource exploitation in indigenous peoples' territories shall be conducted. Additionally, the judgments safeguarded that the requirement of consultation shall be complied with in good faith and under informed consent. Meanwhile, some countries furthermore introduced ordinary norms regarding the proceedings of the consultation.

Simultaneously, in Brazil, indigenous peoples took it on themselves to comply with the obligations, developing specific Protocols describing how consultation should be conducted. Contributing to confront a structural problem of society and law, the efficacy of consultation is thus under development.[8]

Overall, Brazil's enforcement of the requirement of consultation faces severe hindrances to its forthcoming application. The detailed analysis of the data shows the constant lack of enforcement with consultation, undermining the efficacy of consultation by leading to systemic forms of restrictive interpretations of the obligation for the Brazilian judiciary and legislature. Efforts to date mostly shadow the necessary

[7] (1988) Constitution of Brazil.

[8] See e.g. Minda (1995), White (1985), and Baron (1999).

debate on the efficacy of the norm as engrained by the ILO Convention No. 169 in Brazil, not only undermining the self-determination but also the cultural rights' provisions found in Brazil. In sum, this work comprehends self-determination and cultural rights in a practical way through a better applicability of the norm underlying consultation.

The second chapter of the book thus provides an outlook, the structure that is adopted and the methodological aspects that are considered. It sketches out the developments regarding the definition of indigenous peoples followed by assessing the definitions of consultation under international law, the IAHRS, the international treaties and the multilateral financial institutions, as those are contributing to the efficacy of the concept. The goal of this part is to provide the methodological basis and the theoretical framework that will inform the analysis of the legal claims and the legislation, in the IAHRS and in Brazil in the forthcoming chapters.

2.2.1 Structure of the Analysis

The work analyzes the efficacy of consultation with indigenous peoples living in rural and urban areas as set out by the IAHRS, and as it is determined by the legal interpretation and application in Brazil. Most national laws are characterized by a dispersed interpretation and applicability, which often provokes legal uncertainty. The analysis emphasizes an adequate solution for Brazil to guarantee that the administrative and legislative measures directed at indigenous peoples consider consultation as multi-dimensional perspective including self-determination and cultural rights.

2.2.1.1 The Enforcement of International Sentences

The most common standard for assessing the success of the international courts, including the IACtHR, is national enforcement.[9] In particular when it comes to social change, it might seem self-evident to focus mainly on whether states comply with a ruling, as legal systems are logical systems, composed of propositions that refer to life situations created by the most diverse interest.[10]

Although the main proposal is to analyze the efficacy of consultation with indigenous peoples in Brazil and the dialogue with the IAHRS, the debates towards consultation in the international realm together with the analyses of other national legal systems are equally relevant to put the Brazilian judiciary and legislature under scrutiny and to find an adequate solution for indigenous peoples. Furthermore, the

[9] Alter (2014).

[10] See e.g. Pontes de Miranda (1981). Didier (2015), translated by author. On the foundations of the economic legal system see e.g. Kluth (2019).

work consists of legal analyses to rethink and reshape consultation 'beyond rule enforcement models'.[11] Therefore, enforcement is here understood as 'a state of conformity or identity between an actor's behavior and a specified rule',[12] giving efficacy to the international treaties that Brazil ratified when the obligation is at stake.[13]

2.2.1.2 Assessing Efficacy: The Application in the National System

Efficacy here is understood in context of the control of conventionality[14] and its representation to the *pro personae* principle.[15] This means that efficacy entails the degree to which the IAHRS is applied and enforced in the national legal system, taking into account the legal claims, the legislations and the indigenous peoples' Protocols.[16] It is thereby closely related to control of conventionality, which is defined as the requirement for ratifying states to interpret domestic law in accordance with an internationally agreed obligation. In the analysis, efficacy is the 'application of the right in the national legal system',[17] including 'the actual fact that it is effectively applied and observed, the circumstance that a human conduct in accordance with the norm is verified in the order of facts'.[18] Thus, the efficacy in consultation within legal claims and legislation is, then, 'the capacity to bring legal norms closer to social reality. Efficacy concerns the implementation of the conditional program, that is, the implementation of the abstract and hypothetical "if-then" link foreseen in the legal norm'.[19]

In order to not overly restrict the range of efficacy, the analysis adopts the application of a multi-dimensional perspective of consultation. The application here proposed provides an analysis that surpasses consultation, understanding the right to include self-determination and cultural rights. Thus, 'the appraisal of judicial efficacy constitutes a primary thematic concern in the sociology of law, [depending] theoretically on the conceptual and methodological definition of efficacy, and

[11] Engstrom (2017).

[12] Raustiala and Slaughter (2002).

[13] According to the author, 'compliance should be clarified further, to indicate whether the obligation at stake is extensive (e.g., to 'give effect' to treaty rights) or circumscribed (e.g., to give effect to a remedial order)'. Viljoen (2017).

[14] Mac-Gregor (2015), p. 94.

[15] Negishi (2017).

[16] See e.g. Brownlie (1982) and Engstrom (2017).

[17] To see more on effectiveness: By its normative force a norm contributes to the realization of what ought to be. If the norm succeeds in this, one speaks of the effectiveness of (the normative force of) the norm. This does not mean that what *ought to be* normatively and what *is* actually differ from each other by necessity; van Dijik (1987).

[18] Kelsen (2005).

[19] Neves (2011).

empirically on the assessment of domestic courts and other legal organs' performance'.[20]

Application is seen here as the legal system which grounds the decisions on consultation, the capacity of the national system to comply with the international system and if behavior is as is required of the jurisprudence.[21] Thus, the analyses of the international organs' contributions, international courts and other jurisdictions to the debate are also relevant and are taking into consideration.[22]

The work hence seeks to analyze if and to what degree the understanding of consultation as a collective right under the multi-dimensional perspective of self-determination and cultural rights in Brazil is appropriate to design a contribution to the equal participation in Brazil through adequate policies of administrative and legislative measures.[23]

Considering that a norm is adequate, not only if observed by the legal system using the format of jurisprudence but also in case of the law-applying organs,[24] the research is also interested in assessing legislation, translated into legislative acts, as well as the unique creation of the indigenous peoples' Protocols by the indigenous peoples themselves.[25] This constitutes an emancipation where the enforcement with the norms had not been executed as expected, triggering a societal response.

The scope of normative action of consultation extends to different aspects of the life of indigenous peoples. The analysis of the right of consultation thereby transgresses mere legal implications and aims to map out consultation emphasizing its multi-dimensional perspective of self-determination and cultural rights.

Consultation with indigenous peoples and traditional groups 'has become one of the most difficult and controversial issues in national and international human rights law. Indeed, in just two decades, since the adoption of Convention 169 of the

[20]The relevance of the international precedent regards the control of conventionality. According to the author, if any of the governmental bodies or courts at any level have begun to exercise, even sporadically, control of conventionality; if there has been an increase in litigation based on the Inter-American Court's decision; if action by individuals, organizations and social movements based on the Inter-American Court's decision has been stimulated; if institutions, legal procedures, actors and human rights norms have been strengthened; Calabria (2018).

[21]See e.g. Alter (2014), García Ramírez (2015), von Bogdandy et al. (2017), and Mac-Gregor (2015).

[22]See e.g. Gilbert (2006) and Calabria (2018).

[23]Relevant for the debate, according to the author: 'consultation is part of a new corpus of collective rights framed in new principles of relationship between states and indigenous peoples, which seek to overcome the assimilationism and integrationism of the past, and are based on the right of peoples to exist in a certain way, as collective subjects of rights with equal dignity to other peoples and nationalities. (...) The legitimacy of consultation, that is, the binding effect of its results, depends on a clever use of law from a counter-hegemonic point of view'. Mazariegos Rodas (2016).

[24]See e.g. Kelsen (2005), Bobbio (2010), Alexy (2010), Burazin (2019), and Krieger (2000).

[25]Examples of Protocols, see: Wajãpi Indigenous Peoples (2014) Protocolo de Consulta e Consentimento Wajãpi; Munduruku (2014) Protocolo de Consulta Munduruku; Povo Juruna (2017) Protocolo de consulta Juruna (YudJá) da terra Indígena PaquIçamba da Volta grande do rIo XIngu.

International Labour Organization in 1989, it has gone from being a relatively specialized and invisible issue to being the subject of legal, political and social conflicts in which both economic interests and the survival of indigenous peoples and other ethnic communities around the world are at stake'.[26] To this end, an adequate theoretical framework is pertinent to improve the efficacy of consultation to avoid that indeterminacies prevent legal applicability.

Although this analysis is intimately related to a broader topic, which is indigenous peoples' human rights, the inquiry was narrowed down to examine: What constitutes the efficacy of consultation with indigenous peoples in Brazil?

To derive pointed responses, the main question was separated into the following sub-questions: (1) Has Brazil applied consultation with indigenous peoples as required by the Inter-American Court of Human Rights? (2) Has the framework of international law contributed to the efficacy of consultation with indigenous peoples in Brazil? (3) Has the implementation of self-determination and cultural rights strengthened the efficacy of consultation with indigenous peoples in Brazil?

Regarding the research questions, the first question focuses on the role of the IAHRS and its juridical interpretation and the role that the conventionality control plays in Brazil. Recent studies have challenged a formalistic understanding of efficacy by seeking to instill in the concept a broad appreciation of the legal and social impacts produced by adjudicative decisions.[27]

Relevant are also other international organs and the jurisprudence of national systems that adopt the legislation of consultation and the international regional courts as well, which is analyzed in response to the second question. The third question addresses the empirical question brought forward by the advent of consultation with indigenous peoples and the most accurate application in Brazil.

The analysis proposes a way to rethink the requirement of consultation[28] through the application of the multi-dimensional perspective of consultation as relevant to overcome the obstacles to the participation of the indigenous peoples in Brazil based on the international standards of universal human rights protection of non-discrimination and equal rights.

The Control of Conventionality

The IAHRS was established in order to address the structural challenges of the region as to *proteger derechos pero cambiar realidades.*[29] Part of the initiative to transform the inequalities through juridical review was the advent of the control of conventionality. The control of conventionality is a jurisprudence creation of the IAHRS elaborated in the case of *Almonacid Arellano v. Chile* in 2006[30] and more

---

[26] Morris et al. (2010), *translated by author.*

[27] Shany (2016).

[28] Manson and ONeill (2007).

[29] See e.g., Mac-Gregor (2015) and Faúndez Ledesma (2004).

[30] 'The Court is aware that domestic judges and courts are subject to the rule of law and, therefore, are obliged to apply the provisions in force in the legal system. But when a state has ratified an international treaty such as the American Convention, its judges, as part of the state apparatus, are

recently, developed also in the jurisprudence of the *Comunity of Garífuna de Punta Piedra v. Honduras* in 2017.[31]

The interpretation given in the case has been developed by the IACtHR in its case law and the literature as well.[32] The literature theorizes that the domestic norms and practices of the national states are to be consistent with the *corpus iuris* of the Inter-American Human Rights requirements.[33] The judges, justices and all states authorities, in other words, all public agents, must take in their actions the control of conventionality into account as it has been established by rulings in contentious cases and advisory opinions, adjusting the national norms to the human rights standards.[34]

The literature reaffirms the obligations for states under the IAHRS as well as extra-American international legal frameworks. Although there is part of the literature that understands the risks of fragmentation or unreasonable impositions, the theorization of the literature has grown into forms of preventing the contestation of the regional system and repetitive violations.[35]

Many countries in the region have granted a *legal status* to human rights treaties, but not in consistent ways. States granted privileged legal status, constitutional rank or constitutional blocks, or in some other cases the treaties were granted an intermediate ranking—beneath the constitution but above ordinary legislation.[36]

Furthermore, 'the inter-Americanization has contributed to finding answers to the structural challenges of the Latin American region',[37] noting that it is an obligation that the states themselves assumed upon ratifying the American Convention deriving

also subject to it, which obliges them to ensure that the effects of the provisions of the Convention are not diminished by the application of laws contrary to its object and purpose, and which from the outset lack legal effect. In other words, the judiciary must exercise a kind of "conventionality control" between the domestic legal norms that apply in specific cases and the American Convention on Human Rights. In this task, the judiciary must take into account not only the treaty, but also the interpretation made by the Inter-American Court, the ultimate interpreter of the American Convention'. Inter-American Court of Human Rights, *Almonacid Arellano v. Chile*, Judgment of 26 September 2006.

[31] 'Ensure that, if there are pending judicial or administrative remedies filed by the San Juan Garifuna Community, they are resolved in a prompt manner and with a control of conventionality in accordance with the international obligations of the Honduran state under the American Convention'. Inter-American Court of Human Rights, *Comunity of Garífuna de Punta Piedra v. Honduras*, Judgment of 10 2015.

[32] See e.g. Mac-Gregor (2015), Carmelina Londoño-Lázaro and Carrillo-Santarelli (2019), Burgorgue-Larsen et al. (2011), Gomes and Mazzuoli (2010), Mazzuoli (2018), Piovesan (2015), and von Bogdandy et al. (2017).

[33] The Interamerican corpus iuris encompasses the international treaties as the Inter-American System of Human Rights. See e.g. Piovesan (2015). Mazzuoli (2018).

[34] See e.g. Carmelina Londoño-Lázaro and Carrillo-Santarelli (2019).

[35] Regarding the debate on fragmentation, see e.g. Ibid.; Perez-Leon-Acevedo (2020) and Abrusci (2019).

[36] International Labour Office (2009).

[37] Mariela and Alessandri (2017).

from the fundamental principle of compensating harm and the principle of good faith in the observance of the consolidation of the interpretation of the Vienna Convention on the Law of Treaties.[38]

In addition, the IARHS has established a system for monitoring and supervising the international obligations assumed by the states parties. The system works according to a two-phase mechanism, 'inspired historically by the European Convention on Human Rights when it was created'.[39] The first attempt is in the IACHR and its admissibility, as it is established in Article 46.[40] There is then an attempt for a friendly solution, as it is described in Article 48.[41] The so called 'first report' makes reference to the IACtHR to solve the claim, as it is in Article 50.[42]

In the specific case of Brazil, Article 5, §2 of the Brazilian Federal Constitution stipulates the 'open constitutional clause': 'establishes that the rights and guarantees expressed in this Constitution do not exclude others resulting from the system and principles it adopts, or from international treaties to which the Republic of Brazil is a party'.[43]

This obligation concerns the actions of the state as a whole, so that not only must sanctioned norms formally conform to the postulates and provisions set forth in the American Convention, but every other act of power, including the exercise of jurisdiction and the imposition of definitive solutions to particular conflicts, must also conform to the precepts of the *corpus iuris* of the IAHRS.

Nevertheless, the relationship between domestic constitutional law and international human rights law has been particularly affected by the intention of expanding the IAHRS to fulfill the implementation of human rights.

There are three legal grounds for the obligatory exercise of conventionality control by all public agents. The first is the principle of *pacta sunt servanda*, according to which states must abide by their international obligations in good faith. The second is the principle of the useful effect of international treaties, whose efficacy cannot be set aside by internal rules or customs. The last one is the general principle enshrined in Article 27 of the Vienna Convention, according to which states may not, for internal reasons or on the grounds of domestic law, fail to comply with treaties and international judgments.[44]

The contentious jurisdiction of the IAHRS is coadjuvant and complementary to the national jurisdiction of the national states, the reason why the control of conventionality should be performed first by national judges. Only in case of absence or

[38] See e.g. Fitzmaurice et al. (2010), Linderfalk (2007), and Lo (2017).

[39] Pegorari (2017), *translated by the author.*

[40] (2009) Rules of Procedure of the Inter-American Commission on Human Rights.

[41] Ibid.

[42] Ibid.

[43] (1988) Constitution of Brazil.

[44] Sagües (2008).

deficiency of compliance by the domestic jurisdiction with the control of conventionality, will the claim be petitioned in the IACtHR, as a last resort.[45]

It has also been suggested that national states should adopt formal mechanisms for ensuring the efficacy of international decisions, establishing through constitutional, legal or jurisprudential means their binding nature, and that they incorporate in public-policy making and when judging legal cases the standards developed by the IACHR and the Inter-American Court; 'indeed, any judicial decision must be linked lege artis to the basic source of a court's authority, in our case the American Convention on Human Rights'.[46] The national states' public servants are all responsible for enforcement with the control of conventionality in order to contribute to a unified normative legal framework.

The indigenous peoples constitute a marginalized political group and their rights, in spite of being constitutionally established, are of very low efficacy, especially when the highest of the Brazilian institutions is failing in the exercise of its function against the majority of the populations in vulnerable situations. Hence the importance of an international jurisdiction to be able to exercise a true judicial control against the majority, that is, to be able to ensure enforcement to protect fundamental rights.

In this scenario, the control of conventionality appears, even as mandatory, as the best possibility to deal with technicalities of application and enforcement with the treaties and also regarding the efficacy of the decisions. The literature finds this critical to ensure the legitimacy of the IACtHR, which ultimately derives from state decisions.[47]

2.2.2 *Methodology*

The research is based on the analysis of the literature, jurisprudence, international treaties and official data, while leveraging interdisciplinarity by taking into account findings of legal anthropology and sociology. The legal claims and legislation offer an opportunity to rethink and redefine the efficacy of consultation in Brazil by shaping its enforcement.

2.2.2.1 The Conduct of Interviews

Due to the impossibility to conduct field work given the COVID-19 pandemic, online interviews, for background understanding, constituted an important part of

[45] Mazzuoli (2011).

[46] von Bogdandy (2019).

[47] It is relevant that the national states comply with the control of conventionality in order to avoid numerous claims to be petitioned in the Inter-American System of Human Rights. Mazzuoli (2018).

the analysis.[48] The approach provided a 'multi-actors'[49] view and supported an insight into stakeholders' interpretations of the norms of the ILO No. 169, the jurisprudence, legislation and the literature, also considering the 'interconnected context'[50] of natural resource exploitation, the public servants and indigenous peoples. The interviews were conducted following a semi-structured method taking into account the gender diversification and multi-stakeholder representation. The main goal was to gain an in-depth understanding on the underlying aspects of the efficacy of consultation with indigenous peoples by interviewing experts: public prosecutors, judges, academics and indigenous.[51]

The fluidity of the interviews conducted by the semi-structured method takes into consideration the informed consent of the research participants as the center of the ethical research practice.[52] The reflexive approach of the interviews guarantees a 'better dialogue between the researcher and the interview which was also considered for a better engagement'.[53] Although the work was not being conducted at a Brazilian University, it was conducted in accordance with the observance of the Decree No. 510 of 2016 which concerns the parameters and ethics needed to conduct the interviews such as privacy, transparency, consent and non-discrimination.[54]

2.2.2.2 The Criteria Adopted to Choose the Case Studies

Brazil was chosen to be the case study for a set of reasons. The propensity to overcome a problem and dictate the experience led to a greater sensitivity to understand the problems and the years of research to commit to a fresh perspective to a neglected part of Brazilian society. The interpretation of the Brazilian Constitution by the national courts has been gradually aligning with the interpretation of the IAHRS. Regardless of the decisions adopted in response to legal claims, the tendency has been towards taking more often into account international legal frameworks and treaties which thus warrants closer investigation.

It is worth to be analyzed in view of the many indeterminacies caused by the challenging application of consultation. The scenario shows the constant lack of enforcement with the norms, undermining the efficacy of consultation by leading to systemic forms of restrictive interpretation of the obligation provided by the Brazilian judiciary and legislature. Thus, there is the necessity to harmonize both legislative and judicial measures and interpretations with indigenous peoples' rights.

[48] See e.g. Debenham (2007), Middha (2018), Braun et al. (2017), and Lupton (2020).

[49] Little (2006).

[50] de Sousa Santos (1987).

[51] See e.g. The conduction of interviews were embedded with the pluralist and non-Western perspective. Mignolo (2011) and Smith (2012).

[52] Wiles et al. (2006).

[53] Sin (2005).

[54] Brazilian Government (2016) Decree No. 510.

In general, all legal claims and legislation under analysis are related to consultation with indigenous peoples dating from 1985 until 2020. The two criteria to choose the cases are first, the relevance and second, the novelty of the case.

According to the criteria of relevance, the claims and cases were selected because they were useful to better understand the magnitude of the topic, given the concept of consultation. The valuable data regarding consultation provided the best approach to these cases, taking into perspective the relevance and the timeline for each of them. The variety of cases was ensured by glancing through the index of indigenous peoples claims for consultation in natural resource exploitation in their territory. The substantive areas with which the study is concerned are explored and brought up for review. Among these areas, special attention is given to cases related to hydroelectric dams, mining and a special claim regarding a hydro road.

The criterion of novelty relates to the need to ensure a sufficient time frame to ensure proper consolidation of the legal claims and the legislation, as 'this broad temporal coverage will make it possible to observe how time may play a decisive role on the maturing effects of decisions and how efficacy can change over time'.[55] The scrutiny of claims and legislation takes not only the main interpretation but also dissident votes into account, which can be a great asset for the analysis. The consideration that has guided the case selection was therefore the objective for illustrating the variety of legal claims and cases regarding consultation with indigenous peoples relying on the most adequate solution for public policies.

As proposed by the ILO Convention No. 169, the analyses of Brazil take two points: the judiciary and legislature. Those were analyzed as national cases because even though Brazil is composed of federal states, the indigenous public policy is understood as being determined at national level. The legal claims of the Brazilian judiciary originate from the Brazilian Supreme Court and the Brazilian Federal Courts; the analysis of legislation considers the federal sphere.[56]

Therefore, the analyses of the IAHRS take into account first the IACHR procedures and second the IACtHR decisions. Within the recent context of internationalization of indigenous peoples' claims, the IAHRS has played an important role, contributing in part to the rupture with the exclusion and oppression of indigenous peoples in Latin America and also to change the legal order framework.

The IAHRS, the IACHR and the IACtHR are relevant to be addressed given increasing appeals to the IAHRS, particularly by those whose rights have been violated.[57] The analysis compares national legal claims with decisions of the

---

[55] Shany (2016); Calabria (2018), p. 26.

[56] The indigenous peoples' rights, when are collective rights involved, as it is in the cases of consultation, the jurisdiction is the Federal Union matter. For more, see: Brazilian Supreme Court, *Habeas Corpus*, HC 158657, Judgment of 2018.

[57] As a rule, states may not justify violations of indigenous peoples' rights in the name of what so called national development. The basic principle was reaffirmed at the 1993 Vienna World Conference on Human Rights understanding that 'development facilitates the enjoyment of all human rights, the lack of development may not be invoked to justify the abridgement of internationally recognized human rights'. (1969) Vienna Convention on the law of treaties. As a matter of

IACtHR for understanding the behavior of Brazil, as 'in a nutshell, the IAHRS is activated by domestic stakeholders in ways that transcend traditional enforcement perspectives, and that have the potential to provoke positive domestic human rights change'.[58]

The work ultimately calls for more measures to consolidate consultation and thereby to establish the intrinsic value of self-determination and cultural rights in Brazil. There is a potential risk of the inoperative application of the norms as judges may have different understandings of the meaning of an international norm depending on the national concerns at stake. To avoid such legal uncertainty, there is the need to comply with the procedure of consultation as the application is essential when defining Brazilian governmental policies, for the promotion and protection of indigenous peoples' rights.

2.2.3 *Scope and Limitations*

The limitations of the work are on one hand the impossibility to conduct field work and on the other hand discriminatory arguments which are contrary to human rights standards.[59]

Regarding initial plans to conduct field research in person, the COVID-19 pandemic and its severe and long-lasting travel restrictions put insurmountable hindrances in the way. In order to nonetheless comprehensively contribute to the debate and to overcome these obstacles, the research project filled the gap of in-person field work by conducting semi-structured interviews online with experts. The interviews helped to understand the theoretical input provided by the work on consultation with indigenous peoples in Brazil as a mechanism for the fundamental understanding of the equalitarian participation of indigenous peoples in natural resource exploitation. Thus, the interviews helped to build connections between

---

fact, the Inter-American Court of Human Rights also observed that the application of bilateral trade agreements does not justify the non-compliance of a state's obligations under the American Convention, otherwise, their application should be compatible with the Convention.

[58] Engstrom (2017).

[59] However not the main topic of the book, it is relevant to mention that the paths of colonialism and the very same framework that comes of the Western perspective translates into the understanding not of the collective rights, but the individual rights; and also the choices of some national states, including Brazil, to insist on natural resource exploitation activities. This discussion analyzes the binding treaties: American Convention and the ILO Convention No. 169 and how the Inter-American Court of Human Rights adapted the individual rights to collective rights, once there was no prevision on the first treaty. The analysis understands and takes into account the international adjudication and how the mandate of the judges changed in the past years and mostly, the relevance of the consolidation of the interpretation. At the same time, the individual rights can be used as long as it protects the indigenous peoples' self-determination. As an example, has the right to consultation but not to consent. See e.g. de Sousa Santos (1987) and von Bogdandy and Venzke (2016).

the data collected on regional standards, international treaties and the indigenous peoples' Protocols, and the experiences made by those who are working with the subject of the analysis on the ground.

The second limitation is represented by the difficulty to establish—by addressing the positive but not yet sufficient contribution of the Constitution of 1988 and the International Human Rights System—the collective rights, the cultural rights, the social rights, the land rights and more recently, the healthy rights to indigenous peoples. For instance, the 2008 ILO Declaration on Social Justice for a Fair Globalization further acknowledges that 'in a world of growing interdependence and complexity the fundamental values of freedom, human dignity, social justice, security and non-discrimination are essential for sustainable economic and social development and efficiency'.[60]

Specific to the Constitution of Brazil, this is the legal document which confers partial ownership rights over indigenous peoples' territory, once the Federal Union entails the property rights. This measure can be seen as a special protection that was given to the indigenous peoples as a vulnerable group, which needs special attention and measures.

The study also highlights that the Constitution of Brazil establishes the special protection of the collective indigenous peoples' lands and everything that it entails, as it should also be, consultation. Natural resource exploitation in indigenous peoples' territory must therefore be understood and conducted in accordance with indigenous peoples' self-determination and cultural rights.[61] The following applies to any activity conducted in their territory as their way of life, in the 'ecological sense of interaction among natural and cultural elements that set aside a more balanced development of human life'.[62] This work contributes to enlighten and strengthen indigenous peoples' collective rights values, in accordance with ethno-cultural diversity.

[60] International Labour Conference (2008) ILO Declaration on Social Justice for a Fair Globalization.

[61] The author explains: 'in times when the ideological inversion of human rights is an increasingly subtle tactic and the use of criminal law to punish the defense of territories and natural assets an increasingly sophisticated practice, it becomes urgent to bet on a shrewd use of law from a counter-hegemonic point of view. Otherwise, as it is being formalized today by governments, consultation will end with equal subtlety, not necessarily eliminating long-standing community systems and practices, but depoliticizing them, neutralizing the social energy of the subjects of rights, and inverting the discourses on life, territories and nature, against their own holders'. Mazariegos Rodas (2016), p. 224, *translated by author*.

[62] Yamada (2005).

2.3 The Implementation of Indigenous Peoples' Rights

This subchapter will describe the legal definitions that have been elaborated by international organs such as the United Nations (hereinafter, the UN) and the ILO. The literature brought forward the relevance of treating the indigenous peoples and their collective rights in accordance with international human rights standards.[63]

Over the past two decades, the rights of indigenous peoples[64] have become an important component of international law as well as national policy. This has been the result of continues demands by social movements driven by civil society activism; international and national initiatives; and indigenous peoples' marches all over Latin American countries, which present some pertinent examples.[65]

The legal opinion on whether there are indeed fundamental rights exclusive to indigenous peoples or whether they are part of the over-arching body of minorities rights is still inconclusive. While the usefulness of a clear-cut distinction between minorities and indigenous peoples is debatable, indigenous peoples do have specific recognition under international law, which is arguably more comprehensive than international legal instruments associated with minorities rights.[66]

Therefore, the main goal of this subchapter is to review the legal definitions as brought forward in international treaties which contemplate indigenous peoples'

---

[63] See e.g. Scheinin (2005), Xanthaki (2014), and Thomas (2007).

[64] Despite the lack of an authoritative definition, scholars aim to develop the conceptual tools to assess the specific legal situation of indigenous peoples. For instance, José Martínez Cobo proposed the criterion of self-identification of indigenous people as one of a set of criteria in his 'study of the problem of discrimination against indigenous populations, which include: historical continuity with pre-invasion and/or pre-colonial societies that developed on their territories; distinctiveness; non-dominance and a determination to preserve, develop and transmit to future generations territories and identity as peoples in accordance with their own cultural patterns, social institutions and legal system'. Cobo (1982).

[65] In the history of indigenous peoples in Latin America, several marches for different demands have taken place, which had a lasting impact on their perception by governments and the societies at large, for example: Colombia: in 2008, 10,000 indigenous marched from the Colombian Cauca to Bogotá to demand the end of the internal violence against them; Bolivia: between 2011 and 2012, 10,000 indigenous peoples participated in marches against the construction of the highway in indigenous territory (TIPNIS); Ecuador: in 2012, 20,000 indigenous peoples marched demanding respect for their right to water, life and dignity; Brazil: in April 2019, indigenous peoples are protesting using the #atl2029, #abrilindigena and #vailterlutasim hash-tags, protesting for the maintenance of the Indigenous Foundation (FUNAI).

[66] In this regard: 'general human rights have a distinctly integrative function. Minority rights are formulated as the rights of individuals to preserve and develop their separate group identity within the process of integration. Persons belonging to minorities often have several identities and participate actively in the common domain. Indigenous rights, on the other hand, tend to consolidate and strengthen the separateness of these peoples from other groups in society. The underlying assumption is that persons belonging to indigenous peoples have a predominantly indigenous identity and participate less in the common domain. The time may have come for the Sub-Commission to review the issue again'. ¶25, Daes and Eiden (2000).

rights. The analysis of the literature shows the implementation of the definitions and the improvement of them to a mostly accurate legal framework.

2.3.1 *Defining Indigenous Peoples*

Understanding indigenous peoples in the context of consultation is based both on their area of inhabitance and their territory, *i.e.* indigenous peoples living in urban or rural areas,[67] and their inclusion or not as a group in the minority rights sphere. In some countries indigenous peoples are categorized as minority, while in others they constitute in quantitative terms a majority of the population. The distinction is difficult to uphold from a theoretical point of view but is a factual reality in international treaties and documents.[68]

Legal theories build on the 'legitimizing acquisition of indigenous peoples' territories'[69] in the international sphere, which echo the elaboration of fundamental rights in national constitutions. "A people" is one of the concepts in international law that has proven hard or sometimes even unfeasible to define. What is defined, however, is that peoples are the units that posses the right to self-determination (its subjects). Furthermore, they exercise this right as a collective entity.[70]

The use of the term indigenous peoples and its meaning have changed over the times and spaces, once it '[had] gained acceptance in the international context, [apart from] ethnic minority, natives, aborigines or indigenous populations'.[71]

The UN was the first organ to attempt to define indigenous as peoples and nations are those which, having a historical continuity and pre-colonial societies that developed on the territories, determined to preserve and transmit to future generations their ancestral territories and their ethnic identity, in accordance with their own cultural patterns, social institutions and legal systems.[72]

---

[67] Indigenous peoples subjected to this work are those who want the requirement of consultation to take place in their territory, willing to accept the procedure of consultation provided by the national state according to their social organization, customs, beliefs, and traditions.

[68] See e.g. Kymlicka (1999), Daes (2000), and Anaya (2004).

[69] In this regard: 'however, since indigenous peoples claim the right to own land as well as rights to manage and own their natural resources, it is important to keep in mind the implications of 'territory' in understanding indigenous claims.' 'It needs to be stated at the outset that references to 'land' and 'territory' have been used alternatively. Indigenous claims are usually based on both notions. However, there is clear preference for recognition of territorial rather than land rights. A 'territory' refers to the totality of 'the environment of the areas which the peoples concerned occupy or otherwise use'? which is a broader concept than merely the land'. Gilbert (2003).

[70] Rombouts (2014).

[71] Yamada (2005), p. 10.

[72] See e.g. Cobo (1982) and Scheinin (2005).

Another attempt of definition can be found in the ILO No. 169, Article 1 for the countries who ratified the treaty.[73] However, due to the lack of a binding definition provided by the IAHRS, the line taken in the work is that consultation is invaluable for the exercise of self-determination and cultural rights for the indigenous peoples as collective entity when dealing with territory and resources. 'Yet there is no single, universally agreed definition of indigenous and tribal peoples. That said, the Convention No. 169 provides subjective and objective criteria that can be used to identify these groups'.[74]

However still pending a final agreement on the definition, the term indigenous peoples as a collective entity and indigenous person as individuals represent the most appropriate approximation and thus were also chosen as working definition for this research.

2.3.2 *The Implementation of Territorial Rights*

This subchapter presents an analysis of the development of the notion of territorial rights, which reveal an arena of great conflict. This occurs partially because of the difficult process on defining indigenous peoples and tribal communities, and partially because of the resulting entitlements to territory imposing a legal commitment, also as regards consultation. The implementation of the entitlement to territory builds on the assumption that consultation constitutes a mechanism through which indigenous peoples may have recourse to realize matters that affect their population. Besides the resulting obligation for the state to recognize the ownership of the lands occupied by indigenous peoples, it also highlights the requests for restitution of indigenous lands. Here it is relevant to emphasize that the use of the term of territory and not just land, addressing the special relationship of indigenous peoples with their territories as the demarcation of their identity, is an indispensable condition of their existence.

A more suitable approach to defining the right to territory is thus to consider the primary substantive rights of indigenous peoples that may be implicated in natural resource usage. These include, in particular, rights to property, culture, religion, health, physical well-being and to set and pursue their own priorities for development, as part of their fundamental right to self-determination and cultural rights.

The legal approach of the indigenous peoples' stresses 'the dimension of a relationship of dispossession or subordination in relation to another group that arrived later'.[75] As a response to discriminatory and non-egalitarian discourse, over time the international and national legislation began to acknowledge indigenous

[73] See e.g. Tomei and Swepston (1996).

[74] Internationale Arbeitsorganisation (2020).

[75] Scheinin (2005), p. 4.

peoples' rights. 'The question of land rights is an issue of restoring lands that were taken under a past discriminatory enterprise, an issue often linked to an ongoing denial of indigenous peoples' rights. In this regard, human rights law is facing the difficult challenge of reparations for past wrongs. Thus, in many ways, indigenous peoples' land rights are an issue of restoring previously denied rights rather than granting or creating new rights'.[76] Territorial rights also concern the territorial jurisdiction, 'to ensure the full and free development of their cultures and the best interest of their people'.[77]

The process of recognition of indigenous peoples' territory has been far from clear-cut. The guarantee of traditional territory and the access to natural resources they traditionally use is associated with the right of possession and property both collective and/or community, guaranteed by international legal instruments, differentiating it from the notion of property in a strict sense as elaborated in the international treaties and national constitutions'.[78]

Thus, 'the making of treaties and concepts of terra nullius and displacement were the classical ways of dispossession, whereby indigenous territories were legitimately acquired. The position of indigenous peoples in today's society is mostly a consequence of the famous literature of the three Cs, civilization, Christianization and commerce, for which international law, as the legal instrument of colonial conquest, was largely culpable. Today the position of indigenous peoples can be subsumed in one idea: they are the first inhabitants of lands they are not allowed to own or use. Their situation is an illustration on the modern development of theories concerning acquisition of land'.[79] As a matter of fact, the recognition of indigenous peoples' territory or land rights was hence crucial for the establishment of indigenous peoples' rights.

By contrast, some countries understood the measures to guarantee land rights as 'right to occupy traditional lands, [where] indigenous peoples are usually perceived as using public or national lands as a 'gift' from the government'.[80] This inflames another issue of recognition: 'one of the most widespread contemporary problems is the failure of states to recognize the existence of indigenous land use, occupancy and ownership, and the failure to accord appropriate legal status and legal rights to protect this use, occupancy and ownership'.[81] In view of the missing theoretical acknowledgement and the lack of understanding of the legal framework, since the beginning the relationship between indigenous peoples and the states that have emerged on their traditional lands have been far from being balanced.[82]

---

[76] Gilbert (2006).

[77] Kymlicka (2003).

[78] da Silva (2017).

[79] Gilbert (2003), p. 199.

[80] Ibid.

[81] Daes (2000), p. 36.

[82] Young (2020).

The implementation of territorial rights reveals an ongoing progress in direction of improvements, also in view of the general rules of consultation that were explored by the IAHRS. Overall, indigenous peoples' attachment to territory has further dimensions than the use and enjoyment of land as it includes not only the territory per se, but other aspects such as the spiritual, cultural, economic and social aspects of indigenous peoples as individuals and collective. The right to land has a special significance for the self-determination and cultural rights of indigenous peoples due to their so-called cosmovision, which understands cultural and spiritual identity as inseparably connected to traditional territories. These aspects may not be reflected in the definition of territory as previously established in international law but has been successively introduced through the interpretation of the IAHRS and constitutes therefore an important component of the present study.

The United Nations Permanent Forum on Indigenous Issues (hereinafter, the UNPFII) recently noted that land is the foundation of the lives and cultures of indigenous peoples all over the world. Without access to and respect for their rights over their lands, territories and natural resources, the survival of indigenous peoples' particular distinct culture is threatened. Land rights, access to land and control over it and its resources are central to indigenous peoples throughout the world, and they depend on such rights and access for their material and cultural survival. In order to survive as distinct peoples, indigenous peoples and their communities need to be able to own, conserve and manage their territories, lands and resources.[83]

In sum, there is the need to recognize the fundamental importance of indigenous peoples' security of territory, its use and access, and the importance of land rights for consultation processes, which includes ameliorating poverty, conflict prevention and resolution, and better adapted public policies to protect indigenous peoples' rights.

2.3.3 The Self-determination of Indigenous Peoples

Once described as *lex lata/lex obscura paradox*,[84] the right to self-determination was long seen as an obscure right, so that the advent of a mutually agreed definition has certainly enriched international law in general.

The literature applies the right to self-determination as it has two dimensions: the internal and the external dimension. The wide-ranging debates about the legal meaning of self-determination provide the backdrop to the question that is highlighted, thereby helping to ease the debate about the meaning of the legal

[83]¶4 United Nations (2007) Permanent Forum on Indigenous Issues Supplement No. 23.

[84]For Crawford, the uncertainties are not marginal and reach the core of the notion of self-determination of peoples: 'although it is understood that the right to self-determination is lex lata (established right), and not lex ferenda (right in the process of development, still uncertain), its content is still lex obscura, that is, nobody knows exactly what it means, especially outside the colonial context'. Crawford (2001).

norm. Although this work does not engage directly with any of the debates about the meaning of the right to self-determination, some clarification might be in order.

Part of the legal literature has understood self-determination as secession, which does not apply to the fullest extent possible of the right. Self-determination can also be achieved, and this regards indigenous peoples' rights, through internal means, through autonomy, the right to land and resource management. Thus, indigenous peoples have articulated their demands in terms of self-determination as an expression of their desire to preserve their traditional land from expropriation processes and to exercise collective rights. It was first understood in the United Nations Charter of 1945 by those countries signing the treaty.[85]

The human rights approach distinguished from the state-centered approach should be into the direction that the right to self-determination is characterized as a human right which is the cornerstone of indigenous peoples' rights once international law opened the door for a positive next step, offering 'strong legal ammunition for indigenous peoples'.[86] The right can be defined as 'affirmation that all human beings, individually or as groups, have the right to exercise control over their own destinies and to participate with equality in the construction and development of the governmental institutional order in which they live, so that it is compatible with their ways of life'.[87] Self-determination is relevant for indigenous peoples once it can be characterized as a way to counter discrimination and to achieve positive measures for the implementation of indigenous peoples' rights, in which at the heart of self-determination, there is the right to consult.[88] At the moment that self-determination became a relevant principle, the cultural rights of indigenous peoples is also relevant, entailing the 'belief that the right of indigenous peoples to freely practice their culture and traditions in accordance with their own institutional structures and customs is invaluable in protecting them'.[89]

Acceptance of the intrinsic worth of consultation in decision-making, by the international treaties and national states,[90] has a clear relationship with indigenous

[85] The nations pledged to reaffirm the faith in human persons, providing the key rights that grasped human rights as is stipulated nowadays. See e.g. Charters et al. (2010); (1945) Documentary about the founding of the United Nations Organization and the San Francisco Conference in 1945.

[86] Xanthaki (2014).

[87] Daes (2000), p. 81.

[88] Xanthaki (2014).

[89] Rombouts (2014).

[90] 'Much has been said about the historical complicity of international law-or dominant thinking about international law-in the oppression of minority and indigenous peoples and their cultures. So it is perhaps with some irony that groups that are identified as indigenous are now looking to international law as a means of reversing the historical patterns of oppression and securing their cultural identities. Largely as a result of their own advocacy at the international level, indigenous peoples or populations are now distinct subjects of concern within the United Nations (UN), the Organization of American States (OAS) and other international institutions. For several years, efforts have been under way within these institutions to develop new international normative instruments specifically for the benefit of indigenous peoples. Although use of the terms *indigenous peoples* and indigenous *populations* remains contested, both have nonetheless become widely

peoples' right to self-determination, including the state's obligation to consult indigenous peoples in matters that may affect them.[91] These processes for legitimizing self-determination reveal a tense relationship between indigenous peoples and the state, as it may entail disputes over the peoples' autonomy as well as the state's sovereignty.[92]

2.3.4 The Cultural Rights of Indigenous Peoples

As one of the most crucial aspects in the development of international obligations favoring indigenous peoples, cultural rights play a central role in the human rights regime.[93] The strong honored identity of indigenous peoples remains, as 'against all odds, the indignities of colonization, and the lures of modern society, indigenous peoples have survived as communities'.[94]

Cultural rights encompass elements of a very elaborated and a complex right that can be found in several international treaties. In the case of an indigenous peoples considered as a culturally differentiated group, there is the need to a democratic political order in which the group is able to preserve its distinct character and to have this character reflected in the institutions of government.[95] The literature posits that some aspects of the right has implications for civil, political, economic and social rights of the indigenous.[96] Under international human rights law, indigenous peoples

employed. In general, the term *indigenous*is used in association with groups that maintain a continuity of cultural identity with historical communities that suffered some form of colonial invasion, and that by virtue of that continuity of cultural identity continue to distinguish themselves from others. It can hardly be disputed that indigenous peoples have been able to generate substantial sympathy for their demands among international actors. This can be seen in several concrete developments, including the UN General Assembly's designation of an International Decade of the World's Indigenous People, which is ongoing, the International Labour Organisation's (ILO) adoption in 1989 of its Convention on Indigenous and Tribal Peoples, and the efforts at both the United Nations and the OAS to create declarations on the rights of indigenous peoples. Indeed, I and others have argued that international law is developing with particular attention to indigenous peoples in a way that is favorable to their demands. At the same time, there is significant ongoing resistance to the indigenous peoples' agenda'. Anaya (1999).

[91]¶4 A/HRC/EMRIP/2010/2 (2010) Progress report on the study on indigenous peoples and the right to participate in decision-making.

[92]¶66 Tauli-Corpuz (2020).

[93]See e.g. Wiessner (2011).

[94]Ibid.

[95]See e.g. Anaya (2004).

[96]According to the scholar: '1) the right to take part in the cultural life, 2) the right to enjoy the benefits of scientific progress and its application, 3) the right to benefit from the protection of moral and material interests resulting from any scientific, literary or artistic production as the author, and 4) the freedom indispensable for scientific research and creativity activity. The right to preserve the cultural identity of minority groups or indigenous peoples is a significant aspect of cultural rights and has implications for civil, political, economic and social rights'. Yamada (2005), p. 13.

have obtained recognition due to their cultural distinctiveness.[97] Furthermore, the importance of the land transcends the economic interest, as it determines the survival of indigenous peoples 'as a differentiated cultural group'.[98]

It is important to note that the rights of nature, territorial rights and cultural rights of peoples, are integrated into a complex legal web, proper to each people or traditional community, 'composing the intrinsic relationship of ethnobiodiversity or sociobiodiversity, considering that biodiversity belongs to the domain of both natural and cultural, the jusdiversity'.[99]

Consultation presents in the right to culture a way to ensure harmonious relations between governments and indigenous peoples as a crucial element in the application of the international obligation. Thus, the 'cardinal purpose of the consultation is to defend indigenous culture and territory, or rather, to guarantee the corresponding rights'.[100]

According to the Human Rights Committee's General Comment (hereinafter, the HRCGC) on Article 27 of the Human Rights Covenant on Civil and Political Rights (hereinafter, the HRCCPR), 'culture manifests itself in many forms, including a particular way of life associated with the use of land resources'. The Committee on Economic, Social and Cultural Rights (hereinafter, the CESCR) pointed out that the 'strong communal dimension of indigenous peoples' cultural life is indispensable to their existence, well-being and development, and includes the right to the lands, territories and resources which they have traditionally owned, occupied or otherwise used or acquired'.[101]

The concept of consultation contributes to the protection of the cultural integrity of indigenous peoples as a preventive effect once ensuring that indigenous peoples take part in assessing measures with the potential to impact their cultural relationship with their territory and natural resources.[102]

2.3.5 *The Legal Nature of Consultation with Indigenous Peoples*

The legal nature of consultation is that it is a material and procedural right in which the proceedings shall be taken by the state towards indigenous peoples according to the indigenous peoples' customary law.[103] This research analyzes the efficacy of

[97] See e.g. Jouannet (2013).

[98] da Silva (2017), p. 94, translated by author.

[99] da Silva (2017).

[100] Duprat (2015).

[101] ¶ 36 United Nations (2009) General comment No. 21: Right of everyone to take part in cultural life (art. 15, para. 1 (a), of the International Covenant on Economic, Social and Cultural Rights).

[102] See e.g. Cabrera (2017) and Garavito (2012).

[103] See e.g. Cabrera (2017) and Navarro (2021).

consultation considering the variants of claims and legislation and the application by all public servants.[104]

The right to consultation is defined in international law as a principle and by some states as an obligation or a right. The definition taken by states usually sets the tone for consultation to merely embrace consent. The binding international treaties, in which consultation can be found, are the ILO Convention No. 169 and the UNDRIP.

This might be seen as a *legal lacunae*, which let the international courts and the international law to define the parameters of its application. The IAHRS, for instance, understood consultation as property right, while international law defined it as self-determination.

Thus, consultation is not a mere procedure and its nature depends on the result, the legitimization[105] of indigenous peoples as part of the process of decision-making. While the legal notion is the same, it is difficult to acquire comprehensive information of the application from all regions. In this regard, 'mechanisms enabling the participation of indigenous peoples in external, non-indigenous decision-making processes can be problematic for various reasons; they may operate in environments where indigenous peoples are politically, socially and economically non-dominant and, while they enhance indigenous peoples' participation, they do not go so far as to level the playing field with non-indigenous individuals and peoples; they do not allow greater indigenous influence over decisions in practice; because they are poorly implemented, or suffer from previously unforeseeable problems; or because they privilege the participation of certain indigenous individuals over that of others, creating concerns about their ability to achieve equality between individuals.'[106]

The participation in decision-making leads to a broader trend: the dominance of the legality of the governance paradigm which explains the rise of terms such as participation, empowerment and consultation in regulations of all kinds.

Participation and empowerment can be seen in the context of articulating the idea of democracy and inclusiveness for so long pursued by indigenous peoples. However similar, consultation is noted here as a principle that might operate as application of the legal guiding thought (in German, *leitender Rechtsgedanke*) setting the

---

[104]The concept of prior and informed consent originated in the medical field, and its main objective was to establish a dialogue between the doctor and the patient. Relevant international documents are the Nuremberg Code uses the term voluntary consent, while the Declaration of Helsinki and the International Guidelines (World Health Organization) use the terminology of informed consent. The Declaration of Helsinki stipulates that consent must be freely given. In Brazil, there is the Resolution No. 196/96-CNS/MS that gives great emphasis to the consent term, dedicating the whole chapter IV to it. The UNESCO Universal Declaration on Bioethics and Human Rights of October 19, 2005, in its article 6, when dealing with consent, uses the expression prior free and informed consent. Moreover, the same declaration brings into the field of bioethics the protection of the environment, the biosphere and biodiversity, having express reference to the respect for traditional knowledge. See e.g. Manson and ONeill (2007), Perrault (2004), and Faden et al. (1986).

[105]See e.g. Franck (1990).

[106]¶ 10 UN A/HRC/18/42 (2011) Final report of the study on indigenous peoples and the right to participate in decision-making.

relevance and giving efficacy to self-determination and cultural rights with indigenous peoples.[107]

The controversy of the norm that has the first appearance in the ILO Convention No. 169 while the application in states are normally contrary to indigenous peoples' rights, is one of the ramifications of consultation to a better and more profound reflection on its legal use for national public policies.[108] The requirement of consultation understood as a norm focusing on procedural issues, offers a poor solution to the discussion that brings together radically different conceptions of economic development and the good life.[109]

Thus, weak regulation has embodied a poor transaction between legalities and multiculturalism as different as those advocated by the global indigenous movement on the one hand and transnational companies on the other. This is a problem of legal concept that not even the most sophisticated international organizations and bodies were able to give clearance to and to promote the indigenous peoples' rights.[110] The better understanding of the legal concept and the application is highly relevant such that there will not be indeterminacies including with reference to non-enforcement with the norm or/and its use to undermine the indigenous peoples' self-determination or facilitate resource exploitation in their territory.

The debate on the right to consultation has revealed some novel contours over the last years. As a contribution to the modern legal semantics of the indigenous peoples as entitled to territory rights, thus, it amplified an issue once subject to certain legal restrictions. Simultaneously, consultation endeavors endure to further legitimize the self-determination and the cultural rights of indigenous peoples.

2.4 The Legal Analysis of Consultation Under International Law

The international applicability of consultation shall be scrutinized as the work hinges on the analysis of the literature, claims and legislation. Accordingly, this sub-chapter examines the norms and the extent to which there is a need for a more specific legal framework to address indigenous peoples' consultation as self-determination and cultural rights or whether the existing human rights instruments are sufficient. When addressing indigenous peoples' rights under international law, the issue of the

[107] See e.g. Krieger (2000).

[108] The scholar shows 'that ethnicity.gov is a contested process, insofar as the governance paradigm has been controversial from below by the global indigenous rights movement of the last three decades, which claims the principle of self-determination and has also influenced national and international rules on collective rights.' Garavito (2012).

[109] Ibid.

[110] Doyle (2016).

adequacy as well as the unique nature of the claim is relevant to design an accurate application.

2.4.1 The Committee on the Elimination of Racial Discrimination

The Committee on the Elimination of Racial Discrimination (hereinafter, the CERD) is part of the UN body in which experts monitor the implementation of the Convention on the Elimination of All Forms of Racial Discrimination by the states parties which signed the treaty. The participating states are obliged to submit regular reports to the Committee regarding implementation, and some of the General Recommendations are relevant for the understanding of consultation. The interpretation of this human right provision can be found in the General Recommendation (hereinafter, the GR) No. 23.

The GR No. 23 adopts the standard calling on states to 'ensure that members of indigenous peoples enjoy equal rights in respect of effective participation in public life and that no decisions directly relating to their rights and interests are taken without their informed consent'.[111] Relevant to add is that CERD had recommended that the consultation includes discussion of an equitable sharing of benefits.[112]

This document included the necessary enforcement of the state to ensure the informed consent of indigenous peoples as part of consultation. The same interpretation was highlighted by the concluding observations to Ecuador in 2003 regarding the importance of the informed consent of affected peoples before the extraction of natural resources from their lands. Thus: 'the Committee therefore recommends that the prior informed consent of these communities be sought, and that the equitable sharing of benefits to be derived from such exploitation be ensured. Detailed information on land titles of indigenous communities, as well as on remedies available to indigenous people claiming compensation for the environmental depletion of their traditional lands, should be included in the state party's next periodic report'.[113]

[111]¶ 7 Committee on the Elimination of Racial Discrimination (CERD) (1997) General Recommendation No. 23: Indigenous Peoples.

[112]Ibid.

[113]¶ 10, *Concluding observations of the Committee on the Elimination of Racial Discrimination-Ecuador*, 22 September 2008.

2.4.2 United Nations Permanent Forum on Indigenous Issues

The UNPFII interpretation of consultation emphasizes the importance of obtaining the consent of indigenous peoples, rather than offering them a mere opportunity to express their views. This interpretation reveals the necessity to observe the indigenous peoples' own views on how the consultation and consent should be conducted. There is, then, a strong sense of consultation understood as self-determination and observation of cultural rights.

For instance, the conclusions of a work process in 2005 regarding the methodology defining free, prior and informed consent, gave a great opportunity to understand the right. As part of the findings, there was the objective that 'positive developments have been achieved in setting international human rights standards for the rights of indigenous peoples to lands, territories and resources, including by regional human rights mechanisms in Africa and the Americas'.[114] This entailed that consent had to be interpreted together with the right to self-determination and rights over their lands and resources.[115] The significance of the consolidation process of consultation and consent could lead to eventual co-management and joint decision-making by indigenous communities on programs and projects affecting them.

2.4.3 The United Nations Declaration of Rights of Indigenous Peoples and the Free, Prior and Informed Consent

The UNDRIP was adopted by the United Nations General Assembly in September 2007 and, although non-binding, it is the most comprehensive and advanced international instrument on the rights of indigenous peoples and the latest addition to a growing body of indigenous peoples' international law. For the first time in international law, the holders of the rights, the indigenous peoples, played a central role in the negotiations on its content.

Before 1970, the United Nations Commission on Human Rights paid little attention to the issue of minorities and less to the indigenous peoples' claims. After 1970, some government delegates and UN experts decided to draw attention to the continuing human rights problems faced by indigenous peoples in several countries such as recognition of their land rights at the national level or their language rights.[116]

Due to the obstinacy of indigenous peoples around the world supported by civil society organizations, they were able to visit the United Nations headquarters in

[114] ¶ 6 United Nations (2018) Permanent Forum on Indigenous Issues.

[115] ¶ 5 Ibid.

[116] See e.g. Xanthaki (2014).

Geneva to present their claims. Those actions led to the establishment of the Working Group on Indigenous Populations (hereinafter, the WGIP), which produced the first draft of the UNDRIP. 'It is this intrigue, which blended psychological, political, legal and cultural issues with national interests and international diplomacy who played particularly important roles in developing the indigenous rights agenda at the UN for more than a quarter of a century'.[117]

The UNDRIP covers the range of civil, political, economic, social, cultural and environmental rights. The innovative part might be seen in that it expresses the individual and collective rights of indigenous peoples. The understanding is that the free, prior and informed consent is also part of self-determination and cultural rights, for indigenous peoples being able to control their futures, having a transformative influence on international law and 'perhaps, to become emancipated from colonial manifestations of international law. That is an attractive picture, but a troubling one. It is troubling particularly because it does not trouble or problematize the subject of that discourse'.[118]

The right to self-determination plays a central role 'and the multiple elements needed for its implementation, be it control over lands, territories and natural resources; recognition of indigenous self-determined sustainable development; respect for indigenous authorities and justice systems, or implementation of the cultural rights related to indigenous languages, religions or traditional knowledge, among others. Adequate application of this right requires changes in the general governance of states, and this will have a transformational impact in terms of human rights enforcement, remedying racism, discrimination and inequality, more democratic and inclusive societies, and enhanced legitimacy of the state itself. The implementation of indigenous peoples' right to self-determination is also at the core of redress for the past and ongoing human rights violations they have suffered and a foundation for reconciliation'.[119]

The UNDRIP adopts three different approaches to consultation that include (1) reallocation and chemicals (Articles 10 and 29); (2) trigger to redress[120]

[117] For more background information on the history of the UNDRIP, see e.g. Charters et al. (2010).

[118] Young (2020).

[119] Tauli-Corpuz (2020), p. 13.

[120] 'The second reference is in Article 11(2). Article 11 is generally concerned with Indigenous cultural rights. Article 11(2) specifically addresses state obligations to effect redress where cultural property has been taken without the free, prior and informed consent of the peoples concerned. This provision is, in a sense, backward looking; the absence of FPIC historically triggers the present duty'. Article 28, the fourth FPIC reference, bears some similarities to Article 11(2).The overall topic of Article 28 is redress for the loss of lands, territories and resource. The trigger for the duty to redress is the historical circumstance that such lands, territories or resources were taken without the free, prior and informed consent of the peoples concerned. If Articles 11 and 28 adopt a similar FPIC formulation, the same can be said for Articles 10 and 29. Article 29 is generally concerned with the protection of the environment. Within that, Article 29(2) adopts an FPIC provision to address the specific issue of the storage or disposal of hazardous substances. Bankes (2020).

(Articles 11 (2) and 28 (1)) and (3) consultation for natural resource exploitation (Article 19 and 32 (2)).[121]

The consultation mentioned in Article 19 and 32 of the UNDRIP provides the essential elements for the analysis of legal claims and legislation. Of particular note here is Article 46 (2), which suggests that rights may be subject to limitations but only where such limitations 'are determined by law and in accordance with international human rights obligations'.[122] In addition to that, there is 'the effect that the [free, prior and informed consent] presents only one universal standard within the normative framework of the UNDRIP'.[123]

Even though international norms are instruments created by states, there has been the recognition that there is a growing concern about the situation in which indigenous peoples live and the way in which mechanisms to protect their rights are designed for them within the UN system. It is a fact that, despite the resistance of some governments, indigenous peoples have come to be recognized by the international community as subjects of specific rights at the international level. From then on, a process of insertion of these specific rights into international human rights law was inevitable. The points that have been the most hotly debated during all these years have been the right to self-determination, the right to autonomy over their lands, territories and natural resources, collective rights, the right to restitution and the right to free, prior and informed consent.

The base understanding of the FPIC is that it was conceived after the definition of consultation. At first, consultation was seen as a procedural character to migrate the interpretation that it needs to reach standards to become an established right revealing 'how quickly one can become engaged in dissecting, rearticulating and advocating for FPIC so that Indigenous peoples can use it to control what affects them without considering the subject-status of indigenous peoples or how defining FPIC might influence that subject'.[124]

The FPIC can be understood as 'a pre-existing object, which then presupposes styles of legal analysis and disciplinary practices that shape and influence the subjects who are supposed to claim FPIC without having to acknowledge the subjectivity'.[125] The UNDRIP defines in Article 19 that 'states shall consult and cooperate in good faith with the indigenous peoples concerned through their representative institutions in order to obtain their free, prior and informed consent before adopting and implementing legislative or administrative measures that may affect them'.[126]

In addition, Article 32 affirms that 'states shall consult with the indigenous peoples concerned in order to obtain their free and informed consent before approving any project affecting their lands or territories and other resources, particularly in

---

[121] The analysis of the two approaches can be found, see e.g. Ibid.; Barelli (2018).

[122] (2007) The United Nations Declaration on the Rights of Indigenous Peoples.

[123] Barelli (2018), p. 20.

[124] Young (2020).

[125] Ibid.

[126] (2007) The United Nations Declaration on the Rights of Indigenous Peoples.

connection with the development, utilization or exploitation of mineral, water or other resources'.[127]

Setting a stronger tone to the right to consultation of ILO Convention No. 169, the FPIC 'ensure that the response to questions and challenges posed by the modernity's increasingly pervasive reach are provided by indigenous peoples themselves. In doing so, free, prior and informed consent reconstructs the foundations of self-determination which were brutally reputed in the initial colonial encounter'.[128]

The intersection of diverse actors around the FPIC is a 'hybridization of legal regimes which might changes the trajectory and future over land, resources and ethnicity in times of globalization'.[129]

However relevant, the debate of the FPIC emanate of a non-binding treaty and has not a substantial repercussion in Brazil, leaving for the American Convention and the ILO No. 169, the binding treaties, the framework and standards to be followed regarding the application of consultation with indigenous peoples.

If consultation is a procedural right, a right for the procedure to participate, the right to consent originates from self-determination and is a substantive right. The consent is established in the UNDRIP and the American Declaration of Indigenous Peoples. However, as it is going to be shown in the third chapter of this book, the IACtHR made an attempt to analyze and perform the right but stopped short of doing so in the *Saramaka People v. Suriname,* a case indigenous peoples petitioned[130] resulting in a mention but not further elaboration in the case *Triunfo de la Cruz Garífuna Triunfo de la Cruz Community and its members v. Honduras*, a petition made by the Afro-descendants community.[131]

2.4.4 *The International Labour Organization Convention No. 169*

The ILO Convention No. 169 of 1989 emerged from the decision to revisit and adjust the legal framework of assimilationism of the previous Convention No. 107.[132] The idea was to 'replace the emphasis of the Convention on the

[127] Ibid.

[128] Doyle (2016), Preface.

[129] Garavito (2012).

[130] See e.g. Inter-American Commission of Human Rights, *Saramaka People v. Suriname*, Case No 172, Judgment of 28 November 2007; Antkowiak (2013) and Wright and Tomaselli (2021).

[131] Inter-American Court of Human Rights, *Garífuna Triunfo de la Cruz and your members v. Honduras*, Judgment of 9 May 2019.

[132] 'Convention No. 169 concerns the situation of more than 5,000 indigenous and tribal peoples, constituting a population of more than 370 million, living in more than 70 countries in all regions of the world. These peoples possess diverse languages, cultures, livelihood practices and knowledge systems. However, in most countries, they face discrimination and exploitative labour conditions, which are interconnected with their generalized marginalization and poverty situation. The ILO's

objectives of integration with an emphasis on respect for the identity of these populations and the promotion of greater consultation and participation of these peoples in the decisions that affect them'.[133]

Regarding consultation as elaborated in the ILO Convention No. 169, a binding treaty, it left quite open the conditions of its application by stating that 'governments shall consult with indigenous peoples'.[134] This provision can be found in Article 6 and tasks the states themselves to conduct the consultation with indigenous peoples towards any administrative and legislative measure taken. The UNDRIP, a non-binding treaty, on the other hand, characterized consultation as free, prior and informed consent.[135] Therefore, the understanding is that the requirement of consultation is not a self-executing norm, depending on an additional norm elaborated by each state to ensure its efficacy.[136]

Therefore, the ILO Convention aimed at overcoming discriminatory practices which directly affect indigenous peoples enabling them to participate in decision-making that impact on the course of their lives. So that 'the fundamental principles of consultation and participation constitute the cornerstone of the ILO Convention No. 169'.[137] Another important consideration in this respect is that the ILO

---

concern for indigenous peoples dates back to the 1920s and originated in the quest to overcome the discriminatory working conditions they live under. In recognition of the complexities and specificities of indigenous peoples' situations, Convention No. 169 takes a holistic approach covering a wide range of issues that affect the lives and well- being of these peoples. Convention No. 169 has become a global reference point with impact on governance and development policies that spans far be- yond the countries that have ratified it. Further, it is an instrument for governments to foster a favourable environment for the creation of sustainable enterprises'. International Labour Organization (2013).

[133] Garavito (2012).

[134] Article 6: *'In applying the provisions of this Convention, governments shall: (a) consult the peoples concerned, through appropriate procedures* and in particular through their representative institutions, whenever consideration is being given to legislative or administrative measures which may affect them directly; (b) establish means by which these peoples can freely participate, to at least the same extent as other sectors of the population, at all levels of decision-making in elective institutions and administrative and other bodies responsible for policies and programmes which concern them; (c) establish means for the full development of these peoples' own institutions and initiatives, and in appropriate cases provide the resources necessary for this purpose. 2- consultations carried out in application of this Convention shall be undertaken, in good faith and in a form appropriate to the circumstances, with the objective of achieving agreement or consent to the proposed measures' (1989) Indigenous Peoples and Tribal Convention No 169.

[135] Article 10: 'indigenous peoples shall not be forcibly removed from their lands or territories. No relocation shall take place without the free, prior and informed consent of the indigenous peoples concerned and after agreement on just and fair compensation and, where possible, with the option of return.' (2007) The United Nations Declaration on the Rights of Indigenous Peoples.

[136] The scholar pointed out that: 'At what point did indigenous peoples' resistance to being physically and culturally annihilated become a discussion about legal procedures?' Garavito (2012), *translated by author*.

[137] International Labour Organization (2013).

Convention No. 169 also 'provides certain language on the right to self-determination to meet particular needs of indigenous and tribal peoples'.[138]

Article 7 should be carried out together with Article 2 of the ILO Convention No. 169 when it 'specifies that the purpose of government action is to ensure equality in terms of rights and opportunities and eliminate the socio-economic gap between indigenous peoples and other sectors of society while recognizing their special rights, needs and aspirations as peoples. Practically, coordinated and systematic action implies undertaking comprehensive reviews and revisions of laws, policies, programmes and projects to ensure that these are all aligned with the provisions for indigenous peoples' rights as well as the establishment of adequate monitoring mechanisms to continuously assess the situation of indigenous peoples. All such action should be undertaken with the participation of indigenous peoples and with due respect to their social and cultural identity, customs, traditions, institutions, aspirations and ways of life. The provisions on co- ordinated and systematic action are thus naturally linked to those on consultation and participation'.[139]

The state must carry out consultation with the peoples concerned to evaluate their social, spiritual and cultural impact, which must serve as fundamental criteria in the execution of development activities. The intention was to deny the indigenous peoples of the right to veto the projects and measures consulted, since there is not the enforcement with the requirement of free, prior neither informed consent. The only adjustment is to require an adequate participation of indigenous peoples regarding the impacts that the activity may have: 'the achievement of permanent dialogue at all levels, as required by the Convention, would contribute to preventing conflict and building an inclusive model of development'.[140] The mitigation of veto might be understood here as a forced way to achieve an agreement between the natural resource companies, the indigenous peoples and the state. The understanding is that the provisions of the convention do not imply that communities have veto power over development policies. On the contrary, 'it argues that no segment of the national population of any country has the right to veto development policies'.[141] Relevant to note is that 'during the process of revising ILO Convention No. 107, the requirement of consultation with indigenous peoples was often articulated as a principle'.[142]

Together with Article 7, Article 6 is essential in requiring governments to hold genuine consultations in which indigenous and tribal peoples have the right to express their views and influence the decision-making process, which means that

[138] Thornberry (2002).

[139] Programme to promote ILO convention no. 169 (PRO 169) and International Labour Standards Department (2009).

[140] Ibid.

[141] Garavito (2012).

[142] Cabrera (2017).

governments have the obligation to create conditions that enable these peoples to contribute actively and effectively to the development process.[143]

Differently than the UNDRIP, however, the ILO Convention No. 169 does not reflect on the crucial need to take into account the indigenous peoples' opinion about national resource projects in their territory. This leads to the understanding that consent is a result of consultation, a requirement found in Article 7. The interpretation is that consultation is not relevant for the exercise of self-determination, which calls into question the efficacy of the participation of indigenous peoples, 'since an action or policy of the state or of third parties in indigenous ancestral territories can be considered legitimate even without their consent'.[144] Article 15 states that 'consultations on exploitation projects are intended to determine whether and to what extent peoples would be adversely affected'.[145] According to this interpretation, the 'pro-forma consultations or simple information are not sufficient to consider the requirements of the Convention fulfilled. At the same time, such consultations do not imply a right of veto, nor do they necessarily result in agreement or consent'.[146]

Some attempts to clarify the interpretation have been given by the Committee of Experts on the Application of Conventions and Recommendations (hereinafter, the CEACR), which was set up in 1926 to examine the governments reports on matters of the ILO treaties. For those countries which ratified the ILO Convention No. 169, it is expected that they report regularly on the measures and public policies for the implementation and taken practice of the standards given by the Convention. The technical evaluation of the ILO standards can be seen in the development of the understanding of consultation with indigenous peoples.[147]

---

[143] 'In applying the provisions of this Convention, governments shall: (a) consult the peoples concerned, through appropriate procedures and in particular through their representative institutions, whenever consideration is being given to legislative or administrative measures which may affect them directly; (b) establish means by which these peoples can freely participate, to at least the same extent as other sectors of the population, at all levels of decision-making in elective institutions and administrative and other bodies responsible for policies and programmes which concern them; (c) establish means for the full development of these peoples' own institutions and initiatives, and in appropriate cases provide the resources necessary for this purpose. *Article 6(2)* The consultations carried out in application of this Convention shall be undertaken, in good faith and in a form appropriate to the circumstances, with the objective of achieving agreement or consent to the proposed measures. *Article 7(1).* The peoples concerned shall have the right to decide their own priorities for the process of development as it affects their lives, beliefs, institutions and spiritual well-being and the lands they occupy or otherwise use, and to exercise control, to the extent possible, over their own economic, social and cultural development. In addition, they shall participate in the formulation, implementation and evaluation of plans and programmes for national and regional development which may affect them'. Programme to promote ILO convention no. 169 (PRO 169) and International Labour Standards Department (2009).

[144] Garavito (2012).

[145] (1989) Indigenous Peoples and Tribal Convention No 169, p. 169.

[146] International Labour Office (2016) Procedimientos para la celebración de consultas con los pueblos indígenas : experiencias de Noruega.

[147] For blunt analyses of the CEACR's work: International Labour Organization (2019).

The CEACR also stressed the importance of consulting with the indigenous peoples to determine whether and to what extent the interests of those peoples were prejudiced in order to incorporate the criteria received into compensation plans for mining exploration. Thus, 'the Committee reminds the Government that the prior consultations required by Article 6 of the Convention, must be carried out by means of appropriate procedures and in particular through the peoples' representative institutions whenever consideration is being given to legislative or administrative measures which may affect the peoples directly. It accordingly asks the Government to provide information on the manner in which the abovementioned consultations were carried out. Please also provide information on progress in applying the Act, citing specific cases of indigenous communities that have benefited from it. The Committee would also be grateful for information on the measures adopted or envisaged to regularize the situation of indigenous villagers or communities who occupy or use in any other manner lands located on state reservations, protected areas or private property, and on progress made in the preparation of the Land Tenure Act, in consultation with the indigenous peoples.'[148]

As a relevant contribution of the experts has been that before undertaking or authorizing any program of exploitation or exploration of natural resources in indigenous territories, the government must carry out a study in cooperation with the indigenous peoples concerned, and that the results of these studies should be considered as fundamental criteria for deciding on the implementation of activities.

2.4.5 *The Convention on Biological Diversity*

The Convention on Biological Diversity of 1993 (hereinafter, the CBD) is one of the most widely accepted international treaties. Together with the ILO Convention No. 169, the CBD is also a binding treaty and was signed by 188 parties. The treaty is a multilateral environmental agreement that is dedicated to determining a strategy for sustainable development. Albeit highlighting the need for consultation not only with indigenous peoples, the overwhelming majority of states-parties have recognized indigenous peoples' rights which facilitates the efficacy of the Convention at the domestic level.

The recognition of consultation in the draft was established without adoption in 1992. Notably, the lack of participation of indigenous peoples during the drafting moment has not altered the meaning of the text, especially in the Articles 8 (j) and 15.

Article 8 (j) sets the framework for the wider application considering the knowledge, innovations and practices of indigenous peoples with the approval and involvement of the holders of such knowledge, innovations and practices. There is the recognition of consultation as a way to seek the approval of the indigenous

[148] CEACR (2007).

peoples when there are activities planned in their territory. Article 15 is also relevant once it is one of the CBD aims, which is the access to genetic resources, informing how it should be conducted.

Regarding consultation to be performed before or after the activities that affect the indigenous peoples, the Conference of the Parties (hereinafter, the COP) have recognized that the consultation should be conducted before undertaking any activity, notably with respect to access to traditional knowledge, innovations and practices, such as made explicit in the draft.

In order to correct the draft of the treaty in which the indigenous peoples were not able to participate, there was the establishment of the International Indigenous Forum on Biodiversity (hereinafter, the IIFB) in 1996, during the 3rd Ordinary Meeting of the Conference of the Parties to the CBD.

During the COP-5, 2 years after the IIFB, the advisory body provided the Decision V/16 which was an invitation to support the participation of the IIFB in advising the Conference on the implementation of Article 8 (j). The advice provided on the application of legal and other appropriate forms of protection of traditional knowledge and related provisions were relevant for fostering the implementation and giving efficacy to consultation with indigenous peoples.

As posited in Article 1 that 'the conservation of biological diversity, the sustainable use of its components and the fair and equitable sharing of benefits arising out of the utilization of genetic resources',[149] there is a prohibition to states to interfere, injure or steal genetic resources of indigenous peoples, whether constitutes signatory under customary international law.[150] That commitment laid down is necessary for the application of the parameters of CBD.

The protection of traditional knowledge and knowledge associated with biodiversity, at the international level regulated by the Convention on Biological Diversity provides for the conservation of biodiversity, the right to free, prior and informed consent and the fair and equitable sharing of benefits.

Recently, the CBD was introduced in Brazil by Law 13.123 of 2015, which revokes the previous regulation, Provisional Measure 2.186/16 of 2001.[151] The new law is the result of a hasty and uncultivated process, which violates the rights of free, prior and informed consultation and consent and represents a clear setback for indigenous peoples' rights.

Article 6 establishes the Genetic Heritage Management Council as part of the Brazilian Environment Ministry. The Council serves as a deliberative and normative organism, an active voice for the protection of the native genetic patrimony, restoration of the environment and the sustainable use of natural resources. The relevance of the regulation of access and benefit sharing is the promotion of sustainable use of biodiversity. Also, it represents a strategic action for biodiversity conservation and

[149] (1993) Convention on Biological Diversity (CBD).

[150] Phillips (2015).

[151] Brazilian Federal Government (2015) Regulates the Convention on Biological Diversity in Brazil.

an opportunity to assert the self-determination and cultural rights of indigenous peoples.[152]

2.5 Consultation with Indigenous Peoples and Financial Institutions

The legal framework of multilateral and national financial institutions has been adjusted over time to better shape the way that business have been conducted all around the world and especially in the Americas, which are home to pluralistic societies.[153] They have been giving special attention to project participants and others interested in the importance of consultation with indigenous peoples in Brazil considering project development and the expectations of the world market.[154]

This section is dedicated to collecting research and to detect how the World Bank and the Development Bank of Brazil, sources of soft law and the most relevant financial institutions for indigenous peoples in Brazil, are considering consultation with indigenous peoples through their policies and guidelines. Although not part of the control of conventionality yet, there is the attempt to better moulding the relationship between business and human rights by the IAHRS so as by the international system.[155]

The results are ambivalent. There are some aspects that might be taken from the guidelines and policies regarding consultation with indigenous peoples. The financial institutions shall follow international standards and the measures elaborated by them are quite substantial. In this sense, they call for 'requirements for a conciliatory approach based on good faith'.[156] But the reconciliation of indigenous and company interests may have been achieved even though a final land claims agreement had not been reached.

Thus, the level at which financial institutions and the private sector should incorporate the criteria of consultation with the indigenous peoples which are affected by the natural resource exploitation projects in their territory still need to be shaped.

[152] Fraxe (2011).

[153] See e.g. Gilbert et al. (2009) and IFC (1998).

[154] IFC (1998) and World Bank Group (2018).

[155] See e.g. Söderlund (2018).

[156] A/HRC/EMRIP/2009/5 (2009) international workshop entitled on Natural resource companies, indigenous peoples and human rights: setting a framework for consultation, benefit-sharing and dispute resolution.

2.5.1 The World Bank's Conception of Consultation with Indigenous Peoples

The World Bank Group has been assisting clients in enhancing the natural resource exploitation around the world. In countries of Latin America, its performance also has impacts on the social life and the environmental impact of the inhabitants of the territory. The broader segments of the effects that the World Bank's activities have lies in the contribution to support companies through helping to 'overcome the policy, institutional, and technical challenges that prevent them from transforming resource endowments into sustainable benefits'.[157] Therefore, the World Bank's operational policy incorporates an unprotective standard, which simply requires the Bank to listen to the views of those affected and the organizations that accompany them.[158]

The World Bank has several policies, procedures and guidelines, and precedents and best practices regarding the environment have been scattered through the institution and its publications.[159] One of the operational policies, the Operational Policy 4.01 (hereinafter, the OP 4.01) is quite relevant as it requires environmental assessments (hereinafter, the EA) of projects proposed for Bank financing to help ensure that they are environmentally sound and sustainable, to improve the decision-making.[160] The World Bank also stated in its OP 4.01 that projects that may affect indigenous communities should undertake 'at least two consultations with these groups: (a) shortly after the preliminary environmental study and before the terms of reference for the environmental assessment are finalized, and (b) once a draft environmental assessment report has been prepared. In addition, it was stipulated that in these cases the borrower must consult these groups during all phases of project implementation to address issues affecting them'.[161]

In 2013, the World Bank took a step back and launched the Enabling the Business of Agriculture project. The initiative aimed to guide business reforms in the agriculture sector in several countries, including Brazil. According to the project, 'the indicators provide a tangible measure of progress and identify regulatory obstacles to market integration and entrepreneurship in agriculture. With globally comparable data on regulations covering agricultural inputs, plant health, access to finance and markets, the Enabling the Business of Agriculture data shows large disparities across countries on the strength of regulations and the efficiency of their implementation'.[162] The development of a scoring methodology was introduced for measuring regulations in the countries from 2013 until 2017. And the last one, of 2019, was

[157] Liebenthal et al. (2005).

[158] Sands and Galizzi (2004).

[159] World Bank (1991).

[160] Sands and Galizzi (2004).

[161] ¶8 The World Bank (1999) The World Bank Operational Manual: Environmental Assessment OP 4.01.

[162] World Bank, *About Enabling the Business of Agriculture*, 2019.

central to the farms.[163] The initiative considers 'land tenure security can also be threatened on private property if governments arbitrarily dispossess farmers of their land. Particularly in countries with poor regulations and weak safeguards relating to expropriation procedures'.[164] The document continues explaining that: 'expropriation is an act of a government taking possession of private land to facilitate public works'.[165]

The initiative understands that 'customary land rights recognition and legal safeguards relating to expropriation procedures are crucial instruments for governments to protect land rights';[166] and it suggests that 'low-income countries do not manage public land in an effective manner, the Bank prescribes the privatization of public land as the way forward: Governments should become land brokers and transfer public lands with 'potential economic value' to commercial use and private ownership'.[167]

The methodology of scoring the countries according to accessing land for agribusiness represents an aggressive push to privatization and access to land contrary to the international human rights legacy. The long-term results of the initiative are still unclear, however, there is increasing backlash over recent negative developments as regards implementing the right to consultation.

2.5.2 The National Bank for Economic and Social Development and the Establishment of Consultation with Indigenous Peoples

The National Bank for Economic and Social Development (hereinafter, the BNDES) is a Brazilian federal public company whose main objective is financing investments in Brazil. For instance, in 2007, the credits provided by the BNDES reached R$ 64.9 billion, the highest amount in its entire history. This amount is approximately 160 times the total spent by the Brazilian federal government in all its activities for the indigenous peoples in 2007, when R$ 407 million were spent.[168]

The financing of BNDES has different branches but mostly in the natural resource exploitation projects. The BNDES alone invested in companies conducting mining, agribusiness and energy in Brazil. The consensus in the scholarly literature on this is that there is nothing inevitable about the increase of the conflicts between indigenous

[163] World Bank (2019).

[164] World Bank, *Enabling the Business of Agriculture 2019 Data on safeguards for land rights*, 2019.

[165] Ibid.

[166] Ibid.

[167] Mousseau and Sonkin (2019).

[168] The Nature Conservancy and Coordenação das Organizações Indígenas da Amazônia Brasileira (2009).

peoples and natural resource companies: the source of conflicts is the disrespect of laws such as territory rights, leading to calls for consultation.[169]

Regarding indigenous peoples, the BNDES does not have specific guidelines as the World Bank or also the Inter-American Development Bank. The loan records on BNDES as a financial institution reflect the need for clarification on the direct and indirect financing support, while the lack of knowledge on how the companies are conducting the activities may have a huge impact on the indigenous peoples and also the national reputation.[170]

The interest in advancing on the issues listed in this publication will allow for dialogue between indigenous peoples and the BNDES, enabling a bridge for development policy. BNDES shall consider the Brazilian context that has illegal miners (in Portuguese, *grilheiros*) and other local actors, as well as systematically disrespecting the laws that protect indigenous peoples' territories and rights.

Thus, 'there is the need of an internal articulation and with other indigenous peoples movements, the adoption of a transversal policy for indigenous peoples, the creation of special rules for the licensing of projects with impacts on indigenous peoples land, the need of transparency of the information about the projects, and the creation of rules and institutional conditions to meet the needs of financial support of indigenous peoples'.[171]

Furthermore, there is the need to fulfil the constitutional and international oaths and act according to the better programming process of strategy and dialogue with indigenous peoples to achieve public policy objectives.

[169] See e.g. Psacharopoulos and Patrinos (1994), Davis (2002), and MacKay (2004).

[170] 'From this initial query, DONR created a database of 797 judicial cases involving disputes over Indigenous territory demarcation, decisions on land expropriation, eviction and land maintenance processes, revocation of environmental licenses, and compensation for environmental or other damages. From this list, we prioritized cases that met the following criteria: a) cases associated with a legal entity with an active status in the Federal Revenue Service; b) cases in which the legal entity involved was directly or indirectly linked to export chains; c) cases which have been opened in the justice system or which, by some of the parties involved, have undergone updates, advances, or changes between 2018 and 2020. The findings were cross-referenced with reports of operations against deforestation and invasion of Indigenous areas carried out by the Federal Police between 2018 and 2020; pre-existing databases; further corroboration of Indigenous associations' informal and formal public statements denouncing violations in Indigenous Territories during the span of the research; and investigative journalism pieces. Based on these initial results, Profundo researched supply chains and financial links by cross-checking data narrowing the list of companies down to the 11 Brazilian and multinational companies mentioned in this report'. Association of Brazil's Indigenous Peoples (2020).

[171] The Nature Conservancy and Coordenação das Organizações Indígenas da Amazônia Brasileira (2009).

2.6 The Legal Analysis of Consultation Under the Inter-American System of Human Rights

The verification of the impact of territorial right violations as addressed to the IAHRS have shown how the international court is dedicated to the improvement of the right as a construction to implement indigenous peoples' right to consultation. Once the claims were posed, the IAHRS became aware of the problems of interpretation given the lack of enforcement instruments regarding consultation with indigenous peoples in the region. Therefore, the regional treaties offer guidance and legal definitions.

2.6.1 The American Declaration of the Rights and Duties of Man

The American Declaration of the Rights and Duties of Man (hereinafter, the American Declaration) was adopted by the 9th International Conference of American States on 2nd May 1948 in Bogota, Colombia. The signatories were the 21 states that were present in the creation of the Organisation of American States (hereinafter, the OAS) and all member states that have joined since; currently all 35 members of the Americas have ratified the OAS treaty.

The American Declaration was not meant to be binding on states of the OAS, which gives general duties and rights as general principles that should be followed to interpret the rights.[172] The Declaration was the first to approach human rights in the region and constituted another legal support for indigenous peoples in their struggle to preserve physical and cultural survival in the face of natural resource exploitation imposed upon them, sometimes without consultation.

The Preamble of the American Declaration elucidates the rights and freedoms of the individual as an individual in her own right and also as an individual pertaining to the community. The pre-eminence of the individuals and their rights 'prevails in the Declaration to a substantial level, however, at the same time it is further assured through the prescription of duties and obligations on other members of the community and society'.[173]

The fulfillment of duty by each individual is a prerequisite to the achievement of rights. As a legal instrument, the American Declaration has provided the normative framework for human rights and fundamental freedoms in the members states of the OAS.

There is no prevision in the American Declaration regarding consultation, however, it asserts that human rights provisions are universally guaranteed for everyone.

[172] See e.g. Hilton et al. (2016) and Devereux (1995).

[173] Seatzu (2019).

Thus, the usage of the American Declaration as not dependent on nationality but the virtue of being human, 'has given rise to a range of other international and regional agreements, such as the International Covenant on Civil and Political Rights and the American Convention on Human Rights'.[174]

2.6.2 *The American Convention of Human Rights*

The context of the creation of the American Convention on Human Rights (hereinafter, the American Convention) is linked to the pervasiveness of authoritarian governments in Latin America at the time. Between 1960s and 1970s, most countries were under repressive governments. Only from the 1980s onwards, the countries of the region slowly made the transition to democracy mostly using the maxim *nunca más!*, which meant that they never again wanted to have military dictatorships running their countries.[175] 'In the past twenty years, as Latin America has emerged from a period of intense struggle with civil wars, military dictatorships, and massive, state-sponsored human rights abuse, the terms of the principal human rights debates have undergone a dramatic shift'.[176]

After the ratification in 1969 in San Jose, Costa Rica, the American Convention entered into force in July 1978. In this context, 'the Inter-American Court of Human Rights, inspired by the IACHR and minded domestic forces, started interpreting the provisions of the Convention in a specific evolutive manner that led to a distinct approach',[177] the Latin American form of judging and applying the international treaties. The regional human rights tribunals have grown in numbers and activities, and 'now receive ten of thousands of petitions and issues over fifteen hundred judgments on the merits each year. The IACtHR recently tripled the number of cases that it resolves annually'.[178] Worldwide, 'the Convention is perhaps the most important international instrument of this nature, which begs the questions of how such an extraordinary development became possible and whether it is lawful'.[179] Thus, 'the latest and perhaps most unexpected chapter in the implementation of structural reform litigation is international. With the turn of the millennium, the European Court of Human Rights and the IACtHR began ordering reform of government policy and institutions, using remedies for individual rights violations as a platform from which to restructure state policies and institutions'.[180]

[174] IACourtHR (2018) 40 years Protecting Rights.
[175] von Bogdandy et al. (2017).
[176] Cavallaro and Schaffer (2004).
[177] von Bogdandy (2019).
[178] Cavallaro and Brewer (2008).
[179] von Bogdandy (2019), p. 1.
[180] Huneeust (2015).

As introduced in the Preamble to the American Convention, the 'system of personal liberty and social justice',[181] recognizes that there is still a long way to go to guarantee efficacy of all provisions that ensure human rights. The American Convention also recognizes in Article 3 the right to juridical personality, which includes communities or collectivities once indigenous peoples are afforded juridical personality. That can be seen as 'while the recognition of rights should be granted to persons under state jurisdiction, the reality reveals the social ostracism to which members of indigenous communities are often relegated. For this reason, the Inter-American Court, while not neglecting the protection of each individual, has referred to indigenous communities as subjects of rights endowed with their own uniqueness'.[182]

Article 21 also provides a relevant asset for the implementation of indigenous peoples' rights, as there is no specific provision contained in the American Convention consecrating the right of indigenous people to consultation neither to self-determination. In practice, self-determination was achieved through claims to the right of ownership over ancestral lands, in accordance with Article 21 of the Convention.

As Article 21 enshrines the right to property and not consultation, part of the literature finds that there was a limited interpretation given by the IACtHR.[183]

However, the IACtHR has used the broad interpretation of Article 21 of the American Convention together with the ILO Convention No. 169 in order to clarify the content and scope of consultation and considering the context of the consolidation of human rights, the IACtHR interprets consultation together with Article 21 and the ILO Convention No. 169.

It is worth to mention that, with respect to the right to consultation, the IACtHR has partially broken with the position adopted by the states and the ILO Convention No. 169. In cases where the integrity of the indigenous community is affected to a greater extent, it understands that a state has the obligation to not only to carry out prior consultation, but also to obtain the consent of the community.[184]

---

[181] 'On average, Inter-American proceedings require more than seven years from when the petition first enters the system until a final decision. To this, the average period of time that states delay in complying totally or partially with the required remedies (when they do so) is approximately 2 and a half years for final reports, and a little more than a year and a half for Court rulings. These time periods are excessively long and may generate distrust and frustration among the users of the IASPHR. If the large number of petitions and subjects received is considered, it is clear that in many cases, the IASPHR does not offer an effective and timely answer for those affected'. For more: IACourtHR (2018) 40 years Protecting Rights.

[182] §83 Inter-American Court of Human Rights, *Yakye Axa Indigenous Community v. Paraguay*, Judgment of 17 June 2005.

[183] See e.g. Cavallaro and Brewer (2008), Navarro (2019), Antkowiak (2013), and Pasqualucci (2009).

[184] Inter-American Commission of Human Rights, *Saramaka People v. Suriname*, Case No 172, Judgment of 28 November 2007.

2.6.3 *The American Declaration of Indigenous Peoples*

The American Declaration of Indigenous Peoples (hereinafter, the ADIP) was adopted by the OAS on 15th June 2016 after nearly 30 years of negotiation. The ADIP offers specific protection for indigenous peoples in all 35 member states of the OAS. It was the first document in the region to affirm the right of self-determination and the rights to education, health, self-government, culture, lands, territories and natural resources, and it includes provisions that address the particular situation such as including protections for those living in voluntary isolation among others.

The ADIP is a comprehensive and vast instrument and has the potential to become one of the most important instruments of the IAHRS, giving tools for interpretation to the IACtHR and also the IACHR.

Regarding consultation, the ADIP, like the UNDRIP, expects that the states cooperate in good faith with indigenous peoples through their own representative institutions and there is the mention of consent as well. The consultation must be conducted before the resource exploitation company or the state implements legislative or administrate measures that might affect them. However, the ADIP does not require consultation with indigenous peoples before using their lands or territories for military activities. The relocation and storage or disposal of hazardous materials in the lands or territories of indigenous peoples was also left out in the legal document.

The position was already judged by IACtHR saying that 'the state has a duty to obtain the free, prior and informed consent of indigenous peoples in the case of large-scale development or investment projects that would have a major impact within indigenous peoples' territories'.[185] A similar view was provided by the IACHR, which has also recognized that 'indigenous peoples consent is required in the case of displacement and storage or disposal of hazardous materials'.[186]

However, there is still no decision regarding consultation that the ADIP was referred in order to strengthen the IAHRS.

2.6.4 *The Regional Agreement on Access to Information, Public Participation and Justice in Environmental Matters in Latin America and the Caribbean*

The Regional Agreement on Access to Information, Public Participation and Justice in Environmental Matters in Latin America and the Caribbean (hereinafter, the Ezcazú Agreement) was adopted in 2018 and entered into force in Latin America

[185] §134 ibid.

[186] §334 Inter-American Commission on Human Rights (2009) Indigenous and Tribal Peoples' Rights over Their Ancestral Lands and Natural Resources.

and Caribbean on 22nd April 2021.[187] The draft process was considered to be transparent and inclusive to settle at regional level the appropriate means for implementing regional standards related to access to information, public participation and access to justice in environmental matters.[188]

Since the implementation of Principle 10 of the 1992 Rio Declaration and the Aarhus Convention of the pan-European region, this is the second regional legal instrument regarding environmental concerns.[189] The agreement was signed by 24 countries and 12 had ratified at the time of writing, becoming state parties to the treaty.

Consultation is characterized in this treaty in Articles 7 (c) and 13; Article 7 (c) states that 'the procedure foreseen for the participation of the public, including the date on which the procedure will begin and end, mechanisms for participation and, where applicable, the date and place of any public consultation or hearing'.[190] And as established in Article 13: 'each Party shall encourage the establishment of appropriate spaces for consultation on environmental matters or the use of those that are already in existence in which various groups and sectors are able to participate. Each Party shall promote regard for local knowledge, dialogue and interaction of different views and knowledge, where appropriate'.[191]

The efficacy of the Ezcazú Agreement as a regional treaty is not clear yet given its recent agreement, but it is relevant to consider the innovation as part of the agenda that aims for a better implementation of existent provisions.

2.7 Conclusions

The articulations of universal human rights applying to indigenous peoples contextualize rights to the situation of indigenous peoples and take the collective aspects of these rights into account.[192] According to international legal pronouncements, the

[187] United Nations (2018) Regional Agreement on Access to Information, Public Participation and Justice in Environmental Matters in Latin America and the Caribbean.

[188] Stec and Jendrośka (2019).

[189] 'Declaration of the United Nations Conference on the Human Environment, Agenda 21, the Programme for the Further Implementation of Agenda 21, the Declaration of Barbados and the Programme of Action for the Sustainable Development of Small Island Developing States, the Mauritius Declaration and the Mauritius Strategy for the Further Implementation of the Programme of Action for the Sustainable Development of Small Island Developing States, the Johannesburg Declaration on Sustainable Development, the Plan of Implementation of the World Summit on Sustainable Development and the SIDS Accelerated Modalities of Action (SAMOA) Pathway.' United Nations (2018) Regional Agreement on Access to Information, Public Participation and Justice in Environmental Matters in Latin America and the Caribbean.

[190] Ibid.

[191] Ibid.

[192] International Labour Organization (2013).

designing of procedures for conducting consultations established fundamental principles that must be taken into account. Thus, the establishment of consultation processes are to be adapted to the particularities of each case and the cultural characteristics of each people, especially their self-determination.

Consultation must be implemented in such a way as to guarantee the efficacy of the norm respecting their customs and beliefs, with the aim of reaching an agreement. Cultural rights and the self-determination play an important role for ensuring enforcement. Self-determination and cultural rights overlap and it has been argued that 'the reformulation and reinforcement of self-determination in recent decades has had an accompanying impact upon cultural rights'.[193] With regard to cultural rights, 'self-determination has broadly two components: one relates to participation and the other concerns identity. Until recently, contemporary discourse on self-determination has largely centered on the former. Yet, from its earliest conceptions, self-determination has been inextricably tied to notions of identity of peoples and cultural rights'.[194]

Opportunities for dialogue must be supported when individual and collective rights are to be legitimized and recognized. Such dialogue could prevent suffering, repression and confrontation, enabling indigenous peoples to live dignified and fulfilled lives.[195]

This chapter proposes an interrelated analysis of consultation, considering the fundamental aspects of self-determination and cultural rights that are specifically related to indigenous peoples' way of life and identity as a distinct group. For that purpose, a concept of application as a theoretical framework has been created based on the IAHRS to be complied with by Brazil in case of resource exploitation, discussed in Chaps. 3 and 4. Therefore, the analysis explores the possibility of the potential application to strengthen indigenous peoples' participation, and to improve indigenous peoples' human rights' protection.

Brazil has failed to meet the obligations for complying with the requirement for consultation with indigenous peoples persistently. The recent number of administrative and legislative measures undertaken without consultation reveal the lack of efficacy the norm has in the state. The issue aggravates the applicability of the ILO Convention No. 169, having serious repercussions for the self-determination, collective rights, equality and cultural rights of indigenous peoples. The limitation of the comprehension of consultation generates a legal instability among traditional communities in Brazil.

Nevertheless, the IAHRS embraced indigenous peoples' human rights and the reflection on its responses to the theoretical arguments that are going to be used by national judges matter. Moreover, the entitlement of territory became to be legitimized by the legal acceptance of the concept of land traditionally occupied.

---

193 International Labour Organization (2013).

194 Vrdoljak (2008), p. 41.

195 International Labour Organization (2013).

There is an impasse regarding the efficacy of consultation in Brazil. There has been a precarious attempt to mock enforcement with the application of the right to consultation. The evidence on the material content of the right to be consulted is expressed in two relevant dimensions: The first is the self-determination of peoples and the second is cultural rights.

However, as under international law and also in Brazil, the issue of territoriality is one of the main focuses of the states' concerns as the consultation leads to a plurality of legal problems that need to be addressed. The normative character of consultation given by international law for indigenous peoples over their own territory remains a critical issue that needs to be addressed. That being said, the study considers the implications of the IAHRS for Brazil regarding to consultation.

The emergence of indigenous peoples' international law is an unquestionable fact that has drawn attention and increasingly became a focus of interest for indigenous around the world which embraced them to litigate for their rights. Even when ensured by the international treaties and constitutions, the process of entitlement of fundamental rights has often been arduous, albeit being driven by the indigenous peoples' Protocols, the FPIC discussion and the possibility to litigate against transnational corporations which encroach on the natural resources in their entitled land, mostly without consultation.

Thus, the following chapter focuses on the claims brought to the IAHRS regarding consultation. The chapter is mainly theoretical and focusses on the claims of indigenous rights and whether consultation turned from being a heated debate to be left entirely to the discretion of governments in divergence of what has been established by international treaties.

References

Abrusci E (2019) The European Court of Human Rights and its contribution to judicial fragmentation in international human rights law. Proc ASIL Annu Meet 113:92–95. https://doi.org/10.1017/amp.2019.148

Alexy R (2010) The argument from injustice: a reply to legal positivism., 1st paperback ed. Oxford University Press, New York

Alter KJ (2014) The new terrain of international law: courts, politics, rights. Princeton University Press, Princeton

Anaya JS (1999) Superpower attitudes toward indigenous peoples and group rights. Am Soc Int Law Proc

Anaya JS (2004) Indigenous peoples in international law, 2nd edn. Oxford University Press, New York

Antkowiak TM (2013) Rights, resources, and rhetoric: indigenous peoples and the Inter-American Court. Univ Pa J Int Law 2

Association of Brazil's Indigenous Peoples (2020) Complicity in destruction III: how global corporations enable violations of indigenous people's rights in the Brazilian Amazon

Bankes N (2020) The duty to consult in Canada post-Haida nation. Arct Rev Law Polit 11:256–279

Barelli M (2018) Free, prior, and informed consent in the UNDRIP: Articles 10, 19, 29(2) and 32(2). In: Hohmann J, Weller M (eds) The UN Declaration on the rights of indigenous peoples: a commentary, 1st edn. Oxford University Press, Oxford

Baron JB (1999) Law, literature, and the problems of interdisciplinarity. Yale Law J 108:1059. https://doi.org/10.2307/797370

Bobbio N (2010) Teria Geral do Direito, 3rd edn. Martins Fontes, Brazil

Bourdieu P, Nice R (2013) Outline of a theory of practice. Cambridge University Press, Cambridge

Braun V, Clarke V, Gray D (eds) (2017) Collecting qualitative data: a practical guide to textual, media and virtual techniques, 1st edn. Cambridge University Press

Brownlie I (1982) The reality and efficacy of international law. Br Yearb Int Law 52:1–8. https://doi.org/10.1093/bybil/52.1.1

Burazin L (2019) The concept of law and efficacy. Encycl Philos Law Soc Philos

Burgorgue-Larsen L, Úbeda de Torres A, Greenstein R (2011) The Inter-American Court of Human Rights: case-law and commentary. Oxford University Press, Oxford

Cabrera MV (2017) The requirement of consultation with indigenous peoples in the ILO between normative flexibility and institutional rigidity. Brill Nijhoff, Leiden

Calabria C (2018) The efficacy of the Inter-American Court of Human Rights: a socio-legal study based on the jurisprudence of the Inter-American Court of Human Rights concerning amnesty, indigenous rights and rights of detainees. University of Manchester, Manchester

Carmelina Londoño-Lázaro M, Carrillo-Santarelli N (2019) The control of conventionality: developments in the case law of the Inter-American Court of Human Rights and its potential expanding effects in international human rights law. Max Planck Yearb U N Law Online 22: 319–346. https://doi.org/10.1163/18757413_022001013

Cavallaro JL, Brewer SE (2008) Reevaluating regional human rights litigation in the twenty-first century: the case of the Inter-American Court. Am J Int Law 102:768–827. https://doi.org/10.2307/20456681

Cavallaro J, Schaffer EJ (2004) Less as more: rethinking supranational litigation of economic and social rights in the Americas. Hastings Law J 56

CEACR (2007) Direct Request (CEACR) - adopted 2006, published 96th ILC session. ILO

Charters C, Stavenhagen R, Grupo Internacional de Trabajo sobre Asuntos Indígenas (2010) El Desafío de la declaración: historia y futuro de la declaración de la ONU sobre pueblos indígenas. Grupo Internacional de Trabajo sobre Asuntos Indígenas, Copenhague

Clavero B (2005) The indigenous rights of participation and international development policies. Ariz J Int Comp Law 22

Clavero B (2008) Tratados con Pueblos o Constituciones de Estados: Dilema para América. Univ Andina Simón Bolívar

Cobo M (1982) Study of the problem of discrimination against indigenous populations - definition of indigenous populations. United Nations

Crawford J (2001) The right of self-determination in international law: its developments and future. In: Alstor P (ed) Peoples' rights. Collected courses of the Academy of European Law

Silva LAL da (2017) Consulta prévia e livre determinação dos povos indígenas e tribais na América Latina : re-existir para co-existir. Dissertation, Pontifícia Universidade Católica do Paraná, Paraná

Daes E-IA (2000) The spirit and letter of the right to self-determination of indigenous peoples: reflections on the making of the United Nations Draft Declaration. In: Aikio P, Scheinin M (eds) Operationalizing the right of indigenous peoples to self-determination. Institute for Human Rights, Åbo Akademi University, Turku/Åbo, Finland

Daes E-I, Eiden A (2000) Working paper on the relationship and distinction between the rights of persons belonging to minorities and those of indigenous peoples

Davis SH (2002) Indigenous peoples, poverty and participatory development: the experience of the World Bank in Latin America. In: Sieder R (ed) Multiculturalism in Latin America. Palgrave Macmillan UK, London, pp 227–251

de Sousa Santos B (1987) Law: a map of misreading. Toward a postmodern conception of law. J Law Soc 14:279. https://doi.org/10.2307/1410186

Debenham M (2007) Epistolary interviews on-line: a novel addition to the researcher's palette. Jisc TechDis

Devereux A (1995) Should 'duties' play a larger role in human rights? - A critique of western liberal and African human rights jurisprudence. Univ New South Wales Law J 18
Didier Jr (2015) Curso de direito processual civil. JusPodivm, Salvador
Doyle CM (2016) Indigenous peoples, title to territory, rights and resources - the transformative role of the free prior and informed consent. Routledge, New York
Duprat D (ed) (2015) Consulta Indígena: Colombia (y España) entre Derecho Constitucional y Derechos Humanos. In: Convenção n. 169 da OIT e os Estados Nacionais. ESMPU, Brasília, DF
Engstrom P (2017) Reconceptualising the impact of the Inter-American Human Rights System/ Reconceitualizando o Impacto do Sistema Interamericano de Direitos Humanos. Rev Direito E Práxis 8. https://doi.org/10.12957/dep.2017.28027
Faden RR, Beauchamp TL, King NMP (1986) A history and theory of informed consent. Oxford University Press, New York
Faúndez Ledesma H (2004) El sistema interamericano de protección de los derechos humanos: aspectos institucionales y procesales, 3. ed., rev. y puesta al día. Instituto Interamericano de Derechos Humanos (IIDH), San José, Costa Rica
Fitzmaurice M, Elias OA, Merkouris P (2010) Treaty interpretation and the Vienna Convention on the Law of Treaties 30 years on. Brill, Leiden
Franck TM (1990) The power of legitimacy among nations. Oxford University Press, New York
Fraxe JMP (2011) Do geodireito do Conselho de Gestão do Patrimônio Genético- CGEN: caminhos e instrumentos de gestão do conhecimento biotecnológico na Amazônia. Dissertation, Universidade do Amazonas
Garavito CR (2012). Etnicidad.gov: Los recursos naturales, los pueblos indígenas y derecho a la consulta previa en los campos minados. Centro de Estudos de Derecho, Justicia y Sociedad, Bogotá
García Ramírez S (2015) The relationship between Inter-American Jurisdiction and States (National Systems): some pertinent questions. Notre Dame J Int Comp Law 5
Gilbert J (2003) The treatment of territory of indigenous peoples in international law. In: Castellino J, Allen S (eds) Title to territory in international law: a temporal analysis. Ashgate, Aldershot
Gilbert J (2006) Indigenous peoples' land rights under international law: from victims to actors. Transnational Publishers, Ardsley
Gilbert J, Tugendhat H, Couillard V, Doyle C (2009) Business, human rights and indigenous peoples: the right to free, prior and informed consent. SSRN Electron J. https://doi.org/10.2139/ssrn.1403985
Gomes LF, Mazzuoli VdO (eds) (2010) Comentários à Convenção Americana sobre Direitos Humanos: Pacto de San José da Costa Rica, 3a. ed. rev., atualizada e ampliada. Editora Revista dos Tribunais, São Paulo
Harvey D (2005) The new imperialism. Oxford University Press, Oxford
Hilton DJ, Charalambides L, Hoareau-Blanchet S (2016) Reasoning about rights and duties: mental models, world knowledge and pragmatic interpretation. Think Reason 22:150–183. https://doi.org/10.1080/13546783.2015.1076520
Huneeust A (2015) Reforming the State from Afar: structural reform litigation at the human rights courts. Yale J Int Law 40
IFC (1998) Doing better business through effective public consultation and disclosure: a good practice manual. The World Bank
International Labour Office (2009) Application of Convention No. 169 by domestic and international courts in Latin America: a case book. ILO, Geneva
International Labour Organization (2013) Understanding the Indigenous and Tribal People Convention, 1989 (No. 169): handbook for ILO Tripartite constituents. International Labour Office, Geneva

International Labour Organization (2019) Monitoring compliance with international labour standards the key role of the ILO Committee of Experts on the Application of Conventions and Recommendations, Publications Production Unit (PRODOC) of the ILO. Geneva
Internationale Arbeitsorganisation (2020) Implementing the ILO Indigenous and Tribal Peoples Convention No. 169 towards an inclusive, sustainable and just future
Jouannet E (2013) What is a fair international society? International law between development and recognition. Hart Publishing, Oxford
Kelsen H (2005) Pure theory of law. Lawbook Exchange, Clark
Kluth W (2013) Parlamentarische Gesetzgebung im postnationalen Zeitalter, 1. Aufl. Nomos, Baden-Baden
Kluth W (2019) Öffentliches Wirtschaftsrecht. C.H. Beck, München
Krieger H (2000) Das Effektivitätsprinzip im Völkerrecht. Duncker & Humblot, Berlin
Kymlicka W (1999) Theorizing indigenous rights. Univ Tor Law J 49
Kymlicka W (2003) Multicultural citizenship: a liberal theory of minority rights., Repr. Clarendon Press, Oxford
Liebenthal A, Michelitsch R, Tarazona EI (2005) Extractive industries and sustainable development: an evaluation of the World Bank Group experience. World Bank: International Finance Corp.: Multilateral Investment Guarantee Agency, Washington, DC
Linderfalk U (2007) On the interpretation of treaties: the modern international law as expressed in the 1969 Vienna Convention on the Law of Treaties. Springer, Dordrecht
Little PE (2006) Ecologia política como etnografia: um guia teórico e metodológico. Horiz Antropológicos 12
Lo C (2017) Treaty interpretation under the Vienna Convention on the Law of Treaties: a new round of codification. Springer, Singapore
Lupien P (2020) Indigenous politics and resistance in Latin America: continuity and change. In: Oxford research encyclopedia of politics. Oxford University Press
Lupton D (2020) New resource: doing fieldwork in a pandemic
Mac-Gregor EF (2015) Conventionality control the new doctrine of the Inter-American Court of Human Rights. AJIL Unbound 109:93–99. https://doi.org/10.1017/S2398772300001240
MacKay F (2004) Indigenous peoples' right to free, prior and informed consent and the World Bank's extractive industries review. Forest Peoples Programme
Manson NC, ONeill O (2007) Rethinking informed consent in bioethics. Cambridge University Press, Cambridge
Mariela MA, Alessandri PS (2017) The domestic element, 13 Inter-Americanization: its legal bases and political impact. In: von Bogdandy A, Ferrer Mac-Gregor E, Piovesan F (eds) Transformative constitutionalism in Latin America: the emergence of a new ius commune, 1st edn. Oxford University Press, Oxford
Mazariegos Rodas M (2016) Consulta previa a los pueblos indígenas = Prior consultation to indigenous peoples. EUNOMÍA Rev En Cult Leg 11:221–236. https://doi.org/10.20318/eunomia.2016.3289
Mazzuoli VO (2011) The Inter-American human rights protection system: structure, functioning and effectiveness in Brazilian law. Afr Hum Rights J 11
Mazzuoli VdO (2018) Controle Jurisdicional da Convencionalidade das Leis. Forense
Middha B (2018) Everyday digital engagements: using food selfies on Facebook to explore eating practices. Commun Res Pract 4:291–306. https://doi.org/10.1080/22041451.2018.1476796
Mignolo W (2011) The darker side of Western modernity: global futures, decolonial options. Duke University Press, Durham
Minda G (1995) Postmodern legal movements: law and jurisprudence at century's end. New York University Press, New York
Morris M, Rodríguez Garavito C, Salinas NO, Buriticá P (2010) La consulta previa a pueblos indígenas: los estándares del derecho internacional. Programa de Justiça Global y Derechos Humanos, Colombia

Mousseau F, Sonkin F (2019) The highest bidder takes it all: the World's Bank's scheme to privatize the commons. The Oakland Institute

Navarro GCB (2019) The judgment of the case Xucuru People v. Brazil: InterAmerican Court of Human Rights between consolidation and setbacks. Rev Direito Int 16. https://doi.org/10.5102/rdi.v16i2.5958

Navarro GCB (2021) Measuring the effectiveness of the Inter-American System of Human Rights: the case of indigenous territorial rights. Dissertation, Goethe-Universität Frankfurt, Frankfurt am Main

Negishi Y (2017) The Pro Homine Principle's role in regulating the relationship between conventionality control and constitutionality control. Eur J Int Law 28:457–481. https://doi.org/10.1093/ejil/chx030

Neves MCP (2011) A constitucionalizacao simbólica. Editora WMF Martins Fontes, São Paulo

Pasqualucci JM (2009) International indigenous land rights: a critique of the jurisprudence of the Inter-American Court of Human Rights in light of the United Nations Declaration on the Rights of Indigenous Peoples. Wis Int Law J 27:51–89

Pegorari B (2017) A tese do "marco temporal da ocupação" como interpretação restritiva do direito à terra dos povos indígenas no Brasil: um olhar sob a perspectiva da Corte Interamericana de Direitos Humanos. Aracê - Direitos Hum Em Rev 4

Perez-Leon-Acevedo JP (2020) The control of the Inter-American Court of Human Rights over amnesty laws and other exemption measures: legitimacy assessment. Leiden J Int Law 33:667–687. https://doi.org/10.1017/S092215652000028X

Perrault A (2004) Facilitating prior informed consent context of genetic resources and traditional knowledge. Sustain Dev Law Policy 4

Phillips JS (2015) The rights of indigenous peoples under international law. Glob Bioeth 26:120–127. https://doi.org/10.1080/11287462.2015.1036514

Piovesan F (2015) Direitos humanos e o direito constitucional internacional. Editora Saraiva, São Paulo

Pontes de Miranda FC (1981) Fontes e evolução do direito civil brasileiro. Forense, Rio de Janeiro

Programme to promote ILO convention no. 169 (PRO 169), International Labour Standards Department (2009) Indigenous and tribal peoples' rights in practice: a guide to ILO convention numbers 169

Psacharopoulos G, Patrinos HA (eds) (1994) Indigenous people and poverty in Latin America: an empirical analysis. World Bank, Washington, D.C.

Puig SM (2010) The emergence of indigenous movements in Latin America and their impact on the Latin American political scene: interpretive tools at the local and global levels. Lat Am Perspect 32

Raustiala K, Slaughter A-M (2002) International law, international relations and compliance. In: Handbook of international relations. SAGE Publications Ltd, London, pp 538–558

RCA R (2016) Obstacles and resistance to the process of implementing the right to free, prior and informed consultation and consent in Brazil. Doc Prep Audience Requested RCA – Rede Coop Amaz Amaz Coop Netw Vic Tauli-Corpuz U N Spec Rapp Rights Indig Peoples Her Mission Braz March 2016

Rombouts SJ (2014) Having a say: indigenous peoples, international law and free, prior and informed consent. Wolf Legal Publishers, Oisterwijk

Sagües NP (2008) El control de convencionalidad en el sistema interamericano, y sus anticipos en el ámbito de los derechos económicos-sociales: concordancias y diferencias con el sistema europeo. Inst Investifaciones Juridicas

Sands P, Galizzi P (eds) (2004) World Bank Operational Policy 4.01 on Environmental Assessment, January 1999. In: Documents in international environmental law, 1st edn. Cambridge University Press, pp 1097–1108

Santos BdS (1998) Por uma concepção multicultural dos direitos humanos. Rev Crítica Estud Sociais

Scheinin M (2005) What are indigenous peoples? In: Ghanea-Hercock N, Xanthaki A, Thornberry P (eds) Minorities, peoples, and self-determination: essays in honour of Patrick Thornberry. Martinus Nijhoff Publishers, Leiden
Seatzu F (2019) On the meaning and scope of individual human duties and obligations in the American declaration of the rights and duties of man of 1948. Rev Electrónica Iberoam 13
Shany Y (2016) Assessing the effectiveness of international courts. Oxford University Press, Oxford
Sin CH (2005) Seeking informed consent: reflections on research practice. Sociology 39:277–294. https://doi.org/10.1177/0038038505050539
Smith LT (2012) Decolonizing methodologies: research and indigenous peoples, 2nd edn. Zed Books, London
Söderlund E (2018) Transnational corporations and human rights: assessing the position of TNCs within international human rights law, and the appropriateness of an international treaty on business and human rights. Dissertation, Uppsala University
Stec S, Jendrośka J (2019) The Escazú Agreement and the regional approach to Rio Principle 10: process, innovation, and shortcomings. J Environ Law 31:533–545. https://doi.org/10.1093/jel/eqz027
Tauli-Corpuz V (2020) The right of indigenous peoples to self-determination through autonomy or self-government. In: Building autonomies. International Work Group for Indigenous Affairs
The Nature Conservancy, Coordenação das Organizações Indígenas da Amazônia Brasileira (2009) O BNDES e os povos indígenas. The Nature Conservancy (TNC), Brazil
Thomas D (2007) Indigenous rights in Latin America: a legal historical perspective. Max Planck Inst Eur Leg Hist Res Pap Ser 2
Thornberry P (2002) Indigenous peoples and human rights. Juris Pub./Manchester University Press, New York/Manchester
Tomei M, Swepston L (1996) Indigenous and tribal peoples: a guide to ILO Convention No. 169. International Labour Office: International Centre for Human Rights and Democratic Development, Geneva
van Dijik P (1987) Normative force and effectiveness of international norms. German Yearb Int Law 30
Viljoen F (2017) The African human rights system and domestic enforcement. In: Langford M, Rodriguez-Garavito C, Rossi J (eds) Social rights judgments and the politics of compliance. Cambridge University Press, Cambridge, pp 351–398
Bogdandy A von (2019) The transformative mandate of the Inter-American system legality and legitimacy of an extraordinary jurisgenerative process. Max Planck Inst Comp Public Law Int Law Res Pap Ser
von Bogdandy A, Venzke I (2016) In whose name? A public law theory of international adjudication., First published in paperback. Oxford University Press, Oxford
von Bogdandy A, Ferrer Mac-Gregor E, Morales Antoniazzi M, Piovesan F (eds) (2017) Transformative constitutionalism in Latin America: the emergence of a new ius commune, 1st edn. Oxford University Press, Oxford
Vrdoljak AF (2008) Self-determination and cultural rights. In: Francioni F, Scheinin M (eds) Cultural human rights. Martinus Nijhoff Publishers, Leiden, pp 41–78
White JB (1985) The legal imagination, Abridged ed. University of Chicago Press, Chicago
Wiessner S (2011) The cultural rights of indigenous peoples: achievements and continuing challenges. Eur J Int Law 22. https://doi.org/10.1093/ejil/chr007
Wiles R, Charles V, Crow G, Heath S (2006) Researching researchers: lessons for research ethics. Qual Res 6:283–299. https://doi.org/10.1177/1468794106065004
World Bank (1991) Environmental assessment sourcebook, Policies, procedures, and cross-sectoral issues, vol I. The World Bank
World Bank (2019) Enabling the business of agriculture 2019. World Bank, Washington, DC
World Bank Group (2018) Opportunities and challenges for scaling up geothermal development in Latin America and the Caribbean. World Bank, Washington, DC

Wright C, Tomaselli A (eds) (2021) The prior consultation of indigenous peoples in Latin America: inside the implementation gap. Routledge, London

Xanthaki A (2014) Indigenous rights and United Nations standards: self-determination, culture and land. Cambridge University Press, Cambridge

Yamada EM (2005) Collective economic, social and cultural rights approach to indigenous land rights. University of Lund

Young S (2020) Indigenous peoples, consent and rights: troubling subjects. Routledge, an imprint of the Taylor & Francis Group, Abingdon

Chapter 3
Assessing Consultation with Indigenous Peoples in the Inter-American System of Human Rights

3.1 Introduction

The IAHRS features specific legal provisions for the protection of the rights of indigenous peoples, following decade-long discussions towards the elaboration of regional treaties together with the implementation of the international law of indigenous peoples.

The IAHRS was established by the OAS in order to protect and enforce human rights in member states. Those countries that have ratified or acceded to the American Convention and the American Declaration may moreover be subject to the jurisdiction of the IACtHR, but only after the IACHR has completed its consideration of a complaint. 'On average, Inter-American proceedings require more than seven years from when the petition first enters the system until a final decision. To this, the average period of time that states delay in complying totally or partially with the required remedies (when they do so) is approximately 2 and a half years for final reports, and a little more than a year and a half for IACtHR rulings. These time periods are excessively long and may generate distrust and frustration among the users of the IAHRS. If the large number of petitions and subjects received is considered, it is clear that in many cases, the IAHRS does not offer an effective and timely answer for those affected'.[1] In that sense, it is important to note that there is the requirement of member states to also have accepted the jurisdiction of the IACtHR *ipso facto* for all cases.

The IAHRS has emerged as an integral part of the regional institutional landscape of the Americas since the twentieth century as a *mais valia* to fight for human rights in the region. The IAHRS was created and experienced its initial development in a period marked by the Cold War and long phases of repressive and authoritarian rule, from the 1950s to the mid-1980s. During this time, the IAHRS primarily sought to

[1] Basch et al. (2004).

C. Woyames Dreher, *A Legal Assessment of the Efficacy of Consultation with Indigenous Peoples*, https://doi.org/10.1007/978-3-031-50539-3_3

identify general patterns of human rights violations rather than focusing on individual cases.

Since its creation, the institutional development of the IAHRS has given a significant contribution to fostering the enforcement of human rights in the Americas. The IAHRS established the legal obligation under regional and international human rights law for states to protect the rights of citizens, and in the light of failure to do so, to hold states accountable and even more, by creating mechanisms to ensure that the states will cope with the decisions, such as the control of conventionality and including with the possibility of reparations.

The literature understands the consolidation process of the IAHRS as it has adapted from its modest origins to an independent regional international court integrated into an autonomous juridical process to assess whether regional states are in enforcement with international human rights obligations.[2] The access of individuals and regional human rights organizations to the human rights regime has strengthened over time as the system has become increasingly judicialized with a procedural focus on legal argumentation and the generation of regional human rights jurisprudence.

The emergence of the IAHRS has had profound implications for the implementation and protection of the rights of indigenous peoples in the Americas. Over the years, when indigenous peoples felt to not have found justice in their own states' courts, many have filed complaints with the IACHR. The foregoing analysis of the treaty-based provision of the requirement of consultation has received great attention by regional human rights systems in Africa and also in the Americas.

The first two sections of the chapter will therefore discuss a number of cases that cover the consultation with indigenous peoples at the IACHR and the IACtHR. These cases are selected because of their historical significance and according to their subject, by the innovative insight they offer and by the relevance of their consequences for the requirement of consultation with indigenous peoples.

The third section provides an overview of Inter-American cases from 1986 until 2015 in which consultation with indigenous peoples was established highlighting the consolidation character of the decisions regarding the requirement of consultation, giving special attention to the relevance of the interpretation that both, the IACHR and the IACtHR, are using to strengthen its *corpus iuris*.

The chapter reviews legal cases where the requirement of consultation has played an increasingly significant role while considering its basis in international human rights treaties. The cases show that the most significant design change regarding the requirement of consultation was the reiterative way of the application of the principles of (i) good faith, (ii) adequate and accessible consultation and (iii) the self-determination and the cultural rights.

The analysis of the decisions will moreover demonstrate that the right to consultation constitutes more than just a property right, but a means to participation of the

[2]See e.g. Pasqualucci (2003); *Inter-American Court of Human Rights 2019 Annual Report*, 2019; García Ramírez (2015); Huneeus (2011).

indigenous peoples or tribal communities in the decision-making process for fostering their cultural integrity and self-determination. The conclusion of the chapter will further spell out the implications of these findings.

3.2 The Cases of the Inter-American Commission of Human Rights

This section will analyze how the question of the requirement of consultation has been a matter of concern by the IACHR from 1985 until 2010, listing some relevant cases: the case 7615, known as the *Yanomami v. Brazil*, for which the decision was taken on March 5th of 1985; the Report No. 75/02, Case 11.140, known as the *Mary and Carrie Dann v. the United States*, for which the decision was taken on September 27th of 1999; the Report No. 40/04, Case 12.053, known as the *Maya Indigenous Communities of Toledo District v. Belize*, for which the decision dated October 5th of 2004; and more recently, the Precautionary Measure 382/10, known as *Belo Monte v. Brazil*, of July 29th of 2011.

According to Article 106 of the Charter of the OAS, the IACHR is a consultative organ, promoting the observance and protection of human rights. Moreover, Article 41 of the American Convention states that the main function of the Commission '[. . .] shall be to promote respect for and defense of human rights. The IACHR shall develop an awareness of human rights among the peoples of America; make recommendations to the governments of the member states, when it considers such action advisable, for the adoption of progressive measures in favor of human rights within the framework of their domestic law and constitutional provisions as well as appropriate measures to further the observance of those rights; to prepare such studies or reports as it considers advisable in the performance of its duties; to request the governments of the member states to supply it with information on the measures adopted by them in matters of human rights; to respond, through the General Secretariat of the Organization of American States, to inquiries made by the member states on matters related to human rights and, within the limits of its possibilities, to provide those states with the advisory services they request; to take action on petitions and other communications pursuant to its authority',[3] under the provisions of Articles 44 through 51 of the Convention. Specifically, the IACHR shall also submit an annual report to the General Assembly of the OAS.

As part of the *corpus iuris*, the IACHR is held to take into account the regional treaties. The IACHR is not only mandated to analyze and investigate petitions of individuals, but also to bring cases to the IACtHR of alleging violations of human rights, as established in Article 41 of the American Convention. The IACHR's main goal thereby is to develop an awareness of human rights among the peoples of America, by detecting human rights violations in the 35 member states of the OAS.

[3] (1967) Charter of the Organization of American States 'Protocol of Buenos Aires'.

According to Articles 30 and 36 of the Commission's Rules of Procedures, in case a petition meets the admissibility requirements set forth in those Articles, the Admissibility Report is approved. So that, in case there is an Admissibility Report, 'the petition becomes a legal case and it is assigned with a case number and after that, the claim enters the merits stage'.[4]

As a separate instrument, the precautionary measure is a legal mechanism established in the Article 25 of the Rules of Procedure of the IACHR,[5] a document

---

[4](2013) Rules of Procedure of the Inter-American Commission on Human Rights.

[5]'1. In accordance with Articles 106 of the Charter of the Organization of American States, 41.b of the American Convention on Human Rights, 18.b of the Statute of the Commission and XIII of the American Convention on Forced Disappearance of Persons, the Commission may, on its own initiative or at the request of a party, request that a state adopt precautionary measures. Such measures, whether related to a petition or not, shall concern serious and urgent situations presenting a risk of irreparable harm to persons or to the subject matter of a pending petition or case before the organs of the inter-American system. 2. For the purpose of taking the decision referred to in paragraph 1, the Commission shall consider that: a. "serious situation" refers to a grave impact that an action or omission can have on a protected right or on the eventual effect of a pending decision in a case or petition before the organs of the inter-American system; b. "urgent situation" refers to risk or threat that is imminent and can materialize, thus requiring immediate preventive or protective action; and c. "irreparable harm" refers to injury to rights which, due to their nature, would not be susceptible to reparation, restoration or adequate compensation. 3. Precautionary measures may protect persons or groups of persons, as long as the beneficiary or beneficiaries may be determined or determinable through their geographic location or membership in or association with a group, people, community or organization. 4. Requests for precautionary measures addressed to the Commission shall contain, inter alia: a. identifying information for the persons proposed as beneficiaries or information that allows them to be determined; b. a detailed and chronological description of the facts that motivate the request and any other available information; and c. the description of the measures of protection requested. 5. Prior to the adoption of precautionary measures, the Commission shall request relevant information to the state concerned, except where the immediacy of the threatened harm admits of no delay. In that circumstance, the Commission shall review that decision as soon as possible, or at the latest during its next period of sessions, taking into account the information received from the parties. 6. In considering the request the Commission shall take into account its context and the following elements: a. whether the situation has been brought to the attention of the pertinent authorities or the reasons why it would not have been possible to do so; b. the individual identification of the potential beneficiaries of the precautionary measures or the determination of the group to which they belong or are associated with; and c. the consent of the potential beneficiaries when the request is presented by a third party unless the absence of consent is justified. 7. The decisions granting, extending, modifying or lifting precautionary measures shall be adopted through reasoned resolutions that include, among others, the following elements: a. a description of the alleged situation and of the beneficiaries; b. the information presented by the state, if available; c. the considerations by the Commission concerning the requirements of seriousness, urgency, and irreparability; d. if applicable, the time period for which the measures will be in effect; and e. the votes of the members of the Commission. 8. The granting of such measures and their adoption by the state shall not constitute a prejudgment on the violation of any right protected by the American Convention on Human Rights or other applicable instruments. 9. The Commission shall evaluate periodically, at its own initiative or at the request of either party, whether to maintain, modify or lift the precautionary measures in force. At any time, the state may file a duly grounded petition that the Commission lift the precautionary measures in force. Prior to taking a decision on such a request, the Commission shall request observations from the beneficiaries. The presentation of such a request shall not

that was approved by the Commission at its '137th regular period of sessions, held from October 28th to November 13th 2009, and modified on September 2nd in 2011 and during the 147th Regular Period of Sessions, held from March 8th to 22nd March 2013, for entry into force on August 1st 2013'.[6]

As stipulated in Article 2 of the document, there are three possibilities when the decision regarding the adoption of precautionary measure can be taken: In case a situation is considered as serious, which refers to a grave impact that an action or omission can have on a protected right or on the eventual effect of a pending decision in a case or petition before the organs of the Inter-American System; in case there is an urgent situation, which refers to risk or threat that is imminent and can materialize, thus requiring immediate preventive or protective action; and last in case there is evidence of irreparable harm, which refers to injury to rights which, due to their nature, would not be susceptible to reparation, restoration or adequate compensation.[7]

3.2.1 The Yanomami v. Brazil (1985)

The Yanomami is one of the largest and relatively isolated indigenous peoples in South America. They live in the forests and mountains of northern Brazil and southern Venezuela. Their population were estimated to number between '10,000 to 12,000 by 1985 and today there are about 30,000 people'.[8] In Brazil, they live in Roraima and their rights are guaranteed, mainly, by the Federal Constitution of 1988 and the Statute of the Indigenous, Law No. 6.001 of 1973.

In this context, the Indigenous National Foundation (hereinafter, in Portuguese, as FUNAI) was created in 1967 by the Law No. 5.371 is relevant once 'it is

---

suspend the precautionary measures in force. 10. The Commission shall take appropriate follow-up measures, such as requesting relevant information from the interested parties on any matter related to the granting, observance and maintenance of precautionary measures. These measures may include, as appropriate, timetables for implementation, hearings, working meetings, and visits for follow-up and review. 11. In addition to the terms of subparagraph 9 above, the Commission may lift or review a precautionary measure when the beneficiaries or their representatives, without justification, fail to provide a satisfactory reply to the Commission on the requirements presented by the state for their implementation. 12. The Commission may present a request for provisional measures to the Inter-American Court in accordance with the conditions established in Article 76 of these Rules. Any precautionary measures issued with respect to the matter shall remain in effect until the Court notifies the parties of its resolution of the request. 13. In the case of a decision of the Inter-American Court dismissing an application for provisional measures, the Commission shall not consider a new request for precautionary measures unless there are new facts that justify it. In any case, the Commission may consider the use of other mechanisms to monitor the situation'. *Ibid.*

[6] *Ibid.*

[7] *Ibid.*

[8] Inter-American Commission of Human Rights, *Yanomami v. Brazil*, N° 7615, Judgment of 3 May 1985.

responsible to defend, protect and preserve the best interest of the indigenous peoples and tribal communities under Brazilian domestic law'.[9]

Article 2 of the Indigenous Law 6.001 of 1973 establishes that 'the indigenous peoples have the right to possess permanently the lands they occupy, recognizing their right to the exclusive usufruct of the natural resources and all useful things therein existing'.[10] And also in Article 23: 'their land occupied by them in accordance with their customs and tradition, including territories where they carry on activities essential for their subsistence or that are of economic usefulness constituting their territory.[11]

In December of 1980, however, a petition was filed with the IACHR that the Yanomami suffered violations of human rights as stipulated in the American Declaration in 'Article I (Right to Life, liberty and Personal Security); Article II (Right to Equality before Law); Article III (Right to Religious Freedom) and Worship), Article XI (Right to the Preservation of Health and to wellbeing); Article XII (Right to Education); Article XVII (Right to Recognition of Juridical Personality and of Civil Rights); and Article XXIII (Right to Property)'.[12]

The allegations revolved around the construction of a highway in the territory occupied by the Yanomami since 1973. The petition claimed that the invasion was carried out without the adequate consultation with the Yanomami which resulted in a 'considerable number of deaths caused by epidemics of influenza, tuberculosis, measles, venereal diseases and others',[13] mainly diseases carried by the construction workers.

In March 1985, the IACHR declared then, that 'for historical reasons and because of moral and humanitarian principles, special protection for indigenous populations constitutes a sacred commitment of states'. [14] In the same direction, the IACHR therefore recommended that the Brazilian state should give special attention to the suitable training of the officials who are to perform their work in contact with the indigenous who should not be object of discrimination. It noted that the OAS had agreed the importance of the preservation and strengthening of the cultural heritage of these ethnic groups and the struggle against the discrimination that invalidated their members' potential as human beings through the destruction of their cultural identity and individuality as indigenous peoples.

For the last part, the IACHR requested the Brazilian government to provide information on the measures that were taken to implement the recommendations. One of the recommendations to the government of Brazil included 'that the programs of education, medical protection, and social integration of the Yanomami Park

[9](1967) National Indigenous Foundation Law.

[10]*Ibid.*

[11]*Ibid.*

[12]Inter-American Commission of Human Rights, *Yanomami v. Brazil*, N° 7615, Judgment of 3 May 1985.

[13]¶10 b ibid.

[14]*Ibid.*

should be carried out in consultation with indigenous population affected and with the counselling service of competent scientific, medical and anthropological personnel'.[15]

The case did not reach the Inter-American Court, therefore, in 1992, the Yanomani Park was finally demarcated by the Brazilian law, according to the Federal Decree[16] and the Declaratory Order.[17]

However, still nowadays, the Yanomani face the expropriation of their territory and the constant manoeuvres of the manipulative environmental legislation in order to permit resource exploitation activities in their territory.[18]

3.2.2 *Mary and Carrie Dann v. the United States (2010)*

The land of the indigenous communities of which the Dann indigenous community are members is located in the rural community of Crescent Valley, Nevada, United States of America. This land is part of the ancestral territory of the Western Shoshone people and the Dann community and other members of the Western Shoshone. The Western Shoshone nation constitutes a collective of individuals of native descent who have traditionally occupied the vast territory. Regarding the approximately '24,000,000 acres, [there] appears to be no dispute between the parties as to the indigenous status of the Western Shoshone or of their historical occupation and use of this territory and its resources. Moreover, the parties agree that at some point the Western Shoshone had title to this territory as their ancestral lands'.[19]

In the early 1990s, however, United States citizens Mary Dann and Carrie Dann publicly alerted that the administration had interfered several times with these principles by physically removing and threatening to remove the Danns' livestock from the lands. They claimed that the permission of private mining concessions and harmful military activities had harmful consequences for their ancestral lands and had contaminated the ground water in and around Crescent Valley, and that the activities threatened even greater damage as it extended closer to the Danns' household.

Therefore, case No. 11.140 was filed with the IACHR in April 1993 and presented on behalf of Mary and Carrie Dann, sisters and citizens of the United States. The report of the IACHR No.75/02 was dated December 2002. The Dann sisters alleged that the US government needed to be held responsible for violations of 'Articles II (Right to equality before Law), III (Right to religious freedom and

---

[15]¶3 c ibid.

[16](1992) Federal Decree of the Demarcation of the Yanomami.

[17](1991) Declaratory order of the Yanomami Park.

[18]Plummer (2015); Albert (1992).

[19]¶ 100 Inter-American Commission on Human Rights, *Mary and Carrie Dann v. United States*, Case No 11.140, Judgment of 27 December 2002, Report 75/02.

worship), VI (Right to freedom of investigation, opinion, expression and dissemination), XIV (Right to a family and to protection thereof), XVIII (Right to residence and movement) and XXIII (Right to property) of the American Declaration of the Rights and Duties of Man'.[20] In order to support the contention, they also referred in their case to Article 14 of the ILO No. 169, Article 26 of the UNDRIP and Article 27 of the International Covenant on Civil and Political Rights.

It is important to highlight that their claim requested that the state violated ancestral right to the protection of cultural integrity, which they in turn claimed was affirmed in the American Declaration through 'Article XXII (right to property), Article III (right to religious freedom), Article VI (right to family and protection thereof) and Article XIV (right to take part in the cultural life of the community)'.[21] The Dann sisters stressed in particular that the IACHR had recognized the free exercise of these rights as 'essential to the enjoyment and perpetuation of the culture of indigenous peoples'.[22]

They also affirmed that they were unable to exercise their right to self-determination as guaranteed by international law. The right to property of Article XXIII of the American Declaration would have little meaning for indigenous peoples if their property 'could be encumbered without due consultation, consideration, and in appropriate circumstances, just compensation by the state'.[23]

In their claim, they conceded that the state had affirmed that the Dann sisters and other Western Shoshone lost any interest in the lands in question in 1872 as a result of encroachment by non-native Americans and because of that, granted them a compensation for the loss of their lands. The amount was of $26,145,189.89 according to 1872 land values.

However, the Dann sisters argued that the land was considered as customary land tenure system and asserted that this is a 'form of property recognized as original or Indian title by the law of the United States and other common law jurisdictions, as are free standing rights to fish, hunt, gather, or otherwise use resources or have access to lands'.[24]

Most fundamentally, such as in the case of the Yanomami *v.* Brazil, when there was recognition of the collective rights of the Yanomami People in Brazil to the delimitation and demarcation of their territory, the Dann sisters were guided by the Article 13 of the ILO Convention No. 169 that provides that in 'applying the provisions of this Part of the Convention governments shall respect the special importance for the cultures and spiritual values of the peoples concerned of their relationship with the lands or territories, or both as applicable, which they occupy or

[20] *(1948) American Declaration of the Rights and Duties of Man.*

[21] *Ibid.*

[22] ¶59 Inter-American Commission on Human Rights, *Mary and Carrie Dann v. United States*, Case No 11.140, Judgment of 27 December 2002, Report 75/02.

[23] ¶65 ibid.

[24] ¶45 ibid.

otherwise use, and in particular the collective aspects of this relationship'.[25] Thus, the IACHR and other international authorities would have to recognize the collective aspect of indigenous rights, in the sense that rights are realized in part or in whole through their guarantee to groups or organizations of people.[26] And to complement, in the Mayagna (Sumo) Awas Tingni Community *v.* Nicaragua case of 2001, 'the IACtHR of Human Rights has similarly recognized that for indigenous communities the relation with the land is not merely a question of possession and production but has a material and spiritual element that must be fully enjoyed to preserve their cultural legacy and pass it on to future generations'.[27]

Among several communications and other requests for precautionary measures, the Dann sisters sent a letter on October of 1999 to the IACHR, reiterating their willingness to 'enter into a process of friendly settlement with the United States under the Commission's auspices'.[28]

As outlined above, this approach would include 'taking of special measures to ensure recognition of the particular and collective interest that indigenous people have in the occupation and use of their traditional lands and resources and their right not to be deprived of this interest except with fully informed consent, under conditions of equality, and with fair compensation'.[29]

The United States government however strongly objected to the case made by the Dann sisters. It argued that it was not relevant to analyze whether the United States violated general norms of international law since the IACHR would not be an international tribunal. It further laid out that the treaties as cited by the IACHR, including the International Covenant on Civil and Political Rights and the Convention on the Elimination of Racial Discrimination, would not be binding upon the United States to the disputed situation since they were ratified long after the litigation in question was complete.

Ultimately, the IACHR decided that the petition was admissible and placed itself at the disposal of the parties concerned with a view to reaching a friendly settlement in this case. In order to maintain the effect, the Precautionary Measure issued on June 28th 1999, the Commission transmitted the report to the United States, the petitioners and also in its Annual report to the General Assembly to make it public. However, it had failed to find a friendly settlement.

Thus, in the Commission's opinion and in the context of this case, there was not sufficient grounds in order for the state to fulfill its particular obligation to ensure that the status of the Western Shoshone traditional lands was determined through a

---

[25] (1989) Indigenous Peoples and Tribal Convention No 169.

[26] ¶ 128 Inter-American Commission on Human Rights, *Mary and Carrie Dann v. United States*, Case No 11.140, Judgment of 27 December 2002, Report 75/02.

[27] ¶ 149 Inter-American Court of Human Rights, *Mayagna (Sumo) Awas Tingni Community v. Nicaragua*, No. 79, Judgment of 31 August 2001.

[28] ¶ 27 Inter-American Commission on Human Rights, *Mary and Carrie Dann v. United States*, Case No 11.140, Judgment of 27 December 2002, Report 75/02.

[29] ¶ 131 ibid.

process of informed and mutual consent on the part of the Western Shoshone people as a whole. Furthermore, the US rejected the recommendations and the Commission's Report entirely.[30]

3.2.3 *Maya Indigenous Communities of Toledo District v. Belize (2004)*

On August 7th 1998, the Indigenous Law Resource Center and the Toledo Maya Cultural Council petitioned to the IACHR that Belize had violated 'Article XXIII (right to property), the Article III (right to religious freedom), the Article VI (right to family and protection thereof), the Article XIV (right to take part in the cultural life of the community), the Article I (right to life), the Article XI (right to preservation of health and well-being) and the Article XX (right to participate in government) of the American Declaration on Rights and Duties of a Man. And based on the Article 23 of the United Nation Declaration on the Rights of Indigenous Peoples and the Article 14 (1) of the ILO Convention No. 169'.[31] More specifically, the claimers notified that logging concessions as granted by Belize were covering areas of land that included critical parts of the natural environment upon which the Maya peoples depended for subsistence, including vulnerable soils, primary forest growth and important watersheds. They claimed that Belize violated all those legal protections regarding the logging and oil concessions that the government granted to use and occupy their lands.

The claim made the case that Belize was a former British colony, and as such the common law jurisdiction should be deemed to incorporate the common law literature that upheld the property rights of indigenous peoples on the basis of customary land tenure as referred to by common law courts as aboriginal rights or title. These rights had arisen from the longstanding use and occupancy of the territory by the Maya Peoples, which the parties 'have agreed pre-dated European colonization and have extended to the use of the land and its resources for purposes relating to the physical and cultural survival of the Maya communities'.[32]

---

[30] On September 22, 2002, the United States took action to further infringe the rights of the Danns by seizing and confiscating, by action of 40 armed federal agents, approximately 225 head of cattle from their ancestral land which were subsequently auctioned off to the highest bidder several days later. These events took place despite an October 2, 2002 request by the Commission to comply with precautionary measures stipulating the return of said livestock to the Danns and that the authorities should refrain from impounding any additional livestock until the procedure before the Commission was complete, including implementation of any final recommendations that the Commission might adopt on the matter. Goméz (2003), p. 133.

[31] Inter-American Commission of Human Rights, *Maya Indigenous Communities of the Toledo District v. Belize*, Case No. 12.053, Judgment of 10 December 2004, Report No 40/04.

[32] ¶127 ibid.

The Maya People made a reference to the Article 23 of the UNDRIP, in this regard to the fundamental principle of nondiscrimination, which they claimed would prevent an interpretation that would discriminate 'against indigenous peoples regarding to their own modalities and forms of landholding and resource use'.[33]

The logging concession that Belize granted to several companies, covering about 749,222 acres of their territory, were 'contraventions [and] have impacted negatively on the natural environment upon which the Maya people depend for subsistence, have jeopardized the Maya people and their culture, and threaten to cause further damage in the future'.[34]

Lastly, the Maya People contended that Belize denied meaningful consultation before the concession of the logging and oil companies in the Toledo District, which can be established as a violation of the right to consultation, in particular as those concessions affected their interests in lands and natural resources. This provision of 'the right to participate' is implicit in the Article 27 of the ICCPR,[35] under Article XX of the American Declaration, and most relevant, to the principle of self-determination, which is affirmed in multiple international instruments and 'its core means that human beings, individually and collectively, have a right to be in control of their own destinies under conditions of equality'.[36] They also argued that 'this principle establishes at a minimum the right to be genuinely involved in all decision-making that affects them'.[37]

The Maya People asserted that the requirement of consultation with them 'must be more than formalities or simply processes by which they are given information about development projects but must also provide indigenous peoples a full and fair opportunity to be heard and to genuinely influence the decisions before them'.[38]

Thus, the meaningful consultations with the Maya People of the Toledo District had been held without public knowledge with vague and incomplete information, much less in direct consultation with the affected Maya communities. They also claimed 'that any attempts by the Maya themselves to engage in a meaningful dialogue with the Government [had] consistently been rebuffed, resulting in a denial of the Maya's human right to consultation'.[39]

In its verdict, the IACHR acknowledged the failure of Belize to engage in meaningful consultation with the Maya People in connection with the logging and oil concessions in the Toledo District, and the negative environmental effects arising from those concessions, constituting violations of several other rights under

[33] (2007) The United Nations Declaration on the Rights of Indigenous Peoples.

[34] ¶2 Inter-American Commission of Human Rights, *Maya Indigenous Communities of the Toledo District v. Belize*, Case No. 12.053, Judgment of 10 December 2004, Report No 40/04.

[35] *(1976) International Covenant on Civil and Political Rights.*

[36] ¶45 Inter-American Commission of Human Rights, *Maya Indigenous Communities of the Toledo District v. Belize*, Case No. 12.053, Judgment of 10 December 2004, Report No 40/04.

[37] ¶46 ibid.

[38] ¶49 ibid.

[39] ¶57 ibid.

international human rights law.[40] The decision include 'the right to life under Article I of the American Declaration, the right to religious freedom and worship under Article III of the American Declaration, the right to a family and to protection thereof under Article VI of the American Declaration',[41] the right to preservation of health and well-being under Article XI of the American Declaration, and the 'right to consultation implicit in Article 27 of the ICCPR, Article XX of the American Declaration, and the principle of self-determination'.[42]

This case is one of the most relevant for understanding the consolidation of the requirement of consultation because the IACHR emphasized the distinct nature of the right to property as it applies to indigenous people. The analysis of the IACHR rested on the premise that the land traditionally used and occupied by these communities played a central role in their physical, cultural and spiritual vitality; and in line with what the IACHR had previously recognized, it stressed the context 'in respect of the right to property and the right to equality in order to enjoy and perpetuate their culture'.[43]

Likewise, the concept of family and religion within the context of indigenous communities, including the Maya People, was connected with their traditional land, 'where ancestral burial grounds, places of religious significance and kinship patterns are linked with the occupation and use of their physical territories'.[44]

Further, the IACHR specifically concluded in its analysis in this case that the duty of the requirement of consultation 'is a fundamental component of the state's obligations in giving effect to the communal property right of the Maya people in the lands that they have traditionally used and occupied'.[45]

The IACHR understood that Belize violated the right to property enshrined in Article XXIII of the American Declaration[46] to the detriment of the Maya People because they granted logging and oil concessions to third parties to utilize their property and resources. The Commission also requested that the lands must be 'delimited, demarcated and titled or otherwise clarified and protected, in the absence of effective consultations with and the informed consent of the Maya people'.[47]

The IACHR also recommended the adoption of a fully informed consultation as a rule to be included in the domestic law. In accordance with their customary land use practices, and without detriment to other indigenous communities, the Commission recommended to delimitate the land of the Maya People through a legislative,

[40] Anaya (1998).

[41] *(1948) American Declaration of the Rights and Duties of Man.*

[42] *(1976) International Covenant on Civil and Political Rights.*

[43] ¶155 Inter-American Commission of Human Rights, *Maya Indigenous Communities of the Toledo District v. Belize*, Case No. 12.053, Judgment of 10 December 2004, Report No 40/04.

[44] ¶156 ibid.

[45] ¶157 ibid.

[46] *(1948) American Declaration of the Rights and Duties of Man.*

[47] ¶177 Inter-American Commission of Human Rights, *Maya Indigenous Communities of the Toledo District v. Belize*, Case No. 12.053, Judgment of 10 December 2004, Report No 40/04.

administrative or any other measures necessary to title or otherwise clarify that they have a communal property right. By all means, the IACHR also required that Belize should have repaired the environmental damage that resulted from the logging concessions they granted in respect of the territory traditionally occupied and used by the Maya People.

3.2.4 *Belo Monte Precautionary Measure 382 (2011)*

On July 29 of 2011, during its 142nd regular session, the IACHR evaluated the Precautionary Measure 382/10. The request alleged that the life and physical integrity of the indigenous communities that live in voluntary isolation might had been at risk due to the impact of the construction of the Belo Monte hydroelectric dam.[48] The request stressed the impact of the daily construction activities to the indigenous communities of the Xingu River Basin in Pará, Brazil: the Arara of Volta Grande do Xingu; the Juruna of Paquiçamba; the Juruna of Kilómetro 17; the Xikrin of Trincheira Bacajá; the Asurini of Koatinemo; the Kararaô and Kayapó of the Kararaô indigenous lands; the Parakanã of Apyterewa; the Araweté of the Igarapé Ipixuna; the Arara of the Arara indigenous lands; the Arara of Cachoeira Seca; and the Xingu Basin.[49]

Before that, the case was judged in Brazilian Federal Court.[50] The Belo Monte hydroelectric power plant, located in Altamira, Pará, with its installed maximum capacity of 11.233 megawatts (MW) was officially inaugurated on 27th November of 2019.[51] The construction time lasted almost 45 years after first studies were commissioned by Eletronorte for using the Xingu River as a source of electricity.[52]

The official planning for the construction of the Belo Monte dam began in 1975, during the military dictatorship in Brazil.[53] At the time, five large hydroelectric dams were planned in the Xingu basin with an installed capacity of 20.000 MW, but which were estimated to cause a flooding of about 16.000 km^2 of land around the work area.[54] The system of dams was planned to be named *Kararaô*, but the project's high

[48]See e.g. Jaichand and Sampaio (2013); Diamond and Poirier (2010); Fearnside (2006); Atkins (2017).

[49]Jaichand and Sampaio (2013).

[50]In this video, the Federal Prosecutor explains the legal claim from the time that the indigenous peoples Juruna found out that the water level of the river was lower than expected and told him, to the instauration of the whole legal claim against the illegal measures that were taken already without consultation and also not taking into account the Constitution of Brazil and other national laws. For more, see: (2016) Aldeia da Memória-Belo Monte.

[51]de Oliveira Franco and de Alencar Mayer Feitosa (2013).

[52]Hall and Branford (2012).

[53]Zugman (2015).

[54]Federal Court of Pará, *Appeal 'Apelação Cível'*, No. 2006.39.03.000711-8/PA, Judgment of 15 April 2011.

social and environmental risks generated strong protests among indigenous peoples, headed by the *Kayapó* indigenous people, which led to the cancellation of the original project already in 1989.[55]

Since the first studies on the construction of the Belo Monte, civil society organizations, environmentalists, scientists, indigenous peoples' groups and the population leaving close to the river's shores (in Portuguese, *população ribeirinhas*) have denounced the expected social and environmental impact that the dam would bring to the region.[56]

The Belo Monte case was, back the time, one of the few legal claims against natural resource exploitation without the consultation process with the indigenous peoples who live in the territory.[57] The controversial case, at the same time, brought hope for those who wanted to ensure that the requirement of consultation was going to be addressed.

The indigenous peoples initiated their own Protocol of consultation, which raised the awareness of the responsible judges over the necessity to take into consideration indigenous peoples' fundamental rights.[58] There are however still the legal implications regarding the efficacy of the requirement of consultation, which are gradually opening up the debate towards a more thorough constitutional review.

According to the Brazilian Federal Prosecutor's Office, more than 25 legal claims have been filed against the Belo Monte hydroelectric power plant. The litigations were mostly launched in the Brazilian Federal Courts and are still pending decision. The most relevant ones include: the Appeal, in Portuguese, APCIV - *Apelação Cível*, regarding the EIA/RIMA of the Belo Monte and the Appeal No. 5850-73.2001.4.01.3900, in which the federal judge decided on a fixed a fine of R$ 1,000,000.00 (one million Reais) in case of nonenforcement with the decision.[59] And the Appeal No. 2006.39.03.000711-8 towards the legislative Decree No. 788/2005 in respect of the absence of the consultation undertaken by the Brazilian Institute of the Environment and Renewable Natural Resources (hereinafter, the IBAMA) with the indigenous peoples and the refusal to hold informal meetings with indigenous peoples: *Arara, Juruna, Araweté, Parakanã, Xikrin, Xipaya* and *Kuruaya*; all indigenous peoples of the territory.

The federal judge Selene Almeida understood that: 'the consultation is based on the right of the indigenous and tribal populations to decide their priorities regarding their development, to the extent that legislative and administrative acts affect their survival. According to the prescriptions of ILO Convention No. 169, inserted in our

[55] de Oliveira Franco and de Alencar Mayer Feitosa (2013).

[56] See e.g. Ibid.; Watts (2016); (2008) Listing with all the litigations of the Belo Monte case.

[57] Zugman (2015).

[58] See e.g. Povo Juruna (2017) Protocolo de consulta Juruna (YudJá) da terra Indígena PaquIçamba da Volta grande do rIo XIngu; da Silva (2017); Amin Lima da Silva and Mendes (2019); Doyle et al. (2019).

[59] Federal Tribunal 1ª Region, *Appeal 'APCIV Apelação Cível'*, 0005850-73.2001.4.01.3900, Judgment of 2 April 2010.

legal system at the level of constitutional norms, prior consultation (Article 6) and participation (Article 7) constitute the fundamental right that indigenous and tribal peoples have to be able to decide on legislative and administrative measures, when the state permits the implementation of projects. The intention is to protect cultural, social, and economic integrity, in addition to guaranteeing the democratic right to participate in decisions that directly affect these traditional populations'.[60]

The federal judge Herculano Nacif of the city of Altamira, in Pará, reasoned that the indigenous communities could be heard after the Decree was approved by the National Congress, during the course of undertaking the necessary studies for the installation of the dam.[61] The federal judge Selene de Almeida, by contrast, understood, regarding the constitutional consultation, that: 'before authorizing the construction, the Congress needs data to know the extent of damage that will occur and the solutions that must occur to allow the installation of a hydroelectric plant of this size'.[62] She also argued that the opinion of indigenous communities is not to be considered as a potential veto to the whole undertaking, but that their views have certainly to be taken into consideration. federal judge Selene de Almeida also said that public hearings which took place during the environmental licensing process should not replace the prior consultation of the National Congress with the people affected: 'public hearings have a technical character, while the consultation aims to subsidize the political decision'. For her, in addition to being unconstitutional, the Decree that accepted the construction of the Belo Monte dam violated the ILO No. 169 treaty, which Brazil had ratified in 2008.

In 2019, during the drought period in the region, even with 17 of the 18 turbines running production dropped dramatically to only 276 MW, as since the beginning, there were doubts regarding the project. In October, the turbines had to be shut down several times to prevent damage.[63] Also in 2016 during the 65th phase of the Brazilian anti-corruption unit Car Wash, in Portuguese, *Lava Jato*, former Minister Edison Lobão and his son Márcio Lobão were investigated for receiving bribes as part of the construction of the Belo Monte hydroelectric plant.[64]

In sum, in addition to numerous complaints against the dam for environmental and social damage, the controversial issue of the actual functionality of the dam, innumerous ongoing criminal activities, and corruption surrounding the construction of the dam, adds not only the failure to comply with the fundamental right of the requirement of consultation of indigenous peoples but also signals to corporation

[60]Federal Court of Pará, *Appeal 'Apelação Cível'*, No. 2006.39.03.000711-8/PA, Judgment of 15 April 2011., *translated by author*.

[61]Federal Court of Altamira, *Appeal 'Ação Civil Pública'*, No. 709-88.2006.4.01.3903, Judgment of 30 March 2006.

[62]Federal Court of Pará, *Appeal 'Apelação Cível'*, No. 2006.39.03.000711-8/PA, Judgment of 15 April 2011.

[63]ISA (2017).

[64]Watts (2016).

impunity when exploiting natural resources without the need to respect court verdicts.

In response, the IACHR requested that Brazil must immediately suspend the licensing process and any construction work from moving forward of the Belo Monte hydroelectric dam project.

Before that, on April 1st 2011, the IACHR required that Brazil should have conducted consultations, in good faith, informed and culturally appropriate, guaranteeing that the indigenous had access, in their own languages, to the environmental impact study and Brazil should have adopted measures to protect the life and physical integrity of the members of the indigenous peoples of the *Xingu Basin*. The preoccupation in order was 'to prevent the spread of diseases and epidemics among the indigenous communities being granted the precautionary measures as a consequence of the construction of the Belo Monte hydropower plant. This included any diseases derived from the massive influx of people into the region as well as the exacerbation of transmission vectors of water-related diseases such as malaria'.[65]

There are indications, *fumus boni iuris*, that the IACHR will have to refer the case to the IACtHR, in its report on the merits, it will recommend that the Brazilian jurisdiction must adopt the necessary measures to protect the life, integrity and property rights of the indigenous communities affected by the hydroelectric dam. The IACHR should prepare a report in which it concludes whether or not there have been human rights violations and can issue recommendations for Brazil. If it is not heeded, it may refer the case to the Inter-American Court, which has the power to litigate and enforce reparations and costs. Although the dam has been in operation since the beginning of 2015, its construction has not yet been completed due to judicial measures which count more than 25 by now in Pará.[66] The Brazilian state can still avoid further damage, so that the IAHRS is relevant in order to mitigate those violations against indigenous people's rights.

3.3 The Cases of the Inter-American Court of Human Rights

The IACtHR is the juridical organ of the IAHRS.[67] The jurisdiction of the IACtHR shall 'comprise all cases concerning the interpretation and application of the provisions of the American Declaration or other treaties that are in accordance with the human rights'.[68]

[65] Inter-American Commission of Human Rights, *Precautionary Measure PM 382/10: Indigenous Communities of the Xingu River Basin v. Brazil*, Judgment of 4 January 2011.

[66] *Lawsuits Belo Monte.*

[67] Huneeus (2011); Antkowiak (2013).

[68] *(2009) Rules of Procedure of the Inter-American Court of Human Rights.*

The only possible form to litigate is through the IACHR. Only after the IACHR's consideration to review the admissibility criteria determined by the American Convention on Human Rights, the IACtHR may assume a case. And it is also possible, in rare cases, that some cases will be answered only by the IACHR and will not be considered by the IACtHR. Therefore, there can be an attempt to achieve settlement to a dispute by an agreement between the parties putting an end to the claim; or a request can be made for an examination of the merits, which results in a report considering the existence of a human rights violation. There is of course always the contingency of a case being closed when no violation of human rights has been found by the IACHR. In other words, the petition to the IACtHR is the last step of the juridical procedure. This is framed as the last phase before the monitoring of the fulfillment of judgements by the national jurisdiction and then, the analyses of the IACHR, possibly indicating that while violations of human rights have been asserted, no voluntary enforcement with the Commission's recommendations has followed.

According to the IACHR enforcement system, individuals, groups of individuals, and non-governmental organizations recognized in any OAS state members may submit petitions concerning alleged violations of human rights. Over the IACtHR's years of implementation, the commitment with human rights can be considered in an interesting way: its annual case has more than doubled; the IACtHR has adjudicated a significant range of rights protected by the American Convention such as labor, land, and freedom of expression. For instance, the IACHR receives approximately 1500 petitions every year.[69]

The complaint procedures of the IAHRS have historically been designed as a system of individual petitions for alleging violations of human rights. The IAHRS had in general considered the strong prevalence of the civil and political rights, and its assertion as a form of protection also of collective rights. Related to the collective territorial rights that most of the cases focus on, a historical reflection of the struggle of the indigenous peoples since the time of colonization can be detected. In fact, the IAHRS has gained in importance also because of the multifaceted and multicultural character of the American continent. Thus, the decisions as issued by the IAHRS and IACtHR have increasingly shaped the American Convention on Human Rights, revealing violations of human rights of indigenous communities. Regarding one of the thematic areas of the IAHRS, the indigenous peoples, for example, had their first request in the IACHR in 1974.

This first case, the Case 1802, regarding the *Aché Tribe v. Paraguay* of 1974, was about 'denounced, along with the murder of a number of indigenous, the sale of children, the withholding of medical attention and medicines during epidemics, mistreatment and torture, inhuman working conditions, and acts aimed at destroying their culture'.[70] About this matter, the IACHR decided: '1. In application of Article

[69] *The Inter-American Commission on Human Rights Strategic Plan for 2017-2021.*, 2017.

[70] Inter-American Commission of Human Rights, *Aché Tribe v. Paraguay*, No 1802, Judgment of May 1975.

51.1 of the Regulations, to presume the occurrence of the events denounced to be confirmed; 2. To point out to the Government of Paraguay that such acts constitute very serious violations of the right to life, liberty, and personal security (Article I of the American Declaration of the Rights and Duties of Man); of the right to a family and to the protection thereof (Article VI); of the right to preservation of health and to well-being (Article XI); of the right to work and to fair remuneration (Article XIV), and of the right to leisure time and to the use thereof (Article XV). 3. To recommend to the Government of Paraguay that it adopt vigorous measures to provide effective protection for the rights of the Aché tribe. 4. To recommend that the Government punish, in accordance with Paraguayan law, those responsible for the events denounced. 5. To request the Government to advise the Commission of the measures adopted to carry out this resolution, within a period of sixty days. 6. To forward this resolution to the Government of Paraguay and to the claimants. 7. To include this resolution in its Annual Report to the General Assembly of the Organization (Article 9 (bis), c, iii of the Statute)'.[71]

At present 20 state members have opted to accept the IACtHR contentious jurisdiction in accordance with Article 62 of the American Convention.[72] The 20 national states over which the IACtHR may exercise its contentious jurisdiction are: Argentina, Barbados, Bolivia, Brazil, Chile, Colombia, Costa Rica, Dominican Republic, Ecuador, El Salvador, Guatemala, Haiti, Honduras, Mexico, Nicaragua, Panama, Paraguay, Peru, Suriname, and Uruguay. Previously, Trinidad and Tobago and Venezuela had both accepted the IACtHR's jurisdiction but withdrew from that jurisdiction when they denounced the American Convention, in 1998 and 2012, respectively.

The IACtHR began operating in 1979, and soon it issued several advisory opinions, but did not begin exercising its contentious jurisdiction until 1986, when the IACHR submitted the first contentious case: *Velasquez Rodriguez v. Honduras*, 'regarding the claim of violation of the Article 4 (right to life) and the Article 7 (right to personal liberty of the American Convention'.[73]

The data analysis of the cases shows two decades of the IACtHR's jurisdiction recognized in the 20 countries that accepted the IACtHR contentious jurisdiction. During the year of 2019, for instance, the IACtHR delivered 25 judgments, including 21 judgments on preliminary objections, merits, reparations and costs, and 4 interpretation judgments.[74] And still 43 cases are pending a decision.[75] There are 223 cases at the stage of monitoring enforcement, and this entails monitoring 1153 measures of reparation.[76]

[71] *Ibid.*

[72] (1969) American Convention on Human Rights.

[73] Inter-American Court of Human Rights, *Velasquez Rodriguez v. Honduras*, No 7920, Judgment of 29 June 1988.

[74] , *Inter-American Court of Human Rights 2019 Annual Report*, 2019.

[75] Ibid.

[76] Ibid.

The cases below represent those that were considered relevant for the study of the consolidation of the interpretation of the requirement of consultation in accordance the Article 1 of the Statute of the IACtHR of Human Rights that followed the American Convention when it stated that 'the Inter-American Court of Human Rights is an autonomous judicial institution whose purpose is the application and interpretation of the American Convention on Human Rights. The IACtHR exercises its functions in accordance with the provisions of the aforementioned Convention and the present Statute'.[77]

The selected cases include the case *Saramaka v. Suriname*, of 2007; the case *Kichwa de Sarayaku v. Ecuador*, of 2012; the *Povos Kaliña e Lokono v. Suriname*, of 2015 and the *Indigenous Community de la Asociación Lhaka Honhat (nuestra tierra) v. Argentina*, of 2020.

3.3.1 The Saramaka People v. Suriname (2007)

This case was based on Articles 50 and 61 of the American Convention and was divided into preliminary objections, merits, reparations and costs. The relevance of this case resides in the fact that the state's grant of concessions for the exploration and extraction of natural resources found on and within Saramaka's territory violated a range of antecedent rights. The right to property is not an absolute right unless in cases that 'deny the survival of the indigenous and tribal communities and the right to consultation and the duty to obtain consent'.[78]

In this particular case, the restrictions pertained to the issuance of using indigenous peoples' territory for mining and logging. The state was obliged to safeguard the customs and traditions of the Saramaka People, ensuring that they would benefit from any extractions made in their territory and ensuring that there will be state's technical supervision of the impact assessment.

For assessing the case, it is first of all important to note that Suriname recognized the contentious *jurisdiction* of the IACtHR on 12th November 1987. Moreover, Suriname ratified the International Covenant on Civil and Political Rights as well on March 28th 1977 (entered in force March 23rd 1976) and the International Covenant on Economic, Social and Cultural Rights 16th December 1966 (entered in force January 31st 1976).

The Saramaka People are originally from the African continent, and they were brought to Suriname as slaves during the European colonization in the seventeenth century. Some of these facts were recognized only from their testimonies, *e.g.* as laid out by Head Captain and Fiscali Wazen Eduards in the transcription of the public hearing as well as by 'Prof. Richard Price during the hearing at the IACtHR that was

[77] (1979) Inter-American Court of Human Rights Statue.

[78] ¶133 Inter-American Commission of Human Rights, *Saramaka People v. Suriname*, Case No 172, Judgment of 28 November 2007.

held in May of 2007, and the expert opinion of Salomon Emanuels during the public hearing at the IACtHR, also in May'.[79] According to the testimonies, the Saramaka People established their own autonomous community in '12 clans distributed among around 25 thousand to 34 thousand peoples. They are distributed in 63 communities on the Upper Suriname River'.[80]

The Saramaka People organize themselves in 'matrilineal clans (*lös*) and they regulate themselves by their own customs and traditions, being their Head Captains the highest official in the community'.[81] They also maintain a very strong spiritual relationship with the ancestral territory and the land is a source of the continuation of the life, their cultural identity and a link to the history of slavery they were forced into. Thus, this is where they fish, hunt, farm and grow herbs for medicine purpose.

They are not considered indigenous in the region they inhabit because they were brought to the region in Suriname during colonization; therefore, they had to first off assert their rights as tribal peoples with similar characteristics of indigenous peoples, such as 'having social, cultural and economic traditions different from other sections of the national community, identifying themselves with their ancestral territories, and regulating themselves, at least partially, by their own norms, customs and traditions'.[82]

In this case, the IACHR submitted an application on 23rd June 2006 to the IACtHR. The application, No. 12.338 was in order for the alleged violations committed by Suriname against the members of the tribal community living in the Upper Suriname river region. The Commission alleged also that Suriname did not adopt 'effective measures to recognize their right to the use and enjoyment of the territory they had traditionally occupied and used'.[83] In effect, the IACHR requested the IACtHR to determine the international responsibility of the state for the violation of 'Article 21 (Right to Property) and Article 25 (Right to Judicial Protection), in conjunction with Articles 1 (1) and 2 of the American Declaration'.[84]

Some of the significant innovations of this particular case pertain to the special measures of protection owed to members of the tribal community that guarantee the exercise of their rights and the legal base for the right to consultation and the duty to obtain consent. The IACtHR had already determined the need of a special guarantee based on Article 1(1) of the Convention to enable tribal communities' the 'full exercise of their rights, particularly with regards to their enjoyment of property rights, in order to safeguard their physical and cultural survival'.[85] This had been

[79]¶ 80 ibid.

[80]¶81 ibid.

[81]¶ 81 ibid.

[82]¶80 ibid.

[83]¶2 ibid.

[84](1948) American Declaration of the Rights and Duties of Man; ¶2 Inter-American Commission of Human Rights, *Saramaka People v. Suriname*, Case No 172, Judgment of 28 November 2007.

[85]¶85 Inter-American Commission of Human Rights, *Saramaka People v. Suriname*, Case No 172, Judgment of 28 November 2007.

established in the case of the *Mayagna (Sumo) Awas Tingni Community v. Nicaragua*, the case of the *Indigenous Community Sawhoyamaxa v. Paraguay* in 2006 and the case of the *Indigenous Community Yakye Axa v. Paraguay*. In the case *Moiwana Community v. Suriname* the IACtHR, for example, decided that the separate Maroon community, also living in Suriname, was also a tribal community and not an indigenous community because they were settled in the region during the seventeenth and eighteenth century, which had a 'very profound and all-encompassing relationship to their ancestral lands, and the community as a whole'.[86]

Likewise, the IACtHR's decision to this effect had been in accordance with Article 21, 1.1 and 2 of the American Convention, based upon the special relationship that these groups have to their territory, being important to safeguard the physical and cultural survival of tribal communities and indigenous peoples that are living there. Equally important, the IACtHR had decided that the 'indigenous communities might have a collective understanding of the concepts of property and possession in the sense that ownership of the land is not centered on an individual, but rather on the group and its community'.[87]

It is important to highlight that the Human Rights Committee observed that 'the minorities shall not be denied the right, in community with the other members of their group, to enjoy their own cultural (. . .) that may consist in a way of life which is closely associated with territory and use of its resources. This may particularly be true of members of indigenous communities constituting a minority'.[88]

In sum, the IACtHR understood that the Saramaka People had 'the right to enjoy their property in accordance with their system of communal property'.[89]

Regarding the analysis whether Suriname had adopted or not an appropriate framework to give domestic legal efficacy to this right, the IACtHR recalled that the Surinamese law does not recognize and protect the traditional land tenure systems of indigenous and tribal peoples, or their special relationship with the forest. All land and all natural resources are considered to be owned by Suriname itself. About this, the United Nations Commission on Human Rights Special Rapporteur on the situation of human rights and fundamental freedoms of indigenous peoples, Rodolfo Stravenhagen, had observed that Suriname 'does not legally accept the rights of the members of indigenous peoples and tribal communities to their communal land, territories neither resources'.[90]

---

[86]¶123 Inter-American Court of Human Rights, *Moiwana Community v. Suriname*, Judgment of 15 June 2005.

[87]¶149 Inter-American Court of Human Rights, *Mayagna (Sumo) Awas Tingni Community v. Nicaragua*, No. 79, Judgment of 31 August 2001.

[88], *CCPR General Comment No. 23: Article 27 (Rights of Minorities)*, 4 August 1994.

[89]¶97 Inter-American Commission of Human Rights, *Saramaka People v. Suriname*, Case No 172, Judgment of 28 November 2007.

[90]Stavenhagen R, *Report of the Special Rapporteur on the situation of human rights and fundamental freedoms of indigenous people*, UN Doc. E/CN.4/2003/90, 21 2003.

Nevertheless, Suriname understood that as there was no land tenure and the collective rights had not permitted the state to be able to recognize the Saramaka People's rights, as those raised questions regarding the sovereignty and discrimination of the rest of the population in Suriname.

About that matter, the IACtHR decided about the theme, affirming that special measures are necessary to ensure the survival of indigenous and tribal peoples to be able to live in accordance with their traditions and declaring that states have an obligation to take a positive step towards the protection of the minorities as a way to provide equality under the law. As stated by the United Nations International Convention on the Elimination of All Forms of Racial Discrimination in its Article 1.4, 'that special measures taken for the sole purpose of securing adequate advancement of certain racial or ethnic groups or individuals requiring such protection as may be necessary in order to ensure such groups or individuals equal enjoyment or exercise of human rights and fundamental freedoms shall not be deemed racial discrimination'.[91]

Following, the Forest Management Act of 1992 about the 'concessions for the forest exploration and logging',[92] among others and also the Constitution of Suriname of 1987 in its Article 41, '[. . .] natural riches and resources are the property of the nation and shall be used to promote economic, social and cultural development. The nation has the inalienable right to take complete possession of its natural resources in order to utilize them to the benefit of the economic, social and cultural development of Suriname',[93] granted the members of the Saramaka Peoples to use the land but they did not have control over the territory. Suriname argued that the rights regarding the land, in special, the subsoil natural resources were vested in the concessions by the third parties.

The lack of adequacy control was already discussed by the IACtHR in the case Mayagna (Sumo) Awas Tingni Community, the case of the Indigenous Community Yakye Axa, and the case of the Moiwana Community. It was determined that the members of the indigenous peoples and tribal communities had the right to obtain title to their land to guaranteeing their use and enjoyment of the territory, in line with the testimony of Head Captain and Fiscali Wazen Eduards. Nonetheless, the IACtHR had previously agreed that the 'cultural and economic survival of indigenous and tribal peoples depend on their access and use of the natural resources in their territory'.[94]

In sum, the IACtHR decided that Suriname did not accomplish its duty to give domestic legal efficacy to the indigenous peoples in their state, in special, the Saramaka People and their land tenure issue. However, in 2006, Suriname confirmed

---

[91] UN Committee on the Elimination of Racial Discrimination (CERD) (1966) International Convention on the Elimination of All Forms of Racial Discrimination.

[92] (1992) Wet Bosbeheer (Forest Management Act).

[93] (1987) Constitution of Suriname.

[94] ¶120 Inter-American Commission of Human Rights, *Saramaka People v. Suriname*, Case No 172, Judgment of 28 November 2007.

its commitment to improve the legalization of the indigenous peoples' and tribal communities' rights.

Regarding to the Suriname grant of concessions for the exploration and extraction of natural resources found on and within Saramaka territory, both the Commission and the representatives alleged that there was no adequate consultation with the indigenous peoples, thus, violating their right to the natural resources that lie on and within the land.

A separate point of the case as brought to the IACtHR was the matter that the state might grant concessions for the exploration and extraction of natural resources. Although Article 21 protected the members of the Saramaka People's rights over the natural resources that are needed for their physical survival, the interpretation of the Article 21 should not prevent the state to be able to grant concessions for the exploration and extraction of natural resources. The IACtHR gave the example of clean water: 'clean natural water, for example, is a natural resource essential for the Saramaka to be able to carry out some of their substance economic activities, like fishing'.[95] The IACtHR observed that this natural resource is likely to be affected by extraction activities related to other natural resources that are not traditionally used by or essential for the survival of the Saramaka People, and consequently, its members.

The protection of the right to property, according to the IACtHR, 'is not absolute and also does not allow for such a stringent interpretation'.[96] Such that the state may had to restrict the use and enjoyment of the right to property, such as was already decided by the IACtHR in accordance to the case of the Indigenous Community Yakye Axa, the case of *Ricardo Canese v. Paraguay*, the case of *Herrera Ulloa v. Costa Rica*, the case of Ivcher *Bronstein v. Peru* and the case of the Indigenous Community Sawhoyamaxa. They all decided that the 'restrictions to the right to property should be focusing on case it was already established by law, necessity, proportionally and in case of the achievement of a legitimate objective in a democratic society'.[97]

In regard to this specific consultation, it was settled that it can be established to prevent a disregard for human rights. The level of such consultation depended on the specific circumstances. Consultation is not an end in itself but should serve the purpose of respecting the interest of those who used the land. Thus, consultation must be in 'good faith according to culturally appropriate procedures and most important: the interest to achieve an agreement'.[98]

Furthermore, the IACtHR considered that there was the need of the efficacy of the participation in accordance with their traditions and customs. In line with this, the

[95]¶126 ibid.

[96]¶127 ibid.

[97]¶117 Inter-American Court of Human Rights, *Sawhoyamaxa Indigenous Community v. Paraguay*, Judgment of 29 March 2006.

[98]¶131 Inter-American Commission of Human Rights, *Saramaka People v. Suriname*, Case No 172, Judgment of 28 November 2007.

Committee on the Elimination of Racial Discrimination had recommended not only that the prior informed consent of communities must be sought when major exploitation activities were planned in indigenous territories, but also 'that the equitable sharing of benefits to be derived from such exploitation be ensured'.[99]

In the same direction, the Special Rapporteur on the situation of human rights and fundamental freedoms of indigenous peoples has suggested that in order to guarantee 'the human rights of indigenous peoples in relation to major development projects, [states should ensure] mutually acceptable benefit sharing'.[100]

What was related and acknowledged by the IACtHR suggested that the level of consultation with the Saramaka Peoples was not the ideal outcome. Suriname did not complete the environmental and social impact assessments, and neither ensured effective participation in the decision-making process. And because of that, the IACtHR considered that the logging concessions issued by the state in the lands over the Suriname River damaged the environment, making a negative impact on the land and the national resources of the territory traditionally used by the Saramaka People.

In sum, as in accordance with the international law and the Article 63 (1) of the American Convention, by the time there was a violation of an international obligation to prevent damage, there was the need to redress the violation. The IACtHR decided that Suriname had to 'grant the members of the Saramaka People legal recognition of the collective juridical capacity, pertaining to the community to which they belong, with the purpose of ensuring the full exercise and enjoyment of their right to communal property; remove or amend the legal provisions that impede protection of the right to property of the members of the Saramaka People and adopt, in its domestic legislation, and through prior, effective and fully informed consultations with the Saramaka People, legislative, administrative, and other measures as may be required to recognize, protect, guarantee and give legal effect to the right of the members of the Saramaka People; adopt legislative, administrative and other measures necessary to recognize and ensure the right of the Saramaka People to be effectively consulted, in accordance with their traditions and customs, or when necessary, the right to give or withhold their free, informed and prior consent and to adopt legislative, administrative and other measures necessary to provide the members of the Saramaka People with adequate and effective recourses against acts that violate their right to the use and enjoyment of property in accordance with their communal property system'.[101]

In the case of the Saramaka People, the IACtHR indicated that the 'consultation must ensure the effective participation of the members of the Community and that

[99] *Concluding observations of the Committee on the Elimination of Racial Discrimination- Ecuador*, 22 September 2008.

[100] Stavenhagen R, *Report of the Special Rapporteur on the situation of human rights and fundamental freedoms of indigenous people*, UN Doc. E/CN.4/2003/90, 21 2003, p. 66.

[101] Inter-American Commission of Human Rights, *Saramaka People v. Suriname*, Case No 172, Judgment of 28 November 2007, pp. 61–62.

the consultation must be: (i) in good faith and designed to reach an agreement; (ii) in keeping with the community's own traditions and customs and their traditional method of decision-making; (iii) during the initial stages of the project in question, and (iv) following the delivery of all relevant information, including information on possible risks'.[102]

Furthermore, this decision was relevant for some reasons: the international recognition that collective rights are enforceable and the recognition that tribal groups are more akin to indigenous peoples than they are to 'other ethnic, linguist or religious minorities in terms of their rights'.[103]

Regardless, by declaring the need of a prior and independent environmental and social impact assessments, the IACtHR made an important step towards the implementation of one of the essentials pillars of the requirement of consultation as consent, by adopting an evolving principle of international law and setting the tone for future interpretations of Article 21 of the American Convention.

3.3.2 The Kichwa of Sarayaku People v. Ecuador (2012)

Ecuador recognized the American Convention on 28th December 1977 and accepted the binding jurisdiction of the IACtHR on July 24th 1984. Ecuador ratified the International Covenant on Civil and Political Rights as well on 28th March 1977, which entered into force on 23rd March 1976; and the International Covenant on Economic, Social and Cultural Rights 16th December 1966, which entered into force on 3rd January 1976. Ecuador ratified the ILO Convention No. 169, entering into force for Ecuador on 15th May 1999.

A new Constitution of Ecuador was adopted in 2008, which specifically recognizes the collective rights of the indigenous and Afro-Ecuadorian Peoples. According to the Constitution of Ecuador, in its Article 57, 'the indigenous peoples can define themselves as nationalities with ancestral roots.' Moreover, also the requirement of consultation can be found in the Article 57. [104]

Regarding the present case, there was a first petition to the IACHR on 19th December 2003 alleging that Ecuador had permitted a private oil company to establish oil exploration in the territory of the Kichwa Indigenous People of Sarayaku. The exploitation activities had started by using explosives in their territory which was limiting their rights to freedom and cultural expression. Only by 2010, the IACHR submitted to the IACtHR under the allowance of the Articles 51 and 61 of the American Convention, the application No. 12464. Because of the lack of juridical protection and the failure of other judicial guarantees, the IACHR asked

[102]¶133 Inter-American Commission of Human Rights, *Saramaka People v. Suriname*, Case No 172, Judgment of 28 November 2007.

[103]Brunner (2008).

[104]*(2008) Constitution of Ecuador.*

the IACtHR to analyze the petition evolving the international responsibility of Ecuador. The allegation consisted in the violation of 'Article 21 in relation to Articles 12, 23 and 1(1) of the American Convention, regarding private property. The violation of the right to life, judicial guarantees and judicial protection, understood as in Articles 4, 8 and 25 of the American Convention. The right to freedom of movement and residence found in Article 22 and 1(1) of the American Convention'.[105]

The Napo-Kichwa People and the Kichwa People of Pastaza share the same linguistic and cultural traditional and origins of the Kichwa nationality of the Ecuadorian Amazon Basin. They identify themselves as 'runas, which mean persons or human beings and can identify themselves as to the same ethnic identity, or any other than non-Kichwa indigenous peoples'.[106] They can be found in a territory of very limited access in the tropical forest area of the Amazonian region of Ecuador. They are one of the largest populations of the Amazonian Region, with about 1200 inhabitants, and also have organized themselves into different federations: 'Sarayaku Center, Cali Cali, Sarayakillo, Shiwacocha and Chontayacu'.[107] According to the worldview of the Sarayaku People, 'their land is associated with the fact that the nature elements have spirits (*Supay*) which are interconnected. Those sacred places can only be attended by the Yachaks'.[108] Their territory is located 65 km from El Puyo and is one of the most biologically diverse in the world. As other indigenous peoples, around '90% of their nutritional needs come from their subsistence on collective family-based farming, hunting, fishing and gathering'[109] within their territory such as their ancestral traditions.

The case revolves around the *Compañía General de Combustibles S.A.* (hereinafter, the CGC) and the violations vested in its activities in Ecuador, most precisely, in the Sarayaku People territory. According to Sarayaku members, the company's strategy consisted of dividing the communities, manipulating the leaders, and carrying out defamation campaigns to discredit the leaders and organizations. They also allegedly offered money for development projects and jobs for the men in the community. Although Ecuador was not in charge of this meeting, the Sarayaku held a General Assembly, with a presence of the CGC representative and 'they decided to reject the CGC offer'.[110]

However, on 30th July 2001, the Ecuadorian Ministry of Defense signed a Cooperation Agreement on Military Security with the oil companies operating in the country in order to ensure the safety of oil facilities and of the persons who work in them. And according to the Ministry of Energy and Mines, 'from October 2020

[105] Inter-American Court of Human Rights, *Kichwa Indigenous People of Sarayaku v. Ecuador*, No. 185, Judgment of 27 June 2012.

[106] ¶52 ibid.

[107] ¶52 ibid.

[108] ¶57 ibid.

[109] ¶54 ibid.

[110] ¶122 ibid.

until February 2003, there was a 29% advance in the work of the oil company in the Sarayaku territory'.[111] It was also alleged and not contested by Ecuador, that in June 2003, the CGC had destroyed at least one site of a 'very special significance for the spiritual and cultural life of the members of Sarayaku People'.[112] Namely, through this militarization of the territory, Ecuador supported and permitted that the CGC entered the Sarayaku Peoples territory, 'including the destruction of 200 kilometers of primary forest and the destruction of sacred places'.[113] For the Sarayaku People, the destruction of part of the Wichu Kachi Mountain by the arrival of the helicopters caused the suspension of the cultural ancestral events and the ceremonies, the *Uyantsa*. Besides this event, which constitutes the most important festival that takes places on February, the activities serve to renew the links between the territory and their social bonds.

In the merits of the decision, the IACtHR discussed the issue from two different angles: 'the rights to consultation and the indigenous communal property, among the rights to life, to personal integrity and to personal liberty. Thus, the IACtHR analyzed whether Ecuador respected and guaranteed the rights of Sarayaku People in an adequately way. Differently than in the case of the *Mayagna (Sumo) Awas Tingni Community v. Nicaragua*, the case of the *Moiwana Community v. Suriname*, the case of the *Yakye Axa Indigenous Community v. Paraguay*, the case of the *Sawhoyamaxa Indigenous Community v. Paraguay*, the case of the *Saramaka People v. Suriname* and the case of the *Xákmok Kásek Indigenous Community v. Paraguay*, Ecuador had 'fully recognized that the Sarayaku People had the right to their territory'.[114] In this case, and because of this special acknowledgment, the IACtHR decided to analyze the argument of the parties relating to the obligation to guarantee the right to consultation in relation to the rights to communal property and cultural rights in the merits.

Regarding the American Convention, the Ecuadorian Constitution and the ILO No. 169, by the time that Ecuador signed the contract with the CGC, it had the legal obligation to consult with the indigenous peoples of Sarayaku. The IACtHR also mentioned that in a consolidation interpretation of Article 21, which establishes 'that everyone has the right to the use and enjoyment of his property. The law may subordinate such use and enjoyment to the interest of society. And no one shall be deprived of his property except upon payment of just compensation, for reasons of public utility or social interest',[115] and in the cases and according to the forms established by 'law of the Convention as it pertains to indigenous peoples rights, and based on its ratification of ILO Convention 169, Ecuador had the obligation to

[111] ¶101 ibid.
[112] ¶104 ibid.
[113] ¶127 ibid.
[114] ¶128 ibid.
[115] (1969) American Convention on Human Rights.

consult the Sarayaku people in a free and informed manner with specific procedural safeguards before approving the Environmental Impact Assessment'.[116]

The IACtHR also clarified that the state should have provided clear, sufficient and timely information on the nature and impact of the activities to be carried out and on the prior consultation process. The interpretation of the Article 13 together with Article 23, which says that 'every citizen shall enjoy the following rights and opportunities: a) to take part in the conduct of public affairs, directly or through freely chosen representatives',[117] is in a sense that the access to information when actions taken can directly affect the territory of the indigenous or tribal peoples, there is the need to inform and consult.

Moreover, in the case of the *Sawhoyamaxa Indigenous Community v. Paraguay*, the IACtHR decided 'from having access to their traditional health systems and other social-cultural functions, thereby exposing them to poor living conditions and to increased vulnerability to diseases and epidemics, and subjecting them to situations of extreme vulnerability that can lead to the violation of various human rights, as well as casing them suffering and jeopardizing the preservations of their way of life, customs and language'.[118]

The IACtHR established that there was the need to ensure the effective participation to the members of an indigenous community. Such that the state has the responsibility to consult in accordance with the traditions and customs using the right way to reach an agreement, recalling to undertake that in good faith and continuing communication.[119] Considering that Ecuador delegated to the CGC, a private company, the obligation to provide for indigenous peoples the relevant information and conduct adequate consultation as part of its own oil exploration contract is contrary to what is expected of a state.

Furthermore, the IACtHR noted that there was communal ownership of the Sarayaku territory which is exercised by an ancestral manner as it was expressed by an award that Ecuador gave to Sarayaku Peoples in 1992 and also the IACtHR found that was relevant to 'emphasize the profound cultural, intangible and spiritual ties that the community has with its territory, in order to understand more fully the harm caused in this case'.[120]

The IACtHR also addressed the measures of protection to guarantee the right to communal property, noting that there were some guidelines when there is legal conflict between indigenous peoples' territory and private property. In the case of Saramaka v. Suriname, for example, the IACtHR showed the importance of the

---

[116]¶125 Inter-American Court of Human Rights, *Kichwa Indigenous People of Sarayaku v. Ecuador*, No. 185, Judgment of 27 June 2012.

[117]*(1969) American Convention on Human Rights.*

[118]¶73 Inter-American Court of Human Rights, *Sawhoyamaxa Indigenous Community v. Paraguay*, Judgment of 29 March 2006.

[119]¶208 Inter-American Court of Human Rights, *Kichwa Indigenous People of Sarayaku v. Ecuador*, No. 185, Judgment of 27 June 2012.

[120]¶149 ibid.

'conduction of an appropriate and participatory process that can guarantee the right to consultation, the necessity to conduct an environmental impact assessment and to find ways to compensate the exploitation of natural resources in the indigenous people's territories'.[121] However, the community must be able to determine and decide in accordance with their traditions and customs.

The IACtHR observed that, in general, the close relationship between the indigenous communities and their land is an essential component, which is their cultural identity based on their specific worldviews, which, as distinct social and political actors in multicultural societies, must receive particular recognition and respect in a democratic society. Respect for the right to consultation of indigenous and tribal communities and peoples is precisely 'recognition of their rights to their own culture or cultural identity',[122] which must be assured, in any society without denying their right to exist as a people and in particular in a pluralistic, multicultural and democratic society.

The IACtHR indicated that there was the need to understand the human rights instruments as living organisms that reflect on main society. Thus, the interpretation of the IACtHR in regard to Article 21 of the American Convention and the ILO No. 169 Convention, the UNDRIP goes into the direction of domestic law already discussed. Article 21 of the American Convention relating to the use and enjoyment of their territory is considered necessary to guarantee their survival due to the inextricable connection that the indigenous peoples and tribal communities have with their territory. It is closely connected to the natural resources that lie on and within the land.

Given that the present case concerns the rights of members of an indigenous community, the IACtHR found appropriate to recall that, under 'Articles 24 (Right to Equal Protection) and 1(1) (Obligation to Respect Rights) of the American Convention, the states must ensure, on an equal basis, full exercise and enjoyment of the rights of those individuals who are not subject to their jurisdiction'.[123] However, it would be necessary to emphasize that in order to ensure those rights regarding its efficacy, when interpreting and applying their domestic law, the states must take into account the particular characteristics that distinguish the members of the indigenous peoples from the general population and what constituted their cultural rights.

The members of Sarayaku also informed that there was a military presence on their territory while the CGC was conducting oil and mining exploration on the land. The IACtHR criticized the fact that the oil company was the one who carried out the

[121]¶133 Inter-American Commission of Human Rights, *Saramaka People v. Suriname*, Case No 172, Judgment of 28 November 2007.

[122]¶212-217 Inter-American Court of Human Rights, *Kichwa Indigenous People of Sarayaku v. Ecuador*, No. 185, Judgment of 27 June 2012.

[123]*(1969) American Convention on Human Rights.*

consultation and decided that it 'could not be constituted as an appropriate consultation because the company had interest in the case'.[124]

In that sense, the Principle 22 of the Rio Declaration on Environment and Development has recognized that: 'indigenous people and their communities, as well as other local communities, have a vital role in environmental management and development because of their knowledge and traditional practices. States should recognize and duly support their identity, culture and interests and enable their effective participation in the achievement of sustainable development'.[125]

Given the importance of cultural rights, their customs, traditions, worldview and a way of life, the IACtHR considered that it was a 'failure of Ecuador to consult the Sarayaku People in that matter'.[126]

Then, the IACtHR decided that Ecuador had the positive obligation to adopt the legislative measures to guarantee the full exercises of the rights that are established in the American Convention. Therefore, the state must make possible the efficacy of all the rights and freedoms recognized by the American Convention.

Furthermore, Ecuador had argued that there was the intention to harmonize the consultation process in their domestic juridical order. However, as the IACtHR could not observe that there was a real effort on the side of the state on going in accordance with the Article 2 of the American Convention and establishing ways to engage with the right to consultation, cultural identity and property, the IACtHR declared that there was a violation by the state and considered the state responsible for failing to comply with the obligation in adopting domestic legal measures.

Consequently, the IACtHR understood that Ecuador was responsible for the violation of Article 21 of the American Convention on the right to communal property, together with the Article 1 (1) and (2) regarding the right to cultural rights.

The IACtHR considered the remedy of amparo 'in order to resolve the juridical situation of the petitioner'.[127] However, the IACtHR noted that the remedy adopted by the Superior Court of Justice of the District of Pastaza was not an effective protection of the fundamental rights as established in the Articles 27.2, 25.1 and 7.6 of the American Convention on Human Rights. On the contrary, 'the juridical remedy was considered inconclusive'[128] whereas the amparo remedy was not effective because of the negligence of the judicial authorities. Furthermore, Ecuador did not only fail in guaranteeing an adequate remedy to redress the situation, but also did not ensure that the violation of Articles 8 (1), 25 (1), 25 (2) (a) and 25 (2) (c) of the Pact of San José was rectified, namely, the appropriate competent juridical authority to the detriment of the Sarayaku People.

---

[124]¶178 Inter-American Court of Human Rights, *Kichwa Indigenous People of Sarayaku v. Ecuador*, No. 185, Judgment of 27 June 2012.

[125]*United Nations Conference on Environment and Development*, 8 December 1992.

[126]¶220 Inter-American Court of Human Rights, *Kichwa Indigenous People of Sarayaku v. Ecuador*, No. 185, Judgment of 27 June 2012.

[127]¶272 ibid.

[128]¶276 ibid.

Furthermore, the IACtHR decided on the provisions for the reparations according to the Article 63 (1) of the Pact. In accordance with international law, the reparation needed to be adequate. In this case, the IACtHR suggested that the restitution should entail diverse measures of reparations and also have a causal nexus so that the state might redress the violation of human rights in the case that the 'restitution in integrum was not possible'.[129]

The IACtHR decided that the measures of restitution and satisfaction and guarantees of non-repetition would engulf the pecuniary and non-pecuniary measures, in conformity with what was already asked by the IACHR. Among the measures, there was the due prior consultation, the regulation of prior consultation in domestic law and the training of state officials on the rights of indigenous peoples, giving special attention to: 'regarding domestic laws that recognize the right to prior, free and informed consultation, the IACtHR has already observed that, in the evolution of the international corpus juris, the 2008 Ecuadorian Constitution is one of the most advanced in the world in this area. However, the IACtHR has also noted that the right to prior consultation has not been sufficiently and adequately regulated through appropriate norms for its practical implementation. Thus, under Article 2 of the American Convention, the state must adopt, within a reasonable time, any legislative, administrative or other type of measures that may be necessary to implement the right to prior consultation of the indigenous and tribal peoples and communities those measures that prevent its full and free exercise and, to this end, the state must ensure the participation of the communities themselves'.[130]

Lastly, since 2008, the Ecuadorian Constitution is very advanced regarding the prior consultation with indigenous peoples. However, the practical implementation has not been guaranteed by the legislation. And because of that, the IACtHR 'addressed the need to have an adequate regulation in order to ensure enforcement of Article 2 of the American Convention and the prior consultation'.[131] Training the state officials on the rights of indigenous peoples will support the cessation of violating the cultural identity of the Sarayaku People: 'the state must implement, within a reasonable time and with the corresponding budgetary allocation, mandatory programs or courses that include modules on the domestic and international standards concerning the human rights of indigenous peoples and communities, for military, police and judicial officials, as well as others whose functions involve relations with indigenous peoples, as part of the general and continuing training of officials in the respective institutions, at all hierarchical levels'.[132]

The IACtHR noted the manner and sense in which Ecuador had the obligation to guarantee the right to consultation of the Sarayaku People and whether the acts of the concessionary company, which the state indicated as forms of socialization or the search for understanding, satisfied the minimum criteria and essential requirements

---

[129]¶285 ibid.

[130]¶301 ibid.

[131]¶301 ibid.

[132]¶302 ibid.

of a valid consultation process for communities and indigenous peoples in relation to their rights to communal property and cultural identity. It is the duty of the state—and not of the indigenous peoples—to demonstrate effectively, in the specific case, that all dimensions of the right to prior consultation were effectively guaranteed.

In the case of the Kichwa Indigenous People of Sarayaku the IACtHR specified that 'to ensure that the exploration for, or extraction of, natural resources in ancestral territories does not entail a negation of the survival of the indigenous people as such, the state must comply with the following safeguards: (i) conduct an appropriate and participatory process that guarantees the right to consultation, particularly with regard to large-scale development or investment projects; (ii) make an environmental impact assessment, and (iii) as appropriate, reasonably share the benefits produced by the exploitation of natural resources (as a form of just compensation required by Article 21 of the Convention), with the community itself determining and deciding who the beneficiaries of this compensation should be, according to its customs and traditions'.[133]

Another fact was that for the very first time in the IACtHR's history, a delegation of judges conducted a proceeding of a contentious case on the site of the event. The delegation of the IACtHR arrived on the territory of the Sarayaky People, 'crossing the Bobonaza River and arriving at the Tayasaruta (the assembly house) on April 21 of 2012. The President of the IACtHR gave the floor to the members of the Sarayaku People, to their representatives and to the IACHR who presented the observations regarding to this case and to the Secretary of the Legal Affairs of the presidency'.[134] It is relevant to note that the IACtHR had the opportunity to see the

[133]¶156 ibid.

[134]Besides the opportunity to be heard by the President of the Court, the Secretary of the Legal Affairs of the presidency of the state of Ecuador, Alexis Mera, expressed formally that he acknowledge the state responsability regarding this case: '[...] What I am going to say to you, I say not just on my own behalf but on behalf of President Correa, who asked me to come here [...] I do not feel that we are in conflict. Why? Because all the things that have been denounced today, all the testimonies, all the invasive oil extraction activities that occurred in 2003, the Government does not want to challenge them. The Government considers that the state is responsible for the events that occurred in 2003. I want this to be clearly stated and understood. The Government recognizes its responsibility. Therefore, all the actions that occurred, the invasive measures, the actions of the armed forces, the acts against the destruction of the rivers, are all issues that we as a Government condemn, and believe that there is a right to reparation. Therefore, I invite the other party to sit down with us and try to discuss reparations. The State is willing to make all necessary reparations to the community. And I say this in the most direct way possible. In fact, this hearing was convened at the request of the President of the Republic himself: it was the President himself who requested in writing that the President of the Inter-American Court of Human Rights come here to verify the situation of the Sarayaku people, and also to verify that it was this Government that expelled the CGC oil company. When we took office five years ago we discovered all these incidents and all this unease and the serious problem in the block and, as you know, our reaction was, to expel the CGC oil company. It is no longer carrying out exploitation activities. And there will be no more oil exploitation without prior consultation. I saw those who came here to visit, who said "No to round 23." A new round will not begin without informed consultation. And what is this consultation? In particular, it deals with what was said about pollution; what should not be polluted, because rivers and communities cannot be polluted by oil activities; there cannot be pollution, we cannot allow oil

case *in loco*. By recognizing that a violation of human rights was conducted, the IACtHR could address to implement the reparations to the victims.[135]

So on 27th June 2012, the IACtHR unanimously declared that Ecuador was responsible for the violation of the rights to consultation, to indigenous communal property and to cultural identity, in the terms of Article 21 of the American Convention, in relation to articles 1. 1 and 2 thereof, to the detriment of the Kichwa Indigenous People for having allowed a private oil company to carry out oil exploration activities in their territory, since the end of the 1990s, without having previously consulted them.

In sum, while the provision of information and consultation are different concepts, the IACtHR made its first step for a better understanding and clarification of the term. Thus, what is relevant and should specifically be highlighted is the fact that the IACtHR considered that 'consultation is a matter of public interest and vital for the exercise of democratic oversight of the state's administration in relation to exploration and exploitation activities for natural resources in the territory of indigenous communities'.[136]

However relevant, the decision issued an opportunity to amplify the arguments previously made in the *Saramaka People v. Suriname* decision and more, to further development the right to consultation in a more elaborated form adding also the international debates that were formulated already back the time of the decision.[137]

---

exploitation that pollutes. And we must also discuss the situation of the communities themselves. What is the health situation? What about education? When we begin to discuss the oil issue, we could have the best doctors treating the mothers in the communities, we could have the best health teams and best teachers coming from Quito to the area, if there is going to be money generated by oil exploitation. Oil exploitation should benefit the communities. However, the fact is that historically the State has acted behind the backs of the indigenous peoples. That is the historical reality of this country; because the State has acted behind the backs of the indigenous people, oil exploration has been carried out to the detriment of communities. However, we don't want this system, this Government does not want it, and therefore we will not allow any oil exploration to continue behind the backs of the communities. Instead, we will seek dialogue if we decide to resume oil exploration or think about a new oil project here. There will be no oil development without an open, frank dialogue; not a dialogue by the oil company, as has always been denounced. We have changed the law so that the dialogue is initiated by the Government and not by the extractive industry. So, in short, your Excellency, I would like to thank you for allowing me to speak. I reiterate that the State acknowledges its responsibility and is willing to make any reparation arrangement. Lastly, I would like to add a thought. The petitioners accuse us of being the "villains"... I recall that Mr. Cisneros said that we are the "villains".... I don't see it in that way; I believe there has been suffering that must be redressed. And finally, with regard to ancestral knowledge, I see here before me the indigenous leadership. We should work together to bring charges against the companies that steal ancestral rights from indigenous communities. At some point we should begin a frank discussion, and not allow others to take this knowledge that belong to these communities and make themselves rich from it. At some point we must discuss these issues. Thank you, your Excellency'. ¶62 ibid.

[135] ¶62 ibid.

[136] ¶126 ibid.

[137] Verbeek (2012).

3.3.3 The Kaliña and Lokono Peoples v. Suriname (2015)

The case of *Kaliña and Lokono Peoples v. Suriname*, and its merits, reparations and costs was brough forward regarding the alleged violation of Suriname to 'the right to recognition of Article 3 (juridical personality) in relation to Articles 1 (1), Article 2 (right to collective property), Article 21 (right to political rights), Article 23 and Article 25 of the Pact of San José.[138] As a result of these violations, the Kaliña and Lokono People do not have a territory that is delimited, demarcated and titled in their favor, and part of the territory claimed is owned by third parties. Their consultation in the nature reserves that Suriname has established on part of this territory has not been guaranteed and, with regard to a mining project in one of the reserves, their right to participation, by means of a consultation process, has not been respected, which also consists in the violation the right to judicial protection in relation to the obligation to adopt domestic legal provisions and the right of access to information.

As mentioned previously, Suriname ratified the International Covenant on Civil and Political Rights and the International Covenant on Economic, Social and Cultural Rights, on 28th December 1976. The IACtHR is competent to hear this case pursuant to Article 62 (3) of the Convention as Suriname has been party to the American Convention since 12nd November 1987, and accepted the IACtHR's contentious jurisdiction at the same day.

The domestic laws of Suriname do not recognize the right to communal property of the members of tribal people and the state has not ratified the ILO Convention No. 169. It is also an undisputed fact that the laws of Suriname do not recognize the possibility that indigenous peoples may be constituted as legal persons and are therefore not able to hold collective property titles. Emphasis should be put on the fact that the Human Rights Committee 'has examined the obligations of the state parties to the ICCPR, including Suriname, under Article 27 of that instrument, already on the case Saramaka people v. Suriname',[139] which was noted also in this case that 'persons belonging to these minorities shall not be denied the right, in community with the other members of their group, to enjoy their own culture, [which] may consist in a way of life which is closely associated with territory and use of its resources. This may particularly be true of members of indigenous communities constituting a minority'.[140]

In the case *Moiwana Community v. Suriname*, the IACtHR established as a proven fact that 'even though the individual members of the indigenous and tribal communities are recognized as persons in the Suriname Constitution, the laws of the

[138] *(1969) American Convention on Human Rights.*

[139] ¶94 Inter-American Commission of Human Rights, *Saramaka People v. Suriname*, Case No 172, Judgment of 28 November 2007.

[140] ¶123 Inter-American Court of Human Rights, *Pueblos Kaliña y Lokono v. Suriname*, Judgment of 11 February 2015.

state do not recognize these communities as legal entities'.[141] Also, domestic law would not establish collective property rights. In the case of the *Saramaka People v. Suriname*, the IACtHR concluded 'that the state's legal framework merely grants the members of the Saramaka People a privilege to use the land, which does not guarantee their right to control and own their territory without any type of outside interference'.[142]

Regarding the Kaliña and Lokono Peoples, according to domestic records in 2005, the population is composed of eight communities consisting of around 2026 persons.[143] The Kaliña and Lokono Peoples are known as the Lower Marowijne People of the area of the Lower Marowijne River, located in the extreme northeast of Suriname, which borders on French Guiana and has been the territory used and occupied ancestrally by indigenous peoples. The communities that are parties to this case consist of eight villages. The villages of the Kaliña Peoples are 'Christiaankondre, Langamankondre, Pierrekondre, Bigiston, Erowarte and Tapuku, while the two villages of the Lokono people are Marijkedorp (or *Wan Shi Sha*) and Alfonsdorp'.[144] The main subsistence activities of the Kaliña and Lokono People are 'agriculture, fishing, hunting, and gathering non-timber forest products, such as fruits'.[145]

The indigenous peoples that live in the area have a strong spiritual relationship with the Marowijne River, which is an essential element of their 'cultural identity and traditions; thus, they consider that they belong to this place in the same way that it belongs to them'.[146] The Kaliña and Lokono Peoples are vitally important to maintain the balance between man and nature, and this task is the responsibility of the shamans, known as piay or semechichi. According to their world vision, 'the piay is able to discover if anyone has negatively altered the balance between men and nature through the guardians or guiding spirits, known as jakoewa'.[147]

The Kaliña and Lokono Peoples have undertaken plenty of measures to obtain recognition of their rights. They organised various social protests and filed administrative petitions in relation to the territory claimed in this case. And, as the judicial proceedings were dismissed because the members of the indigenous peoples lacked legal standing as a collective entity and did not possess a collective property title to the territory claimed, those measures culminated in sending letters to the president of Suriname: on 31st January 2003, on 22nd March 2004, and on 25th September 2005.

[141]¶86 Inter-American Court of Human Rights, *Moiwana Community v. Suriname*, Judgment of 15 June 2005.

[142]¶115 Inter-American Commission of Human Rights, *Saramaka People v. Suriname*, Case No 172, Judgment of 28 November 2007.

[143]¶31 Inter-American Court of Human Rights, *Pueblos Kaliña y Lokono v. Suriname*, Judgment of 11 February 2015.

[144]¶30 ibid.

[145]¶32 ibid.

[146]¶35 ibid.

[147]¶36 ibid.

'The captains of the Kaliña and Lokono Peoples presented formal petitions to Ronald Venetiaan, under the provisions of article 22 of the Constitution of Suriname. However, there was no formal answer by the state'.[148]

Here it is important to note that three nature reserves were created within the territory that is in dispute in this case, namely: '(i) the Wia Wia Nature Reserve in 1966; (ii) the Galibi Nature Reserve in 1969, and (iii) the Wane Kreek Nature Reserve in 1986'.[149]

Regarding the consultation for the establishment of the nature reserves, several meetings were held with the participation of authorities of the State Forest Management Service, an indigenous people's organization called KANO. However, the representatives indicated that KANO was composed of indigenous individuals from different parts of Suriname who were not traditional authorities or legitimate representatives of the alleged victims in this case. Also, KANO ceased to exist in 1980, around six years before the creation of one of the parks, the Wane Kreek Nature Reserve.

Consequently, the Kaliña and Lokono Peoples were unaware that the reserve had been established until, in 1997, they realized that mining operations were underway in the area. In addition, regarding the prior steps taken by KANO, the representatives of the Kaliña and Lokono Peoples have indicated that, at no time, did KANO either consult or represent them.

Also relevant is that on January 28 of 1958, before Suriname's independence from the Netherlands, the state 'granted a concession to a mining company called Suralco, a subsidiary of the Aluminum Company of America (hereinafter, the ALCOA), to extract bauxite in the eastern part of Suriname, which included the territory of Wane Kreek. The concession was granted for 75 years and will therefore expire in 2033'.[150]

The first environmental impact assessment (Environmental Sensitivity Analysis of the Wane 4 Concession) was made in 2005 by 'a private consultant hired by BHP Billiton, with the intention of starting extracting activities in Wane 4'.[151] The adverse impact of the mining operations in the nature reserve carries implications for 'the hunting and fishing activities, which were traditional in the area, [and] have declined considerably. In this regard, the noise and vibrations caused by the trucks and the dynamite explosions, the contamination of land and streams, and the destruction of fruit-bearing trees caused the wildlife to flee that the indigenous peoples hunted and fished to feed the members of the local communities'.[152]

Regarding the right to collective property in relation to the mining concession within the Wane Kreek Nature Reserve, the IACtHR decided, unanimously, to hold that there was part of Suriname's obligation to ensure 'effective participation,

[148]¶65 ibid.

[149]¶70 ibid.

[150]¶88 ibid.

[151]¶91 ibid.

[152]¶92 ibid.

through a consultation process, applied before any action was taken that could have an important impact on the interests of the indigenous and tribal peoples, such as the exploration and exploitation or extracting stages'.[153] Thus, Suriname had failed to ensure the effective participation, by means of a consultation process, of the Kaliña and Lokono Peoples. Moreover, 'no social and environmental impact assessment was made, and the benefits of the mining project were not shared'.[154]

Lastly, Suriname has not adopted mechanisms to ensure the mentioned safeguards. Consequently, the state was found to have violated Articles 21 and 23 of the Convention, in relation to Articles 1(1) and 2, to the detriment of the Kaliña and Lokono Peoples and their members.

About the 'measures of integral reparation' ordered in the judgment, the IACtHR established that its judgment constituted, of itself, a form of reparation.[155] It also ordered that Suriname, among other measures must have: '(a) grant the Kaliña and Lokono Peoples legal recognition of collective juridical personality; (b) delimit, demarcate and grant collective title to the territory of the members of the Kaliña and Lokono Peoples, and ensure their effective use and enjoyment, taking into account the rights of other tribal peoples in the area; (c) determine the territorial rights of the Kaliña and Lokono Peoples; (d) ensure effective participation processes for these peoples, the execution of social and environmental impact assessments, and the distribution of benefits (e) implement the necessary inter-institutional coordination mechanisms in order to ensure the effectiveness of the measures established above, within three months of notification of this Judgment'.[156]

Particularly with regard to the right to participation through a consultation process, and the recognition of collective juridical personality, the IACtHR judges Humberto Antonio Sierra Porto and Eduardo Ferrer Mac-Gregor Poisot, prepared a concurring opinion. As a matter of fact, 'there is no dispute about the fact that the Kaliña and Lokono Peoples played no part in any of these activities and that the corresponding environmental impact assessment was not made. However, the IACtHR does not have jurisdiction in relation to the award of the mining concession in 1958. Nevertheless, the IACtHR is competent to examine measures taken following the entry into force of its jurisdiction; in particular, the extraction operations carried out as of 1997'.[157]

Such as in the case *Saramaka People v. Suriname* under Article 1.1 of the American Convention, they stressed the guarantees that must be adopted by the state, which exemplify the restrictions imposed on the right to property of the indigenous and tribal peoples owing to the issue of concessions within their territory

[153] ¶9 16 ibid., pp. 85–86.

[154] ¶118 Inter-American Court of Human Rights, *Pueblos Kaliña y Lokono v. Suriname*, Judgment of 11 February 2015.

[155] ¶279 ibid.

[156] Ibid., pp. 85–86.

[157] ¶200 Inter-American Court of Human Rights, *Pueblos Kaliña y Lokono v. Suriname*, Judgment of 11 February 2015.

and that it does not entail a denial of their survival: 'first, it must ensure the effective participation of the members of the [indigenous and tribal peoples], in accordance with their customs and traditions, with regard to any development, investment, exploration or extraction plans implemented within [their territory]. Second, the state must ensure that the members of the [indigenous and tribal peoples] receive a reasonable benefit from the plan implemented within their territory. Third, the state must ensure that no concession will be granted within their territory until independent and technically qualified entities, under the state's supervision, have conducted a prior social and environmental impact assessment. These safeguards are intended to preserve, protect and ensure the special relationship that the members of the [indigenous and tribal peoples] have with their territory'.[158]

They took the plunge of the majority of the IACtHR about the 'state obligation to organize an effective participation process, implemented by means of prior, free and informed consultation'.[159] By addressing the relevance of the requirement of consultation, they considered that one of the most significant contributions of the IACtHR's case law in indigenous and tribal matters has been the interpretation made of Article 21 of the American Convention, as the IACtHR 'has developed an interpretation that protects one of the characteristic situations in the region, the communal ownership of ancestral territories. In this understanding, in the context of major development, investment, exploration, exploitation and extraction projects and plans, the IACtHR has established a solid line of case law concerning the obligation to consult the indigenous and tribal peoples insofar as such projects affect both their territory and their way of life within that territory'.[160]

Equally relevant was that despite the 'indigenous groups, by the fact of their very existence, have the right to live freely in their own territory, the close ties of indigenous people with the land must be recognized and understood as the fundamental basis of their cultures, their spiritual life, their integrity, and their economic survival. For indigenous communities, relations to the land are not merely a matter of possession and production but a material and spiritual element which they must fully enjoy, even to preserve their cultural legacy and transmit it to future generations'.[161]

Thus, the IACtHR considered that, for the effect of this case, the right to consultation was also founded on Article 23 of the American Convention, in light of international standards. This indicated that the state must have available 'mechanisms for the effective participation of the indigenous peoples using procedures that are culturally adapted to the decision-making of such peoples. This is not only a matter of public interest, but also forms part of the exercise of their right to take part in any decision-making on matters that affect their interests, in accordance with their

[158] ¶201 ibid.

[159] ¶3 ibid., p. 92.

[160] ¶4 ibid., p. 92.

[161] ¶149 Inter-American Court of Human Rights, *Mayagna (Sumo) Awas Tingni Community v. Nicaragua*, No. 79, Judgment of 31 August 2001.

own procedures and institutions, in relation to Article 23 of the American Convention'.[162]

In contrast, there was the partially dissenting opinion of the IACtHR judge Alberto Pérez regarding a different approach to Article 23. He affirmed that the transcription of the Article 23 to the judgment was 'partial and biased'.[163] And he argued moreover: 'it only goes as far as the words "public affairs," and omits the passage that states "directly or through freely chosen representatives" as well as subparagraphs (b) and (c) regarding the "rights and opportunities" "to vote and to be elected" and to have equal access "to the public service." Both the elements omitted and the reference to "public affairs" and the name of the rights in question ("Right to Participate in Government") would be sufficient to exclude the application of the norm allegedly violated to a matter concerning private property (Article 21) and not "a matter of evident public interest" (as seen in paras. 13 and 14), but rather a private matter'.[164] Judge Alberto Pérez' interpretation changed the meaning of the political rights and the presumable lack of what constitutes an efficacy participation in relation to the exploitation project within one reserve, by concluding that 'it is not in order to declare a violation of Article 23 of the Convention, but rather sufficient to declare the violation of Article 21 (Right to Property)'.[165] Consequently, he finished his argument affirming that 'was not any violation to the Articles 3, 13 and 23 of the American Convention and that was sufficient to declare the violation of Article 21 (Right to communal property), and the consequent rights to recognition of legal status and to consultation and cultural identity, and Article 25 (Right to Judicial Protection) of the American Convention'.[166]

On 25th November 2015, however, the IACtHR decided that Suriname was ultimately to be held responsible for the violation of the rights to recognition of juridical personality, to collective property, to political rights, and to cultural identity, and of the duty to adopt domestic legal provisions.

Nevertheless, the aspect of the interpretation on collective right is quite relevant. Usually, the international adjudication of the international courts recognizes the individual right of individuals, although, in Kaliña and Lokono, 'the IACtHR did not make a separate body of collective rights enforceable, but instead made individual rights collective'.[167]

The timid development for the protection of the minorities in the region did not overshade the fact the IACtHR continued to use consultation instead of consent, which constitute a stronger right that could also create the possibility of a veto power regarding natural resource exploitation.

---

[162] ¶22 Inter-American Court of Human Rights, *Pueblos Kaliña y Lokono v. Suriname*, Judgment of 11 February 2015, p. 97.

[163] ¶108 ibid., p. 103.

[164] ¶18 ibid., pp. 103–104.

[165] ¶23 ibid., p. 106.

[166] ¶24 ibid., p. 106.

[167] Lixinski (2017).

This position was not adopted by the concurring opinion by the Judges Humberto Antonio Sierra Porto and Eduardo Ferrer Mac-Gregor Poisot and represents a set back towards the possibility of the establishment of the right to free, prior and informed consent in the region by the international adjudication. Thus, given the lack of the IAHRS effort, the control of conventionality of that matter seems more far away.

3.3.4 *Triunfo de la Cruz Garífuna Community and Its Members v. Honduras (2017)*

The case submitted was to the IACtHR in 2013 by the IACHR. The Garífuna Community Triunfo de la Cruz and its members, an Afro-descendant community, alleged international responsibility of Honduras. The case was directed towards the lack of the Community of a suitable and culturally appropriate title to its traditional territory, 'a central problem faced by these communities in Honduras is precisely the various forms of vulnerability of their collective territories'.[168]

The case also refers to the alleged lack of free, prior and informed consultation regarding the adoption of decisions such as the planning and execution of tourism projects and mega-projects, the creation of a protected area, and the alleged sales of community lands. The relevance of 'examining this legal case and the use by the Garífuna community of Triunfo de la Cruz of the IACHR and taking into consideration the implications of the sentence against Honduras, this article analyzes the utility, limits, and possibilities of this type of international legal instrument to defend the multicultural rights of traditional communities'.[169]

The Community has not had recourse that takes into account its particularities with respect to collective property, nor effective access to justice with respect to complaints about alleged sales of traditional lands, acts of threats and harassment allegedly suffered by the authorities of the Community as a result of their activities in defense of the lands, and the situation of insecurity and violence generated by third parties in the territory.

Honduras indicated that, in accordance with Article 346 of the Honduran Constitution, it would have taken measures to protect the rights and interests of the Community, in a progressive manner and in accordance with its legal and economic capacities, as evidenced by the land titles granted to it.[170] Honduras also pointed out that the land titling process for the Garifuna Communities involves three stages: titling, expansion and regulation. Regarding the last stage, he emphasized that it should be taken into account that there are several non-Garifuna occupants in the

---

[168] Agudelo (2019).

[169] Ibid.

[170] §96 Inter-American Court of Human Rights, *Garífuna Triunfo de la Cruz and your members v. Honduras*, Judgment of 9 May 2019.

area in question with legal documents that prove their ownership, who are also protected by national legislation.

The IACtHR understood the right to property enshrined in Article 21 of the American Convention, in connection with Article 1. 1 thereof, to the detriment of the Garífuna Community of Triunfo de la Cruz and its members, by allegedly having carried out decisions regarding measures that affected their territories, without satisfying the requirements established in Inter-American law; such as, carrying out expropriation processes; not threatening the subsistence of the indigenous communities; carrying out prior, free and informed consultations, as well as social and environmental impact studies, and guaranteeing the participation of the indigenous communities in the benefits derived from the concessions granted.

Honduras also carried out a non-consensual methodology and with criteria that reduced the possibilities of a prior, free and informed consultation, replacing it with something called the 'Indigenous Roundtable', which have violated 'the principle of good faith established in Article 6.2 of the ILO Convention No. 169.[171]

As Honduras has ratified the ILO Convention No. 169 in 1996, the state was under the obligation to consult with the indigenous and tribal communities and to include in its internal regulations a procedure that would make the right to consultation efficacy.

The IACtHR decided that Honduras should conduct adequate consultation with the participation of the traditional communities, the legislative or other measures necessary to give efficacy to the right to prior, free, informed and bona fide consultation, in accordance with international human rights standards.[172]

The relevance of this case surrounds the nature of the natural exploitation projects that may affect traditional communities.[173] Although the IACtHR understood the right to free, prior and informed consent and cultural identity, it did so by only addressing the ILO Convention No 169, in which the right is not mentioned. The lack of enforcement with the UNDRIP by not mentioning it and also, not continuing with the definition once established in previous cases, led to a misleading outcome over the possible judicial review of all the national states members of the American Convention.

3.3.5 The Indigenous Community of the Lhaka Honhat (nuestra tierra) v. Argentina (2020)

According to the IACHR, the case concerned the alleged violation of the right of ownership over ancestral territory of the indigenous communities gathered in the Lhaka Honhat Indigenous Communities. The IACHR also indicated that, at the time

[171] §95 ibid.

[172] §275 ibid.

[173] See e.g. Cavallaro and Schaffer (2004); Tremblay-Huet (2019).

of the issuance of the 'Report on the Merits No. 2/12, two decades had passed since the communities submitted the initial application for titling, which was in 1991'.[174] It indicated that, despite this, Argentina did not provide them with effective access to the title to their ancestral territory. And on 1st February 2018, the Commission, by virtue of the foregoing, submitted the case to the IACtHR.

As Argentina had been a party of the American Convention since 5th September 1984 and recognized the contentious jurisdiction of the IACtHR on that same date, under the Article 62 (3), the IACtHR was competent to hear the present case.

The facts of the case referred to a claim by indigenous communities belonging to the *Wichí (Mataco), Iyjwaja (Chorote), Komlek (Toba), Niwackle (Chulupí) and Tapy'y (Tapiete)* peoples, for ownership of fiscal lots 14 and 55, which are adjacent to and together cover an area of approximately 643,000 hectares. In the area referred to, which is within the Province of Salta and borders with Paraguay and Bolivia, 'there has been a constant presence of indigenous peoples and other communities, at least since before 1629'.[175]

Relevant to note that in this case, on 13rd November 2018, Argentina indicated that the 'due diligence in situ was of the utmost importance'.[176] The IACtHR, considering the principle of immediacy, considered it appropriate to conduct the in situ proceeding, which was held on 17th May 2019.

It has been pointed out that the variations in quantity are due to the very characteristics of the indigenous peoples involved, since they are nomadic communities whose ancestral social structure involves the so-called fission-fusion dynamic. Thus 'it is very difficult to calculate the exact number of communities, since this figure is very changeable, given that the processes of fission and fusion of the residential units are part of the main social repertoire aimed at maintaining coexistence'.[177]

Also, there was a constant indigenous presence in the area, and the land was occupied, from close to the beginning of the twentieth century, by people identified as afro-descendants or non-indigenous colonists. In 1902, the Buenaventura Colony was founded, and the national government gave 625 hectares to afro-descendants' families who settled there and according to Argentine, are part of the 'vulnerable and poor population'.[178] However, in 1905, the government of Salta informed the national government that lots awarded as national fiscal lands could be located within the provincial territory. There are 465 afro-descendants' 'families which are small subsistence producers, mainly engaged in raising livestock in open fields and mostly without hiring labour'.[179]

[174]¶1 Inter-American Court of Human Rights, *Indigenous Community de la Asociación Lhaka Honhat (nuestra tierra) v. Argentina*, Judgment of 2 June 2020.

[175]¶1 ibid.

[176]¶10 ibid.

[177]¶34 ibid.

[178]¶135 ibid.

[179]¶52 ibid.

The IACtHR referred to the right of community property, the recognition and determination of property, anything related to the projects and works executed on the claimed territory, the allegations of violations of the rights of movement and residence, the healthy environment, food and cultural identity, also considering the right to water, and the alleged violations of the rights to judicial guarantees and judicial protection in relation to legal actions initiated in the case.

Indeed, Argentina had noted the inadequacy of its legal regime regarding the acknowledgement of the indigenous people's property in its Act No. 26.160 as it '[declared] an emergency with regard to the possession and ownership of the lands traditionally occupied by the country's indigenous communities, whose legal status has been registered with the National Registry of Indigenous Communities or the competent provincial body, or those that already exist',[180] that should not by all means alter the existing legal regime on procedures for recognition of property. The Constitution of Argentina, in its Article 75 (17) 'is directly operative and shows insufficient to solve the problem of the recognition of the indigenous property'.[181]

According to what the IACtHR had indicated previously in the case *Saramaka v. Suriname*, with respect to activities within indigenous territory, the state must observe the 'requirements that are common to any limitation on the right to property for reasons of public utility or social interest in accordance with Article 21 of the Convention, which implies the payment of compensation'.[182] On the other hand, as was stressed by the case of the *Saramaka People v. Suriname*, the case of the *Kichwa Indigenous Peoples of Sarayaku v. Ecuador* and the case of the *Kaliña and Lokono Peoples v. Suriname*, there is the need to comply with following some guarantees such as to ensure the effective participation of the peoples or communities in accordance with their customs and traditions, a duty that requires the state, in this case Argentina, to accept and provide information, and which implies constant communication between the parties. Thus, the consultation must be conducted in good faith, through culturally appropriate procedures, and must aim to reach agreement.

There was thus the need to respect the requirement of good faith. It required the absence of any form of coercion by the state or agents or third parties acting within its authorization or acquiescence such as attempts to disintegrate the social cohesion of affected communities, whether through the corruption of community leaders or the establishment of parallel leaderships, or through negotiations with individual community members. In addition, these peoples should be consulted, in accordance with their own traditions, in the early stages of the development or investment plan. Time was to be allowed for 'internal discussion within the communities and for an adequate response to the state. [The state should] also ensure that members of

[180](2006) Act No. 26.160.

[181](1994) Constitution of Argentine.

[182]¶139 Inter-American Commission of Human Rights, *Saramaka People v. Suriname*, Case No 172, Judgment of 28 November 2007.

indigenous and tribal peoples are aware of possible risks, including environmental and health risks'.[183]

The requirement of a prior environmental impact study was already indicated in Article 7.3 of the ILO Convention No. 169, World Charter for Nature, approved within the United Nations in 1982, by the Principle 11.c, and also the Rio Declaration on Environment and Development of 1992, by the Principle 17. Equally, as in the case of *Saramaka People v. Suriname* and the case of the *Kaliña and Lokono Peoples v. Suriname*, it was established that the requirement of a prior environmental impact study must not be carried out as a mere formality, but should enable the assessment of alternatives and the adoption of impact mitigation measures, 'by being prior to the decision to carry out the project or the implementation of the activity; by being prepared by independent entities, under state supervision; by considering, where appropriate, the cumulative impacts of other existing or proposed projects; and by allowing for the participation of interested or potentially affected persons or communities'.[184] Hence the participation for the 'purposes of environmental and social impact assessment is specific to that purpose, and is not equivalent to the exercise of the aforementioned right of free, prior and informed consultation of indigenous peoples or communities, which is broader'.[185]

After almost 35 years since the first legal complaint had been filed in the domestic realm, on 6th February 2020, the IACtHR issued a decision, by which it declared the international responsibility of the Argentine Republic. On the basis of the provisions of Article 63 (1) of the American Convention, the IACtHR has indicated that 'any violation of an international obligation that has produced damage entails the duty to make adequate reparation, and that this provision reflects a customary rule that constitutes one of the fundamental principles of contemporary international law on state responsibility'.[186] An injured party, within the meaning of article 63 (1) of the Convention, is a person who has been declared the victim of a violation of any right recognized in the Convention. In accordance with the above, the IACtHR considered the 132 indigenous communities as injured parties and stated that the reparation measure was relevant in order to conclude the process. It was also requested the 'IACtHR to order Argentina to provide the human and financial resources necessary for the relocation of the indigenous families. It was understood that a concrete establishment of time limits would favor enforcement with the Judgment'.[187] Therefore, the IACtHR ordered Argentina to adopt and conclude the necessary actions, the legislative, the administrative, the judicial, the registration, the notarial or of any

[183]¶133 ibid.; ¶210 Inter-American Court of Human Rights, *Pueblos Kaliña y Lokono v. Suriname*, Judgment of 11 February 2015.

[184]¶129 Inter-American Commission of Human Rights, *Saramaka People v. Suriname*, Case No 172, Judgment of 28 November 2007.

[185]¶201 Inter-American Court of Human Rights, *Pueblos Kaliña y Lokono v. Suriname*, Judgment of 11 February 2015.

[186]*(1969) American Convention on Human Rights.*

[187]¶310 Inter-American Court of Human Rights, *Indigenous Community de la Asociación Lhaka Honhat (nuestra tierra) v. Argentina*, Judgment of 2 June 2020.

other type of measure, in order to 'delimit, demarcate and grant a collective title that recognizes the property of all the indigenous communities that are victims',[188] and while the representatives request that the different actions be carried out, depending on the case, in two years or less, Argentine maintained that it 'requires eight years to complete the entire process'.[189] However, unanimously, the IACtHR gave six years to 'delimit, demarcate and grant a title that recognizes the ownership of the 132 indigenous communities'.[190]

Regarding the requirement of consultation, the IACtHR decided that the Argentinian state must refrain from carrying out acts, works or undertakings on indigenous territory that could affect its existence, value, use or enjoyment by the victim communities, or to order, require, authorize, tolerate or consent to third parties doing so. It must be preceded, as appropriate, by the provision of information to the indigenous communities that are victims, as well as the holding of adequate, free and informed prior consultations, in accordance with the guidelines set out by the IACtHR in the decision 'according to what the IACtHR has indicated, with respect to works or activities within the indigenous territory, the state must observe the requirements common to any limitation on the right to property for reasons of public utility or social interest in accordance with Article 21 of the Convention, which implies the payment of compensation'.[191] Also, through the above requirements, it sought to preserve, protect and guarantee the special relationship that indigenous peoples have with their territory, which in turn guarantees their subsistence. However, the American Convention does not mention how this can be done, 'the impact of such projects and works cannot in any way deny the ability of members of indigenous and tribal peoples to survive'.[192] This conduct must be observed by Argentina immediately upon notification of the decision. It will be supervised by the IACtHR until enforcement with the measure, previously ordered, 'consisting of delimiting, demarcating and granting a collective title that recognizes the ownership of territory'.[193]

However, the IACtHR decided with only three votes in favor, including that of the President of the IACtHR, and with three against, of the Judges Eduardo Vio Grossi, Humberto Antonio Sierra Porto and Ricardo Pérez Manrique that disagreed and made a dissident vote in regard to the responsibility of Argentine for the 'violation of the rights to participate in cultural life, insofar as it relates to cultural identity, a healthy environment, adequate food and water, established in Article 26 of

[188] ¶327 ibid.

[189] ¶322 ibid.

[190] ¶7 ibid., p. 23.

[191] ¶174 Inter-American Court of Human Rights, *Indigenous Community de la Asociación Lhaka Honhat (nuestra tierra) v. Argentina*, Judgment of 2 June 2020.

[192] ¶175 ibid.

[193] ¶328 ibid.

the American Convention on Human Rights, in relation to Article 1(1) of the same treaty, to the detriment of the 132 indigenous communities'.[194]

For the first time in a contentious case, the IACtHR analyzed the rights to a healthy environment, to adequate food, to water and to cultural identity in an autonomous manner in accordance with their specificities with respect to indigenous peoples, based on Article 26 of the American Convention. It understood that illegal logging, as well as the activities carried out in the territory by the afro-descendants' population, specifically the installation of barbed wire, had affected the environmental assets as well as the traditional way of feeding the indigenous communities and their access to water. The deficit in the argumentative aspect of the decision relies on the fact that the decision poorly explores the aspect of the afro-descendent communities who were also living in the territory and their rights.[195]

Therefore, Argentina was found to have violated Article 26 of the American Convention in relation to its Article 1 (1). Bearing in mind the dissenting votes, however, there is a special need to monitor closely how the sentence will be implemented and enforced.

3.4 The Inter-American System of Human Rights and the Brazilian Jurisdiction

Brazil recognized the IACtHR's mandatory jurisdiction on 10th December 1998. That means that Brazil must comply with the remedies provided by the IACtHR decisions. If this does not occur, and if in consequence there is a conviction to pay a fine, it will be executed in the form of Article 68.2.[196] With regard to the fulfillment of the international sentence, as in other relevant matters of international law, the Brazilian system offers a *non liquet*.[197] Apart from the assumptions of control of conventionality, there is a 'rather frosty stance'[198] treatment give by the Supreme Federal Court towards the IAHRS.

As seen, the right to property pursuant Article 21 of the American Convention on Human Rights thus has singular importance for indigenous and tribal peoples, because the 'guarantee of the right to territorial property is a fundamental basis for the development of indigenous communities' culture, spiritual life, integrity and economic survival—IACHR, Arguments before the IACtHR'.[199]

---

[194] ¶9 ibid., p. 125.

[195] C. de la Fuente (2020).

[196] (1969) American Convention on Human Rights.

[197] de Oliveira Mazzuoli (2011).

[198] Daly (2017).

[199] ¶113 Inter-American Court of Human Rights, *Sawhoyamaxa Indigenous Community v. Paraguay*, Judgment of 29 March 2006.

Presently, however, one of the most challenging demands to the whole of Brazil remains to more closely align outcomes of the Brazilian judgments with the decisions of the IACtHR. That includes all actors that are part of Brazil. It is necessary to understand that Brazil needs to evolve in finding a way to persistently align with the IAHRS cases, guaranteeing that all its citizens are under the sphere of the human rights system. As the IAHRS and its jurisprudence are vital to the process of recognition of human rights, expressedly so in Brazil, it is crucial to understand and revisit how other members of the OAS have merged norms related to consultation with indigenous peoples in their own juridical system.

This subchapter will address cases judged under the IAHRS in which Brazil was one of the parties. The data collected in the cases reveals the relevance of the IACtHR to influence the judgements of the Brazilian contentious jurisdictions.

This subchapter will address cases judged under the IAHRS in which Brazil was one of the parties.

3.5 Legal Claims Against the Brazilian State in the Inter-American Court of Human Rights

The IACtHR is an international body with jurisdictional action, created by the American Convention on Human Rights and charged with interpreting and applying it as mentioned in the Article 62.3 of the Pact of San José.[200] Its functions, however, go beyond this, as it has the jurisdiction to interpret other human rights treaties applicable on the Americas as it is established in Article 64 of the Pact of San José.[201] As a regulation, Article 68.2 of the American Convention may be subject to judicial enforcement of the remedies given by the decisions of the IACtHR.

In its jurisdictional activity, the IACtHR judges who may be denounced by the IACHR on Human Rights, an OAS organ, or by countries party to the Inter-American Convention on Human Rights, that have accepted the jurisdiction of the international court.

According to a decision of the IACtHR itself, the state parties must do everything possible to comply with international verdicts, under penalty of default being submitted to the OAS General Assembly, according to Article 65 of the Pact of San José.[202] This is an international sanction, of a political nature. Moreover, in general, the judgments of the IACtHR are generally complied with: 'for the time being, the encouraging rate of enforcement -casually on a case-by-case basis- with all the judgments of the IACtHR to date is due above all to the good faith and procedural loyalty with which the respondent states have complied with those

[200] (1969) American Convention on Human Rights.

[201] Ibid.

[202] Ibid.

judgments, thus also contributing to the consolidation of the regional system of protection'.[203]

Therefore, the statement applies to Brazil as well: '[…] the great majority of the states parties to the American Convention have not yet taken any action, legislative or otherwise, in this regard. Consequently, the victims of human rights violations in whose favor the IACtHR has declared a right - as to the merits of the case, or reparations in the broad sense - have not yet been fully and legally assured the execution of the respective sentences under the domestic law of the states sued. This situation must be promptly remedied'.[204]

The case Barbosa de Sousa and others *v.* Brazil[205] and the case Workers of the fireworks company and others *v.* Brazil.[206] Brazil has seven cases under supervision in which six were declared by Brazil to be listed as accomplished and therefore, terminated: the case Ximenes Lopes *v.* Brazil,[207] the case Garibaldi *v.* Brazil,[208] the case Gomes Lund and others (know as *Guerrilha do Araguaia*) v. Brazil,[209] the case workers of the Hacienda Brazil Verde *v.* Brazil, the case Favela Nova Brasília *v.* Brazil[210] and the case Xucuru peoples and members *v.* Brazil.[211]

The case Arlei josé Escher and others *v.* Brazil, a case of 2007 regarding illegal telephone interceptions is the only case that Brazil evidently complied with the decision so far. The case Herzog and others *v.* Brazil[212] is still pending of accomplishment. These cases are relevant to understand the extent to which Brazil does not comply with the rules as set out in international treaties, but also show how the state at times complies with the decisions and the remedies provided by the IACtHR.

In some cases, for instance, the Brazilian state has spontaneously accepted the international decisions and its implications. An example of this commitment is what happened in the case Damião Ximenes Lopes *v.* Brazil. Once Brazil was condemned,

---

[203] Trindade (1999), p. 184.

[204] Trindade (1999).

[205] Inter-American Court of Human Rights, *Barbosa de Sousa and others versus Brazil*, Judgment of 2019.

[206] Inter-American Court of Human Rights, *Workers of the Fireworks company and others versus Brazil*, Judgment of 2018.

[207] The Ximene Lopes case of 2006 is about the mistreatment in a mental institution and his killing in 1999, in Ceará; Inter-American Court of Human Rights, *Case of Ximenes-Lopes v. Brazil*, No. 12.237, Judgment of 7 April 2006.

[208] Inter-American Court of Human Rights, *Case of Garibaldi v. Brazil*, No. 13/07, Judgment of 23 September 2009.

[209] Inter-American Court of Human Rights, *Gomes Lund case (Guerrilha do Araguaia) v. Brazil*, Judgment of 24 November 2010.

[210] Inter-American Court of Human Rights, *Favela Nova Brasília case v. Brazil*, 11.566 and 11.694, Judgment of 16 February 2017.

[211] Inter-American Court of Human Rights, *The Xucuru indigenous people and members v. Brazil*, Judgment of 2 May 2018.

[212] Inter-American Court of Human Rights, *Herzgov and others v. Brazil*, No. 71/15, Judgment of 15 March 2018.

there was the regulation of the Decree No. 6.185, of 13rd August 2007, authorizing 'the Special Secretariat for Human Rights of the Presidency of the Republic to comply with the sentence issued by the IACtHR.[213] As the jurisdiction of the IACtHR was accepted by Brazil in 1998 and the American Convention on Human Rights is duly internalized in the legal system, Article 68.2 of the Pact of San José assumes its supralegal value as regards matters relating to human rights. In the following a closer look will be taken at one example case, the *Xucuru people v. Brazil*.

The presence of the Xucuru indigenous people in the Brazilian federal state of Pernambuco dates back to the sixteenth century. Several historical documents describe the areas occupied by the Xucuru throughout the eighteenth century. Currently, the so-called Xucuru People of Ororubá are 'composed of 2354 families, which live in 2265 houses. The Indigenous Land Xucuru is home to 7726 indigenous people distributed in 24 communities within approximately 27,555 hectares, in the municipality of Pesqueira, state of Pernambuco. In addition, approximately 4000 indigenous people live outside the indigenous land in the city of Pesqueira'.[214]

The case Xucuru People *v.* Brazil is the first one where Brazil was condemned by the IACtHR on the matter of indigenous peoples.[215] The decision dates back to February 8th 2018 and because of its Brazilian citizenship, the judge Juez Roberto F. Caldas did not attend the discussion of the judgement according to 19.2 of the Regulation and Article 19.1 of the IACtHR Rulings.

First of all, on October 16th 2002, the Commission received the initial petition submitted by the National Human Rights Movement/Northeast Region, the *Gabinete de Acessoria Jurídica* (hereinafter, the GAJOP) and the Conselho Indienista Missionário (hereinafter, the CIMI) and was then assigned the case number of 12,728. This was followed by the Admissibility Report on October 29th of 2009 and then, on July 28th of 2015 the IACHR gave its concluding remarks and some recommendations aimed at Brazil.

On 16th October 2015, the Commission addressed to Brazil the recommendations with a predetermined timeframe to follow suit. However, after the allotted time had passed, the Commission found that Brazil did not make substantial progress in implementing the recommendations.

Based on the foregoing, the Commission requested the IACtHR on March 6th 2016 to declare the international responsibility of Brazil for the violations of the right to collective property and personal integrity of the Xucuru indigenous people. This violation was caused by some facts: after having waited more than 16 years, from 1989 to 2005, the Xucuru people had their ancestral lands and territory still not

---

[213] (2007) Decree that authorizes the Special Secretariat for Human Rights of the Presidency of the Republic to comply with the judgment of the Ximene Lopes v. Brazil.

[214] Inter-American Court of Human Rights, *The Xucuru indigenous people and members v. Brazil*, Judgment of 2 May 2018¶60.

[215] For more about the leadership of Marcos Xucuru and the relevance of fight against violence that happened in the territory. O 'bem viver' como forma de luta. 'Acima de tudo, coragem'. (2018) Tribo Xukuru do Ororubá.

recognized, titled, demarcated and delimitated, and the allegation of the failure to comply with the reasonable time limit to comply with the entitled the territory to the Xucuru indigenous peoples.

The IACHR understood that this was a violation of the rights to judicial guarantees and judicial protection. Thus, the Commission also stressed that Brazil violated Articles 21, 5, 8 and Article 25 of the American Convention in relation to Articles 1(1) and 2, and thus the right to property, the right to personal integrity and the right to judicial guarantees and protection.[216] That being said, it should be noted that this case is not intimately related to the requirement of consultation but—as it is the first time that Brazil faced a case in the IACtHR—it is relevant to be addressed.

The IACtHR analyzed five preliminary objections brought forward by Brazil regarding the inadmissibility of the case by virtue of the publication of the Fund Report by the Commission; the 'marco temporal' with respect to acts prior to the date of recognition of the IACtHR's jurisdiction; the *ratione temporis* with respect to acts prior to the date of the state's accession to the Convention *ratione materiae* with respect to the alleged violation of ILO Convention No. 169 and the lack of prior exhaustion of domestic remedies.

As to the merits of the case, the IACtHR conducted a legal analysis of the alleged violations of property rights, judicial guarantees, judicial protection, and personal integrity, all in relation to the process of titling, demarcation, and disintrusion (in Spanish, *saneamiento*) of the territory of the Xucuru indigenous people and their members.[217] The legal standoff in the present case, therefore, was based on whether the actions taken by Brazil in this legal dispute were effective in guaranteeing the land entitlement and the impact on it of the delay in the legal proceedings.[218]

Brazil alleged four preliminary exceptions against the IACHR and also alleged that the IACtHR had no jurisdiction over their territory.[219] The allegations were that the jurisdiction ratione temporis in respect of the signature of the Convention was not fulfilled.

The Xucuru case, therefore, demonstrates the possibilities of success of the strategic litigation of indigenous peoples at the international level. Especially, if considering the efficacy of the jurisprudence of the IACtHR in relation to Article 21 of the Convention. This is an understanding that, based on international human and indigenous peoples' rights law, clashes with recent representations in domestic disputes of the Brazilian Constitution estipulated in Article 231, such as the requirement of consultation in the Brazilian Federal Courts and also the litigations pending decision of the Brazilian Supreme Court.

[216]Inter-American Court of Human Rights, *The Xucuru indigenous people and members v. Brazil*, Judgment of 2 May 2018.

[217](2017) Testmonial of Marcos Xucuru during the hearing at the Inter-American Court of Human Rights.

[218]Inter-American Court of Human Rights, *The Xucuru indigenous people and members v. Brazil*, Judgment of 2 May 2018.

[219]Ibid.

Relevant to note is here also that the IACtHR did conduct *in loco* procedures such as in the case Kichwa de Sarayaku *v.* Ecuardor, the case Garífuna de Punta Piedra *v.* Honduras, the case Garífuna Triunfo de la Cruz *v.* Honduras and the case Kaliña y Lokono *v.* Suriname, taking the victim perspective into consideration. According to Article 63.1, the IACtHR established appropriate measures to remedy the suffered damage and to avoid future violations. In respect to the compensation measures, the IACtHR considered the payment of one million dollars to a fund regarding the immaterial damage, however, not stipuling how the fund should be managed by the Brazilian state. The compensation was ruled as 10,000.000,00 dollars.[220]

It should be noted that there was an inherent contradiction in the decision 'between this reparation measure and the IACtHR's merit analysis. In the merit analysis, the IACtHR differentiated conflict between private property and traditional territory (solved by case analysis according to proportionality criteria) from the duty to perform saneamiento (solved by the removal of any interference to an already registered property), framing the present case in the second situation. However, the flexibility granted to the state regarding final delivery of the territory collides with the duty of saneamiento, as it questions the validity of the property registration itself'.[221]

After 17 years of litigation, the Xucuru People found partially closure that clarified their case and also helped to further bolster indigenous peoples' rights under the IAHRS System.[222] In any case, the decision consolidated the jurisprudence of the IACtHR in respect of territorial rights enriching the interpretation of Article 21 and the international obligation of the signature states of the Convention to perform the *saneamiento*[223] of the indigenous peoples' lands. Albeit the IACtHR recognized the cultural identity rights and the prior consultation for the first time with regard to the Brazilian state, which from now on is obliged to follow the precedent to reinforce its human rights system.[224]

Regarding the property rights, the IACtHR places economic limitations on the case of private property, as it was decided in previous cases.[225]

However, the IACtHR established that the state should provide alternative lands, which is against the cultural rights, as the land that the indigenous peoples occupied

[220] Ibid.

[221] Navarro (2019), p. 212.

[222] See e.g. Dodge R (2016) Aldeira da Memória: o caso Xucuru.

[223] *Saneaminento* is a Spanish word that might be translated as the transitory technical-legal procedure aimed at legalizing and perfecting the right to indigenous community lands. It can be found in some legislations in Latin America, such as the Bolivian and the Chilenean, for example. Art. 63 (1993) Chilean Law that establishes standards for the protection, promotion and development of indigenous people; Art. 64 (1996) Bolivian Law of the Agrarian Reform; Aylwin Oyarzun (2002).

[224] Navarro (2019).

[225] Inter-American Court of Human Rights, *Garífuna Triunfo de la Cruz and your members v. Honduras*, Judgment of 9 May 2019; Inter-American Court of Human Rights, *Comunity of Garífuna de Punta Piedra v. Honduras*, Judgment of 10 2015.

is their territory where they maintain a cultural relationship. 'The right to saneamiento is decided when the community already has the property title but there are invaders on their territory. In this scenario, the Xucuru had the title of the property, and the entitlement was already defined by court law. However, the IACtHR understood that also in this case, the state should provide alternative lands.[226]

The IACtHR recognizes the prevalence of indigenous property under the prevalence of private property, and in the case of saneamiento, it does not put any restriction. Once there is no conflict of property right because the property already has the title, there is no need of such possibility provided by the IACtHR.

Yet, the IACtHR missed an opportunity to refer to the American Declaration of Indigenous Peoples Rights. This would have been very relevant for the Brazilian state and also for the strengthening of human rights of indigenous peoples in the whole region.

3.6 Conclusions

The analysis in this chapter reviewed legal cases where the requirement of consultation constituted an increasingly dominant role and analyzed how these cases have been addressed by the IACHR and the IACtHR, under close consideration of the international treaties which formed the base for the legal arguments. In accordance with the foregoing, Article 29 of the American Convention, the Vienna Convention on the Law of Treaties, the ILO No. 169 Convention and the UNDRIP provide the juridical possibility for the interpretation of how human rights treaties at internal and domestic level evolve over time. Such as law adjusts to a changing environment, so should adjust the interpretation of law of international courts, such as the regional IACtHR. This process of consolidation interpretation is consistent with the general rules of international law. This aligns with what ought to be and the normative force of international norms. Moreover, 'by its normative force a norm contributes to the implementation of what ought to be. If the norm succeeds in this one speaks of the efficacy of the (normative force of) the norm by the control of conventionality. These are not purely legal issues. The question as to what should be is, even if the answer can be given in reference to an existing legal norm, a preliminary question which must be answered not from law, but from social necessity, ethics and religion'.[227]

The analysis of the decisions demonstrates moreover that the right to consultation constitutes more than just a property right, but a means to participation of the indigenous peoples or tribal communities in the decision-making process for fostering their cultural rights and self-determination that need to be addressed by the IAHRS. The cases showed that the most significant design change regarding the

[226] Navarro (2021); Interview with Academic Expert No. 01.

[227] van Dijik (1987), p. 15.

requirement of consultation was the reiterative way of the requests for good faith application, the appropriate and accessible consultation and the conduct of environmental impact studies by the successive IACHR and IACtHR decisions. Henceforth, the consultation must be carried out with (i) good faith, the purpose of reaching an agreement, in other words, an (ii) adequate and accessible consultation and the need to have an (iii) environmental impact study. The high number of those concepts appearing are admittedly a crude indicator of their relevance. However, in this sense 'endogenous sources of change—learning about the international judicial system and the development of international jurisprudence, the order to improve the systems' functioning—should contribute to rising litigation levels'.[228] Bringing these three concepts together reveals the architecture of the requirement of consultation, in a way that shows *how* it should be executed.

The principle of (i) good faith can be traced back to the ILO Convention No. 169, in Article 6 (2) stating that 'consultations must be carried out in good faith and in a manner appropriate to the circumstances with the aim of reaching an agreement or obtaining consent regarding the proposed measures'.[229] Consequently, consultation might be a true instrument for participation to achieve consensus between the parties. Therefore, some examples of other jurisdictions may be found in Canada, where the Supreme Court decided that the consultation process must be exercised in good faith and with the intention of considering the interests of the indigenous population whose lands are at stake. In the case Haida *v.* British Columbia (Minister of Forests) '[...] that the honor of the Crown requires that these rights be determined, recognized and respected. The latter requires that the Crown act honorably and participate in negotiation processes. During this process, the honor of the Crown may require a consultation and, where indicated, consider the interests of the indigenous population'.[230] In the same way, the case Rio Tinto Alcan Inc. *v.* Carrier Sekani Tribal Council, the Supreme Court also 'determined that the state's proposed intervention on indigenous territory does not require an immediate impact on the territories or resources of the indigenous communities in order for the duty to consult to arise; it is sufficient that the state's activity potentially will have a negative impact on the territorial rights of the indigenous community'.[231]

The principle of a need of an (ii) appropriate informed consultation that is adequate and accessible, under their own traditions and their own institutions and by the language spoken was a matter of the case Saramaka v. Suriname and the case Sarayaku v. Ecuador, where the use of the cultured appropriate procedures was highlighted as cultural rights. According to Article 12 of the ILO Convention No. 169, the 'measures that members of these peoples can understand and be

[228] Alter (2014), p. 109.

[229] *(1989) Indigenous Peoples and Tribal Convention No 169.*

[230] ¶25 British Columbia, *Haida Nation v. British Columbia (Minister of Forests)*, 29419, Judgment of 18 November 2004.

[231] ¶31,32,33 British Columbia, *Rio Tinto Alcan Inc. v. Carrier Sekani Tribal Council*, 33132, Judgment of 28 October 2010, 2010 SCC 43.

understood in legal proceedings, where necessary through the provision of interpretation or by other effective means'.[232] The same provision can be found in Article 32 (2) of the UNDRIP: 'states, in consultation and cooperation with indigenous peoples, shall take effective measures to facilitate the exercise and ensure the implementation of this right'.[233] Furthermore, there is the Report of the Special Rapporteur on the situation of human rights and fundamental freedoms of indigenous peoples of 5th October 2009 that lists that 'the appropriate nature of the consultation with indigenous communities through their representative institutions does not respond to a univocal formula but depends to a great extent on the scope or sphere of the specific measure which is the object and ultimate goal of the consultation'.[234]

And finally, the principle of conducting (iii) an environmental impact assessment is also relevant as was previously decreed by the ILO Committee of Experts on the Application of Conventions and Recommendations where the term appropriate procedures should be understood as including the environmental impact assessment. As it is mentioned in Article 15 (2) of the ILO Convention No. 169, 'the governments shall establish or maintain procedures through which they shall consult these peoples, with a view to ascertaining whether and to what degree their interests would be prejudiced, before undertaking or permitting any program for the exploration or exploitation of such resources on their lands'.[235] Moreover, the consultation should take place in advance and be aligned with the inherent traditions of the indigenous peoples such as mentioned in the case of the Saramaka People *v.* Suriname, where the IACtHR decided that it was necessary to have sufficient time for an internal discussion with all the community and where an appropriate answer to the state should be provided in the matter they were asked about.

The environmental impact study needs furthermore to be conducted by an independent entity under the supervision of the state in which the indigenous peoples have territory. As it is established in the Article 14 of the Convention on Biological Diversity the goal of the environmental impact is that the 'impact Assessment and Minimizing Adverse Impacts. 1. Each Contracting Party, as far as possible and as appropriate, shall: (a) Introduce appropriate procedures requiring environmental impact assessment of its proposed projects that are likely to have significant adverse effects on biological diversity with a view to avoiding or minimizing such effects and, where appropriate, allow for public participation in such procedures; (b) Introduce appropriate arrangements to ensure that the environmental consequences of its programs and policies that are likely to have significant adverse impacts on biological diversity are duly taken into account; [...]' And in accordance

[232] *(1989) Indigenous Peoples and Tribal Convention No 169.*

[233] (2007) The United Nations Declaration on the Rights of Indigenous Peoples.

[234] ¶28 Anaya JS, *Report of the Special Rapporteur on the situation of human rights and fundamental freedoms of indigenous people - Report on the Situation of Human Rights of Indigenous Peoples in Brazil*, UN Doc. A./HRC/12/34 (2009), 26 September 2009.

[235] *(1989) Indigenous Peoples and Tribal Convention No 169.*

to principle 17 of the Rio Declaration on Environment and Development 'environmental impact assessment, as a national instrument, shall be undertaken for proposed activities that are likely to have a significant adverse impact on the environment and are subject to a decision of a competent national authority'.[236] And also, the principle 20 'environmental issues are best handled with participation of all concerned citizens, at the relevant level. At the national level, each individual shall have appropriate access to information concerning the environment that is held by public authorities, including information on hazardous materials and activities in their communities, and the opportunity to participate in decision-making processes. States shall facilitate and encourage public awareness and participation by making information widely available. Efficacy access to judicial and administrative proceedings, including redress and remedy, shall be provided'.[237]

Furthermore, Article 7 (3) of the ILO Convention No. 169 states that 'the governments shall ensure that, whenever appropriate, studies are carried out, in cooperation with the peoples concerned, to assess the social, spiritual, cultural and environmental impact on them of planned development activities. Therefore, the result of these studies shall be considered as fundamental criteria for the implementation of these activities'.[238] As in the case of the Saramaka People *v.* Suriname, the IACtHR declared that the environmental impact assessments must be conducted in conformity with the international standards and best practices which respects the indigenous peoples' traditions. Thus, there is the obligation of the state to supervise the environmental impact assessment. The IACtHR addressed this by observing that the environmental impact plan: '(a) was prepared without the participation of the Sarayaku People; (b) was implemented by a private entity subcontracted by the oil company, without any evidence that it had subsequently been subject to strict control by state monitoring agencies, and (c) did not take into account the social, spiritual and cultural impact that the planned development activities might have on the Sarayaku People. Therefore, the IACtHR concludes that the environmental impact plan was not implemented in accordance with its case law or the relevant international standards'.[239]

The efficacy of consultation and right to veto typically held by the state carries the obligation to guarantee the right to consent. Thus, 'when indigenous communal property and individual private property enter into real or apparent conflict, the American Convention and the IACtHR's case law provide guidelines to define the admissible restrictions, which must be established by law, necessary, proportionate and aimed at achieving a legitimate objective in a democratic society without

[236] *United Nations Conference on Environment and Development*, 8 December 1992.

[237] Ibid.

[238] *(1989) Indigenous Peoples and Tribal Convention No 169.*

[239] ¶206 Inter-American Court of Human Rights, *Kichwa Indigenous People of Sarayaku v. Ecuador*, No. 185, Judgment of 27 June 2012.

denying their right to exist as a people'.[240] According to Article 1 of the ILO No. 169 Convention, 'the tribal peoples in independent countries whose social, cultural and economic conditions distinguish them from other sections of the national community, and whose status is regulated wholly or partially by their own customs or traditions or by special laws or regulations',[241] and Article 2 of the same Convention: 'the states shall have the responsibility of developing, with the participation of the peoples concerned, coordinated and systematic actions to protect the rights of these peoples and to guarantee respect for their integrity'.[242] Regarding the ILO Convention No. 169, the Articles 6, 15, 17, 22, 27 and 28 are related to the consultation of the indigenous and tribal populations and the Articles 13, 14, 15, 16, 17, 18 and 19 apply to the use of the land and territory.

There is also the necessity of the consultation to be informed in order to clarify all the potential risks of the development of the plan for their territory, including the environmental damages and health risks for the population. This is required for the state to be able to provide information to the indigenous peoples, by constantly informing all involved parties. Given that the indigenous peoples have an intrinsic connection with their territory, the protection of property rights and the use of the enjoyment of the land is necessary. In order to guarantee the security of the control of the natural resources it is necessary in order to maintain their way of living. For this relationship to be considered, this may include the 'traditional or spiritual ceremonial ties, sporadic settlements or cultivation; traditional forms of subsistence such as seasonal or nomadic hunting. Fishing or gathering; use of natural resources associated with their customs or other elements characteristic of their culture'.[243]

The IACtHR's sentences build on proven and undisputed facts such as those given by the affidavit prepared by the current president of the Sarayaku People, Mr. José Maria Gualinga. In his testimony, he 'emphasized that in the living forest there are special noises and phenomena, and it is the inspiration where, when we are in these places, we feel a kind of sign, an emotion, and then when we return to our people, to the family, we feel strengthened'.[244] These were the places providing the necessary resources, potential and energy, they claim, to be able to survive and live.

Equally relevant is the understanding of the progressive effort of the historical construction with regard to human rights and the constant recognition of new social actors that form part of an open and democratic society. The system can maintain itself because it allows for the participation in decision-making of civil society in its varied nature, by overcoming the gap and including marginalized groups such as the

---

[240] ¶144 Inter-American Court of Human Rights, *Mayagna (Sumo) Awas Tingni Community v. Nicaragua*, No. 79, Judgment of 31 August 2001.

[241] *(1989) Indigenous Peoples and Tribal Convention No 169.*

[242] *Ibid.*

[243] ¶154 Inter-American Court of Human Rights, *Yakye Axa Indigenous Community v. Paraguay*, Judgment of 17 June 2005.

[244] ¶152 Inter-American Court of Human Rights, *Kichwa Indigenous People of Sarayaku v. Ecuador*, No. 185, Judgment of 27 June 2012.

indigenous peoples. One of the recent and audacious invention of the indigenous peoples in the region are the Protocols, which were discussed in the previous chapter and will be more detained in the Brazilian legal cases. They are not yet discussed in the IACtHR but were discussed in the IACHR in a public hearing about the requirement of consultation. It is a very interesting instrument of self-determination and cultural rights.

This chapter emphasized the legal consolidation of indigenous peoples' rights within the IAHRS, both in the realm of the IACHR and the IACtHR and showed how case law is contributing to the consolidation process of the requirement of consultation by expanding subject litigations and adding guidelines and juridical remedies. The 'how' that was described here is relevant because it provides the ground rules for the next chapter, which will offer an in-depth analysis of the application of the requirement of consultation in the Brazilian jurisdiction.

References

Agudelo CE (2019) The Garífuna community of Triunfo de la Cruz versus the State of Honduras: territory and the possibilities and limits of the Inter-American Court of human rights verdict. Lat Am Caribb Ethn Stud 14:318–333. https://doi.org/10.1080/17442222.2019.1673069

Albert B (1992) Indian lands, environmental policy and military geopolitics in the development of the Brazilian Amazon: the case of the Yanomami. Dev Change 23:35–70. https://doi.org/10.1111/j.1467-7660.1992.tb00438.x

Alter KJ (2014) The new terrain of international law: courts, politics, rights. Princeton University Press, Princeton

Amin Lima da Silva L, Mendes G (2019) Protocolo juruna de consulta prévia frente aos empreendimentos hidrelétrico e minerário na amazônia: caso belo monte e belo sun. Núcleo Antropol Direito Anais VI ENADIR-GT04

Anaya JS (1998) Maya aboriginal land and resource rights and the conflict over logging in Southern Belize. Yale Hum Rights Dev Law J 1

Antkowiak TM (2013) Rights, resources, and rhetoric: indigenous peoples and the Inter-American Court. Univ Pa J Int Law 2

Atkins E (2017) The multi-dimensional framing of Brazil's Belo Monte dam: dammed and diversionary. Singap J Trop Geogr 38:276–292. https://doi.org/10.1111/sjtg.12206

Aylwin Oyarzun J (2002) El acceso de los indígenas a la tierra en los ordenamientos jurídicos de América Latina: un estudio de casos. Vol. 2: ... Naciones Unidas, CEPAL, Red de Desarrollo Agropecuario, Santiago de Chile

Basch F, Filippini L, Laya A et al (2004) The effectiveness of the Inter-American System of Human Rights Protection: a quantitative approach to its functioning and compliance with its decisions. SUR Rev Int Direitos Hum 1

Brunner L (2008) The rise of Peoples' Rights in the Americas: The Saramaka People Decision of the Inter-American Court of Human Rights. Chin J Int Law 7:699–711. https://doi.org/10.1093/chinesejil/jmn031

C. de la Fuente O (2020) Comentario a la sentencia de la Corte Interamericana de Derechos Humanos en el caso Comunidades Indígenas Miembros de la Asociación Lhaka Honhat (Nuestra Tierra) vs. Argentina. Rev Discusiones 25

Cavallaro J, Schaffer EJ (2004) Less as more: rethinking supranational litigation of economic and social rights in the Americas. Hastings Law J 56 da Silva LAL (2017) Consulta prévia e livre determinação dos povos indígenas e tribais na América Latina: re-existir para co-existir. Dissertation, Pontifícia Universidade Católica do Paraná, Paraná

Daly TG (2017) Brazilian 'Supremocracy' and the Inter-American Court of Human Rights: unpicking an unclear relationship. In: Fortes P, Boratti L, Palacios Lleras A, Gerald Daly T (eds) Law and policy in Latin America. Palgrave Macmillan UK, London, pp 3–20

de Oliveira Franco FC, de Alencar Mayer Feitosa MLP (2013) Desenvolvimento e direitos humanos: marcas de inconstitucionalidade no processo Belo Monte. Rev Direito GV 9:93–114. https://doi.org/10.1590/S1808-24322013000100005

de Oliveira Mazzuoli V (2011) The Inter-American human rights protection system: structure, functioning and effectiveness in Brazilian law. Afr Hum Rights J 11

Diamond S, Poirier C (2010) Brazil's native peoples and the Belo Monte Dam: a case study. NACLA Rep Am 43:25–29. https://doi.org/10.1080/10714839.2010.11725513

Doyle C, Rojas Garzón B, Weitzner V, Okamoto T (eds) (2019) Los protocolos de consentimiento libre, previo e informado como instrumentos de autonomía: Sentando las bases para interacciones basadas en los derechos, Institut für Ökologie und Aktions-Ethnologie (INFOE) e. V. Forest Peoples Programme, Köln

Fearnside PM (2006) Dams in the Amazon: Belo Monte and Brazil's hydroelectric development of the Xingu River Basin. Environ Manage 38:16–27. https://doi.org/10.1007/s00267-005-0113-6

García Ramírez S (2015) The relationship between Inter-American Jurisdiction and States (national systems): some pertinent questions. Notre Dame J Int Comp Law 5

Goméz V (2003) IACHR Report No. 75/02 Mary and Carie Dann. Hum Rights Law Rev 3:128–134

Hall A, Branford S (2012) Development, dams and Dilma: the saga of Belo Monte. Crit Sociol 38: 851–862. https://doi.org/10.1177/0896920512440712

Huneeus A (2011) Court resisting courts: lessons from the Inter-American Court's struggle to enforce human rights. Cornell Int Law J 44

ISA I (2017) Brazil's Amazon Hydroelectrics in the United Nations Clean Development Mechanism (CDM): Defrauding Investors, Cheating the Atmosphere?

Jaichand V, Sampaio AA (2013) Dam and be damned: the adverse impacts of Belo Monte on indigenous peoples in Brazil. Hum Rights Q 35:408–447. https://doi.org/10.1353/hrq.2013.0023

Lixinski L (2017) Case of the Kaliña and Lokono Peoples v. Suriname. Series C, No. 309. Merits, Reparations and Costs. Am J Int Law 11

Navarro GCB (2019) The judgment of the case Xucuru People v. Brazil: InterAmerican Court of Human Rights between consolidation and setbacks. Rev Direito Int 16. https://doi.org/10.5102/rdi.v16i2.5958

Navarro GCB (2021) Measuring the effectiveness of the Inter-American System of Human Rights: the case of indigenous territorial rights. Dissertation, Goethe-Universität Frankfurt, Frankfurt am Main

Pasqualucci JM (2003) Introduction: the practice and procedure of the Inter-American Court of Human Rights. In: Brewer SE, Cavallaro JL (eds) Reevaluating regional human rights litigation in the twenty-first century: the case of the Inter-American Court, 1st edn. Cambridge University Press

Plummer J (2015) The Yanomami: illegal mining, law, and indigenous rights in the Brazilian Amazon. Georget Int Environ Law Rev 27

Tremblay-Huet S (2019) Tourism and the protection of the cultural rights and identity of indigenous communities in the light of the iachr Judgment in the Comunidad Garífuna Triunfo de la Cruz y sus miembros v. Honduras Case. Int J Minor Group Rights

Trindade AAC (1999) Tratado de direito internacional dos direitos humanos. Sergio Antonio Fabris, Porto Alegre

van Dijik P (1987) Normative force and effectiveness of international norms. German Yearb Int Law 30

Verbeek CY (2012) Free, prior, informed consent: the key to self- determination: an analysis of the Kichwa People of Sarayaku v. Ecuador. Am Indian Law Rev 37

Watts J (2016) Brazil: insider claims Rousseff coalition took funds from Belo Monte mega-dam. The Guardian

Zugman DL (2015) O dever de consulta aos povos indígenas e a construção da usina de Belo Monte. Rev Discente Direito Red-GV

Chapter 4
Assessing Consultation with Indigenous Peoples in Brazil

4.1 Introduction

Societal relations in the countries of the Americas have been historically characterized by unequal systems skewed in favour of elites and their governments versus all others living in the territory. For better or for worse, the problems of that part of the hemisphere 'are more unique than they are universal or European. They can only be solved within the framework of their own legal, cultural, political, and social traditions'.[1]

The same delicate problems persist in Brazil where predominantly traditional communities are affected, also in view of continued favoritism for influential third parties such as multinational companies in case their interest conflict with indigenous peoples. Contemporarily, in abusive conflicts over territory, this may translate into violations of fundamental rights of indigenous peoples for the pursuit of national projects[2] in context of resource exploitation.

The Brazilian experience of indigenous peoples' rights has in recent years experienced some significant changes in terms of social and political inclusion.[3] These changes have occurred partially due to the international courts's decisions, the indigenous peoples activism, the Constitution of 1988 and the advent of the 6th Prosecutor Office,[4] regarding the recognition of indigenous peoples' collective

---

[1] Pasqualucci (2003), p. 6.

[2] See e.g. Domingues and Bermann (2012); Heck et al. (2005).

[3] Indigenous peoples in Latin America also tend to be more organized and networked than in other regions. At the same time, violations of their rights—including consultation and consent rights are prevalent across the region. Latin America is also known for an extensive regulatory approach combined with "wide discretionary power for officials", something reflected in a high level of corruption in the natural resource sector and corporate control over politics. See e.g. Doyle et al. (2019), p. 20.

[4] In all regions that have indigenous peoples have their own ways to fight for their rights. The international organs and bodies, the IAHRS are equally relevant. Nevertheless, in Brazil, the

C. Woyames Dreher, *A Legal Assessment of the Efficacy of Consultation with Indigenous Peoples*, https://doi.org/10.1007/978-3-031-50539-3_4

property of ancestral land rights and self-determination, which propel their fundamental rights into a more egalitarian legal status by clarifying ambiguities, filling legal lacunae, and promoting the underlying objectives of the legal obligations. So that, 'the status of all individuals under international law is no longer in doubt: everybody is subject to international law and as such enjoys entitlement of rights. Yet rights are illusory without the procedural capability to enforce them. They are no more than high-minded principles if individuals whose rights have been violated have no avenue for complaint and relief'.[5]

Thus, the increasing resonance of international adjudication within the IAHRS went in conjunction with a set of supportive developments at the regional level. As a matter of fact, consultative aspects of procedures at the IACHR and the IACtHR as part of the IAHRS are of particular relevance. These are the reasons that the once barely acknowledged concepts of self-determination and collective property rights, cultural rights, and more recently also the requirement of consultation, are today being advocated in Brazil. As Brazil is one of the members of the IAHRS, the judiciary has moulded, because of the control of conventionality the national jurisprudence following recent decisions of the IACtHR, and the precautionary measures given by the IACHR.

This role that the IACtHR plays in consolidating and fundamentalizing human rights, as observed in the last chapter, is not only illustrated by addressing the new criteria of interpretation related to international treaties, but it is also exemplified by considering the cases that will be presented in this chapter. In view of the observable correlation between the rise in the number of decisions and recommendations of the IAHRS and the expansion of the jurisdiction of international courts, in this case both the IACHR and the IACtHR assume a leading position.

In this chapter, the analysis' objective is to understand if the set of legal mechanisms of the IAHRS in regarding the efficacy in Brazil is having an impact on the application of the requirement of consultation with indigenous peoples as a way to achieve cultural rights and self-determination in Brazilian national claims (legal and legislation) of resource exploitation.

The legal understanding in the IARHS is that the requirement of consulation is a right in the national realm based on the consolidation of the argumentative criteria provided by Article 21 of the American Convention simultaneously with the interation of the ILO No. 169, which explicitly mention the requirement of

---

indigenous peoples fought for their rights several times. One of the most important was the requirement to include articles (the Popular Amendment with the proposed chapter on the rights of Indigenous Peoples) in the Constiutution of 1988. After over 20 years of dictatorship, it was a legal achievement for the indigenous peoples' rights that only came out of a mobilization of the indigenous peoples for the Brazilian state to recognize their rights as a traditional people of Brazil, such as the demarcation and the rights to territory. They also claimed the Brazilian projects for the indigenous peoples' future in the country. See e.g: Cunha (2012); Dallari (2017); Krenak (1987); (2013) Índio Cidadão?

[5] Pasqualucci (2003), p. 52.

consultation.[6] Thus, the cultural rights and the right to self-determination are included in the American Convention and the ILO No. 169. Nevertheless, the literature and the United Nations organs locates the requirement of consultation approach within an international human rights frame of analysis.[7]

In Brazil, a state that accepted the jurisdiction of the IACtHR and ratified the ILO Convention No. 169, the legal cases involving indigenous peoples may evolve into administrative, criminal, environmental, constitutional and civil proceedings petitioned by the Brazilian Federal Union organs, indigenous peoples themselves or by international and national organizations. The Brazilian Constitution has a sort of consultation, which are the public hearing and the constitutional hearing. However, differently than the consultation of Article 6 of the ILO Convention No. 169, those requirement does not have the void of the efficacy in case of non-enforcement. Another novelty of the Brazilian jurisdiction is that the indigenous peoples Protocols and others traditional communities' Protocols have been claimed as a legal way to conduct the consultation considering their self-determination and cultural rights.

The cases in the chapter have been selected for assessing in detail the problems and juridical tensions underlying the guiding research questions. The cases chosen highlight frequent problems that indigenous peoples in Brazil experience related to the requirement of consultation in the specific context of resource exploitations. They are, of course, translated into the legal claims and inumerous possibilities to appeal. The claims include the building of hydroelectric dams, mining explorations and the construction of highways in indigenous peoples' territories in Brazil; *e.g.*, the (i) the Taparajós case; (ii) the Volta Grande do Xingu case; and (iii) the Polo Naval de Manaus case. The legislative cases are equally relevant and are also going to be addressed in the chapter.

The cases of the *Raposa do Sol* of the Brazilian Supreme Court and the Xucuru people *v.* Brazil of the IACtHR, addressed in the previous chapter, are equally pertinent for the study and will be addressed as well. The case known as *Raposa do Sol*, which was brought to the Brazilian Supreme Court (hereinafter, the STF), is relevant once the decision in this case was responsible for the thesis of time frame (in Portuguese, *marco temporal*), which results from the restrictive interpretation, which implements a chronological line to the characterization of the concept of traditionally occupied land provided by the Brazilian Constitution (hereinafter, the Constitution of 1988).

[6]It is relevant to address that there are generally two interpretations pointed out in the literature: the interpretation of the IACtHR on the consolidation of the right to property, and the interpretation that is broader and promulgated by the international organs of the United Nations, considering the Free, Prior, Informed Consent. The most adequate solution for Brazil is going to be discussed in the sixth chapter of this study. The problem here is that the Brazilian legal system only recognizes the indigenous peoples' territory when they are demarcated already: and the country has only ratified the ILO Convention No. 169 which only considers the requirement of consultation. This indicates that possibly the international approach is not the most adequate for Brazil.

[7]See e.g. Anaya (2005); Doyle (2016); Xanthaki (2014).

The case Xucuru people *v.* Brazil was the first one to be judged by the IACtHR. This case reveals the workings of Brazil with regard to indigenous rights in terms of efficacy, especially, and the binding character of the decision.

In a broader sense, the results of the analysis point into the direction that the role of the control of conventionality of the IAHRS regarding the requirement of consultation has further developed in the Brazilian national jurisdiciton[8] as a 'subsidiary source in prosecutions for human rights' violations'.[9] This process of interaction and iteration with the IAHRS also demonstrates, however, that the consolidation of indigenous peoples rights still has some limitations in the Brazilian judiciary and legislature.

The main goal of this chapter is to analyze the alternatives of interpretation of the requirement of consultation as a self-determinarion and cultural rights provided by legal precendents of the Federal Courts once the discourse of the Higher Tribunals has stalled and limited the understandings and applications of the requirement of consultation in the Brazilian society.

4.2 Indigenous Peoples in Brazil

The section analyzes the legal, anthropological and the historical literature in order to understand the particularities of Brazil with regard to indigenous peoples' fundamental rights. This subchapter describes functional aspects intended to further understand the juridical implications, such as the reasons that the indigenous peoples in Brazil are considered to have guardianship or legal guardian by the federal governamental agencies and the judiciary, the context of resource exploitation, the land tenure issues in Brazil and how this is in a sense intrinsic to the lack of consultation and the absence of indigenous peoples' rights. The results pervade the colonial era and the Republic through several constitutional moments in the history of Brazil, along with possibilities to reconcile and engage in dialogue with different perspectives.[10]

Indigenous peoples' rights in Latin America must be discussed against the backdrop of two historical processes: that of the coloniality of power and that of the imposition of the paradigm of hegemonic Western modernity. It is important to note that development was, in Latin America, the argument that historically served as the basis for a political discourse associated with the logic of modernity and the capitalist model. The concept of development historically adopted by Latin

[8]See e.g. Schumann (2018); Engstrom (2017); Alter (2014); Torelly (2017).

[9]Torelly (2017), p. 345.

[10]In addition to the economic and political dimensions, colonialism brought a strong epistemological dimension that did not end with the independence of the colonies. According to Boaventura, colonialism was responsible for a true epistemicide, that is, the death of alternative knowledge and the consequent liquidation and subordination of the groups that sustained themselves on such knowledge.Santos et al. (2006).

American states and reproduced to the present day is linked to an anti-democratic logic of exploitation of nature and mercantilization of natural resources, justified by a productivist and predatory ethic.[11]

Because of that, a brief detour into fews chosen moments in the Brazilian history may help to further elucidate the emerging legal conceptualization of the requirement of consultation with indigenous peoples.

4.2.1 The Conceptualization of Indigenous Peoples in Brazil

The conceptualization of the indigenous peoples in Brazil occurred via three significant historical events. However, differing in periods, the objective is to understand the origins of the guardianship and the definition of the indigenous peoples in recent times.

The first period refers to the colonial era. The enchantment with the novelty of the territory was notable,[12] which might be one of the reasons that in several moments in the history of Brazilian colonization, marked by a violent process of enslavement, assimilation and integration of the indigenous peoples,[13] here was also part of the history tarnished by attempts of forcing marriage with Portuguese's and catholics missionaries controlling the villages.

In 1507, the Catholic Church had recognized America as a fourth part of the world, inserting the continent into its universalist theology 'the evangelical preacher went forth to sow' the divine word (*Ecce exiit qui seminat, seminare*).[14] For that purpose, the moral foundations of Saint Thomas Aquinas were restructured. This geographic/moral enlargement promoted the formulation of several divergent hypotheses, but they became convergent to assure the spiritual dominion of the new territory. It is important to point out that these reasonings provided the moral and legal support for the conquests and the integration of peoples of the territory into Christianity, as well as having provided credence for colonization strategies of the Iberian crowns. Thus, the works of Hugo Grotius (*De iure belli ac pacis),*[15] Saint Thomas Aquinas (Summa Teologica),[16] Francisco Vitoria (*De indis et De jure*

---

[11] See e.g. Aníbal (2005).

[12] Between 1850 and 1916, five million Europeans left their continent of origin, and 80% of these were destined for the Americas. Most of these people had been relegated to social vulnerability by the double revolution that had been taking place in Europe since the middle of the eighteenth century and saw the chance to obtain better living conditions on their way to a new continent.

[13] For more about the indigenous peoples conflicts with the Europeans, see e.g. Schwarcz and Starling (2019).

[14] Vieira (1998).

[15] Grotius (2005).

[16] Thomas (1265).

belli),[17] Francisco Suárez (*De legibus*)[18] and Padre Antônio Vieira (in Portuguse, *Sermão da Sexagésima*)[19] are fundamental to understand how the natural law and the state domination given by the value-based public international law order had as the main goal mediating between the indigenous peoples and the Europeans during the age of America's colonization. Thus, the law between nations (*jus inter gentes*), understood as an element proper to the international community in substitution for the Christian community, was accepted for the inclusion of the barbarians[20] to the *communitas christiana*. The contents of the *De indis et De jure belli*, as well as Bartolomeu de Las Casas[21] 'removes the indigenous from the Aristotelian justified natural slavery'[22] when Vitoria states 'that the indigenous are not insane, but in their own way they have ratione, which brought up the humanity status for the indigenous peoples'.[23] The base of the neotomistic principle discussion would years later, by the early drafts of the Constitutions in some countries of the Americas and also the public policies adopted by the governments, undergird assumptions that the indigenous are not to be conceived as citizens but as individuals that require guardianship. Thus, as the colonization process in Brazil had an inherent relationtionship to the land tenure regulations and the inclusion of the indigenous peoples in the fundamental rights, years later this would lead to an alteration of the relationship between indigenous peoples and Brazil.[24]

The second moment is the period of dictatorship in Brazil, when, the indigenous peoples were already mentioned in the Constiution Bill, encountered several violations of their rights. The period of 1964 until 1985 recorded over 8000 fatalities among indigenous peoples'[25] and saw the beginning of the construction of projects of national interests such as 'the construction of the Transamazon Highway, the idealization of the Belo Monte hydroelectric dam, the construction of the Itaipu hydroelectric dam, the Perimetral Norte highway, the imprisonment and use of indigenous labor and the sale of indigenous goods'.[26]

The Figueiredo Repport, (in Portuguese, *Relatório Figueiredo*), a document written by Jader de Figueiredo Correia, a federal attorney, reported several violations of human rights: human hunts, deliberate inoculations of smallpox in isolated villages, donations of sugar mixed with strychnine—a poison, among others cruel

---

[17] Francisco (1532).

[18] Suárez (1612).

[19] Vieira (1998).

[20] Medeiros and Regiani (2018), p. 71; Júnior and Tanagino (2020).

[21] Casas (1992).

[22] Aristotle (1981), p. 12.

[23] Vitoria (2016), p. 58.

[24] The blood-brotherhood was considered to be the closest idea of a treaty and a contract. Alexandrowicz (1973).

[25] Government BF (2014) Comissão da Verdade 'Violações aos Direitos dos Povos Indígenas'.

[26] Demetrio and Kozicki (2019).

acts directed against the indigenous peoples.[27] The report features numerous pages detailing the breadths of violations. The violations were discovered as part of the work of the Brazilian Truth Commission (in Portuguse, *Comissão Nacional da Verdade*), a temporary official body set up to investigate human rights violations committed by the Brazilian state during the dictatorship.

In this period, the Brazilian government adopted an integrationist regime with regard to indigenous peoples, in which being indigenous was considered a transitory characteristic that should be overcome at same point. This understanding was contrary to the idea of the collective rights of indigenous peoples, as would emerge soon after.

The last and third moment was the adoption of the Constitution of 1988, which laid the normative foundations for indigenous peoples' legal definition and declared self-determination and cultural rights as fundamental rights. Thus, under the Brazilian legal system, indigenous peoples have thus gone from being considered as slaves, via a transitional social category until today, being entitled to rights.

Nowadays, there are 896,917 indigenous persons in Brazil, distributed among 305 ethnic groups. There are about 274 languages. Among indigenous persons over the age of five, only 37.4% speak an indigenous language, while 76.9% speak Portuguese. Regarding to the rural areas, there are 502,783 individuals and 315,180 who live in urban zones. Currently, there are some 713 indigenous areas, with a total area of 117,387,341 hectares, which means that 13.8% of the lands in the country have been reserved for indigenous peoples.[28]

4.2.2 The Context of Resource Exploitation

The consolidation of resource exploitation in Brazil is reflected in the relationship of territory entitlement, soil and subsoil with the rights and lives of indigenous peoples. Over time, the legal system adapted the laws in order to facilitate exploration of soil and subsoil. There are also few moments in history that determine the route taken to explore the natural resources.

Resource exploitation in Brazil began during the Colonial period, specifically in the aftermath of the Tordesilhas Treaty, when the Portuguese seized the opportunity to exploit the existence of natural resources such as gold and wood by stipulating the division of the territory into hereditary captaincies[29] (In Portuguese, *capitanias hereditárias*), as a way to economically distribute the land among the owners of the land (In Portuguese, *senhores da terra, da religião, do Estado, do dia-a-dia*).[30]

---

[27] Figueiredo Correia J de, *Relatório Figueiredo*, No. CI154/67, 1968.

[28] (2012) Os indígenas no Censo Demográfico 2010 primeiras considerações com base no quesito cor ou raça.

[29] Schwarcz and Starling (2019).

[30] Do Salvador (1627).

Today, the first period analyzed, is known as the beginning of the economic exploitation by Portugal[31] of its colonies and its attempts to enslave the indigenous, via forced marriages and catechesis. The vast lands of the new terra were distributed among few powerful individuals who, as extension of Portugal, wielded governmental powers.[32] The first system of occupation and colonial administration had the objective to provide better organization for the occupation of the territory[33] and had its end by the beginning of the nineteenth century, specifically in 1808 when the Portuguese Royal Family arrived in Brazil in order to announce the United Kingdom of Portugal, Brazil and the Algarves.[34] This is the period when the exploitation of the resources was focused on the wood (*pau-brasil, jacarandá*, among others) and the growth of sugar (in Portuguse, *cana de açúcar*).[35]

The second period analyzed is when D. Pedro I, in 1822, promulgated the freedom of Brazil from Portugal and instituted the country as the Republican state of Brazil,[36] at a time when there was still the commercialization of slaves, woods, and spices such as sugar and tabbaco. Equally important is the Law *Eusébio de Queiró's*, signed in 1850, which prohibited the trade of the slavery and in 1888 when Queen Isabel signed the Law abolishing slavery in Brazil.[37] However, as there was the Law of Lands (in Portuguese, *Lei das Terras*),[38] which was still ensuring that the latifundium owners continued prevailing, as it had the hidden intention to prevent the possession of the land to those who bought their own freedom;[39] in other words, those that had the document, in Portuguese, *Carta de Alforria,* and were not slaves anymore. The Law 'provides on the vacant lands in the Empire, and on those possessed by sesmaria title without fulfilling the legal conditions'[40] and is an expression that the land was still being relevant as a source for exploitation.

The period of Brazil's First Republic lasted from 1889 until 1930, and the predominant resource exploitation during this time was in mining, latex and coffee.[41] As a matter of fact, the end of the nineteenth century saw an end to the understanding of the indigenous peoples as a work force, but rather witnessed the ascent of the purpose of territorial conquest for the use of local soils and subsoils.[42] Indigenous labour remained important only as local and transitory alternative such as

[31] Ibid.

[32] See e.g. Schwarcz (2019); Schwarcz (2017).

[33] Do Salvador (1627), p. 42.

[34] Gomes (2014).

[35] See e.g. Furtado (2007); Schwarcz and Starling (2015).

[36] Gomes (2010).

[37] See e.g. Freyre (2006); Freyre (2004); Holanda (2012); Schwarcz (1993); Schwarcz (2012).

[38] (1850) Disposes of the vacant lands of the Empire.

[39] Thus, the slaves had to get money in order to buy their freedom. See e.g. Schwarcz and Starling (2015); Nequete (1988).

[40] (1850) Disposes of the vacant lands of the Empire.

[41] Schwarcz and Starling (2019).

[42] Cunha (2012).

a work force to the 'extraction of natural rubber from the western Amazon while immigration of workers coming from the northeastern of Brazil had not been established'.[43]

The last period analyzed is from the twentieth century on, as the extractivism developed into new forms of exploitation of wealth,[44] among which numbers coffee, cane, rubber, cattle, mining, construction of highways roads and, more recently, the building of hydroelectric dams. The expansion saw the advance of the agricultural frontier; the growing need to build hydroelectric dams and exploit mineral resources was characterized by the aggressive way in which companies pursued their aims, as they used the exploitation of natural resources to become competitive in national and world markets.[45]

Albeit, as a result, all forms of exploitation have consequences, especially with regard to environmental degradation.[46] The preoccupation over environmental damages caused by the exploitation of natural resources today feeds into international efforts to develop and enforce legislation to prevent climate change,[47] such as the Reducing Emissions from Deforestation and Forest Degradation, also known as REDD+ and other measures.[48]

Besides the environmental issues, Brazil became also more attentive to indigenous peoples' rights in general, starting with the Constitution of 1988, which changed the paradigm of the relationship between the indigenous peoples and the government.[49]

---

[43] Ibid., p. 57.

[44] See e.g Brown (2018); Galeano (1997).

[45] See e.g Santos de Almeida (2015).

[46] See e.g. Browder (1992); Raftopoulos (2017); McKay (2017).

[47] About that: 'traditional communities are highly vulnerable to the impacts of climate change, especially given the connection with nature and its territory. Despite this, traditional knowledge has been recognized as relevant to a better design of climate policies. Furthermore, they bring to the fore that, despite the potential to foster the protection of traditional communities from climate change impacts and to assure the integration of their knowledge into resilience policymaking, the role of law is scantly referred to in articles and the Paris Agreement has not exerted significant influence in the development of new studies with this approach'. Iocca and Fidélis (2021). Thus, 'Indigenous peoples are among the first to face the direct consequences of climate change, due to their dependence upon, and close relationship, with the environment and its resources. Climate change exacerbates the difficulties already faced by indigenous communities including political and economic marginalization, loss of land and resources, human rights violations, discrimination and unemployment'.Department of Economic and Social Affairs Indigenous Peoples (2012) The effects of climate change on indigenous peoples.

[48] For more, see e.g.: Hanschel (2007); Bastos Lima et al. (2017); Schulz (2020).

[49] 'The contact between southern the indigenous peoples Jê with the non-indigenous began in the XVI century, in a mild and rare way, generated from the expansion fronts printed by the Portuguese Crown, these being attempts of catechization by the clergy, in addition to the Paulista flags, which were military expeditions originating from the Captaincy of São Paulo with the objective of exploring the territory and acquiring indigenous captives to be used as slave labor. There are therefore two different indigenous in the 19th Century: the good savage Tupi-Guarani (conveniently a dead indian) who is a symbol of nationality, and a living one who was the object of the

4.2.3 Resource Exploitation in Indigenous Peoples' Territory

Indigenous peoples' societies depend upon the lands, territories and natural resources that they traditionally use. The term, traditional use, can be understood as a construction that was established before the normative form of the major law which in the American continent starts with the signing of the Constitution of the United States on 17 September of 1787. The citizenship and the fundamental rights can be found written in the draft of the Bill: 'we the people of the United States, in order to form a more perfect union, establish justice, insure domestic tranquility, provide for the common defense, promote the general welfare, and secure the blessings of liberty to ourselves and our posterity, to ordain and establish this Constitution for the United States of America'[50] and further that 'the citizens of each state shall be entitled to all privileges and immunities of citizens in the several states'.[51] In the historical point of view, it was the first draft of a Constitution in the north of the American continent that acknowledged indigenous peoples for the purpose 'to regulate commerce with foreign nations, and among the several states, and with the indigenous tribes'.[52]

The first draft of a Constitution in the south of the Americas dates back to 1917, when the United States of Mexico signed the draft saying that 'in the United Mexican States, all individuals shall be entitled to the human rights granted by this Constitution and the international treaties signed by the Mexican state, as well as to the guarantees for the protection of these rights. Such human rights shall not be restricted or suspended, except for the cases and under the conditions established by this Constitution itself".[53] It also stipulates that 'the nation is multicultural, based originally on its indigenous peoples, described as descendants of those inhabiting the country before colonization and that preserve their own social, economic, cultural and political institutions, or some of them. Consciousness of indigenous identity will be the fundamental criteria to determine to whom apply the provisions on indigenous people. An indigenous community is defined as the community that constitutes a

Anthropology. In the context of the state of Brazil, the Brazilian federal government interest in projects are placed as strategic to the large projects to be installed with the hydroelectric plants, ports, mining and highways roads as a resource exploitation mainly in the western region of Brazil. By the time of the military dictatorship (1964–1986), there were profound conflicts among indigenous people, squatters, miners, landowners and entrepreneurs for the use and ownership of their traditional lands. During this period, the II National Development Plan formulated for the year of 1975 until 1979 was created, which considered it necessary to stimulate the development of the region. In 1978, the then Minister of the Interior Rangel Reis sought to get the so-called "Emancipation Decree" accepted. It was a matter of distinguishing between "forest dwellers", understood as Indians who lived according to their "traditions", and "acculturated" Indians, who were already conforming to the customs of most Brazilians and should be emancipated'. Cunha (2018), p. 429.

[50] (1787) Constitution of the United States of America.

[51] Ibid.

[52] Ibid.

[53] (1917) Constitution of the United States of Mexico.

cultural, economic and social unit settled in a territory and that recognizes its own authorities, according to their customs. Indigenous peoples' right to self-determination shall be subjected to the Constitution in order to guarantee national unity. States' and federal district's constitutions and laws must recognize indigenous peoples and communities, taking into account the general principles established in the previous paragraphs, as well as ethnic-linguistic and land settlement criteria'.[54] Regarding title to territory, it states: 'Attain with preferential use of the natural resources of the sites inhabited by their indigenous communities, except for the strategic resources defined by this Constitution. The foregoing rights shall be exercised respecting the forms of property ownership and land possession established in this Constitution and in the laws on the matter as well as respecting third parties' rights. To achieve these goals, indigenous communities may form partnerships under the terms established by the law'.[55]

Futhermore, the literature on the colonization period and the title to territory frames the issue of indigenous peoples' claims to land tenure according to the fundamental rights perspective.[56]

Moreover, already here first foundations were laid for indigenous peoples' right to consultation: the treaties concerned the rights of the inhabitants of the territory or 'historically, it precides the treaties',[57] meaning that indigenous peoples mantained consultation among themselves already during the pre-colonization period. The requirement of consultation was thus 'grounded in the time immemorial right of indigenous peoples to sovereignty and domination over their territories, and is integral to the historical assertion of title of territory under international law, testifies to its indispensable role in the pursuit of indigenous self-determination'.[58] The consultation emanates from their self-determination, their customs and traditional lands feeding into their decision-making, which goes beyond the human rights translating into another way to affirm their self-determination rights.

4.3 The Role of Self-Determination and Cultural Rights in Legitimizing the Requirement of Consultation with Indigenous Peoples

This subchapter addresses legislation of the role of the fundamental rights of self-determination and cultural rights, as in Article 231 of the Brazilian Constitution, in legitimizing the requirement to consultation with indigenous peoples, as in the ILO Convention No. 169 to be analyzed after words.

---

[54] Ibid.

[55] Ibid. *translated by author.*

[56] See e.g. Anaya (2004); Piovesan (2019); Trindade (2015); Xanthaki (2014); Doyle (2016); Thornberry (1991); Mignolo (2011); MacKay (2002).

[57] Clavero (2008), p. 5, *translated by author.*

[58] Doyle (2016), pp. 15–16.

First of all, the Brazilian legal system can be described as a set of rules brought together by a unifying element, which are the axiological elements of the Constitution, the higher legal document which contains the fundamental rights.[59] Brazil is one of the countries influenced by the Romano-Germanic tradition, having the civil law model as the structural basis of its legal system. The legal system, thus, has always had its basis established on the norms, in a broad sense, being the written law as the most important source of the law.[60] The Brazilian Constitution of 1988 expressly reveals the Romano-Germanic origin which was strongly influenced by the positivist legal theory. Even so, the Law of Introduction to the Rules of Brazilian Law, in its Article 4, states that 'when the law might be omitted, the judge will decide the case according to the analogy, the customs and the general principles of law'.[61]

It happens that the legal system, inserted in the world of cultural exchange and globalization, experienced the impact of the already mentioned movement of approximation between the models of the common law and the civil law.[62] That is, the Brazilian reality was not unaware of the trend of changes and adaptations of the legal system, so that a process of relaxation of the positivist rigidity typical of the civil law in favor of a greater autonomy of the judiciary in the interpretation of the laws and appreciation of judicial precedents as a source of law is observed.

Historically, the jurisprudence in Brazil, as in the other nations adopting the *civil law system*, did not have great relevance, functioning only as a tool of literature and persuasion, of moral value. The norm which regulated the creation of another norm is the higher, the norm created in conformity with the former is the lower one.[63] The legal order was not a system of coordinated norms of equal level, but a 'hierarchy of different levels of legal norms'.[64]

This scenario of approximation between the two systems becomes more evident with the phenomenon that the literature calls as the constitutionalisation of the law (in German, *Völkerrechtliche Nebenverfassungen*).[65] Thus, the *civil law* model adopted by the Brazilian legal order, although still having the written law as it is main source, experienced modifications aiming to adapt to the new realities and needs. It brings with it the idea of the normative strength of the constitution, as it is the foundation and limit of the entire legal system.

Thus, this next section will discuss the corpus legis involving the Constitution drafts, the Constitution and the ILO Convention No. 169, the Civil Code, the Decree of the National Policy for Territorial and Environmental Management of Indigenous

[59] See e.g Barroso (2020).

[60] Ibid.

[61] (1988) Constitution of Brazil.

[62] See e.g. Didier Jr et al. (2015); Gomes (2018).

[63] Sampaio Ferraz Jr. (2017).

[64] Kelsen (2005), p. 221.

[65] See e.g. Pernice (2002); Preuss (1994); Alexy and Rivers (2010); Neves (2009); Uerpmann (2003).

Lands, the FUNAI, the Federal Prosecutor Office and the discussion towards the legal validity of the indigenous peoples' Protocols.

4.3.1 The Brazilian Constitution Drafts

Brazil had in total seven different Constitutional drafts and in all of them the legislators reflected the particular historical moment that the country was in. [66] However, regarding indigenous peoples' rights, there are two drafts of the Constitution that mention indigenous peoples and their fundamental rights. It all began with the Federal Constitution of 1934[67] and the Constitution of 1988[68] that introduced citizenship for indigenous peoples and their entitlement as legal entities to hold rights.

The regulatory framework for the right of indigenous peoples to lands of traditional occupation has been stable over the centuries, beginning with the Portuguse royal charter of 1st April 1680—later ratified by the Law of 6th June 1755—which had established the principle of land entitlement.

Article 129 of the Constitution of 1934 was the first one that regulated the issues related to indigenous peoples, providing for the protection of lands where they were permanently located. All subsequent constitutional texts also expressedly recognized their right to the enjoyment of the lands (but not entitlement of land rights), such was in the Article 54 of the draft of the Constitution of 1937, Article 216 of the Constitution of 1946 and the Article 186 of the Constitution of 1967. It should be noted, however, that the clarity of the normative treatment given to the matter was not sufficient to guarantee the efficacy of indigineous peoples' rights. There are several historical records that narrate the most diverse types of violence practiced against the first inhabitants of Brazil, including the expulsion from their lands and the extermination of anyone who resisted the civilizing project of European colonization. For example, the "indigenous searcher" was a work that was mentioned in the Law of 26th July 1596, in the Law of 9th April of 1655 and in the Rules of Missions dating back to 1686, always in the sense of being someone in charge of requesting justice on behalf of the indigenous.

The concept of "relative civil capacity" (in Portuguese, *relativamente incapaz*) was conditioned by the 'low scope of civilization' of the indigenous, and the related legal regime of guardianship, materialized, in a systematized manner, in Decree

[66]To see more of the historical documents of the previsous Constitutions: (1824) Constituição Política do Império do Brazil; (1934) Constituição da República dos Estados Unidos do Brasil; (1937) Constituição dos Estados Unidos do Brasil; (1946) Constituição dos Estados Unidos do Brasil; (1964) Constituição da República do Brasil; (1891) Constituição da República dos Estados Unidos do Brasil.

[67](1934) Constituição da República dos Estados Unidos do Brasil.*translated by author.*

[68](1988) Constitution of Brazil. *translated by author.*

No. 5.484 of 27th June 1928, which regulated the situation of the indigenous peoples that were born on the Brazilian national territory.

Along these lines, the indigenous peoples' policy developed until the advent of the last draft of the Bill of Constitution, in 1988. The idea was in order to make the Brazilian society into one whole, incorporating the indigenous peoples into a process was considered as "civilization". Furthermore, there was the intention of integrating them into the dynamics of the society involved and stripping them of their collective characteristics.

Indigenous peoples' fundamental rights, in this context, were not seen from the standpoint of fundamental community rights. The right to territory, although guaranteed to indigenous peoples in successive normative legal drafts, and, from 1934, in constitutional texts, was not linked to the recognition of other rights to them, but was more related to an idea of territorial confinement of the indigenous peoples by the legal order expanding the occupation of the national territory and the economic development, rather than to guarantee their uses of land according to the indigenous peoples' customs and own forms of social organization.

4.3.1.1 The Brazilian Federal Constitution as of 1988

Brazil has a broad range of traditional communities. According to the latest census by the Brazilian Institute of Geography and Statistics (hereinafter, the IBGE), the indigenous peoples are 0.4% of the Brazilian population. They are distributed in 505 indigenous people's lands, which occupies 12.5% of the national territory.[69] In spite of the not so large segment in relation to the total Brazilian population, the indigenous peoples present immense sociodiversity. Another group part of the traditional communities in Brazil are the Afro-Descendents communites (in Portuguese, *quilombolas*), for instance, there are about 5972 quilombolas communities.[70] According to a study by the Federal Prosecutor Office, 650,234 Brazilian families declare themselves as part of the traditional community.[71]

Thus, the 1988 Brazilian Constitution Bill, recognized for extending individual rights (hereinafter, in Portuguese, the *Constituição Cidadã*), was innovative by devoting an entire chapter to indigenous peoples' rights. The new constitutional order, in addition to reaffirming centuries of the invisibility of the right of the indigenous peoples to traditional territory, titled and valued the right of indigenous peoples to their cultures, self-determination and traditions. Regarding the legal capacity, differently of the previous Constitutions drafts, the legislation in Brazil understands indigenous peoples defined as of pre-Columbian origin that distinguish

[69] (2012) Os indígenas no Censo Demográfico 2010 primeiras considerações com base no quesito cor ou raça.

[70] (IBGE) IB de G e E (2020) Information Base on Indigenous Peoples and Quilombolas | Indigenous and Quilombolas 2019.

[71] Paulo (2019).

themselves in society as a whole and among themselves, with their own identity and organization, specific cosmovision and special relationship with the land they inhabit.[72] The indigenous is the individual who considers himself/herself to belong to a people or community, and is recognized as such by its members.[73] The indigenous community is a local human group, part of one or more indigenous peoples' groupings with an autonomous organization.[74]

The indigenous organizations are characterized as a legal entity under private law, which include one or more indigenous communities or one or more indigenous peoples.[75] The indigenous communities have legal personality and their existence is independent of registration or any act of the government and will be represented judicially and extrajudicially according to their uses, customs and traditions.[76]

Under the IAHRS, for instance, the IACtHR notes that recognition of the legal personality of individual members of the community is necessary for the enjoyment of other rights, such as the right to life, cultural rights, self-determination and personal integrity.[77]

The same can be seen in other jurisdictions such as the African Human Rights System.[78] Same in the international treaty of the UNDRIP which is not ratified in the Brazilian legal system but still represents a source of soft law which: 'recognizing and reaffirming that indigenous individuals are entitled without discrimination to all human rights recognized in international law, and that indigenous peoples possess collective rights which are indispensable for their existence, well-being and integral development as peoples'.[79]

The 1988 Constitution Bill regulated the main aspects of the right to entitlement to territory with the objectives of recovering, preserving and safeguarding the indigenous rights observing the rights of the future generations. Prior to the first drafts of the Brazilian Constitution, the indigenous peoples were under the tutelage of Brazil. Deprived of any fundamental rights, the expected path was a gradual

[72](1988) Constitution of Brazil.

[73]Comissão Nacional de Política Indigenista P da (2009) Draft Bill 'Estatuto dos Povos Indígenas'.

[74]Ibid.

[75]Ibid.

[76]Ibid.

[77]Inter-American Commission of Human Rights, *Saramaka People v. Suriname*, Case No 172, Judgment of 28 November 2007.

[78]This case was the first judgment from the African Commission on Human and Peoples' Rights to address the rights of indigenous peoples and their claims to land and natural resources. The relevance is also regarding the violation of the right to development and that the decision establishes an important precedent. The decion ensured the indigenous peoples the equity and participation in natural resource management and development on their entiled territory. See e.g. African Commission on Human and Peoples' Rights, *Centre for Minority Rights Development, Minority Rights Group International and Endorois Welfare Council (On Behalf Of the Endorois Community) v Kenya*, 276/2003, Judgment of 25 November 2009.

[79](2007) The United Nations Declaration on the Rights of Indigenous Peoples.

assimilation by the rest of the Brazilian population.[80] This governmental choice prevented the indigenous peoples from engaging with the political decision-making process according to their real needs.

Albeit more narrowly than other countries in Latin America, Brazil has two Articles devoted to indigenous peoples' fundamental rights and they both have their efficacy limited to other infra-legal norms. The Constitution recognizes the traditional land rights of the indigenous peoples in Brazil, however, the federal union is the one responsible to demarcate the territory. They are responsible for the exclusive enjoyment (in Portuguse, *posse*) of the riches of the soil, rivers and lakes existing on them.[81] They are inalienable and unavailable lands because they are destined for the future generations as well. The rights over them are imprescriptible, so that the aggressions that have victimized them for centuries do not seal their fate and make the damage caused to them irredemable.[82]

The Constitution, thus, recognizes that the enjoyment of the indigenous peoples over their lands is not related to a physical matter of mere apprehension of an asset, nor it is identified with the notion of private property. In the current model, more than in any other, the enjoyment of terriory in order to be guaranteed to the indigenous peoples is directed to their physical survival and to the preservation of their cultural right. Today, indigenous peoples have recognition of their social organization, customs and traditions, and the 1988 Constitution considers that they have legitimacy and do not have the tutelage to claim for their rights.

The conceptualization of the traditional ocupied lands in Brazil dated backt to the Constitution of the 1988 as well as the Decree No.6040 of 2007.[83] Thus, the Article 231 of the Constitution maintains that 'the indigenous peoples have the right of the land that they traditionally occupy'.[84]

Along with other provisions, the Constitution defines the traditonal lands as 'occupied by the indigenous are those permanently inhabited by them, those used for their productive activities, those indispensable for the preservation of the environmental resources necessary for their well-being and those necessary for their physical and cultural reproduction, according to their habits, customs and traditions'.[85]

In addition to the constitutional text, other international legal instruments guarantee the need to consent of indigenous peoples to carry out activities on their lands, such as Article 8, J, of the CBD, and Articles 6 and 15 of the ILO No. 169.

---

[80] Cunha (2012).

[81] (1988) Constitution of Brazil.

[82] Ibid.; Krenak (1987); Cunha (2018).

[83] The Decree nstituted the National Policy for the Sustainable Development of Traditional Peoples and Communities and recognizes, as such, riverine communities, babaçu coconut breakers, grassroots communities, gypsies, extractivist populations, among others. (2007) Decree that institutes the National Policy for the Sustainable Development of Traditional Peoples and Communities.

[84] (1988) Constitution of Brazil.

[85] Article 231 §1 ibid.

4.3.1.2 The Public Hearings and the Constitutional Hearings

The legislation offers some possibilities of improving the participation of indigenous peoples in the process. Both public hearings and constitutional hearings are legal tools for the indigenous peoples to be heard, applied within a different situation as they are two processes of a diverse legal characterization that are not related to the requirement of consultation. The constitutional hearing can be legally characterized as a form of consultation that was established even before the ILO Convention No. 169, which was 'a legal figure totally unique in the continent, which grants the legislative Branch a fundamental role in the interlocution of the state with the indigenous peoples regarding the exploitation of natural resources specifically from indigenous lands'.[86] Thus, Article 231 stipulates a type of consultation, the constitutional hearing. It can be considered as a daring choice for the Constiution or a way to protect the territory of the Federal Union. Once the constitutional hearing is foreseen by the constitutional text, therefore, the indigenous peoples are entitled to the public hearing, in case they are the major targets of the social and environmental impacts.

The lands have the destination of *posse permanente* and they have the 'exclusive tenure of the soil, rivers and lakes'.[87] However, the use of water resources, including energy potentials, research and the mining of mineral wealth on indigenous lands can only be carried out with the authorization of the National Congress, after consulting with the affected communities, with their 'participation in the results of the mining in accordance with the law'.[88]

The constitutional hearing of the National Congress should authorize, or not, a hydroelectric or mining enterprise that exploits the natural resources in the territory of the federal union. It is also worth considering that the Constitution makes clear that the hearing must be conducted directly by the government with the communities and not by the companies that are conducting the project.

In regard to how the hearing should be carried out, it is stated that it shall preferably take place within the indigenous territory itself, as this will give them a better chance to verify the social, political and economic conditions of the locals, directly evaluate its impacts and hear the opinion of more indigenous peoples that are affected by the project.

The National Congress stresses that it is relevant to check each factual situation,[89] in order to evaluate the rights and interests of the indigenous peoples and the

---

[86]Rojas Garzón et al. (2016), p. 31.

[87]Article 231 §2 (1988) Constitution of Brazil.

[88]Article 231 §3 ibid.*translated by author.*

[89]Thus, 'the regulation of mining on indigenous lands has been under discussion for almost twenty years in Congress. In a way, the subject fell asleep for a few years and was pushed back after the discovery of gemological diamonds in the Roosevelt Indigenous Land, of the Cinta Larga indigenous people. This indigenous peoples territory comprises one of the four villages that make up the Arupuanã Indigenous Park, an area demarcated between the states of Rondônia and Mato Grosso, with approximately 1,500 indigenous. Despite the illegality of the mining activity carried out on

necessity of the practice of those activities, recognizing that the principle of the indigenous peoples' interests is the one that should prevail and then, the National Congress can authorize the project or not.[90]

On the other hand, the public hearing is also established by the Constitution but has a different goal. The Environmental Impact Study (hereinafter, the EIA) is an enviromental licence and it is mandatory for any activity with the potential to generate socio-environmental damage, so it is necessary that it occurs before a mining activity is carried out on indigenous land, together with the Environmental Impact Statement (hereinafter, the RIMA), jointly known as the EIA/RIMA. The RIMA is the concluding report containing the definitions of the technical terms of the analyses of the EIA. The environmental impact assessment is also a constitutional matter, provided for in Art. 225, § 1, Subsection IV of the Federal Constitution, which determines that a prior environmental impact study must be conducted for the installation in the country of works or activities that potentially cause significant environmental degradation.[91] After this phase is concluded, the FUNAI is going to conduct the, in Portuguese, *Estudo do Componente Indígena* (hereinafter, the ECI), a report to identify and analyze the impacts of the project on indigenous territory, in its environmental and social aspects, in accordance with the Decree No. 02 of 2015 (in Portuguese, *Instrução Normativa).*[92]

They both are absolutely essential as the indigenous communities depend on the ecological balance of their entitled land. The legislation states in Article 1: 'for the purpose of this Resolution, any change in the physical, chemical and biological properties of the environment caused by any form of matter or energy resulting from human activities that directly or indirectly affect the environment is considered an environmental impact. I—the health, safety and well-being of the population; II—social and economic activities; III—biota; IV—the aesthetic and sanitary conditions of the environment; V—the quality of environmental resources'.[93] The EIA should also inform the National Congress of the medium and long-term effects of the project, because depending on the conditions and intensity in which it is carried out, the project might put 'at complete risk and may result in the depletion of underground resources, to the detriment of future generations'.[94]

---

indigenous lands, the Cinta Larga people, from practically the first contact with the surrounding society, suffer incursions of non-indigenous garimpeiros on their lands. With a subsoil rich in cassiterite, diamonds and other minerals, the indigenous people were establishing conflicting relations with the invaders and with the so-called development projects that were installed in the region. With the news of the diamond, some 5,000 miners went to the vicinity of the indigenous land, as well as speculators, smugglers and mining companies who are pressing for regulation of the matter'. Curi (2007).

[90] See e.g. Da Silva (2020); Canotilho et al. (2018); Barroso (2020).

[91] (1988) Constitution of Brazil.

[92] (FUNAI) INF (2015) Decree 'instrução Normativa'.

[93] (1986) CONAMA Decree No. 01 for general guidelines for environmental impact assessment.

[94] Curi (2007), p. 237.

It is important to note that it is also necessary to have an anthrophological study of the uses, customs and traditions of the indigenous peoples, and on how the project can impact and generate consequences for their entitled lands. It is also up to the anthropological report to provide the mitigating measures and estimating the financial burden which should be the responsibility of the company conducting the project.

Another relevant actor in the process is the Brazilian Environmental Agency, the CONAMA (hereinafter, the CONAMA). The Decree No. 9 of 1990 has an administrative nature and it regards the public hearing. Article 1 states that: 'the public hearing has the goal to be addressed to the parties interested and it referres to RIMA, solving doubts and gathering information about the environmental licensing'.[95] Article 2 explains that the public hearing will be promoted by the Environment Agency 'whenever deemed necessary, or when requested by a civil entity, by the Public Prosecution Service, or by 50 or more citizens'.[96] The CONAMA Decree No. 237 of 1997 outlines the main types of projects that are subject to environmental licensing and stipulates that a public hearing should be conducted when appropriate, in accordance with relevant regulations.[97]

The best criteria for choosing the company to be authorized to research or conduct national exploitation on the indigenous land is the administrative process, in Portuguese, *licitação*.[98] It is believed that this process is necessary not only to 'ensure that mining on indigenous land is carried out by a company with the best technical skills, but also to ensure that it is carried out by the company that presents the best proposals for environmental preservation and aims to minimize the impact on indigenous communities'.[99]

Artcile 225 stipulates that 'the person who exploits mineral resources is obliged to recover the degraded environment, in accordance with the technical solution required by the competent public body, in the form of the law'.[100] In order to prevent environmental degradation from occurring on indigenous lands, a monetary deposit of a certain amount may be prescribed in a contract for the recovery of the degraded environment. This deposit mechanism has for example also been adopted in

---

[95] (1990) CONAMA Decree No. 9: Provides on the holding of Public Hearings in the environmental licensing process.

[96] Ibid.

[97] (1997) 'Resolução' No. 237 of CONAMA.

[98] Licitação is the Portuguese word for the legal process in which the government negociates regarding the works, services, including advertising, purchases, sales, concessions, permissions and leases when contracted with third parties. This process will necessarily be preceded by bidding, subject to the hypotheses foreseen in this Law (1993) Law that regulates the Article 37, XXI of the Federal Constitution by establishing the rules for bids and contracts of the Brazilian Public Administration.

[99] Santilli (1993).

[100] § 2 (1988) Constitution of Brazil.

Newfoundland[101] in Canada and can serve as a guarantee for the country's indigenous communities that will have to support mining on their lands.

Article 232 states that 'the indigenous peoples, their communities and their organizations are legitimate parties that can pettition in court in case their rights are violated'.[102] The organizations can also petition with the indigenous peoples. Recently, the fact that the indigenous peoples of Brazil have been represented by Brazilian entities, such as *Articulação dos Povos Indígenas do Brasil* (hereinafter, the Apib), represents a break with the legal obstacle that existed before regarding guardianship, overcoming the coloniality of law and reaffirming that all are equal and subject to the law.[103] Relevant to note is here that neither the regime of institutional autonomy nor the self-organizational jurisdiction is guaranteed by the Constitution. In that sense, 'because these territories do not behave as true jurisdictions, the *saneamiento* has not been accompanied by an equivalent process of reflection and reconstruction of their own instances for dispute settlement, increasing levels of institutional autonomy in exercising their own justice, and gradual retrieval of legal practices'.[104]

The question of representativeness within the indigenous or tribal community is also a fundamental issue. Sometimes the hearing is done only through the Chief of the community, in view of their self-organization and respect for their leaders. In that case, the indigenous peoples' Protocols might be a relevant tool to indicate the representative.

In the case of the constitutional hearing, the Brazilian National Congress can directly consult the indigenous communities or delegate consultation to other public bodies, even the Executive Branch. Such delegation is even recommended by the principle of administrative efficiency and practicability, as the executive organs such as the FUNAI, the IBAMA and the Chico Mendes Institute for Biodiversity (hereinafter, the ICMBio) have a better understanding of their cultural identity, in accordance with the CONAMA No. 237 of 1997. An important caveat needs to be added given that the National Congress can only delegate to a governmental organ but not to the private company that is going to conduct the resource exploitation project.

[101] See e.g. Joan K (2005) Canadian Mining Law and the Impacts on Indigenous Peoples Lands and Resources.

[102] Article 323 (1988) Constitution of Brazil.

[103] 'The amicus curiae brief, although known in Roman law, has reached its fullest development under the common law system. The Inter-American Court of Human Rights has accepted amicus briefs from the time of its first advisory opinion request even though al most all of its members are nationals of countries adhering to the civil law system. The European Court of Human Rights modified its Rules in 1983 to permit acceptance of amicus briefs'. Moyer C The role of the Amicus Curiae in the Inter- American Court of Human Rights. 8.

[104] Segato (2011), pp. 359–360.

4.3.2 *The International Labour Organization Convention No. 169*

Megaprojects of natural resource exploitation are very often launched without meaningful participation of all parties envolved. Frequently, these projects represent dire threats to indigenous peoples' rights and existence in the context of large-scale or high-impact development projects.[105] The requirement of consultation is the main legal instrument and it entered the Brazilian legal system after the ratification of the International Labour Convention No. 169 on 20th June 2002 by the Legislative Decree No. 143 of 2002,[106] having entered into force on 25th July 2003 by the Executive Decree No. 5.051 of 2004,[107] which was revoked by the Executive Decree No. 10.088 on 5th November 2019.[108] The Constitutional Amendment No. 45 in that matter reads: 'the international treaties and conventions on human rights that are approved, in each House of the National Congress, in two shifts, by three-fifths of the votes of the respective members, will be equivalent to the constitutional amendments'.[109]

As an international human rights treaty, the ILO Convention No. 169 has supralegal normative status as the interpretation that attributes the characteristic of supra-legality to human rights treaties and conventions seems more consistent. (...) human rights treaties would be infra-constitutional, but given their special character in relation to other international normative acts, they would also be endowed with an attribute of supra-legality, as does the Brazilian Supreme Court decision of 2008.[110] This means that not only any infra-constitutional legislative measure must comply with its provisions, but also that it constitutes an interpretative vector of constitutional norms themselves. It also implies that the requirement of consultation has immediate applicability, to traditional peoples and communities, as stipulated by the ILO Convention No. 169, following Article 5, paragraph 1 of the Federal Constitution, regardless of any additional regulation in order to achieve the effectiveness of the right.

The public policies for traditional communities are recent within the Brazilian state. In Brazil, the Decree No. 6040 of 2007 institutes the National Policy for the

---

[105] See e.g. (2019) Indigenous communities in Brazil protest threats to land and services. Dtsch. Welle; Indigenous peoples in Brazil. IWGIA - Int. Work Group Indig. Aff.; Demetrio and Kozicki (2019); Walker et al. (2016).

[106] (2002) Decree that approves the Convention No. 169 of the International Labour Organization on Indigenous and Tribal Peoples.

[107] (2004) Decree that enacts the International Labour Organization No. 169.

[108] (2019) Decree that consolidates the normative acts edited by the Brazilian Federal Executive Branch that provides for the promulgation of conventions and recommendations of the International Labor Organization ratified already.

[109] (2004) Constitutional Amendment.

[110] Justice Gilmar Mendes, Appeal "Recurso Extraordinário," No. No. 349.703-1 (Brazilian Supreme Court December 3, 2008).

Sustainable Development of Traditional Peoples and Communities. According to Article 1: 'Traditional Peoples and Communities are culturally differentiated and recognized groups that have their own forms of social organization, that occupy and use territories and natural resources as a condition for their cultural, social, religious, ancestral and economic reproduction, using knowledge, innovations and practices generated and transmitted by tradition'.[111]

In Brazil, the traditional communities are, in the Portuguese language: *quilombolas, ciganos, matriz africana, seringueiros, castanheiros, quebradeiras de coco-de-babaçu, comunidades de fundo de pasto, faxinalenses, pescadores artesanais, marisqueiras, ribeirinhos, varjeiros, caiçaras, praieiros, sertanejos, jangadeiros, ciganos, açorianos, campeiros, varzanteiros, pantaneiros, caatingueiros,* among others.[112]

The Constitution of 1988 together with the Decree No. 4887 of 2003, that regulates the procedure for identification, recognition, delimitation, demarcation and titling of land occupied by remnants of quilombola communities were important symbolic steps in order to recognize the rights of those communities, one of the traditional communities, to the demarcation of their lands and territories.[113] Yet despite the government commitment, as happened to the indigenous peoples' territory, 'the cumbersome and somewhat technical procedures mean that demarcation processes regularly take up to 6 years or more'.[114]

---

[111] (2007) Decree that institutes the National Policy for the Sustainable Development of Traditional Peoples and Communities.*translated by author*.

[112] CNDH (2018)

[113] Relevant to hightlight here is the Decree of 2015 which mentions the 'quilombola' territory and the parameters of the licensing. (2015) Decree 'Portaria Interministerial'. Equally relevant is the appeal ADI No. 3223 of 2020 in which reinforces the territorial rights of quilombola communities. Brazilian Supreme Court, *Appeal ' Ação Direta de Inconstitucionalidade"*, No. (ADI) 3239, Judgment of 19 December 2019.

[114] The Special Rappourteur also explains that: 'Indigenous peoples constitute a minority within Brazil. However, given the specific international legal framework developed for the rights of indigenous peoples, I will not focus on the situation of indigenous peoples in Brazil. Given this ethnic, racial and religious diversity, political discourse developed in the 20th century constructed the myth of Brazil as a 'racial democracy'. Yet while it is true that some groups who migrated to Brazil were able to enjoy social and economic success, other groups, most notably the Afro-Brazilians, remain marginalised due to historically rooted patterns of discrimination against them, stemming from centuries of slavery, and racism. Regrettably, some of these attitudes persist and are pervasive in many spheres of social and political life. Indeed, throughout my mission, I observed that Afro-Brazilians are rarely represented in key public and private positions, have lower socio-economic indicators, and are strongly affected by structural problems such as extreme poverty, racial discrimination, exclusion, and marginalization. Poverty in Brazil has a colour. Therefore, while afro-Brazilians do constitute a numerical majority in the country of Brazil with 51% of the population, they remain a political minority. For this reason, a large focus of my visit has been the situation of Afro-Brazilians, including traditional Quilombo communities and Terreiro African religious communities. I therefore view my mission as building upon the work of the United Nations Working Group of Experts on People of African Descent and their 2014 report on Brazil.' Izsák R, *Mission Statement United Nations Special Rapporteur on minority issues*, A/HRC/27/68/ Add.1, 2018.

The reasons are normally legal as the decisions made by INCRA take years and are stalled due to court claims.[115]

4.3.3 The Brazilian Statute Regarding Indigenous Peoples

The Brazilian government launched a Decree on 20th November 1889 in order to delegate the civil responsibility of the indigenous peoples in matter of legal aspects from the federal government to the state governments. For this purpose, the government also established the Ministry of Agriculture, Industry and Commerce, which had as one of its objectives to assist indigenous peoples' issues. In 1910, the Service for the Protection of Indigenous and the National Workers[116] was created to address indigenous issues in Brazil. The intention behind the Decree was to allocate the indigenous as a cheap labor to be exploited to become workers.[117] The strategy was to provide them with work opportunities and a minimum salary, such that they would not be dependend on their territory for subsistence, enabling further agricultural exploitation in surplus land areas.[118]

In 1918 the institution Service for the Protection of Indigenous and the National Workers was changed to Service of Protection of Indigenous. During the peak of the military dictatorship in Brazil (1964–1985),[119] then, there was the establishment of the same institution with a different name, by Law No. 5.371 of 5th December 1967. The indigenous were thus treated under their first legal statute, as strangers, taking the idea that they distinguish themselves and oppose the national interest—under a policy that did not even recognize them as full national Brazilian citizens.[120] In 1973, the Statute of the Indigenous Peoples (hereinafter, the Statute) was promulgated.

The Statute counts 68 Articles containing the legal parameters of the indigenous peoples' rights. With regard to civil and political rights, Article 6 states that 'the rules of Articles 145 and 146 of the Federal Constitution relating to nationality and

[115] In January of 2020, the federal government decided to transfer the demarcation of indigenous and quilombola lands to the Ministry of Agriculture, according to the National Federation of Quilombola Associations. The change made it even more difficult to demarcate the territories of the traditional peoples.

[116] (1910) Decree regarding the Indigenous Protection Service.

[117] Marcon (1994).

[118] Cunha (2012); Marcon (1994); (1910) Decree regarding the Indigenous Protection Service.

[119] 'The discourse of integration and assimilation would serve to legitimize, in the legal and theoretical fields, the usurpation of indigenous lands under the pretext of the loss of the identity of these peoples. Moreover, if the military dictatorship made practices of genocide and ethnocide a public policy, it is also true that mobilization and resistance actions took place'. Government BF (2014) Comissão da Verdade 'Violações aos Direitos dos Povos Indígenas'. *translated by author.*

[120] As another measure taken after the Figueiredo Report, the FUNAI was created in order to protect the indigenous peoples. See: Figueiredo Correia J de, *Relatório Figueiredo*, No. CI154/67, 1968.

citizenship shall apply to indigenous peoples. The exercise of civil and political rights by the indigenous peoples depends on the verification of the special conditions established in this Law and in the relevant legislation.[121]

The Brazilian Indigenous Peoples Statute was intended to provide the tools to clarify the relationship and the tone between indigenous peoples and Brazil. Since Article 231 and Article 232 of the Constituion of 1988 are rules of limited efficacy,[122] the Statute is one of the particular laws that should define the parameters of the legal treatment of the indigenous peoples. In view of an alleged inefficacy of the Statute in protecting the rights of the indigenous peoples, their authority, therefore, before the judiciary has faced deep criticism from the juridical and academic literature.[123]

Thus, based on an intercultural dialogue provided by the paradigm of human rights interculturalism, the literature already recognizes the non-receipt of several provisions of the Statute.[124] It had reflected the ideals of the integrationist paradigm, no longer conceived or tolerated after the Constitution of 1988 and the ratification of the ILO Convention No. 169.

4.3.3.1 The Brazilian Foundation of Indigenous Peoples

Although designed to protect the legal rights of indigenous peoples as laid out in the Statute of the Indigenous Peoples, the FUNAI, has often been considered as an obstacle to the indigenous peoples' claims in the Brazilian legal system. This occurred as the FUNAI, was designated as the entity with the exclusive legal jurisdiction to represent indigenous peoples in legal disputes and to provide guidance. In practice, indigenous peoples could petition for violations of their constitutional rights on their own, something that was not possible in the past and must not be repeted in the present and in the future. It should be emphasized that the FUNAI, which was initially know by the name of the SPILTN in 1919, and then changed the name to Indigenous Protection Service (hereinafter, the SPI) was initially linked to the Ministry of Agriculture, Industry and Commerce. Since the SPI advent, it was also the government agency in charge of regularizing territories occupied by indigenous peoples.

The direct action of public institutions in indigenous politics during the Brazilian dictatorship was initially executed through the SPI, which was replaced from 1967 by the FUNAI. Both bodies were responsible for providing assistance to indigenous peoples in various fields of social life such as health, education, land rights, protection of traditional knowledge, economic development and others.[125]

[121] (1973) Brazilian Indigenous Peoples Statute.

[122] See e.g. Gomes Canotilho (2003); Da Silva (2020); Silva (2007, 2018).

[123] See e.g. Cunha (2012); Cunha (2018); Castro (2016).

[124] Heemann (2017); Albuquerque (2008); Kayser (2010); Oliveira (1972).

[125] Mendes et al. (2018).

As a result of SPI's interference, the body was closed in 1967 by the military government of the president of Brazil, Costa e Silva and replaced by FUNAI, which united the former SPI, the National Council for Indigenous Research (hereinafter, the CNPI) and the Xingu National Park.[126]

With the advent of the Constitutional draft during the military dictatorship in 1969, the indigenous lands were incorporated into the federal union property, and the people who traditionally used them had only the right to enjoy the territory. The same constitutional clause was perpetuated through and kept in the Constitution of 1988, still in force today. In that sense, the FUNAI, which was created after the release of the Figueiredo Report had the role of working on development policies with indigenous populations, often alleged to be putting indigenous interests in second place.[127]

Because of the heritage of the indigenous project, the law required that indigenous peoples that were not yet integrated should be subject to tutelage. For those considered integrated and therefore emancipated, the Brazilian Civil Code entailed their civil capacity.

Article 37 of the Indigenous Peoples Statute, which deals with the defense of indigenous lands, states: 'the indigenous peoples are legitimate parties for ligitating their rights in court, and in this case, they are entitled to the assistance of the Federal Public Prosecutor's Office or the FUNAI.[128]

It should be emphasized that the reference setting used by the Indgenous Peoples National Foundation was the category of 'indigenous land' and not the category 'indigenous society' used most in Anthropology.[129] This is significant, as 'there are situations where several indigenous societies occupy a single indigenous land, such as the Javari River Valley, or the Upper Rio Negro. There are many situations in which an indigenous society occupies an indigenous land, as in the case of the Waimiri-Atroari, the Waiãpi, and the Kadiweu, to give some examples. And there are other situations where an ethnic group occupies several indigenous lands as in the case of the Xavante and the Kayapó'.[130] Another misunderstanding occurred with regard to the assessment of the population density. The low population density of the non-urban Amazon area can be measured not by extension of indigenous tenure lands, but in accordance with the 'Federal Environmental Conservation Units, which are areas destined for the Armed Forces, few people with large land tenure rights and even the extension of rural modules for settlement and agrarian reform'.[131]

In 1999, the government's Guidelines for the Indigenous Education program were created by the Brazilian National Council of Education, as were the rules for

---

[126] Santos de Almeida (2015), p. 90, *translated by author.*

[127] Ibid., *translated by author.*

[128] (1973) Brazilian Indigenous Peoples Statute.

[129] Baines (2001), p. 2.

[130] Ibid., p. 3.

[131] Baines (2001), p. 4, *translated by author.*

the demarcation of indigenous lands, which would be carried out by the Indigenous Peoples Foundation and the National Institute for Agrarian Reform (hereinafter, the INCRA). It is relevant to note that the Brazilian Institute of the Environment and Renewable Natural Resources (hereinafter, the IBAMA) is a federal agency, an administrative arm, linked to the Ministry of the Environment and was created by the Law No. 7735 of 1989[132] and has the legal jurisdiction to fight against illegal deforestation and illegal invasion of the territory as well.

The Special Department for Indigenous Health (hereinafter, the SESAI) was also recently created[133] to implement basic health policies for indigenous populations. It is also only recently that the indigenous population has been included in federal government social programs.[134]

It is still uncertain the role that FUNAI is going to take in the protection of the indigenous peoples and their territory as now the indigenous peoples are legally capable to petition and fight for their rights.[135] In sum, it is necessary to consider indigenous peoples as protagonists of their rights so that they can tell the state how their rights should be implemented, thus changing the paradigm of the state v. the tutelage relationship. The use of international human rights mechanisms drives the true recognition of indigenous peoples as citizens and allows for a dialogue of equals to determine priorities, participate in and influence the public policies that concern them as true subjects of law.[136] The immediate future implies that the violations of the requirement of consultation will be prosecuted once it is unreasonable to comply with indiscrimate resource exploitation in order to engage with the agribusiness only, leaving aside the rest of the population and the environment.[137]

[132] (1989) Environment and Renewable Natural Resources Law.

[133] (2003) Special Department for Indigenous Health Law.

[134] 'The Ministry of Health now directly manages the health care of indigenous people, taking into account cultural, ethnic and epidemiological aspects of the 225 peoples living in Brazil. Before, Funasa was responsible for both health actions and the acquisition of inputs, logistical support, bids and contracts. The new office is divided into three areas: Indigenous Health Management Department, Indigenous Health Care Department and Indigenous Special Sanitary Districts. Sesai also began to provide basic and environmental sanitation to indigenous areas, such as preservation of clean water sources, construction of wells or remote collection in communities without drinking water, construction of sanitation systems, final disposal of garbage and control of pollution from springs'. Garnelo and Pontes (2012); Mendes et al. (2018). *translated by author.*

[135] Since the Parliamentary Commission of Inquiry, the CPI, iniciative in 2015 with the objective to investigate the institutions FUNAI and INCRA in order to analyze the demarcation of indigenous and quilombola lands in Brazil, one of the consequences is the misguided interpretation of the work of anthropologists thus questioning the legitimacy of anthropological knowledge, as well as the autonomy and defense of indigenous people as subjects of law.One of the repercussions is the weakening of the relevance of the anthropological reports. For more, see e.g. Machado et al. (2018); Julia Marques Dalla Costa (2019); Gomes Ferreira (2018); Foblets et al. (2022).

[136] Wapichana (2008).

[137] 'In addition to playing a leading part in the government's ceaseless propaganda war on 'gender ideology', Alves's ministerial remit has been extended to include Brazil's Indigenous Affairs Agency (funai). In this domain, Alves draws on her experience evangelising in Indigenous areas of the country to execute Bolsonaro's horrifying vision of the Amazon, environment, and

4.3.3.2 The Brazilian Public Prosecutor's Office

In addition to the FUNAI, which is an administrative organ, the Brazilian Public Prosecutor's Offices (hereinafter, in Portuguese, the *Minitério Público*, the MP) is a judicial organ that guarantees the efficacy and enforcement of the law. According to the Brazilian Federal Constitution of 1988, the Brazilian Public Prosecutor's Office is essential in order to petition against violations of individual rights, the legal order and the democratic regime. The Brazilian Public Prosecutor's Office is composed of the Public Prosecutor's Offices in the states (acting before state courts), and the Federal Public Prosecutor's Office, which in turn has four branches: the Federal Public Prosecutor's Office, the Prosecutor's Office, the Military Public Prosecutor's Office, and the Federal District and Territories Public Prosecutor's Office. Under the terms of Subsection V of Article 129 of the Federal Constitution of 1988, it is stipulated that the Public Prosecutor's Office has the jurisdiction to defend the rights and interests of indigenous populations. Subsection XI of Article 6 of the Complementary Law No. 75 of 1993 provides that the Public Prosecutor's Office shall be responsible for such attribution, including the filing of appropriate actions. Thus, it is essential that there is an 'adequate dialogue between the *Parquet* and the indigenous people'[138] so that, in case of violations of human rights, the appropriate legal measures can be taken swiftly.

The MP plays a relevant role when there is a violation of the indigenous peoples' rights and its importance and powers have grown more and more extensive, especially after the adoption of the Constitution in 1988, when the MP began to act autonomously.[139] The public institution is guided by anthropological studies on the customs, traditions and needs of the indigenous peoples and guided by the Constitutional norms that establish the plurality of ethnic groups and cultures of Brazil. The MP is the public organ responsible for the legal order: the *custus iuris* and the *custus legis* when it matters to the control of conventionality.[140]

Since the advent of the configuration of the special 6th Coordination and Review Chamber, the MP's intention is to guarantee the implementation of the fundamental rights of the indigenous peoples, the *quilombolas*, the *comunidades ribeirinhas*, among other traditional communities. The public servants are entitled to deal with the bureacreacies of titling, demarcation and land tenure of the traditionally occupied lands. The proportion of the indigenous territory compared to the privately owned territory is 18%.[141] In that sense, the factors preventing the advance of the Brazilian

---

Indigenous territories. A key facet of the president's perspective in this area is the ostensible alignment of Indigenous interests with those of corporate mining and agricultural giants'. Webber (2020); Cunha (1994).

[138] Mattos F da S, *O direito à consulta prévia às comunidades indígenas e a atuação do Ministério Público para a sua concretização*, p. 116.

[139] See e.g. Duprat (2016).

[140] Mazzuoli (2018).

[141] Oliveira (1998).

agriculture are much more complex, involving ‘economic and political variables of another order’.[142]

In which there is the contradictory the discourse of protection with the practice of integration. Attempts to fit situations such as the indigenous collective right over the land they live on into the individual property system, for example, have revealed the difficulty (almost impossibility) of maintaining the unity of law in a society that is not one.[143]

Contrary to the Constitutional and infra-constitutional provisions, the indigenous peoples thus become invisible in the face of the planning of the Brazilian economic ventures on their lands and, later, during the operationalization phase of these proposals, an obstacle to national development.[144]

The 6th Coordination and Review Chamber plays the role, within the MPF,[145] of coordinating, integrating, and reviewing institutional actions aimed at protecting the indigenous population and traditional communities. It is responsible for acting in civil actions related to the defense of the rights and interests of indigenous populations and related to traditional communities.[146]

The main challenge for the prosecutors working on these issues is to ensure the plurality of the Brazilian state from an ethnic and cultural perspective, as determined by the Brazilian Constitution.

The 6th Chamber understands consultation as it is established in international treaties. The consultation is an obligation of the Brazilian state to ask, adequately and respectfully, the indigenous peoples their position on administrative and legislative decisions capable of affecting their lives and rights.[147] It is the right of indigenous peoples to be consulted and to participate in the decisions of the Brazilian state through intercultural dialogue marked by good faith.[148]

The prosecutors of the 6th Chamber understand the necessity of the holistic view of the law and the rights of indigenous people for a dignified life, as well as that

---

[142] Ibid.

[143] Souza Filho (2000).

[144] In order to make the advance of agricultural borders in the North of the country feasible, for example, the measure adopted was often “cleaning up the area,” that is, decimating entire indigenous communities so that the advance could be realized. As an example of these actions, one can cite the Massacre do Paralelo, as it became known the extermination, in the 60s, of villages of Cinta Larga Indians, in the state of Mato Grosso. A tragedy that became internationally known and denounced the practice of indigenous genocide in Brazil. The invasion of indigenous lands by non-Indians for the illegal exploitation of natural resources is a reality that affects almost all indigenous land in the country. Although the Federal Constitution guarantees permanent possession by Indians of the lands they traditionally occupy and the right of exclusive enjoyment over the natural resources existing on them (art. 231, §2), these precepts are not effectively respected, which causes many conflicts and impacts for the communities. Curi (2007).

[145] (1988) Constitution of Brazil.

[146] Brazilian Federal Prosecutor (2021b).

[147] See e.g. Maia and Lira (2018).

[148] Brazilian Federal Prosecutor (2021a).

the development models proposed have curtailed the identity of indigenous peoples. The process of consultation initially started unfavorably for indigenous peoples. The dialogue should be broadly participatory, transparent, free of pressure, flexible to meet the diversity of indigenous peoples and communities, and have a binding effect, in the sense of leading the state to incorporate what is discussed in the decision to be made.[149]

4.4 Legal Claims Regarding the Requirement of Consultation in Brazilian Supreme Court

There are two higher Courts in Brazil, the STF[150] and the STJ (hereinafter, Brazilian Superior Court), idiosyncratic characteristics of the Brazilian legal system. The STF[151] is the higher court, the main jurisdiction of which is to enforce the Brazilian Constitution by hearing some particular kinds of appeals, undertaking concrete judicial reviews, but also engaging in broader measures when reviewing actions that challenge the constitutionality of norms, the abstract judicial review.[152] The STJ holds the jurisdiction of an appellate court, the role of which is to harmonize the

---

[149] Ibid.

[150] The Brazilian Federal Supreme Court (STF), highest judicial body in Brazil, located in Brasília, is composed of eleven Judges, chosen among native Brazilian citizens, who are more than thirty-five and less than sixty-five years old and have renowned legal knowledge and impeccable reputation (article 12, § 3, IV, and article 101, both from the Federal Constitution). The Court has two chambers and the plenary as the bodies responsible for collegiate decisions. Besides live sessions, broadcasted live on TV, radio and internet, the collegiate bodies also deliberate online, through a system known as virtual plenary, in place since 2007 and since then an important and successful technological tool aimed at reducing the backlog of case. The Brazilian Federal Supreme Court and the Superior Courts have jurisdiction over the entire Brazilian territory. The Constitution of 1988, article 102, states that the jurisdiction of the Supreme Federal Court is primarily to safeguard the Constitution. Among matters of its jurisdiction the Court rules on direct actions of unconstitutionality, declaratory actions of constitutionality and allegations of disobedience of fundamental precept from the Constitution itself. The Federal Supreme Court has ruled on 115,603 cases in 2019, among which 17,695 cases were ruled by the plenary and the two chambers, a figure 21.74% higher than the previous year. The virtual plenary has dealt with 14,471 of those collegiate rulings (82% of them) and has been instrumental in tackling the backlog, reduced by 19.12% in 2019, to 31,279 cases, the lowest figure in 20 years. The process of nomination for the life-tenured office of Justice of the Supreme Federal Court is started by the President submitting a name to the Senate, responsible for the approval. Once in office, Justice will only relinquish the position by resignation, compulsory retirement (at seventy-five years old) or impeachment. The Chief Justice serves a two year-term, on a rotational basis which involves all Justices. STF (2020a).

[151] The STF has a peculiar structure of the Justices and ways to conduct the control of irregulaties regarding constitutional rights. However, there has been also a debate regarding the usage of the 'political control' of the claims by the federal government. It is still unclear if this strategy will change the decisions towards indigenous people's rights. See e.g.: Terto Neto (2020); Machado (2020); Torres et al. (2021); Arguelhes and Hartmann (2017); Gomes Esteves (2020).

[152] Barroso (2020).

interpretation of the federal norms in the Brazilial legal system. The cases related to indigenous peoples' rights, following appeals to the decision ruled by Federal Courts, or, in determinated cases, are subject to adjudication in this higher court.

The role that the Brazilian Supreme Court plays is characterized by the protection of fundamental rights through juridical ways to appeal such as, in Portuguese: *Mandado de Segurança, Mandado de Injunção, Habeas Corpus,*[153] *Ação Civil Pública* and *Ação Popular*. Some of those appeals come not in response to international adjudication and are a Brazilian contribution to the constitutional proceedings in order to apply the juridical review. Some others, such as the *Suspensão de Segurança,*[154] are remnants of Brazil's dictatorship period, that still remain and do not comply with the due process of law. Thus, 'the direct application does not only mean that rights, freedoms and guarantees apply regardless of legislative intervention. It also means that they apply directly against the law when it establishes restrictions in disagreement with the Constitution'.[155]

In addition, there are other appeals that might be used as tools to achieve the implementation of fundamental rights that are related to the abstract constitutional control. There are four appeals in total: the Declaration of Unconstitutionality, the Direct Action for the Declaration of Unconstitutionality by Omission, the Action for Declaration of Constitutionality and the Action Against the Violation of the Constitutional Fundamental Rights. Those are all very specific to each legal case.

The outcome of the decision might be the *erga omnes* or the limitated efficacy. It is important to note that in some of these cases, the judges quoted the IACtHR decisions, and they must decide in accordance with the international human rights treaties.

The most relevant case so far in the Brazilian legal system is the Raposa do Sol case in which the Brazilian Supreme Court interpreted the claim as a tempus frame theory. Also relevant are the the cases: *Guyra Roka* of the *Guarani Kaiowá* indigenous peoples, the *Porquinhos of the Canela Apanyekrá* indigenous peoples and the *Terena* indigenous peoples of the *Limão Verde.*

In this subchapter the Brazilian Higher Courts most relevant claims will be analyzed.

[153] Habeas Corpus: it is originally an action destined to guarantee the right of freedom of movement. It is the jurisdiction of the Federal Supreme Court when the constrained party is the President of the Republic, the Vice-President, members of the National Congress, the Court's own Justices and the Procurator-General of the Republic, or when it is to be decided as an appeal in last instance. STF (2020b).

[154] Prudente (2014).

[155] Gomes Canotilho (2003).

4.4.1 The Legal Cases of the Brazilian Supreme Court

Most conflicts involving indigenous peoples' right to territory are judicialized.[156] Those conflicts translated in courts are directly related to facts that have occurred in the past century, already explored in chapter three, when the indigenous peoples have faced physical, psychological and cultural violence. Although the Constitution of 1988 ended the tutelage, this process led to a deceptive process of spoliation of their property title.

Their jurisdiction to be allowed in a court of the justice system as collective subjects of rights did not change the fact that they continued to be tricked by the system. In a recent case, the judiciary led to a violation of human rights when, in 2015, the indigenous peoples were not even called to be parties in the legal process.

The example highlighted was the indigenous peoples *Guarani and Kaiowá*, of the indigenous land *Guyraroká,* in *Mato Grosso do Sul*. In 2009 the Ministry of Justice had declared the entitlement to property to them permanently. However, without a legal subpoena, the Brazilian Supreme Court decided on suspending their entitlement to property.

The Brazilian Supreme Court decided the *Limão Verde* case in 2014 regarding the territory issues of the indigenous peoples *Terena*, in *Mato Grosso do Sul*.[157] Regarding the case, the Federal Prosecutor Deborah Duprat stated: 'much has already been said about the very close relationship between indigenous and land, in nothing comparable to what a non-indigenous person establishes with their real estate. Here, capital, value, are its central elements. It would be possible and legitimate to keep the Santa Bárbara territory under indigenous peoples property and to order the Federal Union to fully indemnify the farmer who pressed charges. What amazes and saddens, in this case, is the indifference as to the fate of a people and their right to a land'.[158]

Regarding the cases of the *Guarani Kaiowá* indigenous peoples, the *Porquinhos* indigenous peoples and the *Canela Apanyekrá* indigenous peoples, there were also plenty of contradictions leading to constant violations of human rights.

The *Porquinhos dos Canela-Apãnjekra* case regarded the loss of part of the entitled territoy of the indigenous peoples: 'allowing this litigation would weaken the principle of legal security, weakening the confidence one should have in the acts of the federal government'.[159]

Justice Dias Toffoli of the Brazilian Supreme Court suspended the decision of the case and also ensured that the *Guarani-Kaiowá* indigenous peoples could stay in the

---

[156] Primor Ribas and Marés de Souza Filho (2014).

[157] Justice Teori Zavascki, Appeal "Recurso Extraordinário com Agravo," No. 803.462 (Brazilian Supreme Court December 9, 2014).

[158] Duprat (2018).

[159] Justice Carmen Lúcia Antunes Rocha, Appeal "Recurso Ordinário em Mandado de Segurança," No. No. 9943034-06.2010.1.00.0000 (Brazilian Supreme Court November 4, 2019), *translated by author.*

territory in order not to contribute to the increase of tensions and agrarian conflicts in the region.[160] As to the efficacy of the decision, the *Guarani-Kaiowá* do not need to vacate the areas, however, after waiting more than 16 years the judgment of the merits is still outstanding.

In the *Kaingang* case, litigation was brought forward by indigenous peoples regarding their constitutional right of entitlement to territory, the *Toldo Boa Vista*, in Paraná.[161] Amending a litigation that took place in 2012, petitioned by a rural landowner who requested that the territory was entitled to him, one of Justices, Justice Rosa Weber reaffirmed in her vote that 'the non-inclusion of the indigenous community as a party in the original litigation made the allegation of procedural defect plausible'[162] in accordance with the Brazilian Procedure Civil Code, Article 966,V.

The *Xokleng* case of 2019 is also important to highlight, as it is going to be decided in the STF regarding the entilement of the *Ibirama-La Klãnõ* territory. As the indigenous peoples in Brazil are not anymore under the guardianship of the FUNAI, they do not have to claim for them to be included in the procedure of the litigation, they have the legitimate claim to be part. However, the validity of this constitutional right has rarely been accepted by the Brazilian judiciary. In this case, the STF understood that the decision has *erga omnes* efficacy. Justice Edson Fachin argued the need of a 'definitive decision on the issue of indigenous lands is necessary, since conflicts are getting worse and the issue is not pacified in society or even in the judiciary'.[163] Moreover, the case is pending due to the COVID-19 pandemic.[164]

---

[160] Justice José Antonio Dias Toffol, Appeal "Suspensão da Reintegração de Posse," No. No. 0007674-18.2015.1.00.0000 (Brazilian Supreme Court February 3, 2020).

[161] Justice Roberto Barroso, Appeal "Medida Cautelar na Ação Rescisória," No. No MC AR 0028329-69.2019.1.00.0000 PR-0028329-69.2019.1.00.0000 (Brazilian Supreme Court November 7, 2019).

[162] Justice Rosa Weber, Appeal "Medida Cautelar na Ação Rescisória," No. No. 2.750 (Brazilian Supreme Court October 1, 2019), *translate by author.*

[163] Justice Edson Fachin, Appeal "Recurso Extraordinário," No. No. RE1017365 (Brazilian Supreme Court September 29, 2020). *translated by author.* See e.g. Silva and Joca (2020).

[164] In the decison: 'It is notorious that the indigenous people, since the first incursions in Brazilian lands, have suffered with the diseases brought, and that these diseases were responsible, until recently, for decimating entire ethnicities in the interior of the country, given the lack of preparation of the immune system of the indigenous to the diseases.Thus, although it is a new disease, whose mechanism scientists and health authorities from all over the world are still trying to understand, the measures of distance and social isolation have been adopted by several countries, with a progressive decrease in the number of infected people and deaths.The maintenance of the process, with the risk of determinations of repossessions, aggravates the situation of the indigenous people, who can suddenly see themselves clustered on the edges of roads, unassisted and without minimum conditions of hygiene and isolation to minimize the risks of contagion by the coronavirus.In this case, the precautionary principle, based on Article 225 of the Constitution, is to require the Federal Government to act towards the mitigation of social and environmental risks, in defense of the maintenance of life and health'.Justice Edson Fachin, Appeal "Recurso Extraordinário," No. No. 1.017.365 (Brazilian Supreme Court May 6, 2020).

To note, in view of the COVID-19 pandemic, indigenous peoples have already suffered previous lethal epidemics of viral diseases over time, and were foreseen more than others to suffer in this pandemic.[165] According to the data provided by the, in Portuguese, *Comitê pela Vida e Memória Indígena* and the SESAI, about 33226 indigenous peoples were contaminated, 826 dead, and 158 indigenous people's communites were affected: 'the first confirmed case of contamination by COVID-19 among Brazilian indigenous was a 20-year-old girl from the Kokama people, on March 25, in the Amazonian municipality of Santo Antônio do Içá. The contagion was done by a doctor coming from São Paulo at the service of the Special Secretariat of Indigenous Health, which was infected with the virus. Today the Kokama are the most affected in cases of death'.[166]

The case of the *Xokleng* indigenous peoples and also several indigenous groups and organizations that petitioned together as *amici curiae* in this litigation, that is efficacy is *erga onmes* (in Portuguese, *repercussão geral*), Justice Edson Fachin also declared the suspension of the land tenure suits against indigenous people and the annulment of the land demarcations.

This same judgment returned to the agenda of the STF on 13rd August. The Supreme Court will define whether or not the suspension, determined by Justice Edson Fachin in May of 2020 is maintained or not. This is in regard to the appeal (in Portuguese, *liminarmente*) that suspended the Decree No. 001 of 2017 of the Federal Advocacy, which confirms the use of the modus ponens and the 'creativity interpretation' of the Constitution by Justices, confirming the thesis of the time frame.[167]

4.4.2 The Raposa do Sol Case (2009)

A detour back to 2009 is relevant to analyze the *Raposa do Sol* case considering its substantive limitations to the indigenous peoples' rights.[168] In 1992, the FUNAI started the proceduree s to identify and demarcate the indigenous peoples' territory known as *Raposa do Sol*, where about 194 indigenous communites were living, the

[165] Justice Edson Fachin, Appeal "Recurso Extraordinário," No. No. 1.017.365 (Brazilian Supreme Court May 6, 2020).

[166] (Apib) A dos PI do B (2020) Covid-19 data of the indigenous peoples that were affected in Brazil.

[167] In the Document: 'the Supreme Court, in the decision 'Raposa do Sol'established the "institutional safeguards for entitlment of indigenous people's lands," which are norms derived from the interpretation of the Constitution and, therefore, must be followed in all processes of demarcation of indigenous lands.Fernandes Mendonça GM (2017) 'Parecer' 0001/2017/GAB/CGU/AGU.

[168] Most of the literature understands that the case was a set back of the recognition of the indigenous peoples territorial rights. Yamada (2008); Silva (2018); Jaichand and Sampaio (2013).

more than 19 thousand indigenous peoples of the *Macuxi*, the *Taurepang*, the *Patamona*, the *Ingaricó* and the *Wapichana'* communities.[169]

However, a group of rice farmers from the south of Brazil declared that they were entitled to the territory and had land tenure over part of the territory that was supposed to be demarcated as indigenous peoples' land and with their claim, they litigated for the entitlement of the territory.

The president of Brazil at the time, Luís Inácio Lula da Silva, signed a Decree saying that those who were not indigenous must leave the territory within one year. Meanwhile, several legal petitions were filed in Federal Courts and also in the STF contesting the demarcation.

Four years later, the STF judged the merits of one of the petitions,[170] filed against the demarcation of the land petitioned by the senator Augusto Affonso Botelho asking for the invalidation of the Decree No. 534 of the Brazilian Justice Department and accepted by the president of Brazil, in 2005.

The *Raposa do Sol* had repercussions because of the resistance from those who did not accept the judicial fact that the territory belonged to the indigenous population, even thought, the lawsuit itself was not complicated. There was no contrary opinion about the fact that the land was entitled to the indigenous peoples and the question of borders had also been revisited long before. What makes the case interesting is the fact that it was even on the STF's agenda. It was an initiative of the Attorney General of the Republic Carlos Fontelles, who saw a legal precedent that made it possible for this claim to be decided in the STF. The Attorney General could then propose the in Portuguese, *Ação Civil Orginária*, arguing federative conflict.[171]

The claim was then judged, and the Justices confirmed that the *Raposa do Sol* was entitled to the land tenure, and the votes of Justices served as a foundation for the implementation of the rights of those indigenous peoples who lived there. Although it changed the normative standard of the *Raposa do Sol*, it also brought forward some discussions regarding the interpretation of the right to territory. The lands traditionally occupied by the indigenous peoples are under the domain of the federal union, being inalienable, unavailable and insurmountable in order to provide the indigenous communities welfare and conditions that are indispensable for their physical and cultural welbeing, according to their uses, customs and traditions.

[169] The Raposa do Sol Indigenous Land has a total surface of one million, seven hundred and forty-seven thousand, four hundred and sixty-four hectares, seventy-eight ares and thirty-two centiers, and a perimeter of nine hundred and seventy-eight thousand, one hundred and thirty-two meters and thirty-two centimeters, located in the municipalities of Normandia, Pacaraima and Uiramutã. (2005) Decree demarcating the Raposa do Sol.

[170] This relationship between law and politics has been called by the literature the judicialization of politics. This phenomenon, which will be better explained below, stems from the strong crisis of representativeness of the legislative Branch, which can be exemplified by numerous decisions of the Federal Supreme Court, such as the demarcation of the Raposa/Serra do Sol indigenous lands and nepotism Primor Ribas and Marés de Souza Filho (2014).

[171] Duprat (2016).

For instance, the Brazilian Supreme Court understood that the right to territory, the demarcation of the land, should be understood under the theory of the time frame.

Power relations in Latin America have historically been characterized by a marked elitist bias reflected in the systematic exclusion of different ethnic groups and the continued favoritism of influential private/business actors (local and transnational) when their interests conflict with those of marginalized groups. Contemporarily, this translates into serious violations of the rights of indigenous peoples and Afro-descendants in the context of land conflicts and extractive and infrastructure megaprojects. Despite the bleak outlook experienced by different indigenous peoples and Afro-descendants in the region, there have been some significant transformations in terms of social and political inclusion in recent years. These changes have occurred partly through the judicialization of several demands from these groups for more egalitarian conditions in multiple areas (political participation in the decisions that concern them, recognition of their ownership of ancestral territories, the fight against racial discrimination, etc.). The process of local judicialization of these demands is directly linked to the jurisprudential developments in the Inter-American sphere. For illustration, it is enough to cite the *Raposa Serra do Sol* judgment of the Brazilian Supreme Court, which was a case of wide national visibility due to the extension of the lands in question and the economic interests involved. In the ruling, the Supreme Court identified 19 normative standards applicable to conflicts over indigenous lands based on Inter-American standards on the right of indigenous peoples to collective ownership of territory. The STF itself cited the Awas Tingni case as an example that the international community will spare no effort to try to apply its positions on collective rights to member states.

The time frame theory can be defined as a limited amount of time stipulated by the Brazilian Supreme Court related to the indigenous peoples' land claims. According to the marco temporal, the only indigenous peoples who can benefit from the recognition of their right to property are those who were occupying their territory on October 5 of 1988, when the Brazilian Constitution was promulgated.

In the *Raposa do Sol*, the Federal Supreme Court held that 'the right to prior consultation with the communities must give way to strategic issues, such as national defense, sovereignty, or environmental protection, which may require prior communication to anyone, including indigenous communities'.[172] Opposing Justice's opinion, the Superior Judge Feliz Fischer, in the decision of the appeal in Porutuese, *Agravo de Instrumento*, argued that there was no granting of rights to have a reasonable time to conduct the requirement of consultation: 'the time frame of a few months that guaranteed the participation of the indigenous peoples affected by the decision, without the establishment of a fixed term to conduct the consultation'.[173]

[172]Supreme Judge Carlos Ayres Britto, The Raposa do Sol case, No. Petition 3.388 (Brazilian Supreme Court September 24, 2009).

[173]Brazilian Superior Court, *Appeal 'Agravo de Instrumento'*, AgRg na Rcl 17224 PA 2014/0062484-0, Judgment of 9 March 2014.

Justice, Menezes Direito decided that: 'there's no indigenous without land. The relationship with the soil is a characteristic mark of the indigenous essence, for all that it is is in the earth and with the land. Hence the importance of the soil in guaranteeing their rights, all connected in one way or another to the land. This is what is understood of the art. 231 of the Constitution. [. . .] It is in and through it that they organize themselves. It is in their relationship with the land that the indigenous peoples forge their customs and traditions. It is by stepping on the ground and exploring their limits that they develop their beliefs and enrich their language, intimately referenced to the earth. Nothing is more imminent to them. The indigenous is thus ontologically earthy, so much so that the autoc-tone and native terms give an idea of something generated and formed in a certain locus. The indigenous peoples are thus, attached, a being of their land'.[174] There would therefore be no point in recognising indigenous peoples' rights without securing their land, identifying and demarcating it.

It should also be noted that some of Justices' votes did not even consider the point brought by the new thesis of the time frame introduced during the trial, such as the vote of Federal Judge Eros Grau.[175] The vote of Justice Joaquim Barbosa was in accordance with the vote of Justice Ayres Britto.[176] Justice Ellen Gracie's statement was brief and did not address the issue.[177]

Justice Carmen Lúcia's vote, on the other hand, reaffirmed the theory of the in Portuese, *indigienato*, without confronting the subject.[178] The Justice expressed the literature theory[179] by the following statement: 'it is understood that indigeneity, however, had been received by the Constitution so that its effects produced independent of express constitutional prevision. The [*indigienato*] therefore, is far from being a ready and finished thesis, capable of being applied to all the other demarcations of indigenous lands, distinct from that which was appreciated in the Petition No. 3.388/RR. After all, the casuistry and the practical problems that would follow that judged—as, in fact, they succeeded—would be the basis for the improvement and development of the multiple topics. The reality shows that the introduction of the thesis of the [*indigienato*] did not contribute to the implementation of the

[174] Justice Carlos Alberto Menezes de Direito, "Raposa do Sol" case, No. Pet 3388 (Brazilian Supreme Court December 10, 2008, *translated by author.*

[175] Justice Eros Grau, "Raposa do Sol" case, No. Pet 3388 (Brazilian Supreme Court December 10, 2008).

[176] Justice Joaquim Barbosa, "Raposa do Sol" case, No. Pet 3388 (Brazilian Supreme Court December 18, 2008).

[177] Justice Ellen Gracie, "Raposa do Sol" case, No. Pet 3388 (Brazilian Supreme Court December 18, 2008).

[178] Justice Carmen Lúcia, "Raposa do Sol" case, No. Pet 3388 (Brazilian Justice December 18, 2008).

[179] The theory of indigenity was developed at the beginning of the 20th century and brought a relevant argument for the theory of indigenous peoples territoty entitlement over traditionally occupied lands. The theory of 'posse permamente' is not regulated by civil law. The theory determins the declaratory nature of the entitlement. Mendes Junior (1912).

constitutional guarantee of the land tenure. On the contrary, it generated great legal insecurity, by serving as a basis for questioning various administrative processes for demarcating indigenous lands and exacerbated the scandal and violence in the countryside, as demonstrated by the various news held in Brazil by the Special Rapporteur of the United Nations for the Rights of Indigenous Peoples and the IACHR on Human Rights'.[180]

The vote of Justice César Peluso, on the other hand, disregarded the singularities of the indigenous peoples' land tenure: 'I can only praise once again the brilliant votes of Justice Menezes Direito and all the others, but above all those two votes that ran for the already defined majority formation. They comfort me and reinforce my convictions regarding the solution of this cause. I accept, because it seems to me absolutely correct the only legal explanation for the criterion of delimitation of indigenous areas, which is what Justice Menezes Direito called an indigenous fact. In fact, the legal entititlement of the territory on the date the Constitution took effect, on October 5th of 1988, corresponds practically to the legal-civil concept of possession, as a factual possibility of economic exploitation of the case'.[181]

In the vote of Justice Celso de Mello some of the reasons were presented that underlie the protective objective of the recognition of indigenous peoples' entitlement to the land: 'it clearly emerges from the constitutional text that the land issue represents the fundamental aspect of the rights and constitutional prerogatives assured to the indigenous, since the latter, without the guarantee of permanence on the lands already traditionally occupied by him, is exposed to the very serious risk of cultural disintegration, the loss of their ethnic identity, the dissolution of their historical, social and anthropological bonds and the erosion of their own consciousness and perception as an integral part of a people and a nation that revere the mystical places of their spiritual worship and celebrate in them the unfathomable mysteries of the universe in which they live.'[182]

In the end, the Supreme Court's effort in the *Raposa do Sol* became a complex demand of the establishment of the so-called time frame thesis as conditioning factor brought legal insecurity (in Portuguese, *insegurança jurídica*) to a series of other subsequent cases, aggravating violence and increasing the vulnerability of indigenous communities.

The Supreme Court understood that 'lands that traditionally occupy, watch out, not those that will occupy. Nor the lands already occupied at other times, but without sufficient continuity to reach the landmark of October 5, 1988'.[183]

---

[180] Justice Carmen Lúcia, "Raposa do Sol" case, No. Pet 3388 (Brazilian Justice December 18, 2008), *translated by author.*

[181] Brazilian Supreme Judge, *'Raposa do Sol' case*, Pet 3388, Judgment of 18 December 2008. *translated by author.*

[182] Justice Celso Mello, "Raposa do Sol" case, No. Pet 3388 (Brazilian Supreme Court December 18, 2008).

[183] Brazilian Supreme Court, *The Raposa do Sol case*, Petition 3.388, Judgment of 24 September 2009.

In another decision of 1998, Justice Marco Aurélio had alread said that in order to avoid what he called to be the "Copacabana Effect", in which all the decisions regarding the entitlement of property of indigenous peoples should be taken into consideration as of the Constitution of 1988.[184] As a matter of fact, the decision was already supported by Justice Soares Muñoz. According to Justice Décio Miranda, a criterion was proposed in order to verify the indigenous peoples land tenure entitlement. In his words: 'assuming that the territory in question is not occupied by the indigenous peoples, or have not been since the 1960s, having verified that the private land entitled coincide with the regular indigenous occupation, the tenure title of the indigenous peoples will prevail and they will be entitled to the land rights'.[185]

The cases so far judged, and *Raposa do Sol* was no different, offered an example of how the narrow interpretation of the Constitution can lead to the juridical insecurity. The increasing participation of indigenous peoples through the requirement of consultation is not only essential to esnure their cultural integrity and self-determination but in this case, as in many others, it was meaningful to restrict easy access to natural resources located in indigenous peoples' territories.

4.5 Legal Claims Regarding the Requirement of Consultation in Brazilian Federal Courts

The traditional idea of civil law given by the supremacy of the Constitution over other sources of law changed in the new establishment, where the judges assume an important role in order to interpret and apply the constitutional fundamental rights.[186] The legislation might not be considered isolated from the legal order but should pursue the fundamental rights and guarantees present in the Constitution, from which it draws its enforcement. In that sense, the Brazilian government and the indigenous peoples' rights have a contentious relationship that translates into a large number of legislations that do not protect violations of indigenous peoples' rights. The "Anti-indigenous Congress", as the Brazilian Congress is known, holds 33 proposals, bringing together over 100 projects, that threaten indigenous rights. A survey taken by the Conselho Indienista Missionário indicates that most of the proposals were made by ruralists (in Portuguese, *Bancada Ruralista*), as the politicians that

[184] Brazilian Supreme Court, *Appeal 'Recurso Extraordinário*, RE 219983/SP, Judgment of 12 September 1998.

[185] 'If it is verified that the lands in question are not occupied by forest dwellers, or have not been since 1960, which seems to have been the time of their transfer to private individuals by the state of Mato Grosso, the deeds, if it is accepted that they have this origin in a regular manner, would overcome any opposition that could be made in this regard. However, if it is verified that the original acquisition, or those that followed, coincide with regular indigenous occupation, the appellants' deeds will lose any force that they may have formally had'. Justice Décio Miranda, Appeal "Recurso em Mandado de Segurança," No. MS 20215 (Brazilian Supreme Court March 5, 1980).

[186] Baron (1999); Poscher (2019); Barak (1993).

advocate for the agribusiness in Brazil are known, and intends to change criteria for demarcation or release exploitation of resources on indigenous lands.[187]

Rendering the right of consultation of indigenous peoples adequate is imperative to the communities involved, since the country's need for development and the increase in its energy mix based on natural resources will require a model for consultation to be established from the outset, which prevents social vulnerability of these communities, the violation of the national legal order to achieve enforcement with the IAHRS standards.

Besides some differences in terms of exploitation activities, all cases share the procedural imbalance in favour of Brazil, struck by the Brazilian Development Bank, that demonstrates the limits of BNDES' Socio-environmental Responsibility Policy (hereinafter, the PRSA), both to assess socio-environmental risks, avoiding support for certain undertakings, and to efficiently monitor the management of risks and socio-environmental impacts involved in case the bank decides to support projects of resource exploitation.[188]

The most relevant cases, the the the *Taparajós* case; the *Volta Grande do Xin*gu case; and the *Polo Naval de Manaus* case are going to be extensively analyzed in separate subchapters showing the need of observance of the requirement of consultation as a cultural right and a self-determination when there is a resource exploitation in the indigenous territory; in those cases: in the subsoil, the soil and the water, as determined by the Brazilian Constitution and the ILO Convention No. 169.

This subchapter will discuss a number of cases in the Federal Courts involving the exploitation of natural resources, which have been launched without the previous consent of the indigenous peoples living in the relevant lands.[189] The cases were chosen because they represent the violation of the consultation right of traditional communities, including indigenous peoples.

---

[187] CIMI (2017).

[188] There are international standards guidelines for the conduction of consultation and also penalties and remedies when the international organization did not comply with the law. See e.g. United Nations Development Programme (UNDP) (2007) Indigenous Peoples and the Human Rights-Based Approach to Development: Engaging in Dialogue; Special Representative of the Secretary-General (2011) Guiding Principles on Business and Human Rights: Implementing the United Nations 'Protect, Respect and Remedy' Framework. In regard to the World Bank, for example, it 'has reviewed its environmental and social policies at a moment of intense production of international instruments dealing with land tenure, all of which take the form of soft law. This endeavour is motivated by the progressive acknowledgement of the importance of secure and equitable access to land for the implementation of human rights and food security. The latest contribution of the World Bank to this debate is of great significance.' Brunori (2019).

[189] Relevant to know is that regarding the legal nature, all cases involving indigenous peoples or traditional peoples are a matter of the Federal Union. Thus 'the Federal Courts may process and judge cases in which the Union, autarchies or federal public companies are plaintiffs, defendants, assistants or opponents – except for those that are related to bankruptcy, work accidents, or those that are the sphere of the Electoral Courts or Labor Courts. It is made up of federal judges and that act in the first instance, of the regional federal courts (appeal), and special courts that rule on crimes that have less dangerous potential and lesser economic value'.Presidency of the Republic of Brazil (2020) Organs of the Judiciary Power.

The cases regarding the requirement of consultation in Brazil perpetrate the juridical and the legislative sphere. The analysis will add relevant insights on the subject matter, also to be compared with the cases already described in this and the previous chapter. The Brazilian Federal Courts have different legal approaches, depending on the federal judges' views, however, in most of the jurisprudence, there is observance of the IAHRS and also the ILO Convention No. 169.

Nevertheless, the Brazilian claims and legislation chosen regarding the violation of the requirement of consultation analyzed in this section are: the case *Educação Escolar Indígena*, the case *Hidrelétrica São Luiz do Tapajós,* the case *Usina Hidrelétrica Teles Pires*, the case *Usina Hidrelétrica São Manuel*, the case *Polo Naval de Manaus*, the case *Parque Nacional of Superagui*, in Paraná, the case *Duplicação da estrada de Ferro Carajás*, the case *Linhão Manaus Boavista*, the case of the resource exploitation of oil, gas and xisto, in Acre, the case *Construção do porto no lago Maicá*, the *Projeto de Lei* which is an alteration in the Law No. 892 of 2013 regarding the indigenous teachers, the case *Belo Monte* and the case *Mineração Volta Grande do Xingu.*

4.5.1 Legal Cases Relevancing the Requirement of Consultation

Relevant to the discussion is that some of decisions of the Federal Courts amply referenced the IACtHR, which provides evidence to the finding that Brazil's federal judges are following the IAHRS interpretation regarding the requirement of consultation to be a way for the indigenous peoples in Brazil to achieve self-determination and the cultural rights. Thus, all of the judgments and decisions refered to the ILO Convention No. 169 and to the requirement of consultation. 'Additionally, Indigenous lawyers and Apib's legal advisors are now a powerful legal defense team on the front lines in Brazil. The unanimous enforcement with the Claim of Non-enforcement with Fundamental Precept (in Portuguese, the ADPF) at Brazil's Supreme Court, presented and led by Apib in partnership with various civil society organizations and political parties, is a historic milestone for the indigenous peoples of Brazil and all Brazilians because it acknowledges that the government failed to protect indigenous people against the pandemic. It is an unprecedented achievement to guarantee the protection of Indigenous peoples and to establish the importance of indigenous Brazilians in building a more just country'.[190]

In the case *Hidrelétrica São Luiz do Tapajós*, in Pará, the Federal Judge ruled that the Brazilian government had the legal obligation to comply with the requirement of consultation and conduct consultations with the indigenous peoples of the *Mundukuru*, the *Santaré-Mawé*, the *Montanha* and the *Mangabal.* The federal judge pointed out that the consultation 'was not only a question of qualifying

[190] Association of Brazil's Indigenous Peoples (2020), p. 6.

democracy (*i.e.*, non excluding minority groups), but also of a qualitative point of view'.[191] He affirmed that: 'ethnically, differentiated groups have perspectives on the measures consulted that other groups could not have, due to cultural alterity. For example, does a hydroelectric power plant have the same meaning for an indigenous people as for a company or for the whole society?'[192] The jurisprudence of this case is rich and this was also one of the reason that it was one of the illustrative cases chosen to be analyzed in this chapter.

The case *Usina Hidrelétrica Teles Pires* regarding to the planning of another dam, in Pará and Mato Grosso, where the federal court decided that the project should be suspended until a consultation with the indigenous peoples *Mundukuru, Kayabi* and the *Apiaká* had been conducted. The federal judge Souza Prudente decided that the lack of the ECI was enough to suspend the EIA/RIMA'.[193]

The case *Usina Hidrelétrica São Manuel*, towards another dam in Pará and Mato Grosso, saw the federal court decide that the Brazilian government should consult with the indigenous people. The IACtHR stated that there was the necessity to asses the multi-faceted impacts of the dams in the region: 'that global impacts produced by the set of projects in the region such as the hydroelectric power plant of Teles Pires the hydroelectric power plant of Colíder, the hydroelectric power plant of Sinop, the hydroelectric power plant of São Manoel, the hydroelectric power plant of Foz do Apiacás, the hydroelectric power plant of Magessi and the hydroelectric power plant of Salto do Apiacás, strengthenen and corroborate the verisimilitude of the allegations of the other actions petitioned at this Court'.[194] Because of that, the federal court: 'determined the holding of public hearings on indigenous lands, aimed at the affected indigenous peoples of the Kayabi, the Munduruku and the Apiacás'.[195] The federal judge Ilan Presser understood that: 'the right of consultation can be seen as a concretization of the neoconstitutionalist paradigm, because, at only one time, it remains materialized: (a) the centrality and normative force of the Constitution (Article 231, 3); (b) the fundamental rights to the preservation of the minorities' way of life are effected; (c) the judiciary exercises its counter-rights role; (d) there is a discursive and argumentative logic; (e) finally, there is the approximation of law with ethics and justice, and the overcoming of the positivist model, in which law was watertight, without interdisciplinarity with other sciences'.[196]

The case *Polo Naval de Manaus,* in the state of Amazon, referred to the mega-project of the construction of a port. The federal court decided that Amazonas must

[191] Itaituba Federal Court, *Appeal 'Ação Civil Pública'*, No. 3883-98.2012.4.01.3902, Judgment of 23 November 2017.

[192] Ibid.*translated by author.*

[193] Federal Court '1ª Região', *Appeal 'Ação Civil Pública'*, No. 3947-44.2012.4.01.3600, Judgment of 10 September 2013.*translated by author.*

[194] Federal Court of Mato Grosso, *Appeal 'Ação Civil Pública'*, No. 14123-48.2013.4.01.3600, Judgment of 6 May 2014.*translated by author.*

[195] Ibid.*translated by author.*

[196] Brazilian Federal Court of Mato Grosso, *Appeal 'Ação Civil Pública'*, No. 17643-16.2013.4.01.3600, Judgment of 28 April 2018.

consult with the indigenous peoples, the *comunidades ribeirinhas* and the fishermen that were affected by the natural resource exploitation project. The court also quoted the ILO Convention No. 169 and the Convention of the Biologocial Diversity. The court then reasoned that as no consultation had been conducted before the realization of the project, this was likely one of the reasons that the *Polo Naval de Manaus* was rejected by the population: 'and how did the repulsion of the traditional communities affected by the beginning of the so-called Polo Naval procedures begin? The MPF itself answered the question at the beginning: the representatives of the traditional riverside communities Puraquequara, *Bela Vista, Colônia Antônio Aleixo, São Francisco do Mainã* and *Jatuarana,* together with representatives of the Environmental Commission of the Legislative Assembly of Amazonas and the non-governmental entity SOS Encontro das Águas, met with the federal public prosecutors and presented reports on the existence of a naval pole construction project that was in progress, about which they had not been informed or consulted before'.[197] And the federal judge observed that: 'the worst and most serious is the lack of free and informed participation of the communities regarding the acceptance of the Polo Naval project and the impacts that the undertaking will cause to the region'.[198]

The case *Parque Nacional do Superagui*, in Paraná, based on the obligation to consult with the fishermen of the *Guaraqueçaba* region regarding a management plan imposed by the government for the *Parque Nacional do Superagui*, a Biosphere Reservation declared by the United Nations Educational, Scientific and Cultural Organization (hereinafter, the UNESCO).

In this very peculiar case, the public defenders petitioned the federal court of Curitiba for the agreement formulated by the fishermen of *Guaraqueçaba*, which consisted of a Protocol of consultation to be incorporated by the ICMBio in the elaboration of a management plan for the region and other acts that involve the traditional community in the region. Thus, 'the Protocol was elaborated collectively by the fishermen, in workshops and assemblies that have been held for two years in the communities involved and consists as an indication of the way in which the community should be consulted'.[199] The federal judge Guilherme Borges reasoned that there was no regulation regarding the management plan and the requirement of consultation, however, as any other case in which the communities are affected by the project, there was the need to abide with the requirement of consultation.[200]

In the case *Duplicação da estrada de Ferro Carajás*, in Pará and Maranhão, the federal court stated that the indigenous peoples *Awá Guajá* should be consulted about a highway project to be realized in their region. The federal judge Höhn Junior

[197] Federal Court of Amazonas, *Appeal 'Ação Civil Pública'*, No. 0006962-86.2014.4.01.3200, Judgment of 16 May 2016.*translated by author.*

[198] Ibid.*translated by author.*

[199] Defenders (2015) Petition.

[200] Federal Court of Curitiba, *Appeal 'Ação Civil Pública'*, No. 5000742-88.2015.4.04.7008/PR, Judgment of 26 May 2015.

argued the need of complying with the ILO Convention No. 169 regarding the requirement of consultation.[201]

The case *Linhão Manaus Boavista* regards an eletric cable passing by the federal state of Amazonas and Roraima. The federal court decided on the necessity of the government to consult with the indigenous peoples *Waimiri Atroari* that will be directly affected by the project. The federal judge Marília Paiva e Sales stated: 'in spite of the petition presented by the defendants, I understand that the essential requirements for the granting the preliminary decison are present, namely, fumus boni iuris and periculum in mora. Once the preliminary environmental license was granted by the IBAMA, the Law No. 522 of 2015, without the prior, free and informed consultation to the *Waimiri Atroari* indigenous people, according to the ILO Convention No. 1699, I decide that there is the need of conducting the consultation with the indigenous peoples'.[202]

Regarding the case of the resource exploitation of oil, gas and schist, in Acre, the federal court also quoted the ILO Convention No. 169 and demanded that 'any activity regarding the project should cease until there is the consultation with the indigenous peoples affected by the resource exploitaiton'.[203]

The case *Construção do porto no lago Maicá* happened in Santarém, Pará. The federal court suspended the environmental license until the conduct of the consultation with the indigenous peoples and the *comunidades ribeirinhas* affected by the project, known as *Terminal Portuário Emphraps*. The court understood that: 'there was the obligation of ceasing the proceeding of the licensing and the authorization of construction of the project until the consultation with the quilombola peoples and other traditional communities located in the territory in where the project was being conducted'.[204]

In view of the successive acknowledgements in the Federal Courts and in the Supreme Court, the judiciary as a whole started the process of the incorporation of international standards in the domestic legal system. Therefore, continuing the necessity of the consolidation of the jurisprudence on the subject, and to be able to improve the decisions by the precedents, gives efficacy to the requirement of consultation.

---

[201] Federal Court of Maranhão, *Appeal 'Ação Civil Pública'*, No. 61827-77.2015.4.01.3700, Judgment of 26 June 2015.*translated by author.*

[202] Federal Court of Amazonas, *Appeal 'Ação Civil Pública'*, No. 0018032-66.2015.4.01.3200, Judgment of 19 February 2016.*translated by author.*

[203] Federal Court of Cruzeiro do Sul, *Appeal 'Agravo de Instrumento'*, No. AI 0008464-86.2016.4.01.0000, Judgment of 5 October 2016.*translated by author.*

[204] Federal Court of Santarém, *Appeal 'Ação Civil Pública'*, No.0000377-75.2016.4.01.3902, Judgment of 10 May 2019.*translated by author.*

4.5.2 The Tapajós Case (2017)

The expansion of the technology for the use of hydraulic power to generate electricity in Brazil, emerged in the beginning of the twentieth century.[205] The Plan for the Economic Valuation of the Amazon Region, foreseen in Article 199 of the Federal Constitution of 1946 and institutionalized by Law No. 1806, of January 6th of 1953, defined among its attributions the establishment of a policy involving the electrification of the main production centers and industry.[206]

The indigenous peoples of *Tapajós*, the *Jamanxim*, the *Juruena* and the *Teles Pires* are situated in the watershed of the same name, which expands through the states of Pará, Mato Grosso and Amazonas, connecting two large biomes, the savana (in Portuguese, *cerrado*) and the Amazon. The government and the private companies have been developing plans regarding the use of the water, such as the construction of hydroelectric dams.

Since the 1980s, the Tapajós Hydroelectric Complex project has been brought forward. The initial proposal was to build five plants—*São Luiz do Tapajós, Jatobá, Jamanxim, Cachoeira do Caí* and *Cachoeira dos Patos*—but only the first two had been built. At least three indigenous territories were considered as 'obstacles' to the implementation of those projects.[207]

The Tapajós hydroelectric complex consisted of seven hydroelectric dams on the Tapajós and Jamanxim rivers. In both scenarios, the socio-environmental costs of the ventures were estimated to reach around US$ 400 million.[208]

From January 2011 to July 2014, the BNDES granted loans for hydroelectric plants in the Tapajós basin totaling about R$ 4.087 billion of Reais. The company Eletronorte built the Balbina Hydroelectric Plant, flooding an area of about 2,928.5 km^2 that was expropriated from the original *Waimiri-Atroari* indigenous peoples' land. This example reveals 'a new strategy of the large mining companies in collaboration with the state—to favor the demarcation and homologation of the indigenous area and exercise their economic power to lure new indigenous leaders, with the connivance of the FUNAI, to sign direct agreements between the indigenous communities and the companies, in the name of 'indigenous self-determination'.[209]

The location of the projected power plants reveals the close association between energy projects and the development of the mineral sector in the Amazon.[210] Unfortunately, at least three indigenous populations' territories are no longer recognized by the Brazilian state and an extractive reserve (hereinafter, the Resex) which was supposed to be built, was no longer build. The reason was that their interests

[205] Ioris (2010).

[206] (1987) Brazilian Federal Government Energy Plan.

[207] Alarcon et al. (2016), p. 22.

[208] Ibid., p. 24.

[209] Baines (1996).

[210] Batista and Miranda (2019).

were colliding with the interests of the company responsible for the hydroelectric plant. The indigenous peoples who inhabit the area of the Tapajós hydroelectric near the *São Luís do Tapajós* and *Jatobá* dam projects have long fought for the official recognition of their lands.

The federal judge understood the consultation as a fundamental right and the necessity to interpret in dubio pro salute and in dubio pro natura, which also applies to the cultural environment according to Article 216 of the Constitution, the UNESCO Convention on the Protection and Promotion of the Diversity of Cultural Expressions and the UNESCO Convention for the Safeguarding of the Immaterial Cultural Heritage.[211] All those international treaties were already internalized by the presidential Decree and endowed with supralegal statue in addition to the Law No. 12.343 of 2010.[212]

The legal treatment of dam licensing and, above all, the impact on indigenous peoples clearly illustrates the barriers preventing the application of existing protections in the Federal Constitution, Brazilian legislation and international conventions, such as the ILO Convention No. 169.

In the claim, the federal prosecutor Boaventura pointed out the need for the internalization of international standards on the topic: 'this last point is particularly important in view of the legislative offense against human rights and environmental licensing corpus juris that has been taking place in the country'.[213]

The federal court pointed out Article 225, paragraph 1 of the Constitution of 1988 regarding the need to ensure the effective implementation of the right of all citizens to an ecologically balanced environment. Also mentioned was the relevance of ILO Convention No. 169, which breaks out with the 'current tutelage displaces from the state to the indigenous and tribal peoples giving the possibility of themselves to deciding about their lives and their form of development'.[214] According to the Federal Court, this is important to the comprehension and establishment of the right of self-determination and cultural identity, which was also referred to in the International Covenants of Rights Civil and Political Rights and Economic, Social and Cultural Rights, ratified in 1996 in Brazil by Decree No. 591 of 1992.[215]

The informed consultation is an essential right in the context of the new relationship promoted between national states and indigenous and tribal peoples. And in respect to the federal court decision, this was based on the ILO Convention No. 169 and as well to be found in the Constitution of 1988.

The federal prosecutor also quoted the IACtHR decisions: the case Saramaka *v.* Suriname, the case Kichwa de Sarayaku *v.* Equador, the case Garífuna Community

---

[211] Itaituba Federal Court, *Appeal 'Ação Civil Pública'*, No. 3883-98.2012.4.01.3902, Judgment of 23 November 2017.

[212] (2010) National Information System and Cultural.

[213] Itaituba Federal Court, *Appeal 'Ação Civil Pública'*, No. 3883-98.2012.4.01.3902, Judgment of 23 November 2017.

[214] Ibid.*translated by author.*

[215] Enacting the International Covenant on Economic, Social and Cultural Rights.

de Ponta Pedra *v.* Honduras and the case Kaliña e Lokono People *v.* Suriname. As pointed out by the Brazilian Federal Prosecutor: 'the IACtHR recognizes the consultation as an international right, implying that the national states should adjust their norms and institutions to consult indigenous peoples and tribals peoples in an effective manner, always in enforcement with the standards international on the subject, in order to generate efficacy and reliable channels of dialogue with these groups'.[216]

He also mentioned that: 'the IACtHR also reaffirmed the right to consultation as a general principle of international law, meaning that it is the right of indigenous and tribal peoples in all countries that have ratified the American Convention, regardless of whether they have ratified the ILO Convention No. 169 and/or are signatories to the two aforementioned Declarations. (...) The Court established specific guidelines to be observed by member countries during the concrete application of the law and that the Court's interpretation must necessarily be considered by national judges'.[217]

The federal prosecutor understood that: 'through the technique of consolidation ary and dynamic interpretation of international treaties, as well as the so-called multicultural method of interpretation, the IACtHR understands the consultation as a corollary of the right to property provided for in Article 21 of the American Declaration'.[218]

4.5.3 The Polo Naval de Manaus Case (2016)

Rivers have always been an important source of subsistence, income and power. In these terms, the waters were also formed as an element of dispute, especially in the formation processes of the national states when, in addition to supplying the demands of the society, rivers were also established as traffic routes, opening the possibility of a hydrobusiness.[219]

In Brazil, this could be attested by the Plan for the Economic Valuation of the Amazon Region, foreseen in Article 199 of the Constitution of 1946 and institutionalized by the Law No. 1806, of January 6th of 1953, defining among its attributions the establishment of a policy that involves the rivers as the main production centers for the development of the country.[220]

This law was revoked later but the perception of water as an abundant and apparently inexhaustible element has continued to be reflected deeply in government plans for the region of the Amazon, with several implications for the relationship

[216] Itaituba Federal Court, *Appeal 'Ação Civil Pública'*, No. 3883-98.2012.4.01.3902, Judgment of 23 November 2017.

[217] Ibid.

[218] Ibid.

[219] Batista and Miranda (2019).

[220] Plano de Valorização Econômica da Amazônia (1953) Law 1806.

between society and nature. In fact, the Amazon, due to its dimensions and presence of a large quantity of bodies of water, has been superlatively qualified in the literature, in the government speeches, in the administrative reports, in the government plans, among others.[221]

However, considering the need to still explore the natural resource as the water of the rivers, the government of Amazonas decided by Decree No. 32.875 of 2012 to conduct the Manaus's hub (in Portuguese, the *Polo Naval de Manaus*) without considering a consultation with the more than 19 communites[222] that were living in the area. The federal judge Jaíza Freixo understood that the ideia was: 'at first, I notice that the main objective of the naval hub is to provide a transportation and fluvial access system, with port and terminals, including energy, gas, water and telecommunications supplies, all geared towards the flow of the pipeline production'.[223] However, the Kaolin Project, as it was known, hid that, exactly on the route of the Manaus hub, from the city of Manaus to the city of Boa Vista, in another state, there was an extraordinary kaolin reserve.

The decision of the federal judge was precise on suspending the Decree regulating establishement of the Manaus hub, once it could be also applied to the resource exploitation of this exquisite industrial mineral.

Regarding the requirement of consultation, the federal judge Jaíza Freixo understood the need of the requirement of consultation in accordance with the ILO Convention No. 169 mostly because: 'in turn, the creation of a naval hub decontextualized from the social accomplishment in which the traditional unheard populations live for centuries, is providing in a conflicting way a laboratory for the social sciences, as it produces a scenario of social struggles for a cartographic justice in the Amazon. At this point, the emergence of cartographies with names such as new social cartography, participatory cartography, action cartography or countermapping, are distinguished by the representation of aspects of reality little valued in the spatial cartographic representations hegemonic—aspects transformed into 'non-existences'.[224] The federal judge opposed the development model of the new economy in the heart of the Brazilian Amazon without consulting the indigenous peoples and the 'comunidades ribeirinhas' who live there.

The federal judge understood that: 'the geographic space comes to be a set of geographic objects (natural elements humanized and human works) with certain purposes assigned by society. Thus, an economic company cannot destroy or alter a

[221] Federal Court of Amazonas, *Appeal 'Ação Civil Pública'*, No. 0006962-86.2014.4.01.3200.

[222] The communities: 'São Francisco do Mainã, Jatuarana, União e Progresso, São Francisco do Tabocal, São Raimundo, Nazaré, São Pedro da Costa do Tabocal, Santa Luzia do Tiririca, Bom Sucesso, São Francisco do Caramuri, Santa Rosa, Monte Horebe, Nova Esperança, Nossa Senhora do Perpétuo do Socorro, Nova Vida e Canaã'. Ibid.

[223] Federal Court of Amazonas, *Appeal 'Ação Civil Pública'*, No. 0006962-86.2014.4.01.3200, Judgment of 16 May 2016. *translated by author.*

[224] In order to understand the 'cartografia social' and the territories in a pluralistic view, see: Federal Court of Amazonas, *Appeal 'Ação Civil Pública'*, No. 0006962-86.2014.4.01.3200; Almeida and Farias Júnior (2013); Santos (2016); Anderson (2016); McCall (2021).

traditional space (humanized natural elements and human works) without the prior manifestation and authorization of the people involved. The Amazonian ethos is not a styrofoam model or a graphic computer program that can be reproduced in the existing amusement parks of the developed world, only with the use of technology'.[225]

She quoted the federal Prosecutor's Deborah Duprat work in which she explained the relevance of the case Saramaka people *v.* Ecuardor in the IACtHR, as it provided the important distinction between consultation and consent, requiring the latter in the hypothesis of large enterprise projects that cause loss of territory or serious commitment with respect to the access, use and enjoyment of the fundamental resources to the physical and cultural existence of the group. She understood that the consultation is required for eventual consent.[226] The federal judge then explained that the consultation would be conducted as it is in Articles 6 and 7 of the ILO Convention No. 169.

In 2016, the federal judge extended this chapter of the Manaus hub determining that the Decree No. 32.875 of 2012 was illegal. Nonetheless, the government of Amazonas continues trying to find a legally permissible way, through the public-private partnership with international multinationals for the restructuring of the *Polo Naval de Manaus*, still defying the ruling that in order to implement such a naval hub, there would be first the need to consult with those who live in the region.

4.5.4 The Mining Volta Grande do Xingu Case (2017)

The region of *Volta Grande do Xingu* is located in the same region as impacted by the Belo Monte Hydroelectric Plan and it is inhabited by fishermen, *comunidades ribeirinhas* and indigenous people. It is home to three indigenous communities, whose inhabitants depend on the seasonal flow of the Xingu river.

A mining company called Belo Sun Mining Ltda a subsidiary of the Canadian Belo Sun Mining Corporation (hereinafter, the BSX.TO), had received a preliminary license to operate what is said to be the largest open-pit gold mine in Brazil.

According to the BSX.TO: 'Belo Sun has a large property within a greenstone belt. The Volta Grande Gold Project has a measured and indicated gold mineral resource and a long-term exploration potential. The project has a phased development approach with a strong production profile and robust economics. The construction licence was received in February 2017'.[227]

---

[225] Federal Court of Amazonas, *Appeal 'Ação Civil Pública'*, No. 0006962-86.2014.4.01.3200. *translated by author.*

[226] Duprat (2014); Federal Court of Amazonas, *Appeal 'Ação Civil Pública'*, No. 0006962-86.2014.4.01.3200.

[227] BSX.TO Mining Corp BS (2017) Gold Project, Volta Grande, Brazil.

The licensing process was underway with potential impact on the indigenous lands affecting the Paquiçamba, the Arara do Maia and the Ituna/Itatá. In this context, the MPF filed an appeal against the license given to the BSX.TO.

The federal judge Aram Meguerian suspended the license in his decision. He also quoted Article 231, VI, 3 of the Constitution saying that there is the need for the authorization of the National Congress and the observance of Articles 6, 7 and 15 of the ILO Convention No. 169 regarding the requirement of consultation of indigenous peoples before executing projects of natural resource exploitation. According to the federal judge, the elaboration of the ECI did not remove the need of the 'prior, free and informed consultation of indigenous peoples, in the form of the ILO Convention No. 169, since they are institutes that do not confuse with each'.[228]

Relevant to highlight is the fact that not even the FUNAI nor the MPF recommended to give the license to the Volta Grande Project without consultation. The mining was going to affect the same region affected by the Belo Monte dam. 'Once compared, the six years of monitoring the impacts of the Belo Monte hydroelectric plant have not elapsed'.[229]

According to BSX.TO, the company, continuous updating the mining project in light of the new regulatory guidelines. In regard to the ECI, the company affirms that it was conducted according to the FUNAI parameters. However, the licence remains suspended while the merit of the petition is under the judicial analysis.

4.6 Legislative Cases with Respect to the Requirement of Consultation

Regarding the legislative side, over the years several attempts have been brought forward to alter the legislation regarding the fundamental rights and the international rights of indigenous peoples. The challenges regarding the effectiveness of the requirement of consultation are constantly spurred by the Brazilian legislature and executive, which may issue regulations and decrees revoking the IAHRS, the internationational treaties and even the Constitution of Brazil.

Among the legislations, as example, there are: the application of Article 6, which was described, erroneously, as the public hearings of the Article 231 of the Brazilian Constitution following the interpretation of the Decree No 303[230] of 2012 (in Portuguese, *Portaria Interministerial*); there is the Decree No 289[231] of 2013

[228] Tribunal Regional Federal 1ª Região, *Appeal 'Ação Cível'*, 0002505-70.2013.4.01.3903/PA, Judgment of 19 December 2017.*translated by author*.

[229] Rojas Garzón et al. (2016), p. 35.*translated by author*.

[230] This Decree (in Portuguese, *Portaria),* limit the usage of the indigenous peoples territory. Advocacia Geral da União (2012) Portaria No 303.

[231] This Decree (in Portuguese, Portaria) determined how the construction of highways should be conducted and mention Ministério do Meio Ambiente (2013) Decree 'Portaria' No 289.

(in Portuguese, *Portaria*); and there is the Order No 2[232] (in Portuguse, the *SEAV/COGAB/PRES/2019*) among other legislative indeterminacies.

The case *Educação Escolar Indígena* occurried in the city of Santarém, Pará and the case refers to the Decree No. 001 of 6th January 2014 on the consultation with the indigenous peoples regarding the organizational structure of the schools in the city of Santarém. The federal judge Pablo Zuniga Dourado decided (in Portuguese, *liminarmente*) that: 'it is known that the subsunctive activity is extremely complex, so that the difficulty is not always located on the major premise [normative]—there is no doubt that the norms of the 1988 Constitution and infra-constitutional require the implementation of indigenous schools (...) In fact, prior consultation will better equip the process for the final decision, especially given the knowledge of the opinions of all the indigenous communities involved and better clarifications about the real situation of the municipal schools'.[233]

There is also the Constitutional Amendment Bill No. 76 of 2011, with the objective to alter Article 176 and Article 231 of the Constitution, which ensure the indigenous peoples profit share in the use of water resources on their entitled lands, is an example of this attempt.[234]

Second, the Constitutional Amendment Bill No. 71 of 2011 constitutes an alteration to the Article 231, § 6° of the Federal Constitution allowing a monetary grant for the holders of title deeds related to lands declared as indigenous.[235]

Third, the Constitutional Amendment Bill No. 227 of 2012 permits the alteration of Article 231 paragraph 6. This change in the Constitutional draft regards the possible division of indigenous lands for the use of hydroelectric plants, farms, and others, without taking into consideration neither the environmental licences nor the requirement of consultation.[236]

Fourth, the Constitional Amendment Bill No. 5807 of 2013 aimed at changing the new Mining Code expecially with regard to the mining in indigenous and *quilombola's* lands without the requirement of consultation.[237]

---

[232]This Order limit the assistance of indigenous peoples to the resources provided by the Indigenous Peoples Foundation (FUNAI) for only those who live in the territory already demarcated by the state. However, there are several indigenous peoples territory who were not demarcated yet. Fundação Nacional do Índio (FUNAI) (2019) Order No. 2.

[233]Santarém Federal Court, *Appeal 'Ação Civil Pública'*, No. 378-31.2014.4.01.3902, Judgment of 26 February 2014.*translated by author.*

[234]Maggi SB Constitutional Amendment Bill altering the Article 176 and the Article 231 of the Constitution which ensure the indigenous peoples profit share in the use of water resources on their entitled lands.

[235]Bauer SP Amendment to the Constitutional Bill altering the Article 231, § 6°, of the Federal in order to allow for the indemnification of holders of title deeds related to lands declared as indigenous.

[236]Pereira CH (2012) Complementary Bill that defines what are the assets relavant to the Brazilian state.

[237]Government BF (2013) Bill of Law that set parametres on the mining activity, hereby establishesthe National Council of Mineral Policy and the National Mining Agency.

Fifth, the Constitutional Amendment Bill No. 1216 of 2015 on Article 231 of the Constitution, in which, by the alteration, the indigenous peoples who, due to expulsion of the territory, did not occupy their lands at the time of the promulgation of the Constitution of 1988, would not have the entitlement to the territory.[238]

Last but not least, the current Brazilian president, Jair Bolsonaro, oversaw the drafting of a Bill in 2020 regarding the alteration of Article 176 of the Constitution for excluding consultation with indigenous peoples from the conditions for conducting research and mining of mineral and hydrocarbon resources and for the use of water resources for generating electricity on indigenous lands, instituting compensation for the restriction of the indigenous lands. The legislative file is still pending in the House of Representatives.[239]

Moreover, there was also a draft bill, which would increase the size of the territory, mostly of the farms and latifundium owners, that can be regularized without previous inspection.[240] Among other measures, the draft has not brought any innovation to combat illegal mining (in Portuguese, *grilheiros*), a serious issue to the physical integrity of the indigenous peoples and an issue that commonly concerns deforestation.

However, there was an attempt, between the years of 2012 and 2014, to conduct discussions on regulating the right to consultation. The proposals brought forward by the Brazilian National Congress received several criticisms from indigenous and tribal peoples, both in terms of the draft process and the content as well. The lack of consultation, the insufficient participation, and the change in scope, without prior notice, of meetings that were merely informative, had weakened the undertaking.[241]

In summary, while legislative discussions ceased and rather aimed at curtailing the requirement of consultation, the judiciary has successively recognized the right to consultation, quoting the ILO Convention No. 169, the decisions of the IACtHR and starting the debate settled by the UNDRIP regarding free, prior and informed consent.

[238] Filho CC Bill tha regulates the Article 231 of the Federal Constitution, providing the procedure for the demarcation of the indigenous lands and revokes Decree No. 1.775 of 1996.

[239] Government BF (2020) Bill that regulates § 1 of art. 176 and § 3 of art. 231 of the Constitution to establish the specific conditions for conducting research and mining of mineral and hydrocarbon resources and for the use of water resources for generating electricity on indigenous lands and institutes compensation for the restriction of the indigenous lands.

[240] Silva CZ (2020) Draft Bill that modifies social and environmental legislation.

[241] Grabner (2015).

4.7 Conclusions

The preamble of the Constitution of Brazil states that the country ensures the exercise of social and individual rights, freedom, security, well-being, development, equality and justice as supreme values of a fraternal, pluralist and unprejudiced society, which culminating in the expression of the self-determination.

Article 225 deals with the protection of cultural heritage, manterial and immaterial. The former regards the exercise of cultural rights and manifestations, which the Brazilian state must protect, as well as the valuation of ethnic diversity. For this reason, it states that the right to consultation is the recognition of pluralist, multicultural and democratic societies.[242] In this scenario, pluralism should be understood in the terms in which the Constitution established it as the foundation of the Republic as a fundamental right to difference in all areas and expressions of human coexistence with different social and cultural choices.

The expression of the requirement of consultation should be a valuable tool in order to achieve equality. Thus, it is possible to derive the principles of self-determination and cultural integrity of indigenous peoples, which is an expression of the requirement of consultation with indigenous communities in regard of natural resource exploitation.

This realignment can be seen in the discussion on the requirement of consultation in the ILO Convention No. 169, the UNDRIP and the recent practices of the IAHRS System, the African Human Rights System and the Human Rights Committee, the Committee on the Elimination of Racial Discrimination and the Commitee on Economic, Social and Cultural Rights and more recently, in some jurisprudence of the Brazilian Federal Courts and the Brazilian Supreme Court.

The efficacy of the IAHRS and the international treaties, thus, the control of conventionality, do not represent an obstacle to national development, as the next chapter will show. And the indigenous peoples' Protocols are an adequate way to strengthen and ensure the application of the requirement of consultation, as a bridge between the IAHRS interpretations and the Brazilian legal system.

Thus, the application of indigenous peoples' consultation is an imperative for Brazil in view of the country's eagerness for development. Natural resource exploitation will require a model for consultation to be established from the outset, which avoids the legal insecurity for all traditional peoples and communites, and any kind of violation of human rights.

[242] Duprat (2014); Segato (2011).

References

Alarcon DF, Brent M, Mauricio T (eds) (2016) Ocekadi: hidrelétricas, conflitos socioambientais e resistência na bacia Tapajós. International Rivers ; [Santarém, PA] : [Universidade Federal do Oeste do Pará], Brasília, DF

Albuquerque AAU do L (2008) Multiculturalismo e direito à autodeterminação dos povos indígenas. Porto Alegre: Sérgio Antonio Fabris, 2008. Sérgio Antonio Fabris, Porto Alegre

Alexandrowicz CH (1973) The European-African confrontation: a study in treaty making. Sijthoff, Netherland

Alexy R, Rivers J (2010) A theory of constitutional rights, Repr. Oxford University Press, Oxford

Almeida AWB de, Farias Júnior E de A (eds) (2013) Povos e comunidades tradicionais: nova cartografia social. UEA Edições, Manaus

Alter KJ (2014) The new terrain of international law: courts, politics, rights. Princeton University Press, Princeton

Anaya JS (2004) Indigenous peoples in international law, 2nd edn. Oxford Uiversity Press, New York

Anaya SJ (2005) Divergent discourses about international law, indigenous peoples, and rights over lands and natural resources: toward a realist trend. Colo J Int Environ Law Policy 16

Anderson BRO (2016) Imagined communities: reflections on the origin and spread of nationalism, Revised edn. Verso, London

Aníbal Q (2005) El "movimiento indígena" y las cuestiones pendientes en América Latina. Tareas 119

Arguelhes DW, Hartmann IA (2017) Timing control without docket control: how individual justices shape the Brazilian Supreme Court's Agenda. J Law Courts 5:105–140. https://doi.org/10.1086/690195

Aristotle (1981) The politics, Rev. edn. Penguin Books, Harmondsworth, England, New York

Association of Brazil's Indigenous Peoples (2020) Complicity in Destruction III: how global corporations enable violations of indigenous people's rights in the Brazilian Amazon

Baines SG (1996) Energia na Amazônia. In: A usina hidrelétrica de Balbina e o deslocamento compulsório dos Waimiri-Atroari. Museu Paraense Emílio Goeldi, Belém, pp 747–759

Baines SG (2001) As terras indígenas no Brasil e a "regularização" da implantação de grandes usinas hidrelétricas e projetos de mineração na Amazônia. Sér Antropol 300:1–16

Barak A (1993) Hermeneutics and Constitutional interpretation. Cardozo Law Rev

Baron JB (1999) Law, literature, and the problems of interdisciplinarity. Yale Law J 108:1059. https://doi.org/10.2307/797370

Barroso R (2020) Curso de Direito Constitucional Contemporâneo, Saraivajur

Bastos Lima MG, Visseren-Hamakers IJ, Braña-Varela J, Gupta A (2017) A reality check on the landscape approach to REDD+: lessons from Latin America. For Policy Econ 78:10–20. https://doi.org/10.1016/j.forpol.2016.12.013

Batista IM d S, Miranda LM (2019) Os "Hidronegócios" nos rios da Amazônia. Rev Bras História 39:117–139. https://doi.org/10.1590/1806-93472019v39n81-06

Brazilian Federal Prosecutor (2021a) 6ª Câmara - Populações Indígenas e Comunidades Tradicionais

Brazilian Federal Prosecutor (2021b) Protocolo de Consulta Prévia dos Povos Indígenas e Comunidades Tradicionais

Browder JO (1992) The limits of extractivism. BioScience 42:174–182. https://doi.org/10.2307/1311822

Brown MT (2018) Latin American inequalities and reparations. In: Ystanes M, Strønen IÅ (eds) The social life of economic inequalities in contemporary Latin America. Springer International Publishing, Cham, pp 253–272

Brunori M (2019) Protecting access to land for indigenous and non-indigenous communities: a new page for the World Bank? Leiden J Int Law 32:501–516. https://doi.org/10.1017/S0922156519000232

Canotilho JJG, Mendes GF, Sarlet IW, et al (eds) (2018) Comentários à Constituição do Brasil, 2a edição. Saraiva Jur : Almedina, São Paulo, SP

Casas B d l (1992) A short account of the destruction of the Indies, 1st edn. Penguin Books, New York

Castro AR d (2016) Fundamentos para uma crítica do estatuto do índio: raça e história de lévi-strauss. Rev Eletrônica Curso Direito UFSM 11:275. https://doi.org/10.5902/1981369420970

CIMI O (2017) Congresso anti-indígena: 33 propostas, reunindo mais de 100 projetos, ameaçam direitos indígenas

Clavero B (2008) Tratados con Pueblos o Constituciones de Estados: Dilema para América. Univ Andina Simón Bolívar

CNDH CN dos DH (2018) Povos livres, territórios em luta: relatório sobre os direitos dos povos e comunidades tradicionais. Brazilian Federal Government, Brasília

Cunha MC (2018) Índios na Constitutição. Novos Estud CEBRAP 37

Cunha MC d (1994) O futuro da questão indígena. Estud Av 8:121–136. https://doi.org/10.1590/S0103-40141994000100016

Cunha MC d (2012) Índios no Brasil: história, direitos e cidadania. Claro Enigma, São Paulo, SP

Curi MV (2007) Aspectos legais da mineração em terras indígenas. Rev Estud E Pesqui FUNAI 4

Da Silva JA (2020) Curso de Direito Constitucional Positivo, 43ª. Malheiros Editores/Juspodivm

Dalla Costa JM (2019) O "agir temerário, fraudulento e tirânico": a antropologia e os antropólogos segundo a CPI da Funai e do Incra (2015-2017). Dissertation, Universidade de Brasília, Brazil

Dallari D d A (2017) Índios e Direitos Agredidos. J Bras

Demetrio A, Kozicki K (2019) A (In)Justiça de Transição para os Povos Indígenas no Brasil. Rev Direito E Práxis 10:129–169. https://doi.org/10.1590/2179-8966/2017/28186

Didier F Jr, Sarno Braga P, Alexandria de Oliveira R (2015) Curso de direito processual civil. JusPodivm, Salvador

Do Salvador FV (1627) História do Brasil

Domingues MS, Bermann C (2012) O arco de desflorestamento na Amazônia: da pecuária à soja. Ambiente Soc 15:1–22. https://doi.org/10.1590/S1414-753X2012000200002

Doyle C, Garzon BR, Weitzner V, Okamoto T (2019) Free Prior Informed Consent Protocols as Instruments of Autonomy: Laying Foundations for Rights Based Engagement. Institut für Ökologie und Aktions-Ethnologie (INFOE) e. V, Köln

Doyle CM (2016) Indigenous peoples, title to territory, rights and resources - the transformative role of the free prior and informed consent. Routledge, New York

Duprat D (2014) A Convenção 169 da OIT e o Direito à Consulta Livre. Prévia e Informada, Cult Juríd, p 1

Duprat D (2016) Film: Aldeia da Memória: Evolução das Ações

Duprat D (2018) O marco temporal de 5 de outubro de 1988 – TI Limão Verde. In: Carneiro da Cunha M, Barbosa S (eds) Direitos dos Povos Indígenas em Disputa. Unesp, São Paulo, pp 43–74

Engstrom P (2017) Reconceptualising the Impact of the Inter-American Human Rights System / Reconceitualizando o Impacto do Sistema Interamericano de Direitos Humanos. Rev Direito E Práxis 8. https://doi.org/10.12957/dep.2017.28027

Foblets MC, Goodale M, Sapignoli M, Zenker O (eds) (2022) The oxford handbook of law and anthropology. Oxford University Press, New York

Francisco de V (1532) De Indis De Jure Belli. Ernest Nys. Oceana Publications Inc., Wildy & Sons LTD, New York, London

Freyre G (2004) Ordem e progresso. Global, São Paulo

Freyre G (2006) Casa-grande & senzala: formação da família brasileira sob o regime da economia patriarcal, 51a edição, 10a reimpressão. Global Editora, São Paulo

Furtado C (2007) Formação econômica do Brasil, 34. ed. Companhia das Letras, São Paulo

Galeano E (1997) Open veins of Latin America: five centuries of the pillage of a continent, 25th anniversary ed. Monthly Review Press, New York

Garnelo L, Pontes AL de M (eds) (2012) Saúde indígena: uma introdução ao tema. Unesco, Organização das Nações Unidas para a Educação, a Ciência e a Cultura, Representação no Brasil : SECADI-Secretaria de Educação Continuada, Alfabetização, Diversidade e Inclusão, Ministério da Educação, Governo Federal Brasil, Brasília, DF

Gomes Canotilho JJ (2003) Direito constitucional e teoria da constituição, 7. ed. Almedina, Coimbra

Gomes Esteves LF (2020) Onze ilhas ou uma ilha e dex ilhéus? a presidência do STF e sua influência na atuação do Tribunal. Rev Estud Inst 6

Gomes Ferreira FM (2018) Povos Indígenas Brasileiros: a CPI da FUNAI e do INCRA e a Criminalização de Antropólogas (os). Rev Idealogando 2

Gomes L (2010) 1822: como um homem sábio, uma princesa triste e um escocês louco por dinheiro ajudaram D. Pedro a criar o Brasil ; um país que tinha tudo para das errado. Nova Fronteira Participações, Rio de Janeiro

Gomes L (2014) 1808: como uma rainha louca, um príncipe medroso e uma corte corrupta enganaram Napoleão e mudaram a história de Portugal e do Brasil, 3. Edição. Globo Livros, São Paulo

Gomes LAE (2018) The Influences of Common Law on the Brazilian New Code of Civil Procedure. SSRN Electron J. https://doi.org/10.2139/ssrn.3204827

Grabner ML (2015) O direito humano ao consentimento livre, prévio e informado como baluarte do sistema jurídico de proteção dos conhecimentos tradicionais. Bol Científico ESMPU 14

Grotius H (2005) The rights of war and peace. Liberty Fund, Indianapolis

Hanschel D (2007) The future of the climate regime – how does the institutional design matter? In: Rodi M (ed) Implementing the Kyoto protocol: chances and challenges for transition countries: proceedings of the Summer Academy 'Energy and the Environment'. lexxion, Der Juristische Verlag, Berlin

Heck E, Loebens F, Carvalho PD (2005) Amazônia indígena: conquistas e desafios. Estud Av 19: 237–255. https://doi.org/10.1590/S0103-40142005000100015

Heemann TA (2017) Por uma releitura do direito dos povos indígenas : do integracionismo ao interculturalismo. Rev Doutrina E Jurisprudência Trib Justiça Dist Fed E Territ 109

Holanda SB de (2012) Roots of Brazil

Iocca L, Fidélis T (2021) Traditional communities, territories and climate change in the literature – case studies and the role of law. Clim Dev 1–20. https://doi.org/10.1080/17565529.2021.1949573

Ioris A (2010) Da Foz às nascentes: análise histórica e apropriação econômica dos recursos hídricos no Brasil. In: Almeida A (ed) Capitalismo globalizado e recursos territoriais. Lamparina, Rio de Janeiro, pp 211–255

Jaichand V, Sampaio AA (2013) Dam and be damned: the adverse impacts of Belo Monte on Indigenous Peoples in Brazil. Hum Rights Q 35:408–447. https://doi.org/10.1353/hrq.2013.0023

Júnior AG, Tanagino PID (eds) (2020) Democracia e estado de exceção entre o temporário e o permanente. CRV, Curitiba

Kayser H-E (2010) Os direitos dos povos indígenas no Brasil: desenvolvimento histórico e estágio atual. Antonio Fabris, Porto Alegre

Kelsen H (2005) Pure theory of law. Lawbook exchange, Clark, NJ

Krenak A (1987) Índio Cidadão? Interview

Machado LZ (2020) From the time of rights to the time of intolerance. The neoconservative movement and the impact of the Bolsonaro Government. Challenges for Brazilian anthropology. Vibrant Virtual Braz Anthropol 17:e17458. https://doi.org/10.1590/1809-43412020v17d458

Machado LZ, Motta A, Facchini R (2018) Quem tem medo dos antropólogo(a)s? Práticas científicas em novos cenários políticos. Rev Antropol 61:09. https://doi.org/10.11606/2179-0892.ra.2018.145509

MacKay F (2002) Guide to Indigenous peoples' Rights in the Inter-American Human Rights System. Denmark, Copenhagen

Maia LM, Lira Y (2018) Controle de Convencionalidade: temas aprofundados. Juspodivm

Marcon T (1994) O Serviço de Proteção ao Índio. In: A Trajetória Kaingang no Sul do Brasil. Universidade de Passo Fundo, Passo Fundo, pp 47–92

Mazzuoli V de O (2018) Controle Jurisdicional da Convencionalidade das Leis. Forense

McCall MK (2021) Radical cartographies: participatory mapmaking from Latin America. Soc Nat Resour 1–3. https://doi.org/10.1080/08941920.2021.1881195

McKay BM (2017) Agrarian extractivism in Bolivia. World Dev 97:199–211. https://doi.org/10.1016/j.worlddev.2017.04.007

Medeiros K, Regiani A (2018) História Indígena Em Perspectiva: Representações Neotomistas Ainda Presentes No Ensino De História. Rev Temporis 18:61–79

Mendes AM, Leite MS, Langdon EJ, Grisotti M (2018) O desafio da atenção primária na saúde indígena no Brasil. Rev Panam Salud Pública 42. https://doi.org/10.26633/RPSP.2018.184

Mendes Junior J (1912) Os indigenas do Brasil: seus direitos, individuais e politicos. Hennies Irmãos, São Paulo

Mignolo W (2011) The darker side of Western modernity: global futures, decolonial options. Duke University Press, Durham

Nequete L (1988) O escravo na jurisprudência brasileira: magistratura e ideologia no segundo reinado. Rev Trib

Neves M (2009) Transversale Verfassungen? Konstitutionalismus: Vom Staat zur Weltgesellschaft. In: Brunkhorst H (ed) Demokratie in der Weltgesellschaft, Soziale Welt, Sonderheft 18. Nomos, Baden-Baden

Oliveira JP (1998) Demarcação e reafirmação étnica: um ensaio sobre a FUNAI. In: Indigenismo e Territorialização: Poderes, Rotinas e Saberes Coloniais no Brasil Contemporâneo. Contra Capa, Rio de Janeiro, pp 69–123

Oliveira RC d (1972) A sociologia do Brasil indígena: ensaios. Universidade Federal do Estado de São Paulo, Rio de Janeiro, Tempo Brasileiro

Pasqualucci JM (2003) Introduction: the practice and procedure of the Inter-American Court of Human Rights. In: Brewer SE, Cavallaro JL (eds) Reevaluating regional human rights litigation in the twenty-first century: the case of the Inter-American Court, 1st edn. Cambridge University Press

Paulo PP (2019) '650 mil famílias se declaram "povos tradicionais" no Brasil; conheça os kalungas, do maior quilombo do país'. G1

Pernice I (2002) Multilevel constitutionalism in the European Union. Eur Law Rev

Piovesan F (2019) Direitos humanos e justiça internacional: um estudo comparativo dos sistemas regionais europeu, internamericano e africano. Saraiva, São Paulo

Poscher R (2019) Hermeneutics and law. In: Forster MN, Gjesdal K (eds) The Cambridge companion to hermeneutics, 1st edn. Cambridge University Press, pp 326–353

Preuss UK (1994) Revolution, Fortschritt und Verfassung: zu einem neuen Verfassungsverständnis, Erw. Neuausg. Fischer Taschenbuch, Frankfurt am Main

Primor Ribas GP, Marés de Souza Filho CF (2014) A Judicialização das políticas públicas e o Supremo Tribunal Federal. Rev Direito Estado E Soc

Prudente FJAS (2014) A suspensão de segurança como instrumento agressor dos tratados internacionais

Raftopoulos M (2017) Contemporary debates on social-environmental conflicts, extractivism and human rights in Latin America. Int J Hum Rights 21:387–404. https://doi.org/10.1080/13642987.2017.1301035

Rojas Garzón B, Yamada EM, Oliveira R (2016) Direito à consulta e consentimento de povos indígenas, quilombolas e comunidades tradicionais. Due Process of Law Foundation, São Paulo

Sampaio Ferraz Jr. T (2017) Introdução ao Estudo do Direito: Técnica, Decisão, Dominação. Atlas, Brazil

Santilli J (1993) Aspectos jurídicos da mineração e do garimpo em terras indígenas. In: Santilli J (ed) Os direitos indígenas e a Constituição. Núcleo de Direitos Indígenas e Sérgio Antônio Fabris Editor, Porto Alegre, pp 145–160

Santos B de S (2016) Epistemologies of the South: justice against epistemicide. Routledge, London New York

Santos B de S, Menezes MPG, Nunes JA (2006) Conhecimento e transformação social: por uma ecologia dos saberes. Rev Direito Ambient Amaz 6

Santos de Almeida C (2015) Tempo, memória e narrativa kaingang no oeste catarinense: a tradição kaingang e a proteção tutelar no contexto da transformação da paisagem na terra indígena Xapecó. Santa Catarina Federal University

Schulz C (2020) Forest conservation through markets? A discourse network analysis of the debate on funding mechanisms for REDD+ in Brazil. Environ Commun 14:202–218. https://doi.org/10.1080/17524032.2019.1631869

Schumann C (2018) Framing prior consultation in Brazil: ethnographic perspectives on limits of participation and multicultural politics. Transcript, Bielefeld

Schwarcz LM (1993) O espetáculo das raças: cientistas, instituições e questão racial no Brasil, 1870-1930. Companhia das Letras, São Paulo, SP

Schwarcz LM (2012) Nem preto nem branco, muito pelo contrário: cor e raça na sociabilidade brasileira. Claro Enigma, São Paulo, SP

Schwarcz LM (2017) Lima Barreto: triste visionário. Companhia das Letras, São Paulo, Brazil

Schwarcz LM (2019) Sobre o autoritarismo brasileiro. Companhia das Letras, São Paulo, Brazil

Schwarcz LM, Starling HMM (2015) Brasil: uma biografia. Companhia das Letras, São Paulo, Brazil

Schwarcz LM, Starling HMM (2019) Brazil: a biography

Segato RL (2011) Que cada pueblo teja los hilos de su historia. El pluralismo jurídico en diálogo didáctico con legisladores. In: Chenaut V, Gómez M, Ortiz H, et al. (eds) Justicia y diversidad en América Latina: pueblos indígenas ante la globalización, Primera edición. FLACSO Ecuador ; CIESAS, Quito, Ecuador : México, D.F

Silva EC de A (2018) Povos indígenas e o direito à terra na realidade brasileira. Serviço Soc Soc 480–500. https://doi.org/10.1590/0101-6628.155

Silva JA daa (2007) Aplicabilidade das normas constitucionais, 7a. ed. Malheiros Editores, São Paulo, SP

Silva LAL da, Joca PM (2020) Failure to comply with autonomous during Covid-19 in Brazil. Debates Indígenas

Souza Filho CFM de (2000) O renascer dos povos indígenas para o direito, 1a. ed., 2a. tiragem. Juruá Editora, Curitiba

STF O (2020a) The History of the Brazilian Federal Supreme Court

STF O (2020b) About the Brazilian Federal Supreme Court. Judic Rev

Suárez F (1612) Selections from three works of Francisco Suárez, S.J: De legibus, ac deo legislatore, 1612 ; Defensio fidei catholicae, et apostolicae adversus anglicanae sectae errores, 1613 ; De triplici virtute theologica, fide, spe, et charitate, 1621. W.S. Hein, Buffalo, N.Y

Terto Neto U (2020) Bolsonaro, populism and the fascist threat: the role of human rights defenders in protecting Brazilian democracy. Kairos J Crit Symp 5

Thomas A (1265) Summa Theologica, 1995th edn. Sophia Institute Press, Manchester

Thornberry P (1991) Minorities and human rights law. Minority Rights Group, London

Torelly M (2017) Transnational legal process and Fundamental Rights in Latin America: how does the Inter-American human rights system Reshape domestic constitutional rights? In: Fortes P, Boratti L, Palacios Lleras A, Gerald Daly T (eds) Law and policy in Latin America. Palgrave Macmillan UK, London, pp 21–38

Torres TJF, Sousa Junior AR de, Freire VT (2021) As características e os impactos da narrativa de Jair Messias Bolsonaro. https://doi.org/10.5281/ZENODO.4553171

Trindade AAC (2015) A Humanização do Direito Internacional

Uerpmann R (2003) Völkerrechtliche Nebenverfassungen. In: von Bogdandy A (ed) Europäisches Verfassungsrecht. Springer, Berlin, pp 339–371

Vieira A (1998) Sermão da sexagésima. Vega, Lisboa

Vitoria F de (2016) Relectiones: sobre os índios e sobre o poder civil. Editora Universidade de Brasília : Fundação Alexandre de Gusmão, Brasília

Walker RS, Kesler DC, Hill KR (2016) Are Isolated Indigenous Populations Headed toward Extinction? PLOS ONE 11:e0150987. https://doi.org/10.1371/journal.pone.0150987

Wapichana J (2008) A implementação dos instrumentos internacionais – desafios e fortalecimento dos povos indígenas. In: Franco F (ed) Um olhar indígena sobre a Declaração sobre os Povos Indígenas das Nações Unidas

Webber JR (2020) A great little man: the shadow of Jair Bolsonaro. Hist Mater 28:3–49. https://doi.org/10.1163/1569206X-12342801

Xanthaki A (2014) Indigenous rights and United Nations standards: self-determination, culture and land. Cambridge University Press, Cambridge

Yamada EM (2008) International human rights law in the context of Indigenous Peoples: moving from legislation to implementation: lands rights' cases at the Brazilian Federal Supreme Court. Dissertation, Arizona University, Arizona

Chapter 5
Assessing the Application of Consultation and Indigenous Peoples' Protocols

5.1 Introduction

The number of legal claims and legislation undertaken without due consultation reveals the lack of efficacy of the requirement in the Brazilian state, as seen in the last chapter. The issue impedes the application of the ILO Convention No. 169 and the body of the IAHRS System, having serious repercussions including as regards the self-determination and cultural rights of indigenous peoples, but also for collective rights, equality and development. The limited comprehension of consultation generates legal instability with respect to traditional communities in Brazil. Thus, questions remain regarding the capacity of Brazil to successfully guarantee the efficacy of indigenous peoples' consultation.

In order to compare different legal system and the way they address consultation this chapter proposes to analyze the application across different countries subject to the IAHRS. Furthermore, to increase the comparative validity, the discussion will also consider states under the African Human Rights System. The main goal is to determine how and to what extent the different states accommodate indigenous peoples' specific claims regarding consultation.

Given this context, the chapter is divided in two parts. The first part analyzes to what extent the indigenous peoples' practices in some countries support the implementation and protection of indigenous peoples' consultation rights. The second part assesses the contribution of indigenous peoples' Protocols to the discussion regarding the application of consultation.

The indigenous peoples' Protocols can be understood as documents in which the indigenous peoples themselves formalize the procedures on how to undertake consultation. Thus, the Protocols emerged as a response to the lack of enforcement of certain states with the application of the requirement of consultation provided by the ILO Convention No. 169 and also from a relevant possibility for indigenous peoples' self-determination. In this chapter, the analyses of the Protocols of Brazil and of Paraguay support the better understanding of the legal nature of the Protocols,

C. Woyames Dreher, *A Legal Assessment of the Efficacy of Consultation with Indigenous Peoples*, https://doi.org/10.1007/978-3-031-50539-3_5

as they may be expressed by national norms and acknowledge by the legal system; and by contrast, the Brazilian legal system will be considered, where the Protocols are not part of the *corpus legis*, but instead are being advocated by state judges.

The results of this chapter are key to an improved comprehension of consultation, to identify how other states comply with the norm, respect its application as well as the Protocols. The implementation of self-determination and cultural rights as translated into practices might be seen as an affirmation of consultation with indigenous peoples. Taking place within the normative framework of states, it may provide the basis for the development of a strong corpus of specific measures for indigenous peoples and by indigenous peoples.

5.2 Assessing Consultation with Indigenous Peoples Under the Inter-American System of Human Rights

This subchapter approaches the question on how some sovereign states that ratified the Organization of American States' Charter comply with the requirement of consultation with indigenous peoples in their own national legislation. For this matter, it is relevant to interpret Article 21 in conjunction with Articles 1.1 and 2 of the American Convention, which oblige states to positively adopt special measures to guarantee the equal exercise within the territories, which the indigenous peoples have traditionally used and occupied. Once consultation is broken up to a bundle of rights such as self-determination and cultural rights, a holistic view emerges in this part and in the second part of the chapter.

The states under analysis were chosen because of constitutional reforms occurring and relevant political mobilization, including legislative renewal following the abolishment of authoritarian regimes and the implementation of democratic institutions—accompanied by the ratification of international treaties. These ratifications had taken place in a context of the monist tradition that sets up the relationship between international and state laws, as international human rights standards became part of their domestic laws, translated sometimes even as fundamental rights.

Many of the reforms were reinforced through constitutional control as exercised by the newly established supreme courts with a broader judicial review procedure. The most relevant effect of this expansion of national courts was the increasing reliance on the rulings by the IACtHR, as analyzed in Chap. 3. Yet this process is far from finished and it is therefore essential to analyze relevant cases in these states and how they are complying with the IAHRS System, and international standards in general.[1]

The analysis addresses national legislation and, in some cases, the court decisions and how national judges were invoking and solving the application of consultation

[1] See e.g. Barié (2014); de Sousa Santos (2004); Assies et al. (2002); Guevara Gil and Cabanillas Linares (2020).

with indigenous peoples in some countries of the region. The 'citations to the jurisprudence of neighboring country courts over the past decade are not necessarily based on the authority and international recognition of the referenced court, but in many cases attempt to explore how a common legal problem was resolved within the regional human rights system'.[2]

For instance, the African Human Rights System as in the IAHRS have reports on natural resource exploitation and territory rights issues regarding indigenous peoples.[3] Therefore, there are also elements that enforce the similarities between the international adjudication system, but differently than the IACtHR the 'African Court does not restrict itself to considering human rights violations exclusively under the regional human rights system under which it was established'.[4] This indicates the advanced stage of the African Human Rights System when, in the Endoris case, the jurisprudence of the IACtHR—the Sawhoyamaxa case—is quoted, and gives another interpretation to the Article 60 of the African Charter, providing a new line to the possibilities of interpretation and assessments of sources of international law.[5]

The set of lessons taken from assessing consultation across these six additional Latin American countries provide useful insights also as regards the cases studied of Brazil. By assessing the application of consultation with indigenous peoples provided by the IACtHR, makes clear that the procedural safeguards analyzed in Chap. 3 are not sufficient to achieve the level of protection of indigenous peoples towards the *pro persona* principle.[6] Furthermore, a clear indication of the relevance of comparative studies is that in contrast, citations of the jurisprudence of neighboring country courts over the past decade are not necessarily based on the authority and international recognition of the referenced court, but in many cases attempt to explore how a common legal problem was resolved within the regional human rights system.[7]

5.2.1 Application of Consultation in Argentina

There are 35 different officially recognized indigenous peoples in Argentina which 'legally hold specific constitutional rights at the federal level and in various

---

[2]Mera (2015), p. 855, *translated by author*.

[3]Talbot (2017).

[4]Jansen Reventlow and Curling (2019).

[5]See: Talbot (2017); Inter-American Court of Human Rights, *Sawhoyamaxa Indigenous Community v. Paraguay*, Judgment of 29 March 2006; African Commission on Human and Peoples' Rights, *Centre for Minority Rights Development, Minority Rights Group International and Endorois Welfare Council (On Behalf Of the Endorois Community) v Kenya*, 276/2003, Judgment of 25 November 2009.

[6]Medellín Urquiaga (2013); Negishi (2017).

[7]Mac-Gregor (2015).

provincial states'.[8] Argentina also ratified the ILO Convention No. 169, the International Covenant on Civil and Political Rights, the International Covenant on Economic and Social and Cultural Rights and the UNDRIP. Also, currently a number of draft bills are pending which propose laws through which indigenous communal ownership could be implemented.[9]

Argentina, through the National Constitution of Argentina of 1994 in Article 75.17, recognizes 'the ethnic and cultural preexistence of the Argentine indigenous peoples, the legal status of their communities and their communal possession and ownership of the lands they traditionally occupy, [and] declar[es] that none of these shall be sold, transferred or subject to liens or embargoes'.[10]

However, according to Article 75.22 of the Constitution, for a treaty to obtain constitutional status it requires the approval of two-thirds of the members of the legislature, unless it is included in the list of human rights instruments contained in such provision. In this case, the ILO No. 169 does not hold a constitutional status.[11]

While the right to consultation in Argentina has not been implemented by a specific law, some advancements towards the recognition of indigenous peoples' Protocols[12] can be registered in certain national laws such as Law No. 26.160 on the Emergency of Community Property[13] and Law No. 26.331 on Minimum Standards for the Environmental Protection of Native Forests.[14]

The Decree 672 of 2016 moreover creates the Consultative Council of Indigenous Peoples of Argentina and establishes 'that consultation is the right of indigenous or original peoples to be able to intervene in advance on legislative or administrative measures that directly affect their collective rights, on their physical existence, cultural identity, quality of life or development. It also corresponds to carry out the consultation regarding the plans, programs and projects of national and regional development that directly affect these rights in respect to legislative or administrative measures that directly affect them.'[15]

---

[8] Mamo (2020).

[9] Ibid.

[10] (1994) Constitution of Argentine.

[11] Cabrera (2017).

[12] For more, see e.g. 'the Consultation Protocol is the result of the struggle, projection and organization of the Indigenous Peoples' Territorial Organizations, who have taken up the legacy of our ancestors and assumed the commitment to take the future of our peoples into our own hands. The National Meeting of Territorial Organizations of Native Peoples -ENOTPO, is a space currently formed by 45 organizations that brings together 27 pre-existing peoples and more than 1500 communities, with representation in 20 provinces. We were constituted in 2009 as a space for the articulation of indigenous territorial policy at the national level with a fundamental objective: to go beyond mere resistance to take into our own hands the definitions concerning the present and future of the Indigenous Peoples'. Encuentro Nacional de Organizaciones Territoriales de Pueblos Originarios –ENOTPO Protocolo de Consulta Previa, Libre e Informada a Pueblos Originarios.

[13] Argentina Government (2006) National Law No. 26160.

[14] Argentina Congress (2007) Law No. 26331.

[15] Justice Ministry of Argentina (2016) Decree No. 672/2016.

The goal of the legislation is thus to establish the conditions for ensuring the efficacy of the intercultural dialogue,[16] so that the legislative and the administrative measures that directly affect them must have afforded indigenous peoples' prior intervention, including the decision-making processes, good faith actions and a manner appropriate to the circumstances, with the purpose of reaching an agreement or achieving consent about the measures.

Under this framework, then, indigenous peoples in Argentina can realize the right to be consulted through their representative institutions and appropriate mechanisms, whenever a legislative or administrative measure affecting them regarding a natural exploitation activity is to be approved. It thus becomes a fundamental right for indigenous peoples that functions as a tool to preserve their cultural identity and self-determination, although there is still the need to put these legislative measures into effect.

5.2.2 *Application of Consultation in Bolivia*

The Bolivian Plurinational State has been one of the original members of the United Nations, although only recently it has accepted the jurisdiction of the ICERD. This relates to a more recent decision, for instance, the abolishment of the death penalty in 2013.

In 1948, Bolivia signed the Charter of the Organization of American States and in 1979 it ratified the ACHR. More recently, in 1991, the Plurinational State of Bolivia ratified the ILO N° 169, changing the curse of the protection of indigenous peoples under the domestic legal system.[17]

The Constitution of Bolivia recognizes, in Article 30.II.15, the right of indigenous peoples to be consulted through appropriate procedures, and in particular through their representative institutions, whenever legislative or administrative measures are considered that may affect them. In this context, the right to compulsory prior consultation conducted by the state, in good faith and with consensus, with regard to the exploitation of non-renewable natural resources in the territory they inhabit shall be respected and guaranteed. Bolivia has also the Law 3058 of May 19, 2005, which is relevant for the matter.[18] Article 78 of Environmental Law 1333 of April 27, 1992, and Executive Decree No. 29033 of February 16, 2007, regulates the process of consultation. Important to note is that Article 4 refers to the principles of comprehensiveness and participation, which set the tone for the parameters of consultation as well as the procedures.

The Bolivian Constitutional Court ruled in June 2006 that the 'rights enshrined in the ILO Convention No. 169 should be considered as a norm that is part of the

---

[16] Alvarez (2009).

[17] Tomaselli (2016).

[18] (2005) Bolivian Hidrocarbons Legislation.

constitutionality block, insofar as it enshrines the rights of indigenous and tribal peoples, and is therefore a parameter for verifying the constitutionality or otherwise of a law(...). In conclusion, what the norm under analysis [Article 15(2) of Convention 169] imposes is an obligation on the state to consult on the existence of effects on the interests of indigenous and tribal peoples, taking into account their particular sociological circumstances, consultation is an unavoidable duty of the state'.[19] Thus, 'prior consultation with indigenous peoples in Bolivia is directly supported by at least the twelve articles of the Constitution: Articles 1, 2, 5, 9, 13.IV, 256, 257.I, 410.II, 30.II.15, 98.I, 352 and 403, to which must be added a block of an even larger number of related provisions. There is no doubt that this is an extraordinary and solid constitutional support'.[20]

The current challenges of the Bolivian Plurinational State to engage in dialogue with the indigenous peoples through consultation processes is based on the search for consensus. It is far from clear, however, if the indigenous peoples are not only observers of their own future, or if the legislature and juridiciary give the base for them to also be the architects of it.

5.2.3 Application of Consultation in Chile

Chile has an indigenous peoples' law, the Law No. 19.253 of 1993 that says that 'when addressing matters that affect or are related to indigenous issues, the services of the state administration and local organizations shall hear and consider the views of the indigenous organizations recognized by this Law'.[21]

Regarding consultation, the first regulatory effort to regulate indigenous peoples' matters dates back to 2009, through Supreme Decree No. 124 of the Ministry of Planning, having transitory nature and was issued just as the ILO Convention No. 169 entered into force in Chile.

The complementary regulations, the Supreme Decree No. 66 of 2013, of the Ministry of Social Development and the Supreme Decree No. 40 of 2012, of the Ministry of Environment established the grounds for a mandatory application of consultation. Those regulations 'address the principles established in the Convention for prior consultation and interpret the concepts of direct impact that determine the need to carry out or not a consultation'.[22]

Meanwhile, another factor has set the framework for the efficacy of consultation in Chile, which is the judicialization of natural resource exploitation projects that had

[19] Constitutional Court of La Paz, *Constitutional decision 0045/2006*, 2005-12440-25-RDI, Judgment of 2 June 2005.

[20] Böhrt Irahola (2015).

[21] (1993) Legislation for the standards on the protection, promotion and development of indigenous peoples, and creates the national indigenous development corporation.

[22] International Labour Organization (2016).

been approved without consultation. The data collected by an ILO report shows that '45 projects have been brought to court in relation to indigenous consultations, of which 5 have been discarded, 4 have been paralyzed and subsequently have had to face consultation processes, and the rest have been approved after legal proceedings, or are still being processed before the Courts of Justice'.[23]

The Chilean Constitutional Court had two relevant decisions regarding the interpretation of the ILO Convention No. 169: in relation to a petition of unconstitutionality and the review of constitutionality. On both occasions, the Chilean Constitutional Court referred to the existence of two types of norms that may be present in an international treaty: self-executing norms and non-self-executing norms. Thus, in April of 2008, the Chilean Constitutional Court declared constitutional and self-executing Article 6, No. 1, 'a' and No. 2, and Article 7, No. 1. The result is that the consultation with indigenous peoples defined in Article 6 of Convention No. 169 must be executed and implemented as soon as the Convention enters into force in Chile, even when its application is not fully regulated.[24]

5.2.4 *Application of Consultation in Colombia*

The Constitution of Colombia of 1991, in its Article 330, stipulates that 'exploitation of natural resources in indigenous territories shall be undertaken without harming the cultural, social and economic integrity of the indigenous communities. In decisions taken with regard to such exploitation, the Government shall encourage the participation of representatives of the respective communities'.[25]

The Colombian Constitutional Court is the most advanced in Latin America with regard to the protection of the cultural integrity of indigenous peoples, having developed an entire jurisprudence on the duty of the Colombian state to consult. Thus, 'on the construction of transformative constitutionalism in the region; the IACtHR and the Constitutional Court of Colombia have become a kind of beacons irradiating principles and supranational values. In other words, these two courts have set up a supranational dialogue beyond hierarchical or vertical preconceptions'.[26]

In February 1997, the Court ruled that the ILO Convention No. 169 was a Constitutional norm that aimed to ensure the efficacy of the implementation of consultation. The Court considered that the institution of consultation with indigenous communities that may be affected by the exploitation of natural resources required the adoption of relations of communication and understanding, marked by mutual respect and good faith between them and the public authorities. In some national cases, the Court granted appeals of injunctions suspending the

[23] Ibid.

[24] Ibid.; Astudillo Becerra (2017).

[25] (1991) Constitution of Colombia.

[26] Herrera (2019).

environmental license and ordering the execution of consultation. In the case of Colombia, the Ministry of the Interior is responsible for the implementation of prior consultation. In particular, consultation on investment projects is coordinated through the Directorate of Prior Consultation, a specialized agency for this type of consultation, which is part of this Ministry. Consultations on legislative measures, other administrative measures or public policies are carried out by the Directorate of Indigenous Affairs and Minorities of the same Ministry.[27]

In the same vein, the Colombian Constitutional Court ruled in November 1998 on the construction of a hydroelectric plant, concluding that there had been a violation of the fundamental rights of the Embera-Katío people of Alto Sinú, since the consultation that should have been made formally and substantially was omitted. The Constitutional Court ordered the national government and the company to consult the indigenous people about the project. This was to compensate the indigenous peoples' for the damages already caused, to adopt measures that would ensure their survival and respect their cultural integrity, and to ensure the informed participation of the indigenous people in decision-making aimed at minimizing the impact of the project on the community. In sum, the ruling required the compensation of the indigenous peoples for the inevitable consequences of the construction of the hydroelectric plant.

In another case concerning the delimitation of indigenous mining areas according to the Colombian Mining Code, the Constitutional Court ruled in May 2002 that when it comes to mining exploration and exploitation by third parties, the law must be harmonized with the ILO Convention No. 169 in terms of consultation. The Court made an integrated interpretation of the Mining Code, the Constitution and the Convention No. 169 in order to carry out the consultation process. The advancement in the decisions can be seen in the interpretation given to legal cases of mining and hydroelectric plants.[28]

There are in fact a number of cases that shaped consultation with indigenous peoples in Colombia. The decision T-652/98 about the right to survival of the indigenous peoples Embera-Katio del Alto Sino can be considered a relevant case in response to the lack of prior consultation on case of a construction of a hydroelectric plant. The decision points 3, 4, 7, 9 and 11 affirm that the consultation should be carried out. In particular, point 4 of the decision states that the 'terms already agreed upon for the representatives of the indigenous peoples and their communities to draw up their own list of impacts of the filling and operation of the dam must be respected; the negotiation of an agreement on the prevention of future impacts, mitigation of those already present and foreseeable, compensation for the loss of the use and enjoyment of part of the lands of the current resguardos, participation in the benefits of the exploitation of the natural resources, and other issues included in the agenda of the consultation, shall be advanced within the three (3) months following the notification of this review ruling; this term may only be extended, at

[27] International Labour Organization (2016).

[28] Garavito and Salinas (2010).

the request of the Embera-Katío people of Alto Sinú, the company that owns the project, the Ombudsman's Office or the Agrarian Attorney's Office, for a reasonable period of time, which in no case may exceed twice the period established in the previous guideline; if in that time it is not possible to reach an agreement or consensus on all the issues, the decision of the authority must be devoid of arbitrariness and authoritarianism; consequently, it must be objective, reasonable and proportionate to the constitutional purpose that requires the state to protect the social, cultural and economic identity of the indigenous community. In any case, the necessary mechanisms must be arbitrated to mitigate, correct or restore the effects that the authority's measures produce or may generate to the detriment of the community or its members'.[29]

The case C-418 assessed participation as the instrument for ensuring the efficacy of other constitutional rights. The case addressed an authorization of a natural resource exploitation in a mining zone in indigenous peoples' territory without their prior consultation. Among other relevant aspects, the decision builds on the fact that prior consultation on decisions is an obligation expressly required by the paragraph of Article 330 of the Political Constitution and by Articles 6 and 7 of ILO Convention No. 169, for which it constitutes a real participation mechanism for those consulted to express their points of view and influence the administration's decision-making.[30] The decision also refers to the decision SU-039 of 1997 in order to argue that prior consultation is a 'fundamental right in favour of the indigenous community not only because it represents a manifestation of the fundamental right to participation, but also because it constitutes the means by which their physical and cultural integrity will be protected in such cases'.[31] According to the argument of the decision, the ILO Convention No. 169 together with Article 40-2 of the Constitution constitutes a 'constitutional block, by virtue of the provisions of Articles 93 and 94 of the Charter'.[32]

According to official information provided by the Directorate of Prior Consultation, it is noteworthy that of the total number of processes registered, only 17 have ended without agreement in the prior consultation. Thus, out of the total of '4496 Protocolizations, the processes protocolized without agreement are equivalent to only 0.37% of the processes protocolized, establishing an effectiveness factor of 99.62%'.[33]

However, Colombia suffers from a paradoxical situation in terms of the right to prior consultation.[34] Between the important reception of international law, the legal system contrasts with the deficiencies in implementing the recognized rights of the

[29] Constitutional Court of Colombia, *Provisional Measure T-652*, T-652, Judgment of 1998.

[30] Constitutional Court of Colombia, *Legal regime of participation and special protection with respect to soil and subsoil exploitation*, C-418/02.

[31] Ibid. *translated by author.*

[32] Ibid. *translated by author.*

[33] International Labour Organization (2016). *translated by author.*

[34] Garavito and Salinas (2010).

international treaties, due to the lack of political will. The lack of a specific legislation, however, may well be made up for by an important set of jurisprudential rules on the basis of which adequate consultation processes can be carried out. The regulatory framework for consultation includes laws, decrees and presidential directives that, due to their number, diversity and lack of consensus, generate legal uncertainty.

In addition, Colombia has negotiated and is currently negotiating free trade agreements that would facilitate the exploitation of natural resources in indigenous territories, which makes it necessary for such agreements to include adequate protections for the efficacy of the right.

5.2.5 Application of Consultation in Nicaragua

The Constitution of Nicaragua in its Article 89 establishes that 'the state recognizes communal forms of land ownership of the communities of the Atlantic Coast. Equally it recognizes their enjoyment, use and benefit of the waters and forests of their communal lands'.[35] Article 180 stresses that 'the communities of the Atlantic Coast have the right to live and develop themselves under the forms of social organization that correspond to their historic and cultural traditions. The state guarantees these communities the benefits of their natural resources, the effectiveness of their forms of communal property and the free election of their authorities and representatives. Furthermore, it guarantees the preservation of their cultures and languages, religions and customs'.[36] Regarding the requirement of consultation, there is the Law on the communal property regime of the indigenous peoples and ethnic communities of the autonomous regions of the Atlantic coast of Nicaragua and of the Law 445.[37]

In its Article 3, the Law stipulates that consultation consists of the 'delivery of technical information regarding the operation of the project, followed by a process of discussion and a decision thereon, during which communities shall have translators to translate what has been said during this process into their languages and be assisted by experts in the field'.[38] Besides regulating the communal property regime of the indigenous peoples' entitlement to territory and to guarantee the recognition of the rights of communal property, use, administration, management of traditional lands and their natural resources, the legislation also contains provisions for demarcation and titling of ancestral lands, and for indigenous land reclamation (in Spanish,

---

[35](1987) Constitution of Nicaragua. *translated by author.*

[36]Ibid. *translated by author.*

[37](2002) Law of the Regime of Communal Property of the Indigenous Peoples and Ethnic Communities of the Autonomous Regions of the Atlantic Coast of Nicaragua and of the Bocay, Coco, Indio and Maíz Rivers.

[38]Ibid. *translated by author.*

Saneamiento). This is the last step of Law 445 and requires clearing of the indigenous territories and also the ethnic communities (the Afrodescendant communities) of non-indigenous who are living and using the territories without a legal title or a lease agreement with the community.[39]

5.2.6 Application of Consultation in Paraguay

The Constitution of Paraguay recognizes an elevated hierarchical position for international treaties, above the domestic legislation yet below the Constitution.[40] In the Paraguay Constitution of 1992, Articles 63 and 64 address consultation. Article 64 states that 'indigenous peoples have [the] right to communal ownership of the land [propiedad comunitaria], in [an] extension and quality sufficient for the preservation and the development of their particular forms of lifestyles. The state will provide them gratuitously with these lands, which will be non-seizable, indivisible, non-transferrable, imprescriptible, not susceptible to guarantee contractual obligations nor to be leased; likewise, they will be exempt from taxes. The removal or transfer of [the indigenous peoples] from their habitat without their expressed consent is prohibited'.[41] Also, in the Constitution it is stipulated that Spanish and Guaraní, an indigenous tongue, are the two official languages recognized in the state. The indigenous language thus forms part of the nation's cultural heritage.[42]

This Constitution develops the content, principles and procedure of the right to consultation of indigenous or original peoples with regard to legislative or administrative measures that affect them directly. In Article 2 it establishes that 'indigenous or aboriginal peoples have the right to be consulted in advance on legislative or administrative measures that directly affect their collective rights, whether over their physical existence, cultural identity, quality of life or development'. The consultation referred to in this Act is implemented by the state on a mandatory basis. In Article 4, there is the guiding principle of the right to consultation that must be the followed by '[the] opportunity, interculturality, good faith, flexibility, reasonable time, absence of co-responsibility or conditioning and timely information'.[43]

With the ratification of the ILO No. 169, by Law 234 of 1993, the Paraguayan state reinforced the constitutional principle by adhering to the provision of the ILO No. 169, confirming that in applying the provisions, governments shall consult the indigenous peoples concerned through appropriate procedures and in particular

[39] Renshaw J (2007) Nicaragua: Documento para Discusión sobre los Pueblos Indígenas y Afro-Descendientes.

[40] (1992) Constitution of Paraguay.

[41] Ibid. *translated by author.*

[42] Ibid. *translated by author.*

[43] Ibid. *translated by author.*

through their representative institutions whenever consideration is being given to legislative or administrative measures which may affect them.

5.3 Assessing Consultation Under the African Human Rights System

The legal instrument that inaugurated the African Human Rights System (hereinafter, the AHRS) is the African Charter on Human and Peoples' Rights (hereinafter, the Banjul Charter or African Charter), which was adopted on 27 June 1981 and entered into force on 21 October 1986. The African Charter emerged under the auspice of the Organization of African Unity (hereinafter, the OAU, which was established in 1962 and replaced by the African Union, AU, in 2002) and imposed supra-national accountability for states as regards violations of human rights. The African Charter created the African Commission on Human and Peoples' Rights (hereinafter, the African Commission), and together with the OAU, they served to promote human and peoples' rights and ensure their protection in Africa. According to Article 31 of the Banjul Charter, 'the Commission shall consist of eleven members chosen from amongst African personalities of the highest reputation, known for their high morality, integrity, impartiality and jurisdiction in matters of human and peoples' rights; particular consideration being given to persons having legal experience'.[44] And in accordance with Article 45, the African Commission had the right to 'interpret all the provisions of the present Charter at the request of a state party, an institution of the OAU or an African Organization recognized by the OAU'.[45]

The AHRS represents a source of soft law: 'recognizing and reaffirming that indigenous individuals are entitled without discrimination to all human rights recognized in international law, and that indigenous peoples possess collective rights which are indispensable for their existence, well-being and integral development as peoples'.[46] It is thus characterized by the recognition of groups as human rights holders. The collective rights of peoples are understood as relevant and essential, setting the ground for rights as among others the right to existence, the right to culture, the right to self-determination, the right to freely dispose of their wealth and natural resources.

Article 17 of the Banjul Charter establishes that 'the promotion and protection of morals and traditional values recognized by the community shall be the duty of the state',[47] which places importance on the cultural rights for peoples and individuals.

[44] African States members of the Organization of African Unity (1981) African Charter on Human Rights and Peoples' Rights.

[45] Ibid.

[46] (2007) The United Nations Declaration on the Rights of Indigenous Peoples.

[47] African States members of the Organization of African Unity (1981) African Charter on Human Rights and Peoples' Rights.

As regards peoples, Article 22 notes that 'all peoples shall have the right to their economic, social and cultural development with due regard to their freedom and identity and in the equal enjoyment of the common heritage of mankind. States shall have the duty, individually or collectively, to ensure the exercise of the right to development'.[48]

Regarding the right to consultation, Article 21 enlightens that 'all peoples shall freely dispose of their wealth and natural resources. This right shall be exercised in the exclusive interest of the people. In no case shall a people be deprived of it. In case of spoliation the dispossessed people shall have the right to the lawful recovery of its property as well as to an adequate compensation. The free disposal of wealth and natural resources shall be exercised without prejudice to the obligation of promoting international economic cooperation based on mutual respect, equitable exchange and the principles of international law'.[49]

The jurisprudence of the African Commission has been influenced in turn by the vast jurisprudence regarding indigenous peoples provided by the IAHRS System.[50] Equally, the African Commission's Working Group of Experts on Indigenous Population has contributed on how to address to indigenous peoples claims through the AHRS.

One of the decisions of the African Commission, the claim of the violation of the right to development of indigenous peoples, established an important precedent. The decision ensured indigenous peoples the equity and participation in natural resource management and development on their entitled territory.[51] The African Commission understood that the Endorois people had the right to participate in case of major development or investment projects that affected the community, and that free, prior and informed consent was essential for the protection of human rights of indigenous peoples in such cases.

Accordingly, the Advisory Opinion of the African Commission on the UNDRIP of 2007 confirms the 'the right to be consulted in the drafting of laws and programmes concerning them and [that it] is compatible with the unity and territorial integrity of the state members'.[52]

More recently, already in 2016, the African Commission adopted a Resolution regarding indigenous peoples. The document mentions Articles 21 and 22 of the Banjul treaty in where there is the recognition of the right to all peoples to their economic, social and cultural development, so as the right to freely dispose of their

---

[48]Ibid.

[49]Ibid.

[50]Viljoen (2017); Ankumah (1996).

[51]African Commission on Human and Peoples' Rights, *Centre for Minority Rights Development, Minority Rights Group International and Endorois Welfare Council (On Behalf Of the Endorois Community) v Kenya*, 276/2003, Judgment of 25 November 2009.

[52]African Commission on Human and Peoples' Rights (2007) Advisory opnion of the African Commission on Human and People's Rights on the United Nations Declaration on the Rights of Indigenous Peoples.

wealth and national resources. There is also the recognition that the state should ensure the exercise of those rights.

The draft reflects the concern over the deteriorating situation of indigenous peoples in Africa and, in order to prevent more violations of human rights, especially, the forceful evictions. The document proposes the national states to: 'adopt policies and laws that secure the rights of indigenous populations/communities to own, control and manage their ancestral lands in the forests and protected areas; adopt policies and laws that will promote and enhance the rights of indigenous populations/communities to access and benefit from social and economic programmes and projects; adopt policies, laws and measures to promote and protect the rights of indigenous populations/communities from marginalization, discrimination and poverty; respect and promote the rights of indigenous populations/communities to security and ownership of their ancestral lands, right to development, and right to their culture and language'.[53]

5.4 Assessing Indigenous Peoples' Protocols

The growing response of indigenous peoples to the violation of the requirement of consultation has resulted in the codification of their 'own laws and governance rules by developing their own autonomous rights-based consultation and consent Protocols based on their experience in the national context'.[54] This process of broadening the forms of participation echoed experiences suffered in the recent past. From a legal perspective, the requirement of consultation has not only had impacts on the legal procedure stipulated in the ILO Convention No. 169 and the Constitution and other norms.

It has also led to the establishment of specific consultation Protocols, with the purpose to ensure the necessary freedom to articulate and provide space for deliberations without neither external nor internal pressures, which usually accompany consultation processes as conducted by state authorities or private companies. In their own terms, the indigenous peoples thus attempted to ensure their claims were heard without coercion to artificially legitimize any natural resource project that was not in their best interest.

This subchapter is going to assess the potentialities of the application of consultation through the indigenous peoples' Protocols in general, and in particular in two countries: Brazil, where there is no regulation as regards the Protocols and in Paraguay, where such regulation can be found.

[53] African Commission on Human and Peoples' Rights (2016) 334 Resolution on Indigenous Populations and Communities in Africa.

[54] Rodríguez Garavito and Andrés Baquero Díaz (2018).

5.4.1 The Advent of the Indigenous Peoples' Protocols

The Protocols can be defined as 'documents that formalize the engagement rules and procedures in relation to consultations'.[55] They have been developed as legal redress to realize consultation with indigenous peoples often proved controversial and the practiced reality turned out to be far away from the initial concept of consultation 'which has its grounds on the people's self-governance, territorial and cultural rights'.[56] The Protocols are thus a response to the lack of observance of indigenous peoples' rights.

The literature identifies several waves of developing the consultation Protocols already since the early 2000s.[57] The first wave translated into the Canadian First Nations practices, when they were negotiating directly with mining companies.[58]

The case dates back to 2006 and involved the Platinex Inc., a junior mining company that intended to set up a drilling in the traditional territory of Kitchenuhmaykoosib Inninuwug (hereinafter, the KI), a small, remote First Nations Community in Canada, without their consent. The community members protested at the campsite which obliged the company to leave the territory; however, subsequently the KI was sued. Justice Patrick Smith granted the injunction 'a remedy very rarely awarded to Aboriginal litigants who object to resource development on their traditional lands—and thus the decision attracted the attention of government, First Nations communities and political organizations, industry, lawyers and academics'.[59]

A relevant lesson from the Supreme Court of Canada can be taken in that one of the fundamental purposes of the Constitutional Act was the 'recognition of existing

---

[55] Doyle et al.

[56] 'Indigenous peoples have shown good faith in developing FPIC Protocols. states, corporations, financers and international organizations now need to show good faith by respecting them. Until this happens, and the necessary preconditions are in place for rights-based consultations to take place, FPIC Protocols will continue to act as tools for resistance, education and strengthening self-governance. Project proponents should:respect FPIC Protocols, follow their guidance and ensure that they are fully addressed as part of human rights due diligence, impact assessments, agreements and monitoring; develop a public policy commitment to respect international standards on indigenous peoples' rights, including the right to consultation and FPIC; recognize that FPIC is a process to be defined and managed by indigenous peoples; and acknowledge that FPIC Protocols reduce long-term investment risk exposure and encourage states and other corporate actors to respect FPIC Protocol implementation. International Organizations should: share and examine of experiences with other indigenous peoples of FPIC Protocol development and implementation; consider a range of topics outlined in the report as part of Protocol development, including whether FPIC Protocols should be used in place of, or in conjunction with, national regulation; collaborate nationally and internationally to amplify the collective impact of their FPIC Protocols; and insist that as rights-based normative self-governance tools, FPIC Protocols must serve as educational instruments for all actors engaging with indigenous peoples.' Ibid., p. 11.

[57] Ibid., p. 23.

[58] Ariss and Cutfeet (2011).

[59] Ibid.

aboriginal and treaty rights. The s.35.(1) The existing aboriginal and treaty rights of the aboriginal peoples of Canada are hereby recognized and affirmed'.[60] In the case R. v. Van der Peet, it was declared 'the reconciliation of the pre-existence of distinct Aboriginal societies with the assertion of Canadian sovereignty'.[61] Along with the common-law perspective, the reconciliation is accomplished via the elaboration of the indigenous peoples' rights, which were determined by the Supreme Court: 'true reconciliation will, equally, place weight on each'.[62]

According to the official Canadian guidelines, 'consulting is an important part of good governance, sound policy development and decision-making. Through consultation, the Crown seeks to strengthen relationships and partnerships with Aboriginal peoples and thereby achieve reconciliation objectives. In addition to pursuing policy objectives, the federal government consults with Aboriginal peoples for legal reasons. Canada has statutory, contractual and common law obligations to consult with Aboriginal groups. The process leading to a decision on whether to consult includes a consideration of all of these factors and their interplay'.[63] In the Haida and Taku River decisions in 2004 that 'it arises when a Crown actor has knowledge, real or constructive, of the potential existence of the Aboriginal right or title and contemplates conduct that might adversely affect it. This in turn may lead to a duty to accommodate Aboriginal concerns. Responsiveness is a key requirement of both consultation and accommodation. The scope of the duty to consult is proportionate to a preliminary assessment of the strength of the case supporting the existence of the right or title, and to the seriousness of the potentially adverse effect upon the right or title claimed'.[64] And in the Mikisew Cree decision in 2005, the Supreme Court of Canada held that 'the duty to consult is an obligation that flows from the honour of the Crown, a foundational principle of Aboriginal law which governs the relationship between the Crown and Aboriginal peoples. This duty requires the Crown to consult Aboriginal peoples before taking action that may adversely affect their asserted or established rights under s. 35 of the Constitution Act, 1982 and ensures that the Crown acts honourably by preventing it from acting unilaterally in ways that undermine s. 35 rights'.[65]

[60] (1985) Constitutional Act.

[61] Supreme Court Judgments, *R. v. Van der Peet*, 23803, Judgment of 21 August 1996, [1996] 2 SCR 507.

[62] Ibid.

[63] *Aboriginal Consultation and Accommodation - Updated Guidelines for Federal Officials to Fulfill the Duty to Consult*, 2011.

[64] Supreme Court of Canada, *Taku River Tlingit First Nation v. British Columbia (Project Assessment Director)*, 2004 SCC 74, Judgment of 18 November 2004, [2004] 3 SCR 550.

[65] Supreme Court of Canada, *Mikisew Cree First Nation v. Canada (Governor General in Council)*, 2018 SCC 40, Judgment of 10 November 2018, [2018] 2 SCR 765.

The second wave of Protocols emerged in the late 2000's in the context of the Convention on Biological Diversity. The implementation of access and benefit sharing agreements under Article 8(j) [66] was crucial for countries such as Honduras,[67] India,[68] South Africa,[69] among other countries that developed their own Protocols.[70] Similar consultation Protocols in Belize made clear that orientation seminars were not sufficient to meet the requirement of good faith consultation, once 'the Maya People did not give consent to the REDD+ Program or R-PP'.[71] In a letter to the World Bank, they demonstrated that in any context of implementing projects involving forest carbon stocks, they 'must be align[ed] with the Maya Consultation Protocol'.[72]

Those initial experiences with autonomous Protocols demonstrate their potential to contribute to 'tackling critical shortcomings in existing law and practice around consultation and consent'.[73]

The start of the elaboration of the Protocols and ways to invoke them to engage with corporations has inspired indigenous peoples around the world, such as has been the case in Suriname.[74] Other Protocols that overcome limitations seen in the

---

[66]According to the Article 8, j: "(j) Subject to its national legislation, respect, preserve and maintain knowledge, innovations and practices of indigenous and local communities embodying traditional lifestyles relevant for the conservation and sustainable use of biological diversity and promote their wider application with the approval and involvement of the holders of such knowledge, innovations and practices and encourage the equitable sharing of the benefits arising from the utilization of such knowledge, innovations and practices" (1993) Convention on Biological Diversity (CBD).

[67](2012) Protocolo bio-cultural del Pueblo Indígena Miskitu: el derecho al consentimiento libre, previo e informado en nuestro territorio de La Muskitia Hondureña.

[68](2009) Lingayats Bio-cultural values.

[69]Shrumm and Harry (2012).

[70]Reinforcing that the traditional the cultural knowledge is a tool for the Protocols, Alaska designed their own guidelines. (2000) Guidelines for Respecting Cultural Knowledge.

[71](2013) Position of Maya Leaders on Belize UN-REDD+ Project and R-PP Submission.

[72]Ibid.

[73]Rodríguez Garavito and Andrés Baquero Díaz (2018), p. 83.

[74]'The Saramaka and Lokono case studies both illustrate a number of points in relation to FPIC, both in general and as related to issued specific to the CBD. These points are: Indigenous and tribal peoples' rights to lands, territories and resources must be secured in law and these lands and territories must be properly delimited, demarcated and titled for FPIC to be effective; While it may be time consuming, the identification of indigenous and tribal institutions and customary norms concerning FPIC is nevertheless essential. This is the case both for indigenous and tribal peoples and for those who seek to interact with them; The 'take me to your leader' approach is not necessarily an appropriate avenue in relation to FPIC, although it may be a place to start; FPIC needs to be incorporated into domestic law to be effective. As shown in the Lokono case, companies will hide behind deficient national laws to evade respect for indigenous and tribal peoples' rights; Mechanisms to verify that FPIC has been given need to be in place; It is important that indigenous and tribal peoples are proactive in identifying potential threats to their territories and resources as well as in defining for themselves what are the elements of an FPIC process. The Lokono attempted to do this by drafting a Protocol on traditional rights and FPIC and trying to get the companies to agree to the terms. Even when the companies refused, they communities incorporated their Protocol

existent Protocols in Brazil include those of countries such as Peru, Mexico, Ecuador, as well as Colombia, the latter being a country that is considered to have had a more successful trajectory in the field.[75]

The Protocols' legitimacy bases on their recognition by national and international courts, as well as international oversight and administrative bodies. In 2006, the Ontario Superior Court of Justice addressed the Resource Development Protocol developed by the KI. [76] And, in 2016, the Constitutional Court of Colombia, quoted the Embera Chamí's Protocol.[77]

Only in the year of 2018, the Federal Court in Brazil required that the future consultations with the Juruna people should respect the *Juruna (Yudjá) da Terra Indígena Paquiçamba da Volta Grande do rio Xingu'* Protocol.[78] The decision states and recognizes that the consultation process must observe the Protocol drawn up by the indigenous people themselves. The relevance of the precedent is highlighted, as it is the first case in which the Brazilian judiciary recognized an autonomous Protocol of consultation, as an instrument that dictates the rules that should guide the processes.

Furthermore, in the year of 2019, the federal court in Amazonas determined the Mura indigenous peoples to elaborate their own Protocol, the first one elaborated due to a judicial process.[79] A new hearing on the process was scheduled for September of 2019 for the parties to analyze the Protocol and also to alter it, since the court have adopted the principle of binding the Protocol.[80]

The Protocols are also an instrument of self-determination: 'the [indigenous peoples' Protocols of the] *Wajãpi and Munduruku*, strengthen the alliance between villages and traditional political leaders; the Xingu Protocol, approved by the Xingu Indigenous Territory Management Plan, represents the internal governance agreement between 16 peoples who share a single indigenous land; and the Protocol of the traditional Mangabal Mountain communities on the Tapajós River, which, through

into a village regulation that they insist outsiders must respect if they are to engage in consultation and other processes with the communities.' Forest Peoples Programme (2007).

[75] 'Through a combination of the Constitutional Court's jurisprudence and ethnic movements' and social organizations' insightful political and legal use of FPIC, Colombia is often considered a model to emulate how to regulate, litigate, and claim this right. Although these are notable and well-known advances, in this chapter we also want to highlight the swings, uncertainties, gaps, and tensions in the application of FPIC in the country so that the comparison with other national cases is more fruitful and accurate'. Rodríguez Garavito and Andrés Baquero Díaz (2018).

[76] Ontario Superior Court of Justice, *Platinex v. Kitchenuhmaykoosib*, 06-0271, Judgment of 28 July 2006.

[77] Constitutional Court of Colombia, T-530/16, Judgment of 27 September 2016.

[78] Tribunal Regional Federal 1ª Região, *Appeal 'Ação Cível'*, 0002505-70.2013.4.01.3903/PA, Judgment of 19 December 2017.

[79] Conselho Indígena Mura, Autazes, Organização das Lideranças Indígenas Mura de Careiro da Várzea (2019) TRINCHEIRAS: YANDÉ PEARA MURA Protocolo de Consulta e Consentimento do Povo Indígena Mura de Autazes e Careiro da Várzea, Amazonas.

[80] Ministério Público Federal (2019) MPF: Povo Mura entrega protocolo de consulta à Justiça Federal do Amazonas.

the definition and public presentation of their own consultation Protocol, demand recognition as legitimate subjects of the right to consultation, and ILO Convention No. 169 as a whole'.[81]

Finally, at the Geneva Free, Prior and Informed Consent Protocol Workshop on occasion of the 7th United Nations Forum on Business and Human Rights in Geneva on 24th November of 2018, some national courts, such as those in Canada, Colombia and Brazil, recognized the indigenous peoples' Protocols as a legitimate tool to fulfill the requirement of consultation.[82]

5.4.2 Assessing Indigenous Peoples' Protocols in Paraguay

Paraguay has a legal framework that guarantees a fairly wide range of rights to indigenous peoples in the national jurisdiction and also has ratified relevant international human rights treaties.

The Constitution of the Republic of Paraguay, in its Chapter V on Indigenous Peoples, explicitly incorporates the principle of participation by peoples based on their cultural values, by establishing that the 'indigenous peoples are guaranteed the right to participate in the social, political, and cultural life of the country, in accordance with their customary practices, this Constitution, and national laws'.[83] However, the normative framework given by the Constitution has not offered sufficient guidelines to translate the 'legislative, administrative or other measures needed to ensure the enjoyment by indigenous peoples of their human rights, in particular their fundamental right to self-determination and their rights to their lands, territories and natural resources. The lack of access to justice and the persistence of racism and discrimination are also causes for concern'.[84]

In August 2010, the Paraguayan Indigenous Institute adopted the Resolution No. 2039/2010 where the obligation is established to request the intervention of the Paraguayan Indigenous Institute for all consultation processes in indigenous

[81] Rojas Garzón et al. (2016).

[82] 'At the same time, indigenous peoples are increasingly developing their own Protocols and policies, which provide guidance to states and corporations on how to consult with them and seek their FPIC in accordance with their right to self-determination and their customary decision-making practices. Communities from the Murut Tahol Community in Alutok, Ulu Tomani, Tenom, Malyasia as well as the Juruna People in the Brazilian Amazon and the Embera Chami in Colombia, are among those who have developed such Protocols. These Protocols reflect the community's identity, culture, ways of life and the interconnection of territories, peoples and nature. They highlight the central importance of respect for indigenous peoples' rights, including their self-determination right to decide their own plans, priorities and visions for their futures and the related right of communities to make decisions on externally proposed projects in or near their territories'. United Nations Forum on Business and Human Rights (2018).

[83] (1992) Constitution of Paraguay.

[84] Tauli-Corpuz V (2015) Report of the Special Rapporteur on the rights of indigenous peoples in Paraguay; Miranda and Alonso (2017).

communities, which states that consultation must be prior, free, informed and in good faith. However, it recognizes the need to continue advancing along this path in order to contribute to the effective and timely fulfillment of the rights of indigenous peoples as regards participation.[85]

There has been significant progress over the recognition of indigenous peoples in Paraguay. As an example of the initiative for quotas, Law No. 5347 of 2014 was elaborated in order to guarantee access to universities for indigenous peoples.[86]

Persons belonging to indigenous communities who are qualified to occupy the positions available pursuant to the provisions of this Law, shall be appointed by the competent authority and shall be assigned positions and duties according to their capacity and suitability and the provisions set forth in Law No. 1626, its amendments and regulations.[87]

These improvements to access are attributed to the influence of the 'Inter-American parameters at the regulatory level, which include the adoption of Protocols that aim at achieving increased access to justice for indigenous peoples. On the other hand, regarding decisions issued in contentious cases, there has been a low level of protection of territorial rights, with a persistent denial of legal parameters established by the IACtHR, even though conventionality control is widely accepted for several topics'.[88]

Related to the access to justice, Paraguay took a step towards a more egalitarian process through the establishment of the Ethnic Rights Division, which is part of the Federal Prosecutor. The main goal of this division is to intervene in criminal proceedings as a technical consultant to prosecutors in cases in which indigenous persons are parties, either as victims or perpetrators. It also guarantees the application of indigenous customary law, contemplated in the Constitution and international conventions and ensures collaboration with prosecutors, rendering the legal provision of the special procedure related to indigenous peoples effective, which establishes the mandatory presence of a technical consultant from the beginning to the end of the investigation.[89]

[85] Programa de las Naciones Unidas para el Desarrollo (PNUD (2013) Propuesta de protocolo para un Proceso de Consulta y Consentimiento con los Pueblos Indígenas del Paraguay.

[86] Paraguay Legislation (2014) Provides free access to indigenous applicants to universities for tertiary level careers.

[87] Paraguay Legislation (2019) Law that guarantees the participation and access of all persons belonging to indigenous communities to the exercise of non-elective public office.

[88] Navarro (2021), p. 204.

[89] 'Advises the indigenous communities on their rights, while analyzing the facts within the indigenous cultural framework and providing elements of judgment in the fiscal investigation. Determines the most favorable solution for the preservation of harmony within the indigenous community. Intervenes as a link between the indigenous communities and the Public Prosecutor's Office. Guarantees differentiated attention to indigenous peoples, ensuring respect for their procedural rights and constitutional guarantees, as well as respect for the culture and customs of indigenous peoples. At the request of prosecutors, it prepares a technical, legal and anthropological opinion that determines the motive for the behavior of members of indigenous peoples in criminal

In 2018, Paraguay took another important step and developed the Decree No. 1039 of 28th December regarding the indigenous peoples' Protocols. The law refers to the UNDRIP and also to the ILO Convention No. 169 regulating the process of consultation under free, prior and informed consent with the indigenous peoples living in Paraguay, while establishing the responsibility of the Paraguayan Institute of the Indigenous to guarantee the efficacy of enforcement with the Protocol, with the collaboration of the indigenous peoples.[90]

The Decree ensures the participation of the affected people as regards natural resource exploitation projects, which implies the acceptance that the consultation and consent processes with indigenous peoples will be carried out on the basis of the recognition and acceptance of some guidelines. For the purposes of efficacy of the consultation, the Protocol protects the area of the traditional territory of the indigenous peoples concerned on which they depend for their cultural, spiritual and physical existence, their subsistence and survival as a people. In general, the Decree is well written and can be considered essential for the states, which still have not yet adopted a more elaborated legislation regarding the application of consultation with indigenous peoples. This can be seen as part of the efforts of organizations and indigenous peoples' groups facing less judicialization in the IAHRS, including lack of enforcement as regards indigenous peoples' rights rulings.

So far, after a relatively optimal experience of enforcement with a negotiated agreement in 1999, involving the Lamenxay and Kayleyphapopyet communities, the Sanapaná People, the Yakye Axa and Sawhoyamaxa, both of the Enxet People, and of Xákmok Kásek of the Sanapaná People were taken to a decision by the IACtHR. The decision was obtained against Paraguay in 2005, 2006 and 2010, respectively. The Kelyenmagategma of the Enxet people had a friendly settlement in 2011.[91]

The Decree No. 1039 stipulates consultation as an obligation of the Paraguayan state to be conducted on any project that may affect indigenous peoples' lands, territories, natural resources and traditional livelihoods. This includes the right of the affected indigenous peoples to give or withhold their free, prior and informed consent on the proposal, as well as to decide whether they want to participate in the consultation or terminate the consultation at any time.[92]

The Decree also states that the indigenous peoples concerned have the right to own, control, manage, participate in and consent to any project that may affect the lands and resources of the area in question. This includes the right of affected

cases. For this purpose, he places the investigators in the cultural context and makes well-founded suggestions as to the applicable legislation'. Ministerio Publico of Paraguay (2021).

[90] Paraguay (2018) Decree No. 1039.

[91] Miranda and Alonso (2017); Inter-American Court of Human Rights, *Yakye Axa Indigenous Community v. Paraguay*, Judgment of 17 June 2005; Inter-American Court of Human Rights, *Sawhoyamaxa Indigenous Community v. Paraguay*, Judgment of 29 March 2006.

[92] Paraguay (2018) Decree No. 1039.

peoples to, in good faith, be consulted as well as to decide whether they want to participate in the negotiation process or not at any time.[93]

Furthermore, it is interesting to notice that the law on voluntary isolation or initial contact was also quoted in the Decree, as the peoples shall legitimately exercise this right and shall not be contacted or subjugated by the project proponents.[94]

Although the objective of the consultation should be to seek an agreement between the parties, this does not mean that all the negotiation processes will culminate in the consent and approval of the project, either totally, partially or with modifications, by the affected peoples.[95]

Besides the good faith and the required achievement of consent, Article 3.11 lays out that there is the possibility of indigenous peoples to ask for another party, as mediator, facilitator or observer. Thus, 'this third party may be a national or international entity and must be invited with the consent of the parties. Either party may invite a third party only to observe the consultations, without intervening. It does not need the consent of the other, except in the circumstance in which the parties previously agreed not to include a third party (or particular persons) or if the presence of the third party in certain circumstances will be detrimental to the norms or customs of the affected people'.[96]

The absence of coercion and unauthorized contracts and promises is equally relevant for the efficacy of the Protocols, as is confirmed in Article 3.12 which is to ensure 'that the consultation and consent processes are fair and that indigenous peoples do not make decisions under any form of coercion, until the affected indigenous peoples give their consent to the commencement of the project, the project proponent shall refrain from any activity and any act that may lead to one of its agents, or third parties under its control and acting with its consent, affecting the existence, values, use or enjoyment of the lands, territories and their natural resources over which the members of the affected indigenous peoples have rights'.[97]

Similar to the recommendations of the Constitution of Brazil, Article 3.19 stipulates the necessity of previous social and environmental impact studies 'in order to ensure that the project does not imply a denial of the traditions and customs, or threaten the subsistence of the affected people, and preserve, protect and guarantee the special relationship that the members of the affected people maintain with their territory, which, in turn, guarantees their survival as a people, a detailed and transparent study on the cultural, social and environmental impacts must be conducted by independent and technically capable entities, with the approval and supervision of the parties before any decision is taken by the affected indigenous peoples to consent, in whole or in part, to the initiation of the proposed project. This

---

[93] Ibid.

[94] Ibid.

[95] Ibid.

[96] Ibid.

[97] Ibid.

study must be prepared in consultation and with the effective participation of the affected indigenous peoples'.[98]

The innovative part of the Decree can be found in Article 3.25, which provides further clarity on how to conduct consultation. States normally do not provide clear guidance on the actual processes to be followed, which not only increases the lack of transparency towards the application of consultation and possible efficacy of the norm, but also renders it inoperative heightening the case for non-enforcement. The Paraguyan Decree sets out what must be the minimum informational content provided to the community by the state and the natural resource exploitation company. Specifically, the document must include: '(a) the nature, size and scope of the project; (b) the duration of the project (including the construction phase, where applicable); (c) the locality of the areas and resources that will be affected; (d) the rights, duties and obligations of all parties under Paraguay's national laws, international laws and other voluntary duties and obligations subscribed to by the project proponent; (e) a preliminary study of the project's potential negative and positive impacts (direct and indirect both cumulative); (f) the reasons or purpose of the project; (g) the national consultation and consent processes, if any, used to determine the need or desirability of the project; (h) the personnel likely to be involved in all stages of the project (including local people, research institutes, sponsors, consultants, etc; (i) the specific procedures that the project proponent will require (e.g. measures to mitigate damages and adverse impacts, to resolve disputes, to monitor implementation and to terminate the project upon completion); (j) the potential risks and adverse impacts presented by the project (direct and indirect both cumulative), but not limited to social, environmental, cultural and health risks, and impacts such as interference with sacred areas, environmental contamination, interference with breeding, hunting or gathering patterns; (k) all implications that can actually be foreseen, including community benefits (e.g. commercial, economic, environmental, cultural)'.[99]

The Decree also determines the minimum reasonable period of time, something which has also been extensively discussed in the literature and courts in Brazil. Article 3.26 states that 'all information required for scheduled meetings should be provided sufficiently in advance to facilitate their exchange. The parties should agree on a reasonable period of time (if there is no prior agreement, at a minimum, two to four weeks) prior to any scheduled meeting. The proponent will be responsible for providing sufficient copies of the information to be distributed to the members and communities that make up the indigenous peoples concerned'.[100]

This legislation dates from 2018 and was drawn up over a period of more than nine years of joint work by representatives of indigenous organizations, indigenous peoples and the government.[101] It has proven as an important opportunity for

[98] Ibid.

[99] Ibid.

[100] Ibid.

[101] Fondo para el Desarrollo de los Pueblos Indígenas de América Latina y El Caribe (FILAC) (2019).

Paraguay to repair the lack of norms and political will towards the implementation of indigenous peoples' rights.[102] At this point, it can be said that the legislation reveals unique contours to shape the indigenous peoples' Protocols under the umbrella of the legal system, proving that it is possible to guarantee the jurisdiction of the Protocols within national judicial systems, ensuring the efficacy of consultation with indigenous peoples.

5.4.3 Assessing Indigenous Peoples' Protocols in Brazil

The Constitution in 1988 allowed the increase of the formalization of indigenous organizations that grew in various regions of the country, with directors elected in assemblies, statutes registered in a notary's office, and their own bank accounts. This is, strictly speaking, the incorporation, by some indigenous peoples, of mechanisms of political representation by delegation, to be able to deal with the institutional world, public and private, of national and international society, and to deal with territorial demands (demarcation and control of natural resources), welfare (health, education, transportation, and communication), and commercial demands (placing products on the market).[103]

The interpretation of indigenous peoples themselves of the requirement of consultation sparked a broad debate about the efficacy and of the provision's internal validity. While it does not exclude a constitutional remedy to the issue, it extends the necessity of acknowledging indigenous peoples' self-determination and cultural rights in the Brazilian legal system. More than that, the indigenous peoples' Protocols should be invoked to settle a dispute, support and harmonize the extension of the constitutionally and internationally ordained right of the requirement of consultation.

In the case of Brazil, the elaboration of those Protocols deals with the collision between the Brazilian legal system and the IAHRS having 'directly impacted the lives of communities and organizations that invoke it within their political strategies'.[104] Brazil has more than 50 Protocols which have resulted form several conflicts between the indigenous and the government, which has the duty to conduct the consultation. The Protocols in Brazil are not only those of indigenous peoples but extend among others to *comunidades ribeirinhas*, *quilombolas, comunidades pesqueiras*.

Following this demarcation, the 'comunidades tradicionais' also encounter the same lack of streamlining and efficiency regarding the consultation process. They

[102] Paraguay (2018) Decree No. 1039.

[103] Ricardo (1991).

[104] Rodríguez Garavito and Andrés Baquero Díaz (2018), p. 1.

claimed during the 177th Session of at the IACHR of Human Rights, that consultation was not being promoted by the Brazilian government.[105] The representative, Cláudia Regina Sala de Pinho informed that, due to conflicts between the 'comunidades tradicionais' and the government, they had decided to propose their own Protocols. She noted that there were over 50 Protocols in which the communities, embedded with the constitutional and the ILO No. 169 entitlement, respected the traditional organizations and living. The Protocols inform how the consultation should proceed in a more efficient process.[106]

Thus, in the next section, one of the most relevant cases regarding the features of the indigenous peoples' Protocols in Brazil will be analyzed. It is an example of a legislative initiative and a court case that show the judicialization[107] of the application of consultation.

5.4.3.1 Assessing Legislative Enforcement with Consultation

This subchapter addresses the application of consultation in case of the Brazilian legislature. In Brazil, there are not many examples of legislation in which traditional communities are recognized. The Ethnoeducational Territories[108] and the Indigenous Environmental and Territorial Management Policy are examples of this initiative, which also featured the Decree of the National Policy for Territorial and Environmental Management of Indigenous Lands of 2016.

The establishment of the Indigenous Environmental and Territorial Management Policy (hereinafter, the GATI) was a joint accomplishment of the Brazilian indigenous peoples, the FUNAI and the Brazilian Ministry of Environment (hereinafter, the MMA). The United Nations Development Program (hereinafter, the UNDP), The

---

[105] The Brazilian representatives in the meeting were: 'Rede de Povos e Comunidades Tradicionais do Brasil (REDE PCTS); Articulação dos Povos Indígenas do Brasil (APIB); Coordenação Nacional de Articulação das Comunidades Negras Rurais; Quilombolas (CONAQ); Observatório de Protocolos Comunitários de Consulta e Consentimento Livre Prévio e Informado; Rede de Cooperação Amazônica (RCA); Rede Cerrado; Rede KÔDYA - Comunidades Organizadas da Diáspora Africana pelo Direito à Alimentação; Articulação Rosalino de Povos e Comunidades Tradicionais do Norte de Minas; Movimento dos Atingidos pela Base Espacial de Alcântara (MABE); Movimento dos Atingidos e das Atingidas por Barragem (MAB); Coalizão Negra por Direitos Centro de Pesquisa e Extensão em Direito Socioambiental; (CEPEDIS); Associação Nacional das Defensoras e Defensores Públicos (ANADEP); Terra de Direitos; Instituto Socioambiental (ISA); Instituto de Pesquisa e Formação Indígena (Iepé); Operação; Amazônia Nativa (OPAN); Conselho Indigenista Missionário (CIMI) Cáritas Brasileira and Federação de Órgãos para Assistência Social e Educacional (FASE)'. (2020) El derecho a la consulta y el consentimiento previo, libre e informado de los pueblos indígenas.

[106] Ibid.

[107] For more on the situation of judicialization of laws regulating indigenous peoples in Brazil: CIMI - Indigenous Missionary Council (2016); de Oliveira Iago (2016); Zoettl (2016).

[108] More: Brazilian Ministry of Education (2009) Decree about the Ethnoeducational territory; Bergamaschi and Sousa (2015).

Nature Conservancy (hereinafter, the TNC) and the Global Environment Facility (hereinafter, the GEF) were also part of the project that was executed between 2010 and 2016 in Brazil and was granted with US$ 6 million from the GEF[109] to develop the project.

Initially, the GATI was designed based on the concepts of biodiversity conservation and the sustainable use of forests, however, nowadays its scope has brought contributions to 'climate change and prevention of environmental degradation, and to the cultural, social and economic strengthening of indigenous peoples'.[110] The most relevant contribution of the GATI was the strengthening of practices and debates that led to the establishment of the Decree of the National Policy for Territorial and Environmental Management of Indigenous Lands (hereinafter, the PNGATI). The innovative aspect of this policy is that it involves multistakeholders such as governmental agencies, indigenous organizations, civil society organizations and international organizations, offering ways to fulfil planned milestones to advance the implementation of the PNGATI. One of the hallmarks of the GATI project has been indigenous participation. From the beginning of its elaboration until its implementation, indigenous participation was encouraged and supported. The views of indigenous peoples on the management of their lands, in all aspects, from social to economic issues, were discussed extensively by the indigenous participants of the Project.[111]

The PNGATI was established as a Decree on 5th July of 2012 based on the ILO Convention No. 169, promulgated by Decree n° 5.051, of April 19, 2004.[112]

The first Article of the National Policy for the PNGATI was thereby instituted, with the objective of guaranteeing and promoting the protection, recovery, conservation and sustainable use of the natural resources of indigenous lands and territories, ensuring the integrity of the indigenous heritage, improving the quality of life and the full physical and cultural reproduction conditions of current and future generations of indigenous peoples, respecting their socio-cultural autonomy, under the terms of current legislation.

5.4.3.2 Assessing Enforcement of Indigenous Peoples' Protocols

In this section, two relevant indigenous peoples' Protocols of Brazil are to be scrutinized: the Wajãpi Protocol and the Juruna (Yudjá) Protocol. These Protocols are understood as a mechanism to seek to make up for the omissions, deficiencies or correct the violations that state law incurs on the rights of indigenous peoples, and in

[109] Vianna et al. (2016).

[110] Ibid.

[111] Bavaresco et al. (2016).

[112] (2012) The National Policy for Indigenous Land Territorial and Environmental Management (PNGATI).

particular, the lack of recognition of the indigenous peoples' own law.[113] The Juruna (Yudjá) was the first to be examined by a Brazilian Court while Brazil still remains with no regulation regarding the Protocols, which leaves the judicialization and Court decisions to achieve the implementation of consultation as self-determination and cultural rights.

5.4.3.2.1 The Wajãpi Protocol

The increase of human rights violations and the difficulties caused by government bodies in even maintaining good communication, the Wajãpi indigenous peoples began to draw up their own Protocol, defining the rules for a legitimate and respectful dialogue with national and international actors regarding exploitation of natural resources that affect their land and their way of life.

Once the Wajãpi had taken their decisions collectively, among the set of chiefs and representatives of all the villages, the Protocol was drawn up based on their social organization. Among other things, the Protocol also aims to guarantee translation into the indigenous language and a good understanding of the proposals. In addition, the consultation is organized in stages, so that there is enough time for the Wajãpi to decide on the themes, valuing and respecting their knowledge, practices and wishes for the future.[114]

Therefore, in May 2017, the First Meeting of the Wajãpi Prior Consultation took place. The Consultation was carried out by the Brazilian National Institute of Colonization and Agrarian Reform and the Amapá State Forestry Institute on the recommendation of the Federal Public Ministry, at the request of the Wajãpi Council—the Apina.[115] In this process, the government agencies were following the rules defined by the Wajãpi Protocol for Consultation and Consent, drawn up by the indigenous group itself in 2014.

The relevance of this Protocol is that it was the first time that a Protocol of consultation has been carried out in the manner proposed by the indigenous group in Brazil, as recommended by ILO Convention No. 169 and the UNDRIP. It was the first time that the indigenous peoples engaged themselves in the process of the application of consultation in Brazil, as the ones holding the right to prior consultation. Thus, the Brazilian state had the duty to consult the indigenous people. This meant that it was the indigenous peoples who decided whether to accept the proposal

[113] Joca (2020).

[114] Wajãpi Indigenous Peoples (2014) Protocolo de Consulta e Consentimento Wajãpi; Instituto do Patrimônio Histórico e Artístico Nacional (2017) Iphan participa de protocolo de consulta inédito do povo Wajãpi. Iphan - Amapá; Insituto Socioambiental (ISA) (2017) O Dever de Consulta Prévia do Estado Brasileiro aos Povos Indígenas.

[115] Instituto do Patrimônio Histórico e Artístico Nacional (2017) Iphan participa de protocolo de consulta inédito do povo Wajãpi. Iphan - Amapá.

or not, indeed whether or not they wanted to accept any project before the Brazilian government took its decision'.[116]

5.4.3.2.2 The Juruna (Yudjá) da Terra Indígena Paquiçamba da Volta Grande do rio Xingu Protocol

Another relevant Protocol designed by the indigenous was the Juruna (Yudjá) da Terra Indígena Paquiçamba da Volta Grande do rio Xingu' Protocol. This one is essential in showing the possibility of application of the Protocols assessing the ILO Convention No. 169 and the UNDRIP and not depending on a national norm for its efficacy.

The content of the claims regards civil procedural law and constitutional law cases with regards to the appeals filed by the Belo Sun Mining company and the federal state of Pará against a sentence issued by the Federal Judge of the Court in Altamira, Pará. The decision came out in favor of the appellants, suspending the environmental licensing of the Volta Grande, a mining project. The judge considered that 'the Environmental Impact Study and respective Environmental Impact Report (EIA/RIMA) of the Volta Grande de Mineração Project must consider the interests of indigenous communities (possible socio-environmental damage) located around the area of work'.[117]

According to Article 23, XI of the Brazilian Constitution: 'it is the common jurisdiction of the Union, the States, the Federal District and the Municipalities to register, monitor and inspect the granting of research rights and exploitation of water and mineral resources in their territories'.[118]

Under the terms of Paragraph 3 of Article 231 of the Constitution: 'the use of water resources, including energy potentials, research and the mining of mineral wealth on indigenous lands can only be carried out with the authorization of the National Congress, after listening to the affected communities and ensuring their participation in the results of the mining, in the form of the law'.[119]

At the international level, the ILO Convention No. 169, which was promulgated by the Decree No. 5.051 of 19th April of 2004, Articles 6, 7 and 15 lay out the obligation of consultation with indigenous peoples in the implementation of exploitation projects of existing resources in their lands.[120]

---

[116] Baniwa (2012).

[117] Tribunal Regional Federal 1ª Região, *Appeal 'Ação Cível'*, 0002505-70.2013.4.01.3903/PA, Judgment of 19 December 2017. *translated by author.*

[118] (1988) Constitution of Brazil.

[119] Ibid.

[120] 'Article 6 1. In applying the provisions of this Convention, governments shall: (a) consult the peoples concerned, through appropriate procedures and in particular through their representative institutions, whenever consideration is being given to legislative or administrative measures which may affect them directly; (b) establish means by which these peoples can freely participate, to at least the same extent as other sectors of the population, at all levels of decision-making in elective

This was in accordance with the decision of another case provided by the Federal Judge Souza Prudente: 'the elaboration of the ECI does not remove the need for prior, free and informed consultation of indigenous peoples, in the form of ILO Convention No. 169, once they are not confused with one another, as they are different'.[121] Following the same interpretation, the Federal Judge Jirair Aram Meguerian partially granted the appeal filed by the defendants. He also rejected the prior license of the *Projecto Volta Grande do Xingu*, conditioning the validity to the elaboration of the ECI required by the FUNAI to the free and informed consultation of the indigenous people affected, in accordance with the Juruna Protocol.[122] The decision follows a common situation that indigenous peoples in Brazil face, the judicialization, when there are conflicts involving the territory related to 'facts that have occurred in the past century, a time when the indigenous communities have faced physical, psychological and cultural violence, followed by a deceptive process

institutions and administrative and other bodies responsible for policies and programmes which concern them; (c) establish means for the full development of these peoples' own institutions and initiatives, and in appropriate cases provide the resources necessary for this purpose. 2. The consultations carried out in application of this Convention shall be undertaken, in good faith and in a form appropriate to the circumstances, with the objective of achieving agreement or consent to the proposed measures. Article 7 1. The peoples concerned shall have the right to decide their own priorities for the process of development as it affects their lives, beliefs, institutions and spiritual well-being and the lands they occupy or otherwise use, and to exercise control, to the extent possible, over their own economic, social and cultural development. In addition, they shall participate in the formulation, implementation and evaluation of plans and programmes for national and regional development which may affect them directly. 2. The improvement of the conditions of life and work and levels of health and education of the peoples concerned, with their participation and co-operation, shall be a matter of priority in plans for the overall economic development of areas they inhabit. Special projects for development of the areas in question shall also be so designed as to promote such improvement. 3. Governments shall ensure that, whenever appropriate, studies are carried out, in co-operation with the peoples concerned, to assess the social, spiritual, cultural and environmental impact on them of planned development activities. The results of these studies shall be considered as fundamental criteria for the implementation of these activities. 4. Governments shall take measures, in co-operation with the peoples concerned, to protect and preserve the environment of the territories they inhabit. Article 15 1. The rights of the peoples concerned to the natural resources pertaining to their lands shall be specially safeguarded. These rights include the right of these peoples to participate in the use, management and conservation of these resources. 2. In cases in which the state retains the ownership of mineral or sub-surface resources or rights to other resources pertaining to lands, governments shall establish or maintain procedures through which they shall consult these peoples, with a view to ascertaining whether and to what degree their interests would be prejudiced, before undertaking or permitting any programmes for the exploration or exploitation of such resources pertaining to their lands. The peoples concerned shall wherever possible participate in the benefits of such activities, and shall receive fair compensation for any damages which they may sustain as a result of such activities'. (1986) Indigenous and Tribal Peoples Convention.

[121] Tribunal Regional Federal 5ª Turma, *Appeal 'Ação Cível'*, AC 0005891- 81.2012.4.01.3600/ MT, Judgment of 29 October 2013.

[122] Tribunal Regional Federal 1ª Região, *Appeal 'Ação Cível'*, 0002505-70.2013.4.01.3903/PA, Judgment of 19 December 2017. *translated by author.*

of spoliation of their property and their land, promoted under the aegis of the state'.[123]

In the same line of thought, the Special Rapporteur of the United Nations, Victoria Tauli-Corpuz, when she was visiting Brazil, had identified the indigenous peoples' Protocols and understood them as 'examples of good practice'.[124] In her official mission in 2016, she encouraged the Brazilian government to ensure that they were respected.

Victoria Tauli-Corpuz visited the Juruna people on the Xingu River who were affected by the Belo Monte dam. The project was surrounded by controversy for the comunidades ribeirinhas[125] who lived there. One of the points was that the indigenous groups and non-governmental organizations had complained that the Belo Monte project was being carried out with neither adequate mitigation measures nor consultations with the affected indigenous communities who lived there and demanded to be heard.

The United Nations Special Rapporteur noted the good practices and proactive approaches on the part of the indigenous peoples to pursue the implementation of their rights. Some of the positive measures and initiatives included were 'the development of consultation Protocols incorporating the consultation and free, prior and informed consent procedures developed by the Wajãpi in Amapá and the Munduruku in Pará; the self-demarcation of lands; the formation of alliances with the Quilombola and Ribeirinho communities to strengthen land and self-governance rights such as in Oriximiná in Pará; the self-protection of territories, for example, through the use of indigenous forest guards set up by the Ka'apor in Maranhão; and partnerships with judicial bodies to strengthen indigenous conflict-resolution systems, such as that between the indigenous peoples of Roraima and the Federal Supreme Court, and to defend their rights, such as that between the Yanomami and the Public Prosecutor's Office for their right to health'.[126]

Those recommendations were relevant because they had been echoed by the United Nations Expert Mechanism on the Rights of Indigenous Peoples in the Report on Free, Prior and Informed Consent in 2018, which identified respect for the indigenous peoples' Protocols as central to the conduct of good faith consultations having repercussions for the indigenous peoples' human rights. In that sense: 'the consultation Protocols elaborated so far in Brazil have demonstrated how this instrument also promotes the strengthening of internal alliances among peoples, the

[123]CIMI - Indigenous Missionary Council (2016). *translated by author.*

[124]Tauli-Corpuz V (2016) Report of the Special Rapporteur on the Rights of Indigenous Peoples on her mission to Brazil.

[125]The 'comunidades ribeirinhas' are a Portuguese term to define the people who live along the rivers. In cases of the Inter-American Court of Human Rights, those who live primarily along the coasts and rivers have also the right to reparation in case of the violation of human rights.

[126]Tauli-Corpuz V (2016) Report of the Special Rapporteur on the Rights of Indigenous Peoples on her mission to Brazil.

definition of political arrangements among them, and the reaffirmation of the legitimacy itself'.[127]

The judges decision set a precedent. However, it was based on thin ice in the sense that the indigenous peoples' Protocols have not yet been established in national legislation. It is imperative that the Brazilian state legally affirms the Protocols allowing for cases regarding consultation to be processed according to the expression of their will on how to conduct the procedure of consultation without the risk that the decision may be annulled by higher courts.

5.5 The Ongoing Debate on the Veto Power Argument

The debate over providing indigenous groups with veto power over natural resource exploitation projects has been reduced to an 'ideological discrepancy with the manner in which the consent requirement has been framed under the human rights jurisprudence'.[128] It has to be noted that the discourse of advocating a veto power for indigenous peoples aligns with the debate on the harmonization of international and national norms. Thus, there is the urge for making this key connection which plays a catalytic and reinforcing role in the discussion on the requirement of consultation.

On the one hand, the UNDRIP addresses concerns regarding a veto power in Article 32; on the other, Article 6 of the ILO Convention No. 169, the only binding treaty in force in Brazil, understands consultation as a tool but does not mention the need to free, prior and informed consent, neither the veto. However, Article 231 of the Brazilian Constitution of 1988 indeed contains fragments for a possible reconciliation of the legal and regulatory frameworks for ensuring the protective rights for indigenous peoples. Some noteworthy engagement with the veto argument can also be found in the draft of the Committee on the Elimination of Racial Discrimination (hereinafter, the CERD) as the CERD's General Recommendation XXIII as well as in the jurisprudence of some legal orders.[129]

The Constitutional Court of Colombia, for instance, decided that: 'for the Court, the criteria that allow these extremes [the veto and the consultation] to be reconciled depend on the degree of which consultation and consent may be determined, as the least harmful measure, as a measure to protect the indigenous peoples' communities. Therefore, any process must be qualified according to the characteristics of each specific case, since what is at stake is not only the expectation of receiving certain

[127] Rojas Garzón et al. (2016), p. 57. *translated by author.*

[128] Doyle (2016), p. 165.

[129] The Court also decided that: 'The principle of pro personae interpretation imposes the application of legal norms that are more favorable to human beings and their rights; in other words, the imposition of that interpretation that favors respect for human dignity and consequently the protection, guarantee, and promotion of human rights and the fundamental rights contemplated in the Constitution.' Constitutional Court of Colombia, *Multiculturalism and minorities*, No. T-129/11, Judgment of 2011. *translated by author.*

economic benefits from an economic project, but also the understanding and recognition that what is at stake is the present and future of a people, of a group of human beings that has the right to self-determination and to defend its physical and cultural existence, however "absurd or exotic" its customs and ways of life may seem to some. On this point, the Court emphasizes the need for the discussion not to be posed in terms of who is to veto whom, but rather, above all, as a possibility for discussion among equals in the midst of differences, an opportunity for the state agencies and the state concessionaires to explain in a concrete and transparent manner what the purposes of the work are, and for the community to be able to present its needs and points of view in relation to the project'.[130]

However, the Brazilian Supreme Court maintained in the words of Justice Gilmar Mendes that: 'the relevance of consulting with indigenous communities does not mean that the decisions are formally dependent on the acceptance of indigenous communities as a requirement of the project's validity. The indigenous must be heard and their interests must be honest and seriously considered. From this, however, it cannot be deduced that the decision taken in the end can only be valid if it counts on their acquiescence. In a democracy, differences are normal and expected. No individual or social group has the subjective right to determine the decision of the state's future by themselves'.[131] The interpretation of the Justice is narrow considering that the discussion should be amplified as it has been in other countries of the region as well as by the international organs.

Consultation brings indigenous peoples to the center of participatory democracy. As a constitutional norm, the fundamental right refers to the optimization of the long debated indigenous peoples' international rights. Nevertheless, the Brazilian judiciary suffers under the limitations of the discussion over the existence of veto power over state activity that is subject to consultation. One needs to remember that this occurs in a country such as Brazil, which as of December of 2015 had witnessed more than 3000 resource exploitation projects with environmental licensing processes.[132]

While these projects included the participation of the FUNAI, none of them respected the requirement of consultation and carried out the necessary outreach prescribed in international human rights standards.[133]

---

[130] Ibid.

[131] Justice Gilmar Mendes, Raposa do Sol case, No. Pet 3388 (Brazilian Supreme Court 2009), *translated by author.*

[132] The quantitative reseach included the federal and statewide licencing that were concluded in all states of Brazil. The research analyzed that until 13rd October of 2020, there were 5279 licences process concluded. PNLA PN de LA (2020) Licenciamento ambiental. *translated by author.*

[133] A more complete data set can be obtained of the Brazilian Citizen Information Service of the Federal Government, however only by special request. On the other hand, the data was analyzed in 2015: 'the projects affect the indigenous people at the Funai, and 198 licenses were being processed at the Palmares Cultural Foundation that would affect quilombola communities (43 transmission lines, 35 highways, 17 railroads, 23 mines, 18 electric power plants, 12 gas pipelines and

Within the legislative branch, the situation is equally disquieting, as several bills and constitutional amendments are being processed in order to alter the normative framework of indigenous and tribal peoples' rights, without the consultation provisions being integrated. Thus, the conceptual enhancement of consultation as a self-determination and cultural right and its way to improve the effective implementation of the fundamental rights of indigenous peoples should be taken into consideration in Brazil. In addition, two vetoes were proposed to the Presidency of the Republic regarding the flexibility of prior, informed consent by means of an official body opinion and the waiving of prior informed consent in the case of access to samples of genetic heritage and traditional knowledge related to agriculture. Therefore, it can be seen that the legal framework has reduced the obligations of users and the rights of traditional peoples, at least with regard to access and referral policies.

According to the International Labour Organization, 'there is an imminent risk of provoking a dynamic of veto players not only for future projects, but in general for legitimate public policies in a democratic system. This generates a profound distortion in the decision-making dynamics of the states, breaking the balances necessary for a democracy to function'.[134]

In order to add to the analysis a more elaborated view on the relevance of being able to say no, it does reflect the implementation that power patterns are more pronounced that mere linguistic mismatches.[135] Preventing the right to veto implies the lack of dialogue and attempt to lead the negotiation without a reasonable base on a good faith consultation.

The debate is still ongoing. According to the IACtHR, however, the aim of consultation is the consent which implies a permanent dialogue, presenting arguments based on the truth to get the consent. The efforts to achieve consultation must be the persistent duty of the states together with the private actors to, through communication and dialogue, get the consent of the indigenous peoples. Thus, the focus is on consultation—but in case of the impossibility to achieve consent, the state has to abstain of natural resource exploitation.

5.6 Conclusions

The findings in this chapter provide new evidence of the need to improve the theoretical framework of the requirement of consultation, considering the IACtHR decisions, the ILO Convention No. 169 and also considering the indigenous peoples' Protocols as a way to achieve enforcement by the states. It is clearly not an

50 "various companies") in Brazil. There is no consolidated data on projects that affect traditional peoples and communities'. Rojas Garzón et al. (2016), p. 7, *translated by author.*

[134] International Labour Organization (2016).

[135] Habermas (2015).

impossible goal, once the states become aware of the Protocols and can thus adjust towards the more adequate application of consultation.

Drawing from the analysis of the application of consultation, the framework in some countries and the analyses of the Protocols and the evolving normative framework of consultation pertaining to the rights of indigenous peoples, one of the considerations is that the IACtHR needs to be aware of the necessity to make adjustments to embed the Protocols.

This needs to consider the non-limited interpretations of the American Convention on Article 29 (b) in which indigenous peoples must declare their own view in this ruling, together with the protection of indigenous territories in accordance with Article 21 as well as Article 6 of the ILO Convention No. 169. Therefore, the IACtHR concluded that, based on previous human rights law and jurisprudence of indigenous peoples, that Article 21 of the American Convention brought up the following considerations: The first one is to guarantee the right of indigenous peoples to determine and freely enjoy their social, cultural, and economic development. The second consideration points to the guarantee of the right to enjoy the particular spiritual relationship indigenous peoples maintain with the territories they have traditionally occupied and used. Thus, state parties that have ratified the American Convention are obliged to respect indigenous territories composed of lands and natural resources according to Article 21.

It is worth noting that, within the international consensus on the disclosure of the content of the right of consultation with indigenous peoples as well as some national practices, the restorative mechanisms of self-determination and cultural rights were understood as part of the consultation process.

Good faith and the transparency of the process of consultation are the legal base of self-determination in the consultation process. As consultation is seen as a fundamental collective right, the state is legally obliged to carry out consultation; neither with indigenous peoples in general nor all national resource exploitation companies, but with indigenous peoples directly affected by resource exploitation projects.

The consultation, which is not a merely public hearing or informative session, must take place before the legislative or the administrative procedure that grants the state concessions for the elaboration of any project in the indigenous peoples' territory. Cultural rights are seen to preserve appropriate procedures and must involve all the steps of consultation to reach the agreement in an objective, impartial, technical, scientifical, and truthful manner in relation to the matter in question that is to be consulted on; as well as the risks that may implicate social, cultural, environmental, health, legal, and political aspects and the territory. Consultation must be conducted in a non-discriminatory way, using the language that is spoken and understood in the territory with regard to the customs and traditions of the indigenous peoples concerned.

The temporal scope of the consultation is equally relevant as it ensures the necessary time for discussion, reflection and responses without external pressures. As the process must be one of constant communication, the time for possible additional clarifications shall be taken into consideration as well.

References

Alvarez L (2009) La cuestión indígena en Argentina: de la efectividad a los contextos de producción. Perfiles Latinoam 17

Ankumah EA (1996) The African commission on human and peoples' rights: practice and procedures. Nijhoff, The Hague

Ariss R, Cutfeet J (2011) Kitchenuhmaykoosib Inninuwug First Nation: mining, consultation, reconciliation and law. Indig Law J 10

Assies W, Van der Haar G, Hoekema AJ (2002) Los pueblos indígenas y la reforma del Estado en América Latina =. Papeles Poblac 8

Astudillo Becerra LF (2017) ¿Cumple Chile los estándares internacionales en materia de consulta a los pueblos indigenas? Estud Const 15:129–152. https://doi.org/10.4067/S0718-52002017000100005

Baniwa AF (2012) El Derecho a la Consulta Previa de los Pueblos Indígenas en América Latina Beatriz Cajías de la Vega Claudia Heins. Fundacion Konrad Adenauer (KAS), Bolivia

Barié CG (2014) Nuevas narrativas constitucionales en Bolivia y Ecuador: el buen vivir y los derechos de la naturaleza. Rev Estud Latinoam 59

Bavaresco A, Menezes M, Miller R et al (eds) (2016) A experiência do Projeto GATI em terras indígenas. IEB, Instituto Internacional de Educação do Brasil, Brasília, Distrito Federal, Brazil

Bergamaschi MA, Sousa FB (2015) Territórios etnoeducacionais: ressituando a educação escolar indígena no Brasil. -Posições 26:143–161. https://doi.org/10.1590/0103-7307201507709

Böhrt Irahola C (2015) El derecho a la consulta de los pueblos indígenas, el Tribunal Constitucional y el TIPNIS. Rev Juridica Derecho 2

Cabrera MV (2017) The requirement of consultation with indigenous peoples in the ILO between normative flexibility and institutional rigidity. Brill Nijhoff, Leiden

CIMI - Indigenous Missionary Council (2016) Assessment of Brazil under the UN's Universal Periodic Review Mechanism: the human rights situation of indigenous peoples – focusing on access to justice, criminalization and legal barriers to effectively demarcating Brazilian indigenous peoples' land (time frame). CIMI, FIAN Brazil, Justiça Global and Association of Judges for Democracy

de Oliveira Iago M (2016) Indigenous peoples and land demarcation in Brazil: a never-ending process? Oxf Hum Rights Hub

de Sousa Santos B (ed) (2004) Corte constitucional y emancipación social en Colombia. In: Emancipación social y violencia en Colombia, 1. ed. Grupo Editorial Norma, Bogotá

Doyle CM (2016) Indigenous peoples, title to territory, rights and resources - the transformative role of the free prior and informed consent. Routledge, New York

Doyle C, Garzon BR, Weitzner V, Okamoto T Free prior informed consent protocols as instruments of autonomy: laying foundations for rights based engagement. Institut für Ökologie und Aktions-Ethnologie (INFOE) e. V, Köln

Fondo para el Desarrollo de los Pueblos Indígenas de América Latina y El Caribe (FILAC) (2019) Paraguay aprobó histórico protocolo de consulta a pueblos indígenas

Forest Peoples Programme O (2007) Free, prior and informed consent: two cases from suriname. Forest Peoples Programme and Association of Saramaka Authorities

Garavito CR, Salinas NO (2010) La paradoja de la consulta previa en Colombia. Rev Fund Para El Debido Proceso Leg 14

Guevara Gil A, Cabanillas Linares C (2020) Mineralizing the right to prior consultation: from recognition to disregard of indigenous and peasant rights in Peru. Glob Jurist 20:20190019. https://doi.org/10.1515/gj-2019-0019

Habermas J (2015) The theory of communicative action: 1. Reason and the rationalization of society. Polity Press, Place of publication not identified

Herrera JC (2019) Judicial dialogue and transformative constitutionalism in Latin America: the case of indigenous peoples and afro-descendants. Rev Derecho Estado 43. https://doi.org/10.18601/01229893.n43.08

International Labour Organization (2016) Convenio núm. 169 de la OIT sobre Pueblos Indígenas y Tribales en Países Independientes y la consulta previa a los pueblos indígenas en proyectos de inversión. Reporte regional: Colombia, Costa Rica, Guatemala, Chile. Oficina Regional para América Latina y el Caribe, Lima

Jansen Reventlow Y-O (Nani), Curling R (2019) The unique jurisdiction of the African Court on Human and Peoples' Rights: protection of human rights beyond the African Charter. Emory Int Law Rev 33

Joca P (2020) In: Hernández SM (ed) Protocolos Autónomos de Consulta Previa Indígena en América Latina: Estudios de Casos en Bolivia, Brasil, Chile, Colombia, Honduras, México y Perú, Ford Fundation. IWGIA, Denmark

Mac-Gregor EF (2015) Conventionality control the new doctrine of the Inter-American Court of Human Rights. AJIL Unbound 109:93–99. https://doi.org/10.1017/S2398772300001240

Mamo D (ed) (2020) The Indigenous World 2020. International Work Group for Indigenous Affairs (IWGIA), S.l.

Medellín Urquiaga X (2013) Principio pro persona

Mera MEG (2015) Judicialização da discriminação estrutural contra povos indígenas e afrodescendentes na América Latina: conceptualização e tipologia de um diálogo interamericano / Juridicalization of structural discrimination against indigenous peoples and afro... Rev QUAESTIO IURIS 8. https://doi.org/10.12957/rqi.2015.16908

Ministerio Publico of Paraguay (2021) Ethnic Rights Division

Miranda MM, Alonso JC (2017) Mejorando los derechos de los pueblos indígenas a través de sistemas regionales de derechos humanos: el caso de Paraguay. 1 Instituto Internacional de Medio Ambiente y Desarrollo (IIED), United Kingdom

Navarro GCB (2021) Measuring the effectiveness of the Inter-American System of Human Rights: the case of indigenous territorial rights. Dissertation, Goethe-Universität Frankfurt, Frankfurt am Main

Negishi Y (2017) The pro homine principle's role in regulating the relationship between conventionality control and constitutionality control. Eur J Int Law 28:457–481. https://doi.org/10.1093/ejil/chx030

Ricardo CA (1991) Quem fala em nome dos índios? Instituto Socioambiental (ISA), Brasil

Rodríguez Garavito C, Andrés Baquero Díaz C (2018) The right to free, prior, and informed consultation in Colombia: advances and setbacks. High Commissioner for Human Rights

Rojas Garzón B, Yamada EM, Oliveira R (2016) Direito à consulta e consentimento de povos indígenas, quilombolas e comunidades tradicionais. Due Process of Law Foundation, São Paulo

Shrumm H, Harry J (eds) (2012) Biocultural community protocols: a toolkit for community facilitators. Integrated participatory and legal empowerment tools to support communities to secure their rights, responsibilities, territories, and areas. Natural Justice: Lawyers for Communities and the Environment, Cape Town

Talbot M (2017) Collective rights in the Inter-American and African Human Rights Systems. Georget J Int Law 163

Tomaselli A (2016) Indigenous peoples and their right to political participation: international law standards and their application in Latin America, 1st edn. Nomos, Baden-Baden

United Nations Forum on Business and Human Rights (2018) Integrating indigenous peoples rights in human rights due diligence: what does it mean in practice?

Vianna F, Siqueira J, Menezes M, Miller R (eds) (2016) Gestão Ambiental e Territorial Indígena no Brasil: Contribuições do Projeto GATI. Brazilian Government, Brasília

Viljoen F (2017) The African Human Rights System and Domestic Enforcement. In: Langford M, Rodriguez-Garavito C, Rossi J (eds) Social rights judgments and the politics of compliance. Cambridge University Press, Cambridge, pp 351–398

Zoettl PA (2016) The (Il)legal Indian: the Tupinambá and the juridification of indigenous rights and lives in north-eastern Brazil. Soc Leg Stud 25:3–21. https://doi.org/10.1177/0964663915593412

Chapter 6
Towards Efficacy: Between the Legal Uncertainty of the Requirement of Consultation and Its Most Adequate Application for Brazil

6.1 Introduction

Worldwide, indigenous peoples are being affected by activities of natural resource exploitation in their territories. In the aftermath of the era of colonization, indigenous peoples continue to not hold entitlement for the territories they have occupied for centuries. Compounded by the fact that indigenous peoples represent minorities in contemporaneous states, these territorial conflicts are marked by both legal and illegal activities.

International human rights law developed legislations and policies to amend these situations and attempted to encourage a better understanding of the imbalanced relationship among indigenous peoples, their states and transnational companies. Notwithstanding the legal protection given to indigenous peoples, however, the persistent gap between their rights as granted by international law and the national application of their rights leads to rising numbers of land evictions and violence against indigenous and those who come out in support of human rights.

As the preceding discussion has shown, only with a sustained harmonization in the application of the requirement of consultation, accompanying also the indigenous peoples' Protocols and national initiatives, will the promotion of the right to consult achieve efficacy.

In this work, normative premises and the different approaches to forms of consultation were inspected in order to understand the procedural framework of the right to consultation and its peculiarities as embedded in international law and the IAHRS.

The selection of cases illustrated the diverse elements surrounding the requirement of consultation in different countries and regions, as well as the provisions of international courts to ensure consistent application.

Therefore, this work aimed to provide an exhaustive review of the different applications, while taking additionally into account the novel instrument of the indigenous peoples' Protocols as well as their application in Brazil.

C. Woyames Dreher, *A Legal Assessment of the Efficacy of Consultation with Indigenous Peoples*, https://doi.org/10.1007/978-3-031-50539-3_6

In order to not overly restrict the range of efficacy as it is assessed, the analysis considered a multi-dimensional perspective of the application of consultation. This work thereby rethinks the standard application and offers an analysis that surpasses mere procedural consultation, understanding the requirement to include self-determination and cultural rights. Although this analysis is intimately related to the broader topic of indigenous peoples' human rights, the inquiry was narrowed down to examine what constitutes efficacy as regards the requirement of consultation with indigenous peoples in Brazilian law.

For this purpose, the main question was separated for addressing the efficacy, the control of conventionality and its application in Brazilian law, the contributions of international law to understand the extent to which the variants of self-determination and cultural rights contribute to the efficacy of its application in Brazilian law, as extensively analyzed in the previous chapters.

This chapter provides a thorough discussion on the degree to which the application of the requirement of consultation achieves efficacy. This part of the work is also shaped by engaging with multistakeholders, who hold close knowledge of the decision-making processes at the national, regional and international level. The concluding findings will be summarized at the end of the chapter, discussing its implications for theory as well as for their practical application.

6.2 Assessing Consultation in the Inter-American System of Human Rights

This section draws on two detailed tables and highlights the use of litigation regarding the requirement of consultation with indigenous peoples and the cases that were addressed under the IAHRS. All of them were granted to be considered and featured some dissident votes, in total four litigations at the IACtHR and four resultant recommendations at the IACHR regarding consultation with indigenous peoples.

The tables provide a succinct overview of relevant cases discussed in Chap. 3 offering a visualization per case of the core rights subject to contentious litigation, their new and innovative character as well as a tracing of how the decisions were taken. This will offer a comprehensive view and further supports the argument explored in more detail in the chapter, concerning the consolidation interpretation of the requirement of consultation under the IAHRS and how it has interacted with Brazilian cases through the control of conventionality.

From what has been established in all cases of the Inter-American Human Rights complaint system under analysis here, the dialogue must be based on a consensus-building process between the efficacy planning to the actual consultation phase according to the international standards, observing the prior nature of the consultation and the aim to reach an agreement observing cultural identity, self-determination, equal protection, development, information provision and good faith (Table 6.1).

The cases featuring a consideration of the requirement of consultation span the years 1985 until 2020, revealing an incremental consolidation in the interpretation of the IAHRS. Specifically, the IACtHR established a peculiar and essential view towards the interpretation of the American Convention in its Article 21, this includes considerations regarding individual and collective rights, self-determination and cultural rights, as identified in the cases considered for analysis of the IACHR and the decisions approved by the IACtHR.

The data collected shows that since 1985 cases involving Brazil support allegations that consultation has not been conducted as required. These includes recommendations to the Brazilian state to comply with as well as in 2011 a precautionary measure towards the construction of Belo Monte; all in all, despite the state's ratification of ILO No. 169, Brazil has poorly complied with the requirement of consultation. More than any other country in the region, Brazil chose to evade complaints raised in the IACHR.

Since the Mayagna (Sumo) Awas Tingni Community *v.* Nicaragua, in 2001,[1] the IACtHR has adopted normative standards of the ILO Convention No. 169, which has led to a convergent line of interpretation between national courts and the regional court without having direct dialogues on these issues. In other words, 'the courts of the Inter-American system have experienced a 'parallel' convergence'.[2] Thus, when the IACtHR began to incorporate normative standards from the universal system on indigenous rights there were already relevant developments at the national level in several countries of the IAHRS—both in their constitutions and in constitutional jurisprudence, especially with respect to collective rights and social rights.

There is an unequivocal understanding in the literature regarding the breakthroughs realized by the IACtHR.[3] The IACtHR has channelled the values of international human rights while at the same time maintaining a dialogue with national courts. The consistency and continuity of the advanced jurisprudence gave contours to the interpretation of Article 21 of the American Convention, in as much as that 'when traditional lands are involved, the right to property has become the Court's structural basis for indigenous rights'.[4]

However, as the cases reflected in the overview table reveal, the right to property brings concerns regarding the safeguarding of rights of indigenous peoples as 'the right to property inherently has difficulty providing even basic protection for ancestral lands because domestic and international law grant states wide latitude to

[1] Inter-American Court of Human Rights, *Mayagna (Sumo) Awas Tingni Community v. Nicaragua*, No. 79, Judgment of 31 August 2001.

[2] Mera (2015), p. 837, *translated by author.*

[3] See e.g. Antkowiak (2013), Mac-Gregor (2015), von Bogdandy and Venzke (2016), Alter (2014), Alter et al. (2015), Alter et al. (2018), and Mazzuoli (2011).

[4] Antkowiak (2013), p. 120.

Table 6.1 Overview of cases as considered by the Inter-American Commission of Human Rights

Enforcement System of Human Rights	Year	Case	Core issue of the violation	Innovative character	Decision
IACHR	1985	The Yanomami v. Brazil	Violations of the Article I (Right to Life, liberty and Personal Security); Article II (Right to Equality before Law); Article III (Right to Religious Freedom) and Worship), Article XI (Right to the Preservation of Health and to wellbeing); Article XII (Right to Education); Article XVII (Right to Recognition of Juridical Personality and of Civil Rights); and Article XXIII (Right to Property) of the American Declaration on the Rights and Duties of Man, in respect of a construction of a highway.	c) That the programs of education, medical protection, and social integration of the Yanomamis be carried out in consultation with the indigenous population affected and with the advisory service of competent scientific, medical, and anthropological personnel.	Granted
IACHR	2004	Maya Indigenous Communities of Toledo District v. Belize	Violation of the Articles I (Right to Life, liberty and Personal Security), Article II (Right to Equality before Law); Article III (Right to Religious Freedom) and Worship); Article VI (Right to freedom of investigation), Article XX (Right to vote and to participate in government), Article XI (Right to the preservation of health and to well- being) and Article XXIII (Right to Property) of the American Declaration on the Rights and Duties of Man in respect of lands traditionally used and occupied by the Maya people, by granting logging and oil concessions.	¶19. In particular, the Petitioners claim that the state has granted logging concessions and oil concessions on the Maya lands without meaningful consultations with the Maya people and in a manner that has caused substantial environmental harm and threatens long term and irreversible damage to the natural environment. ¶37. The Petitioners also allege that the state's practice in granting logging and oil concessions without adequate consultation. ¶ 46. (...) and their right to consultation found in part under Article XX (right to participate in government) of the Declaration. ¶55." In particular, the Petitioners argue that the right to be consulted in a meaningful way	Granted

				about any decision that may affect Maya interests in lands and natural resources is implicit in the human rights provisions that protect these interests, including Article 27 of the ICCPR, the right to participate in government under Article XX of the American Declaration, and the principle of self-determination. According to the Petitioners, self-determination is a principle of general international law.	
IACHR	2002	Mary and Carrie Dann v. United States	Violations of the Article II (the right to equality before the law), Article XVII (the right to recognition of juridical personality and civil rights), and Article XVIII (the right to a fair trial) of the American Declaration on the Rights and Duties of Man. And violation of the Article 1 (right to full enjoyment, as a collective or as individuals, of all human), Article 8 (prohibition of promote or incite racial or ethnic discrimination directed against indigenous), Article 21 (improvement of their economic and social conditions), Article 24 (traditional medicines health practices), Article 25 (spiritual relationship with their traditionally owned or otherwise occupied and used lands, territories, waters and coastal seas and other resources) of the Universal Declaration of Indigenous Peoples Rights.	¶32. In support of their arguments, the Petitioners provide examples of environmental damage caused and threatened by the concessions granted to Toledo Atlantic International, Ltd. and Atlantic Industries. ¶55 (. . .) violation of the "right to consultation." In particular, the Petitioners argue that the right to be consulted in a meaningful way about any decision that may affect Maya interests in lands and natural resources is implicit in the human rights provisions that protect these interests, including Article 27 of the ICCPR, the right to participate in government under Article XX of the American Declaration, and the principle of self-determination. According to the Petitioners, self-determination is a principle of general international law that is affirmed in multiple international instruments, and at its core means that human beings, individually and collectively, have a right to be in control of	Granted

(continued)

Table 6.1 (continued)

Enforcement System of Human Rights	Year	Case	Core issue of the violation	Innovative character	Decision
				their own destinies under conditions of equality. The Petitioners argue that for indigenous peoples, this principle establishes at a minimum the right to be genuinely involved in all decision-making that affects them. ¶56. The Petitioners assert that the required consultation with indigenous peoples must be more than formalities or simply processes by which they are given information about development projects, but must also provide indigenous peoples a full and fair opportunity to be heard and to genuinely influence the decisions before them. ¶80. (. . .) resulted in the alleged violations of their rights to life, property, cultural integrity, a healthy environment, consultation or equality before the law. ¶143. (. . .) at the same time, the Commission is concerned that, according to the information available, the state did not prescribe clear standards or requirements for these consultations, including, for example, information that must be shared with the communities concerned or the extent of community support necessary to permit a license to be issued. ¶154. Finally, the Commission notes the Petitioners' contention that the failure of the	

				state to engage in meaningful consultation (. . .) and the "right to consultation" implicit in Article 27 of the ICCPR, Article XX of the American Declaration, and the principle of self-determination.	
IACHR	2011	Precautionary Measure 382/10—Belo Monte	Precautionary measure alleges that the life and physical integrity of the beneficiaries is at risk due to the impact of the construction of the Belo Monte hydroelectric power plan.	The state must (1) conduct consultation processes, in fulfillment of its international obligations—meaning prior consultations that are free, informed, of good faith, culturally appropriate, and with the aim of reaching an agreement—in relation to each of the affected indigenous communities that are beneficiaries of these precautionary measures; (2) guarantee that, in order for this to be an informed consultation process, the indigenous communities have access beforehand to the project's Social and Environmental Impact Study, in an accessible format, including translation into the respective indigenous languages; (3) adopt measures to protect the life and physical integrity of the members of the indigenous peoples in voluntary isolation and to prevent the spread of diseases.	Granted

interfere with property'.[5] It must be added that the constant but not fully determined use of Article 21 might underlay a strengthening of the inadequacy of the right, and consequently, the right to consultation.

The proposal of this work is therefore to anchor the requirement of consultation in a stronger configurative source in order to solidify the right. The right to self-determination and cultural rights shall serve as a broader and more accurate legal mechanism to achieve the implementation of consultation as a right that is the central part of the redress of indigenous peoples for violations that started with colonization and persist through until nowadays, when, still in 2021, there was a large number of grants to give concessions to natural resource exploitation projects in indigenous peoples' territory, overshadowing continued violence against indigenous leaders and human rights defenders in Brazil, as can be seen in Table 6.2.

The analysis shows that all the decisions granted revealed some innovative character, which reinforces the case for self-determination and cultural rights to become the framework according to which the decisions shall be taken; hence, control of conventionality plays an essential part in addressing the countries that ratified the American Convention, especially Brazil.

This measure shall underscore the development the requirement of consultation underwent through the decisions of the IACtHR, which reconceptualized its application to introduce the *cogent* indigenous peoples' participation towards the decisions regarding natural resource exploitation, underscoring abuses and displacements inflicted by settlers.

From the findings in the previous chapters follows that, in order to realize indigenous peoples' rights, the IACtHR should adopt a more attuned approach towards the requirement of consultation with indigenous peoples, in which the central points are based on the control of conventionality of American and extra-American *corpus iuris*.

6.3 The Divergence of the Inter-American System of Human Rights and the International-Based Normative Framework and the Implications for Assessing the Requirement of Consultation

Regarding the role of the IAHRS and the juridical interpretation and the role that the conventionality control plays in Brazil, it is relevant that other international organs and the jurisprudence of national systems adopt the legislation of the consultation and the international regional courts as well to lead to the most adequate application in Brazil.

[5] Ibid.

Table 6.2 Overview of cases as decided by the Inter-American Court of Human Rights

Enforcement System of Human Rights	Year	Case	Core issue of the violation	Innovative character	Decision
IACtHR	2007	Saramaka *v.* Suriname	Violation of the Article XXI (Right to Property) and Article XXV (Right to Judicial Protection) of the American Declaration on the Rights and Duties of Man and Article 32 (development or use of their lands or territories) of the United Declaration on Indigenous Peoples Rights. In this particular case, the restrictions pertained to the issuance of using their territory for mining and logging.	¶124. The Commission and the representatives alleged that land concessions for forestry and mining awarded by the state to third parties on territory possessed by the Saramaka people, without their full and effective consultation, violates their right to the natural resources that lie on and within the land. ¶133. These consultations must be in good faith, through culturally appropriate procedures and with the objective of reaching an agreement. Furthermore, the Saramakas must be consulted, in accordance with their own traditions (. . .) consultation should take account of the Saramaka people's traditional methods of decision-making. ¶134. the State has a duty, not only to consult with the Saramakas, but also to obtain their free, prior, and informed consent, according to their customs and traditions. The Court considers that the	Granted

(continued)

Table 6.2 (continued)

Enforcement System of Human Rights	Year	Case	Core issue of the violation	Innovative character	Decision
				difference between "consultation" and "consent" in this context requires further analysis. ¶136. States must obtain the consent of indigenous and tribal peoples to carry out large-scale development or investment projects that have a significant impact on the right of use and enjoyment of their ancestral territories. ¶137.(. . .) the safeguard of effective participation that is necessary when dealing with major development or investment plans that may have a profound impact on the property rights (. . .). ¶148. The evidence before the Tribunal suggests not only that the level of consultation referred to by the State was not enough to guarantee the Saramakas' effective participation in the decision-making process, but also that the State did not complete environmental and social impact assessments prior to issuing said concessions (. . .).	

				¶174. (. . .) in consultation with the Saramaka people and fully respecting their traditions and customs, the judicial and administrative conditions necessary to ensure the recognition of their juridical personality, with the aim of guaranteeing them the use and enjoyment of their territory in accordance with their communal property system, as well as the rights to access to justice and equality before the law. ¶191. (. . .) and through effective and fully informed consultations (. . .). p. 57 c) remove or amend the legal provisions that impede protection of the right to property of the members of the Saramaka people and adopt, in its domestic legislation, and through prior, effective and fully informed consultations with the Saramaka people, legislative, administrative, and other measures as may be required to recognize, protect, guarantee and give legal effect to the right of the members of the Saramaka people. The necessity to have a social and environmental impact study. Surinam demanded the	

(continued)

Table 6.2 (continued)

Enforcement System of Human Rights	Year	Case	Core issue of the violation	Innovative character	Decision
				interpretation of the Court sentence, according to Article 67.	
IACtHR	2012	Kichwa de Sarayaku *v.* Ecuador	The violation of Article 21 (Right of assembly), Article 22 (Right of association) in relation to Article 12 (Right to education) and Article 23 and 1 (Right to property) of the American Declaration on the Rights and Duties of Man, regarding to property. The violation of the right to life, judicial guarantees and judicial protection, understood on Articles IV (Right to freedom of investigation, opinion, expression and dissemination), Article 8 (Right to residence and movement) and Article 25 (Right of protection from arbitrary arrest) of the same Convention.	¶159. Respect for the right to consultation of indigenous and tribal communities and peoples is precisely recognition of their rights to their own culture or cultural identity, which must be assured, in particular, in a pluralistic, multicultural and democratic society. ¶164. (...) refer to the importance of consultation or of communal property. In addition, several domestic courts of States of the region that have ratified ILO Convention No. 169 have referred to the right to prior consultation in accordance with the latter's provisions. ¶165 In other words, nowadays the obligation of States to carry out special and differentiated consultation processes when certain interests of indigenous peoples and communities are about to be affected is an obligation that has been clearly recognized.	Granted

				¶166. Thus, States must incorporate those standards into prior consultation procedures, in order to create channels for sustained, effective and reliable dialogue with the indigenous communities in consultation and participation processes through their representative institutions. ¶172. Although the State had an obligation to guarantee the right to the effective enjoyment of the property, in accordance with the communal tradition and taking into account the inherent particularities of their indigenous identity in their relationship to the land, prior to the ratification of the said Convention, it assumed an international commitment to guarantee the right to consultation upon ratifying ILO Convention. ¶178. (...) the right to consultation and whether the actions of the concessionaire company, which the State described as forms of "socialization" or attempts to reach an "understanding," satisfy the minimum standards and essential requirements of a valid consultation process. ¶185. According to	

(continued)

Table 6.2 (continued)

Enforcement System of Human Rights	Year	Case	Core issue of the violation	Innovative character	Decision
				the provisions of ILO Convention No. 169, consultations must be "carried out [. . .] in good faith and in a manner appropriate to the circumstances, with the aim of reaching an agreement or obtaining consent regarding the proposed measures (...)". ¶186. In addition, the consultation must not only serve as a mere formality, but rather it must be conceived as "a true instrument for participation," "which should respond to the ultimate purpose of establishing a dialogue between the parties based on principles of trust and mutual respect, and aimed at reaching a consensus between the parties. ¶208. As indicated previously, the consultation must be informed, in the sense that the indigenous peoples must be aware of the potential risks of the proposed development or investment plan, including the environmental and health risks. And	

				also, in this case, the decision was towards the guarantees of non repetition, the Court also recalled that the processes of participation and prior consultation must be conducted in good faith at all the preparation and planning stages of any project of this nature, the need for regulations of prior consultation in the domestic law and that the states should training of State officials on the rights of indigenous peoples.	
IACtHR	2015	Kaliña Peoples and Lokono *v.* Suriname	The violation of the Article 3 (right to recognition of juridical personality), in relation to Articles 1 (1) (any discrimination for reasons of race, color, sex, language, religion, political or other opinion, national or social origin, economic status, birth, or any other social condition), Article 2 (Where the exercise of any of the rights or freedoms referred to in Article 1 is not Article 21, Article 23 and Article 25 of the American Convention on Human Rights.	¶170. The state's obligations to carry out free, prior and informed consultation, as well as to allow and promote access to the corresponding public information by the affected indigenous communities, were also not fulfilled. ¶184. Therefore, it violated to their detriment the right to property and participation, in relation to the State's obligations to respect and guarantee rights. ¶351. They also requested that the Court order the State to sanction and implement the national and provincial regulations (domestic law) allowing for the proper registration of the Lhaka Honhat Association and other	Important to say that in the case, part of the decision was taken unanimously and part of dissidents votes about: the state responsibility for the violation of the right to property, the violation of the right to property and political rights, the violation of the right to judicial guarantees, the violation of the right to recognition as a person before the law or of the freedoms of thought and expression, association, movement, and residence, the violation of the right to judicial guarantees.

(continued)

Table 6.2 (continued)

Enforcement System of Human Rights	Year	Case	Core issue of the violation	Innovative character	Decision
				indigenous organizations and associations of its nature.	
IACtHR	2020	Indigenous Community of the Lhaka Honhat (nuestra tierra) *v.* Argentine	Violations of the right of community property, the recognition and determination of property, anything related to the projects and works executed on the claimed territory, the allegations of violations of the rights of movement and residence, the healthy environment, food and cultural identity, also considering the right to water, and the alleged violations of the rights to judicial guarantees and judicial protection in relation to legal actions initiated in the case.	After almost 35 years since the first legal complaint had been filed in the domestic realm, on February 6 of 2020, the IACtHR of Human issued a decision, and also, a case related to the responsibility of Argentine. Also for the first time in a contentious case, the Court analyzed the rights to a *healthy environment*, to adequate food, to water and to cultural identity in an autonomous manner in accordance with their specificities with respect to indigenous peoples, based on Article 26 of the American Convention. It understood that activities carried out in the territory by the afro-descendants' population had affected the environmental assets as well as the traditional way of feeding the indigenous communities and their access to water.	Important to note that the dissidents votes of the Judges Eduardo Vio Grossi, Humberto Antonio Sierra Porto and Ricardo Pérez Manrique that disagreed and made a dissident vote in regard to the responsibility of the state of Argentine for the '*violation of the rights to participate in cultural life, insofar as it relates to cultural identity, a healthy environment, adequate food and water, established in Article 26 of the American Convention on Human Rights, in relation to Article 1(1) of the same treaty, to the detriment of the 132 indigenous communities.*

The analysis and the application of the multi-dimensional perspective that considers self-determination and cultural rights as essential for consultation is relevant to overcome the obstacles to the participation of the indigenous peoples in Brazil based on the international standards of universal human rights protection.

On one hand, the requirement of consultation became a critical aspect for the implementation of indigenous peoples' rights as it represents one of the most important concepts in contemporary international law concerning indigenous peoples.

On the other hand, the same right is also one of the most contested in the context of international law, as embedded in the ILO No. 169 and the IAHRS. The models and procedures for the application of the requirement of consultation are still under development across different states, but, fortunately, genuine and suitable application can change the landscape of constant violations of human rights, spiraling into violent conflicts and further backlashes against indigenous peoples' rights.

An objection towards the lack of enforcement with the international human rights paradigm might be construed by the understanding that Western imperialism has little place in indigenous cultures.[6] This approach recognizes as a threat to indigenous peoples concepts conflicting with their fundamental rights.

The urgently needed harmonization should rectify the lack of enforcement with the norm and guarantee the participation of indigenous peoples. This work brough together legal claims and legislations from different states, revealing the legally relevant perspectives on the requirement of consultation with indigenous peoples.

6.4 Assessing Consultation Under the Control of Conventionality: Between the Inter-American System of Human Rights and Brazil

The controversies surrounding indigenous peoples' rights, especially the right to territory, have acquired the prominence of international court decisions in all countries which ratified the American Convention, such as Brazil. It must be noted however that the IACtHR is not an appellate court, while the judges decisions demand an enforcement that must be followed by domestic actors in accordance with the Brazilian constitutional law.

The successful efficacy of the requirement of consultation and all the decisions ultimately depends on the relationship between the IACtHR and Brazilian law. The international system for the protection of human rights has its own legal orders that guides national states as well as individuals. In that matter, indigenous peoples are bound to two or more legal systems, at least including the national and the international level. The meaning of the ratification of the American Convention is that the contemporary legal culture, which is dedicated to the protection and promotion of

[6] See e.g. Ibid.; Anaya (2004).

human dignity, became the ethical-legal reference that guides national, regional, and international legal orders.[7] Thus, the plurality of legal orders and normative sources requires overcoming the old traditional conception of monist law. Relevant are also the attempts of the region to guarantee access to people in vulnerable conditions beyond the IAHRS. For instance, 'the 100 Brasilia Rules were born at the Ibero-American Judicial Summit, within the framework of the work of its XIV edition, and their central concern is access to justice for people in vulnerable conditions'.[8] Thus, 'the agreement explicitly cites neither the American Convention, nor the IACtHR's precedents, but it adopts the same parameters established by the Court regarding access to justice'.[9]

The control of conventionality understands national legal systems and international human rights law as different, but interconnected and interdependent, systems, that will enable the use of legal instruments existing in Brazilian law to ensure respect for and the application of the decisions of the IACtHR; the American Convention; and at the domestic level, the Brazilian Federal Constitution of 1988.

Nevertheless, the Constitution of 1988, in Article 5, §2, establishes the possibility of opening the national legal system to the international legal system, especially in matters of human rights, allowing the dialogue between the internal legal system and the IAHRS through the control of conventionality.[10]

The hierarchical relationship between them depends on the text of the treaty and if it is in conformity with the constitutional text. The norm of the treaty to be valid needs to be materially compatible with the Constitution of 1998. In case of no compatibility, the norm will not have any validity in the Brazilian legal system. Thus, the norm not valid will be removed through constitutionality by the Brazilian courts.[11]

Since the trial of Almonacid Arellano et al. *v.* Chile, the IACtHR has a growing tendency to apply conventionality control.[12] Back in 2006, the IACtHR in this case affirmed the binding force of its precedents, that is, the binding efficacy of the *ratio decidendi* or determining grounds of its decisions, so as to oblige national judges and courts to adopt the meaning it has attributed to the American Convention.

Thus, 'the interpretative efficacy of the conventional norm must be understood as the possibility of achieving a regional minimum standard of efficacy of the American Convention to be applicable by all authorities at the national level'.[13]

---

[7] Barroso (2020).

[8] Ribotta (2012).

[9] Navarro (2021), p. 204.

[10] Piovesan (2018).

[11] Mazzuoli (2011).

[12] Kirmser (2014).

[13] Mac-Gregor (2013).

Furthermore, Brazil has the obligation to adopt the necessary legislative, administrative and judicial measures to ensure the efficacy of the human rights enshrined in the American Convention.[14]

6.5 The Legal Infrastructure of Self-determination and Cultural Rights for the Application of Consultation with Indigenous Peoples

The result of the exclusion of indigenous peoples endured throughout history[15] underlay the absence of their participation in both state-building and national decision-making. Despite these limitations imposed over the years, the requirement of consultation has nowadays advanced from the once forgotten Article 6 of the ILO No. 169 to central discussions over indigenous peoples' rights, embedded in guidelines to apply for financial institutions' grants and the elaboration of a possible veto power and the indigenous peoples' Protocols. These instruments thus provide a new structural basis for realizing indigenous rights towards consultation. In order to achieve the normative force needed for the applicability of consultation, its interpretation shall be tied up with self-determination and cultural rights as the multidimensional character of consultation that was explained in the first three chapters of this work.

Land rights have been discussed at the IACtHR in which decisions were concluded that possession of the land should suffice for indigenous peoples' lacking title to property. This included the first time that the IACtHR applied the interpretation of Article 21 which recognizes the ownership of indigenous peoples' territory;[16] an interpretation that has yet to find a comparable measure in either the African Human Rights System[17] or the European Court of Human Rights.[18] Thus, 'the legal protection of indigenous territory receives constitutional status in almost all involved countries. Furthermore, the almost unanimous constitutional recognition of territorial rights is evidence of an international consensus and even a customary principle of international law. The IACtHR has used that allegation when affirming property rights over traditional territory'.[19]

Self-determination is not a jarring proposition, however according to different interpretations it is 'grounded in the idea that all are equally entitled to control their

[14]Ibid.

[15]Anaya (2004).

[16]Inter-American Court of Human Rights, *Mayagna (Sumo) Awas Tingni Community v. Nicaragua*, No. 79, Judgment of 31 August 2001.

[17]Devereux (1995).

[18]Koivurova (2011).

[19]Navarro (2021), p. 14.

own destinies'.[20] The understanding of self-determination is towards remediating social, economic and political inequalities.[21] The IACtHR has stressed the relevance of self-determination repeatedly.[22]

According to the IACtHR, human rights treaties are live instruments that through interpretations shall adapt to the consolidation of the times and the current living conditions.[23] In further support to communal property, the IACtHR also took a huge step when concluding that the provision forged in Article 21 an elegant, but also contradictory way, to resolve the consultation legal issue that was brought to the appreciation of the IACtHR.

As a result of the expanded interpretation of Article 21, the IACtHR decided using Article 1 on self-determination and Article 27 of the ICCPR regarding cultural integrity, under consideration of Article 29 which abolishes the restrictive interpretation of rights.[24] Yet activities such as logging on traditional lands are not enough to constitute a violation of Article 27 of the ICCPR. Thus, cultural rights should not be seen as cultural preservation only but also paying tribute to the tolerance and respect to indigenous peoples' forms of existence. The IACtHR understood that indigenous groups are peoples who identify themselves with their ancestral territories and who regulate themselves by their own norms, customs and traditions.[25] Vivid demonstrations of violation of cultural rights such as the breaching of the ancestral lands in the context of the natural resource exploitation however often reveal dissatisfying efficacy.

Ultimately, there was a radical turn[26] towards the utility of Article 21, as it did not incorporate the necessity of a broader interpretation of self-determination and cultural integrity, not merely as cultural survival, which would lead to a more elaborated conceptualization of self-determination and cultural rights.

This first step taken by the IACtHR was later reorganized into the concept of participation as the core for the right to consultation.[27] That was the first time that the concept was used more elaborately, also recognizing the norm of the ILO Convention No. 169 provision for opening the possibility to the interpretation of consultation as a general principle of international law.[28]

---

[20] Anaya (2004).

[21] Anaya J (2012) Report of the Special Rapporteur on the rights of indigenous peoples.

[22] Inter-American Court of Human Rights, *Xákmok Kásek Indigenous Community v. Paraguay*, Judgment of 24 August 2010.

[23] Inter-American Court of Human Rights, *Mayagna (Sumo) Awas Tingni Community v. Nicaragua*, No. 79, Judgment of 31 August 2001.

[24] Inter-American Commission of Human Rights, *Saramaka People v. Suriname*, Case No 172, Judgment of 28 November 2007.

[25] Ibid.

[26] Antkowiak (2013).

[27] Inter-American Court of Human Rights, *Kichwa Indigenous People of Sarayaku v. Ecuador*, No. 185, Judgment of 27 June 2012.

[28] Ibid.

However, the application of consultation did not embrace the extension of the right to any administrative and legislative measures that affect indigenous peoples' land. The protection of the territorial rights was only relevant once 'the lack of legal protection of communal lands leaves the community in a vulnerable position to protect its lands and invoke its rights'.[29]

These limits in the interpretation have already been mentioned in another decision: 'an international human rights tribunal can never by itself lower the international protection standards, more so when the parties are in a flagrantly vulnerable position, if not abandoned, condemned —many of them since birth— by their fellowmen to social exclusion, and to chronic poverty, which, as I see it, constitutes, the deprivation of all human rights'.[30]

In this case, self-determination was considered as participation, although cultural rights were understood together with the UNDRIP and the ILO No. 169 provisions, as 'fundamental right that should be respected in a multicultural, pluralistic and democratic society'.[31] The conclusion of the IACtHR was imperative to stress that participation of indigenous peoples in projects of natural resource exploitation in their territory should ensure that severe consequences for their cultural identity and self-determination could be addressed: 'this means that states have an obligation to ensure that indigenous peoples are properly consulted on matters that affect or could affect their cultural and social life in accordance with their values, traditions, customs and forms of organization'.[32]

Thus, the IACtHR solidified its posture towards the interpretation of Article 21 based on the idealized imaginary of traditional communities, in which the ancestral lands have not changed over the years.

On the other hand, the interpretation provided by the international law in the framework of the UNDRIP, the American Declaration on Indigenous Peoples Rights and the ILO No. 169 leads not to a narrow possibility of categorization but to a broader and unlimited framework; this includes the endangering of a stronger and more adequate protection of the right to consultation, indispensable to indigenous people's survival, development and possibility to achieve equal rights.

The IACtHR missed few opportunities to address a more elaborated format of the right to consultation within the lacunae of efficacy in participation, good faith and in the impact assessments to ensure an adequate application of consultation to be followed by the region. In the case of a general principle of international law, the concept without a framework accompanying its application would lead to an inoperative norm. Thus, what could have become the chance for the strengthening of self-determination and cultural rights might ultimately become empty rhetoric.

---

[29] Monteiro de Matos (2018).

[30] Judge Antonio Cançado Trindade, Sawhoyamaxa v. Paraguay, No. Separate Opinion (Inter-American Court of Human Rights March 29, 2006).

[31] Inter-American Court of Human Rights, *Kichwa Indigenous People of Sarayaku v. Ecuador*, No. 185, Judgment of 27 June 2012.

[32] Ibid.

6.5.1 Overview of Legislative Cases in Brazil

Brazil has approximately 900,000 indigenous people and 305 ethnic groups and more than 274 languages that were not legally accepted by the Constitution.[33] The indigenous peoples mostly live in their lands, which are demarcated areas of collective and exclusive usufruct for indigenous peoples, while most of them are not declared as entitlement territories.

The indigenous peoples represent on average 0.5% of the Brazilian population and can largely be found in the north of the vast Brazilian territory.[34] Their central claims have always evolved around their territorial rights, which can be understood as the rights to traditionally occupied lands essential for their physical and cultural survival, to access, use and manage of natural resources present in their territories, as well as the right to be consulted in a free, prior and informed manner about acts that may affect their permanence in and management of their territories.

In recent years, a certain number of indigenous ran for office, were elected and are representing their constituents' interests in the Brazilian administrative and legislative system. In 2020, for instance, a total of 237 representatives of indigenous peoples had been elected to the positions of councilman, deputy mayor and mayor, an increase of 28% as compared to the previous municipal election.[35] These developments notwithstanding, however, at the same time the amount of bills in the Brazilian congress with the intent to delimit indigenous peoples' access to lands and also to use their territory without their consultation for natural resource exploitation kept increasing as well.[36]

The requirement to consider the enabling of consultation in legislative texts is engrained in Article 6 of ILO Convention No. 169. As the past has shown, also as brought forward in the IACtHR, in Brazil there is the need to constantly review proposed bills as to whether they contain the required clauses. The legislature is home to a strong and influential number of legislators in all instances which granted preferential access to instances of natural resource exploitation either to themselves or for foreign investments and transnational companies operating in Brazil.[37] This encompasses an intricate international network that enables the actors that are

---

[33] (2012) Os indígenas no Censo Demográfico 2010 primeiras considerações com base no quesito cor ou raça.

[34] Indigenous peoples in Brazil. IWGIA—Int. Work Group Indig. Aff.

[35] See e.g. Lupion (2020), Souza et al. (2020), and Tribunal Superior Eleitoral (2019).

[36] This study is broader and starts from 2014, but the data shows the number of proposal for legislations and also the amount of money that the legislators had earned: 'in the game of setbacks and maintenance of privileges, the FPA, with 207 deputies, is united against the indigenous populations with the mining (23 deputies), bullet (35 deputies), evangelical (197 deputies), business (208 deputies), and contractors and construction companies (226 deputies). The survey mapped the main funders of deputies and senators proposers through the Consultation on Donors and Suppliers of Candidates Campaign of the Superior Electoral Court. In the 2014 elections, donors are also included for party funds (National and State directories)'. The CIMI (2017).

[37] Simionatto and Costa (2012) and Luís Castilho et al. (2020).

responsible for invading, occupying, looting and destroying the indigenous peoples', territories and cultural rights.[38] Often, the indigenous peoples are considered as "obstacle to development", which enables the government to be actively instigating human rights violations against indigenous peoples.[39]

There is a lack of studies as regards Brazilian draft law proposals and the requirement of consultation with indigenous peoples.[40] Until today, the exact number of proposed bills in that respect, or possible subsequent alterations of bills, is still unclear. It is discernible from the below examples of bills that there is an encouragement of the federal government towards disregarding indigenous peoples' fundamental rights guaranteed by the Constitution of 1988 and by international treaties.

For instance, in 2020, the federal government referred to the Congress the proposal of Bill No. 191. Of all the proposals discussed in Chap. 4, this ranks by far as the most concerning.[41] The proposal refers to the regulation of mining, water resource exploitation and other commercial activities in indigenous peoples' territories.

The proposal is concerning for different matters: The first concern constitutes the lack of fulfilling the requirement of consultation before the proposal was even drafted. This also matters secondly because of the environmental aspect as if passed the bill would certainly lead to an increase of the deforestation in the regions in which the federal bill is implemented.

In the region of Amazon, for example, where there is the largest extent of indigenous peoples' territory, the long-term consequences of past projects have proven catastrophic. The data of recent studies warns that the accelerated destruction of the region would turn the forest into a savanna, releasing billions of tons of carbon stored in the atmosphere.[42]

The third serious issue regards violence against indigenous peoples. In the case that this proposal would become rule of law, the natural resource exploitation of indigenous territories, without the already hard to achieve standards of protection, would be facilitated and allow for even more invasions and deforestation in these territories. Finally, added to those direct environmental impacts, the 'continued assault upon forest peoples can be detrimental to the Amazon considering that they are proven to be the best stewards of the rainforest. Studies show that [indigenous territories] are the ultimate barrier against deforestation and forest degradation'.[43]

[38] Rech (2007) and Instituto Socioambiental (2018).

[39] Association of Brazil's Indigenous Peoples (2020).

[40] According to the CIIMI: 'since 2015, 18 legislative propositions seek to approve laws with the purpose of retroceding rights constituted in 1988, in the Federal Constitution. Today, among the main themes covered by the amendments are the exploitation of natural resources and the attempts to redefine the criteria for demarcation of Indigenous Lands, which have the Proposal for Amendment to the Constitution (PEC) 215/2000 as its flagship'. CIMI (2017).

[41] Canineu and Cavalho (2020) and The Guardian (2020).

[42] Scherer (2020) and Walker et al. (2019).

[43] Association of Brazil's Indigenous Peoples (2020), p. 5.

Consequently, the weakening of environmental enforcement results in illegal deforestation. This aligns with other actions taken by the current government aimed at reducing environmental protections and disregarding the environment and the rights of indigenous peoples. According to the Indigenous Missionary Council from January to September 2019 alone, there were 160 cases of incursions into indigenous lands in the country by people involved in possessory invasions or illegal exploitation of natural resources, such as timber theft and illegal mining (in Portuguese, *grilheiros*).[44]

Furthermore, the growing health issues are of equal concern. According to a study conducted by the Oswaldo Cruz Foundation, many indigenous already suffer from mercury contamination. Analyses of hair samples of two Yanomami villages found mercury concentrations well above the thresholds considered as safe as established by the World Health Organization.[45]

Although there was no consideration of indigenous peoples' interest, not to speak of complying with the requirement of consultation in the proposal of the draft bill, the federal government claims that the proposal would benefit indigenous people. However, as seen in past attempts to violate the right to consultation, Brazil will likely break with international law, trigger more domestic legal claims against the natural resource exploitation, and incur further economic damages and socioambiental problems to the whole nation, as seen in Table 6.3.

6.5.2 Overview of the Legal Claims in Brazil

The Constitution of 1988 represented a change of outlook and a hope for justice for Brazilians after the era of dictatorship. The period thereafter is known in Brazilian history as a period of redemocratization of the country. In the text of the Constitution, there are a couple of Articles, including Article 231 and Article 232, that provide a high-level framework conceptualizing indigenous peoples and the most tormented problem regarding their rights: the right to territory.

Despite its importance, the right to have indigenous peoples' territory recognized, demarcated and protected has been constantly violated. Demarcation processes take years to be completed, affecting indigenous groups' survival as a people in many ways. The deterioration of living conditions of indigenous peoples can be traced back to the lack of understanding related to their territory, which needs to guarantee their self-determination as there is a profound relationship of indigenous peoples with their lands.

The process of identifying, declaring, demarcating, and approving the boundaries of indigenous lands has been slow, sensitive to pressure from large landowners and the backward parcel of agribusiness. The Brazilian state legitimizes appropriation

[44] Rangel (2018).

[45] Basta (2016).

Table 6.3 Legislatives cases in Brazil affecting indigenous peoples

Bill number	Bill alteration	Text alteration
Constitutional Amendment Bill No. 76 of 2011	Article 176 and the Article 231 of the Constitution	Ensure the indigenous peoples profit share in the use of water resources on their entitled lands is an example of this attempt.
Constitutional Amendment Bill No. 71 of 2011	Article 231, § 6° of the Federal Constitution	Monetary grant for the holders of title deeds related to lands declared as indigenous.
Constitutional Amendment Bill No. 227 of 2012	Article 231, § 6° of the Federal Constitution	Use of the lands entitled to the indigenous peoples without the need of licenses and constitutional measures.
Bill No. 5807 of 2011	The previous Brazilian Mining Code	One of the new considerations of the Code is going to be the non necessity of the requirement of consultation for mining activities.
Constitutional Amendment Bill No. 1216 of 2015	Article 231 of the Constitution	The indigenous peoples who, due to expulsion of the territory, did not occupy their lands at the time of the promulgation of the Constitution of 1988, would not have the entitlement to the territory
Bill No. 191	Article 176 of the Constitution	Regarding the conditions for conducting research and mining of mineral and hydrocarbon resources and for the use of water resources for generating electricity on indigenous lands and institutes compensation for the restriction of the indigenous lands. The President proposed the alteration without the indigenous peoples' consent.
Bill No. 2633	New legislation	Increases the size of the territory, mostly of the farms and latifundium owners, that can be regularized without previous inspection. Among other measures, the draft has not brought any innovation to combat illegal mining.

instead of legitimizing traditional knowledge and culture.[46] And even on those lands that are already homologated, in many cases the federal government has not completed the *saneamiento*—the withdrawal of those who unlawfully occupy the land, the *grilheiros*.

Another aspect relates to the constant lawsuits which indigenous peoples face with the purpose to slow the process of the rightful demarcation of the land. This process has had hardly positive results, rather resulting in more violence against the indigenous leaders. Moreover, these actions fostered 'irreversible environmental impacts that significantly compromise their use, even though they are still cultural and spiritually necessary spaces for indigenous peoples. This environmental degradation affects not only the indigenous peoples of the forests, but humanity as a

[46] Ioca (2019).

whole, since the conservation of biodiversity is fundamental to the climate and human survival, and the peoples and their territory have a fundamental role in this history'.[47]

The Brazilian judiciary has not yet recognized indigenous rights as a possibility to be exercised outside of specific actions, for example, as a defense in possessory actions where one asks for the unoccupied areas of land or set of unoccupied apartments on the outskirts of cities. It has not yet recognized, therefore, that collective rights can oppose individual rights in ordinary actions and especially property and possession rights.

Towards the international arena and the relationship with the Inter-American System of Human Rights, Brazil has adopted a posture of allegedly good will international recommendations. Thus, the wide gap between the IAHRS and the Brazilian state can be shortened by the control of conventionality.

Already analyzed in Chap. 4, the legal claims related to consultation decided in the Brazilian judiciary reveal the different positions adopted by the judges, in the Federal Courts and the Higher Courts. Nevertheless, in this subchapter, the same data is translated into tables providing another view on the lack of enforcement with the mandatory parameters of the Inter-America Human Rights System and the binding international treaties.

The crucial role that indigenous peoples play in advocating their rights and also the environmental rights has nonetheless been influential. In all the main cases studied, the mining, the hydroelectric dam and the construction of the road, the indigenous peoples together with the *Ministério Público* and national and international organizations organized themselves to make their voices heard in the process of planning and conducting natural resource exploitation projects.

The same regards the legislature, where the non-compliance with the requirement of consultation led to legal claims and possible international violations of human rights. The compensatory measures for the damages inflicted those states are obliged to provide are not only pecuniary but also include a broader range of measures of restitution, rehabilitation and satisfaction (Table 6.4).[48]

6.6 Towards Efficacy of Consultation and a More Adequate Application in Brazil

There are some main obstacles to the application of consultation in some countries of the region and especially Brazil. One of them is the level of trust.[49] After years of violations and disregarding of international obligations, there is considerable mistrust between the indigenous peoples and the private sector as well as governmental

[47] Yamada (2011).

[48] See e.g. Donoso (2010), Navarro (2021), and Antkowiak (2013).

[49] Mendes Junior (1912).

Table 6.4 Legal cases in Brazil affecting indigenous peoples

Case	Violation of the requirement of consultation	Decision
The case Belo Monte Appeal 'Ação Civil Pública'	YES	Most of the 25 litigations have found violations of environmental and constitutional rights. The Federal Judges quotes the ILO Convention No. 169 regarding the requirement of consultation
Raposa do Sol case	NO	However, the indigenous peoples are elaborating their own Protocols of consultation.
The Xucuru People case	YES	The IACtHR recognized the cultural identity rights and the prior consultation.
The case 'Educação Escolar Indígena' Appeal 'Ação Civil Pública' 378-31.2014.4.01.3902	YES	The Federal Court decided in favor of the requirement of consultation.
The case 'Hidrelétrica São Luiz do Tapajós' Appeal 'Ação Civil Pública' 3883-98.2012.4.01.3902	YES	The Federal Court quoted the IACtHR, the ILO Convention No. 169 and suspended the project until there is the consultation with the indigenous peoples of the region.
The case 'Usina Hidrelétrica Teles Pires' Appeal 'Ação Civil Pública' 3947-44.2012.4.01.3600	YES	The Federal Court decided for the suspension of the project until the requirement of consultation is done.
The case 'Usina Hidrelétrica São Manuel' Appeal 'Ação Civil Pública'14123-48.2013.4.01.3600	YES	The Federal Court understood the necessity of the requirement of consultation.
The case 'Polo Naval de Manaus' Appeal 'Ação Civil Pública' 6962-86.2014.4.01.3200		The Federal Court decided in favor of the requirement of consultation with the indigenous peoples and the 'comunidades ribeirinhas', as observed by the Constitution, the ILO Convention No. 169 and the IACtHR.
The case 'Parque Nacional of Superagui Appeal 'Ação Civil Pública' 742-88.2015.4.04.7008	YES	The Federal Court decided for the requirement of consultation. In the petition, the public defenders quoted the indigenous peoples' Protocols and the Fishermen, indicating their right to consult. The Federal Judge understood that there was no regulation regarding the management plan and the requirement of consultation, however, as in any other case in which the communities are affected by the

(continued)

Table 6.4 (continued)

Case	Violation of the requirement of consultation	Decision
		project, there was the need of the requirement of consultation.
The case 'Duplicação da estrada de Ferro Carajás' Appeal 'Ação Civil Pública' 61827-77.2015.4.01.3700	YES	The Federal Court understood the importance of complying with the ILO Convention No. 169 and the requirement of consultation.
The case 'Linhão Manaus Boavista' Appeal 'Ação Civil Pública' 18408-23.2013.4.01.3200 and Appeal 'Ação Civil Pública' 18032-66.2015.4.01.3200	YES	The environmental license was granted before the consultation and the Federal Court understood to suspend the project until there was the consultation with the communities affected by the project.
The case of the resource exploitation of oil, gas and schisto, in Acre. Appeal 'Ação Civil Pública' 1849-35.2015.01.3001	YES	The Federal Court recognized the ILO Convention No. 169 and suspended the project until is fulfiled the requirement of consultation with the indigenous peoples.
The case 'Construção do porto no lago Maicá' Appeal 'Ação Civil Pública' 377-75.2016.4.01.3902	YES	The Federal Court decided for the suspension of the project until there is fulfilled the requirement of consultation with the indigenous peoples, the 'comunidades ribeirinhas' and the 'quilombolas' of the region.

representatives. The lack of trust hinders dialogue and the possibility of agreements, and its traces can be found before and after the advent of the Brazilian Constitution of 1988. The level of trust could of course be improved, in case notably state actors would adopt clear stances as regards allowing for permanent spaces for dialogue between the state and the indigenous peoples before granting permits to projects of natural resource exploitation.

Another obstacle is the absence of systematized information on indigenous peoples, their traditions, activities and cultural sites, which renders difficult identifying and measuring the impact that a natural resource exploitation activity may have. In order to solve that problem and avoid indeterminacies in court decisions, the help of anthropologist studies and local leaders can be an asset to guarantee the efficacy of consultation on a local level.

The high costs involved in the implementation of a consultation can be considered as a third relevant issue.[50] For ensuring efficacy of consultation, the state must act in good faith and understand the importance of the right of consultation. In this context, the state has to respond satisfactorily to the need for sufficient resources and that if the process of consultation has been delayed or ignored altogether, the

[50] Garavito (2012).

consequences have not only participatory and democratic implications, but also social and economic ones.

The social consequence of a further violation of indigenous peoples' human rights as guaranteed in international treaties will further decrease the already fragile level of trust of indigenous peoples towards the state administration and the legislature. This may add to the increase of violence in the region, also in view that usually no studies on the social impact of these projects are conducted.[51]

The economic consequences relate to the fact that international as well as national courts in the past already decided in favor of the necessity to conduct consultation, the absence of which may lead to the embargo of such natural resource exploitation projects. Thus, the delay in the implementation of consultation processes in those projects has a direct impact on the local economy, labor, and lost profits. In the specific case of energy and infrastructure investment projects, impacts are generated on energy costs and prices, as well as public infrastructure and the connectivity of people and cities.

Another stumbling block consists of the high expectations of indigenous peoples regarding the consultation processes and their results.[52] In this context, the transfer of responsibilities from the state to transnational and/or private companies is another aspect identified during the readings as one of the main difficulties in terms of clarifying expectations of indigenous peoples.

Both the state and the transnational companies have slowly come to understand that consultation is not only to inform and propose compensation measures, but in many cases to make important changes to the natural resource exploitation projects, incorporating indigenous peoples' expressions of their self-determination and cultural rights.

In relation to the institutional aspects, the official procedures should also be streamlined for increasing the efficacy of consultation. Thus, there is the need of trained and capable teams of specialists to develop the processes in order to bring an informative mechanism into practice, based on good faith and non-discriminatory consultation.[53]

Taken together, being attentive to all these aspects may give grounds to aspire to a further improved situation, as the lack of enforcement of the Brazilian government, legislature and judiciary with the requirement of consultation has proven hazardous in the daily life of indigenous peoples in all parts of Brazil.

In order to summarize the recommendations to Brazil, Table 6.5 indicates the different types of consultation: the public hearing, the constitutional hearing and the requirement of consultation in the Brazilian legislation that were discussed in Chap. 3. The intention is to facilitate the understanding and to avoid the legal indeterminacies of the legal concept.

---

[51] Jaichand and Sampaio (2013).

[52] Liebenthal et al. (2005).

[53] Morris et al. (2010).

Table 6.5 Types of consultation in Brazil [a]

Format	Public hearing	Constitutional hearing	Requirement of consultation
Law	Federal Constitution, Law No. 9.784 of 1999; CONAMA Resolutions No. 01 of 1986 and 09 of 1987	Federal Constitution	ILO No. 169, UNDRIP, Biodiversity Convention and American Declaration on the Rights of Indigenous Peoples
Object of the Law	Civil society	Indigenous peoples	Traditional communities
Responsible for the execution	Environmental agency responsible for the environmental licensing	National Congress	Brazilian state
Participation of the private sector	Yes	No	Yes
Juridicity	Right to information and participation	Right to exclusive use of natural resources and territory	Right to self-determination and cultural rights
Reason to conduct	Activity that modifies the environment	Use of water resources, including energy potentials, and research and mining of mineral wealth on indigenous peoples' territory	Administrative and legislative measures likely to affect the traditional communities to achieve a consent
When to conduct	Whenever the licensing agency deems necessary or when requested by a civil entity or the Public Prosecution Office	Whenever it is in the indigenous peoples' territory	Whenever there is an impact on the collective rights of a culturally differentiated community
Execution of the Law	After the RIMA	After the EIA and before the National Congress authorization of the Legislative Decree	At the earliest stages of natural resource project planning and also during the EIA
Method to conduct	Representative of the licensing agency after an objective exposition of the project and its respective RIMA	A mixed commission designed by the National Congress to go in loco	Procedures shall be conducted by the indigenous peoples considering the self-determination and cultural rights
Efficacy	Add value to the RIMA and the analysis and final opinion regarding the project's environmental feasibility	There are three distinct positions: (I) the National Congress is not bound by the deliberation of the indigenous people; (II) in cases where there will be aggressive impact, Congress cannot authorize the enterprise; (III) the manifestation of the	The legal efficacy of the requirement of consultation is the consent of the indigenous peoples regarding the natural resource exploitation in their territory. The UNDRIP provides for the possibilities in which the consent is required

(continued)

Table 6.5 (continued)

Format	Public hearing	Constitutional hearing	Requirement of consultation
		indigenous people will condition the deliberation of the National Congress	(Articles 10; 11, 2; 28, 1; 29, 2; 32, 2). The IACtHR requires consent when dealing with projects that are likely to have profound impacts on the rights of the community. See e.g. Case of the Saramaka People v. Surinam. However, the American Declaration on Indigenous Peoples Rights is based on the consent
In case of non enforcement with the Law	Invalidity of the license granted	Unconstitutionality of the Legislative Decree	Void of the state authorization

[a] This table was first created by the Federal Prosecutor Felício Pontes, which was amended for current purposes. See also: Duprat (2015)

6.7 Recommendations to International Organizations, Transnational Companies, and Multilateral Financial Institutions

A parallel consolidation can be observed towards the integration of international law and sustainability initiatives, leading to a globally growing awareness of the co-constitutive relationships of involved multistakeholders; both the implementation of indigenous peoples' rights and environmental sustainability are influenced by the interactions of transnational companies, indigenous peoples, governments as well as the financial institutions that provide loans for financing projects of natural resource exploitation. For these set of actors, a range of recommendations can be deduced from this work's findings.

The present work examined documents, stakeholder accounts and a range of data points in its analysis of enforcement at the regional and national level with the requirement of consultation with indigenous peoples. Ultimately, the results of the analysis reveal that across countries, all initiatives to ensure an adequate application of consultation could not ensure a continued harmonization of the process but rather did not prevent a less comprehensive approach, a situation which must fundamentally change to provide the general observation of the right to consultation.

Although the obligation of the requirement of consultation requires that the state shall oversee and ensure the application of the norm, transnational companies themselves are not exempt from the responsibility to do all in their power to enable its efficacy, given their close involvement in the relevant projects.[54] Then, it is indeed the transnational companies which shall safeguard the appropriate application by defining and scheduling the most appropriate time plan, ahead of executing the project with close attention to due process.

A further recommendation emerges from the context of establishing a better relationship with indigenous peoples who live in the territory, by developing the internal capacities of the company to engage with indigenous peoples, establishing a connection and promoting the dialogue.[55] For mutually beneficial outcomes, such preemptive mediation could prevent the judicialization of the conflict and raising of legal claims, and thus avoid the associated legal, social, and financial costs.

For both international and national counterparts, to maintain channels of communication constantly open with contact points representing indigenous peoples, the respect of their forms of organization, leadership and interaction is another essential aspect. This dialogue should always take place through institutional and regulated mechanisms for this purpose, with the presence of the member of the state, in order to generate transparency and to avoid mutual mistrust at all costs.[56] At the same time, it has been recorded that in some cases companies do not recognize early on all the impacts they generate, which affects the trust of the indigenous peoples and the success of fulfilling adequate consultation processes.

Nonetheless, there is also the need of the members of government, national and international organizations that are advising indigenous peoples to maintain their high capacity and engagement with negotiations, demonstrating to companies that any failure to comply with the requirement of consultation, as previously informed, might have not only legal and social consequences but also considerable economic costs.[57]

6.8 Conclusions

Seizing upon this momentum in which the requirement of consultation has been at the center of discussions, this work instills it with the potential of a normative force. The application of consultation as mechanism to realize self-determination and cultural rights fills the gaps that the indigenous peoples have perennially emphasized as need to achieve their claims. The possibility to embrace and redress the lack of enforcement with the norm brought into international and national legal systems originated from the ILO No. 169.

[54] Garavito (2012).

[55] Davis (2002).

[56] (2016) Aldeia da Memória-Belo Monte.

[57] Garavito (2012).

The cases assessed in this book involving the requirement of consultation with indigenous peoples brought the preoccupation to the fore, that the lack of definition on how to conduct the consultation leads to its inefficacy and consequently, the inoperability of the norm.

Between the international human rights law and the IAHRS, this work encountered another critical factor: the indigenous peoples' Protocols. Through the chapters, the work addressed the question as to what would constitute efficacy of consultation with indigenous peoples in Brazil. As discovered by analyzing cases in some countries, international courts and Brazilian's legislative draft bills and legal claims, there was a direct relationship with projects of natural resource exploitation and the rights granted and (lack of) obligations imposed by states on transnational companies. One of the most consequential aspects of consultation is the effects it has on the parties and on the viability of the administrative or legislative measure, and on the implementation of the natural resource exploitation project in question.[58]

Under the requirement of consultation, indigenous peoples have the right to have their voices heard as a condition for making a general decision or carrying out a natural resource exploitation project that affects them. A higher standard could set a condition that indigenous peoples shall give their opinion based on good faith.

Agribusiness, hydroelectric dams, mining, among other natural resource exploitation projects, also too often turned out to be a threat, as observable in the increase of the numbers of new draft legislations, which may not be aligned with the Brazilian Constitution and clearly undermine indigenous peoples' consultation rights.[59] These developments are closely related to the increase of the pollution of the waters, land encroachment, deforestation and increase of the violence in some regions.[60]

In further support of indigenous peoples' rights, the recognition of the most adequate application of the requirement of consultation reinforces the need for a more suitable legal protection to guarantee the peoples' self-determination and cultural rights. In addition, the proposed framework fills in some gaps that are left by merely considering the requirement of consultation without the consideration of the self-determination and cultural rights approach.

Some of the inadequacies resulting from the ILO No. 169 and the UNDRIP leading to the lack of incorporation of indigenous peoples' language, the confused veto power and the FPIC also give no direction to the application in national states. In this sense then these international treaties leave more questions than answers to the already complex process of consultation.

[58] Morris et al. (2010).

[59] Those who are in favour of this model of development can rarely be found in the literature, but rather in the promotional videos of those engaged in natural resource exploitation. For more, see e.g. (2019) UHE Belo Monte; Usina Hidroelétrica de Belo Monte (2019) UHE Belo Monte: geração de energia e desenvolvimento sustentável para o crescimento no Brasil; (2019) The Biggest Challenges Facing Miners, According To One CEO; (2017) Brazilian Agribusiness—Entrepreneurship, Preservation and Transformation.

[60] de Area Leão Pereira et al. (2020) and Sauer (2019).

The engagement of indigenous peoples in the process of the construction of the requirement of consultation became a tailor-made exercise of their self-determination. In that sense, the check-list proposed by some international organizations and financial institutions is an approach which may not be the most accurate to discern the unique character of each indigenous peoples' cultures and particularities regarding to their self-determination and should be avoided by those who are conducting the consultation process.[61] The reason is that the usefulness of the same approach to different natural resource exploitation projects and indigenous who live in the territory is limited. Ambiguity and divergent aspects across situations may render the application of a standardized approach to consultation as not adequate, as different problems require different solutions that cannot be wholly addressed by a mere check list previously established by state and non-state actors without considering the indigenous peoples' needs.

Central to achieve the efficacy considering the application of consultation remains the question over the clear definition of the right.[62] The ILO No. 169 left the definition and the process quite open and for discussion, leaving a relevant, not if the most essential and crucial right for indigenous peoples, to be discussed by the states and transnational companies.

The lack of compromise left the discussion open in a time in which most countries in the region could have ratified the only binding treaty as regards the establishment of the requirement of consultation. The problem of definition remained for years to come, also addressed by the UNDRIP, that related to the FPIC and the veto power.[63] The IAHRS subsequently advocated consultation in an elegant, however complicated, format considering the right to property. The problems of using Article 21 of the American Convention were innovative in a sense that the judges only had the Convention to guarantee consultation but also considering that their interpretative attribution is advanced, formulating a forward-looking jurisprudence that shaped the legal order of the region.[64] Those different practices were extensively discussed in this work.

Most of the indigenous peoples' legal complaints as raised during the consultation processes referred to questions as to where the traffic roads were going to go or how the mineral or petroleum exploitation was going to take place. However, the implementation of these activities stood not in question, because the mining or

---

[61] Rombouts (2014).

[62] Young (2020) and Cabrera (2017).

[63] See e.g. Doyle (2016) and Antkowiak (2013).

[64] See e.g. Inter-American Commission of Human Rights, *Saramaka People v. Suriname*, Case No 172, Judgment of 28 November 2007; Inter-American Court of Human Rights, *Sawhoyamaxa Indigenous Community v. Paraguay*, Judgment of 29 March 2006; Inter-American Court of Human Rights, *Xákmok Kásek Indigenous Community v. Paraguay*, Judgment of 24 August 2010; Inter-American Court of Human Rights, *Garífuna Triunfo de la Cruz and your members v. Honduras*, Judgment of 9 May 2019; Inter-American Court of Human Rights, *Comunity of Garífuna de Punta Piedra v. Honduras*, Judgment of 10 2015; Inter-American Court of Human Rights, *Indigenous Community de la Asociación Lhaka Honhat (nuestra tierra) v. Argentina*, Judgment of 2 June 2020.

petroleum policy was not in question. On the other hand, as an exercise of the right to participation, the peoples began to intervene from this stage, from the discussion of the mining and oil policies. In this way, the indigenous peoples must not only be consulted to decide, but the government must also guarantee that the peoples participate jointly with other authorities in the decision-making of these development policies and programs, that is the concrete measures for the execution of the development policies and programs.[65]

Lastly, one of the persisting obstacles leading to non-enforcement with the application of consultation surrounds the economic aspect of providing the tools to execute the norm, considering the location that most of the indigenous peoples live, to organize the meetings and to provide information, good faith and transparency in the process. Otherwise, the analysis of the data and the literature gave different indications, that, indeed, the non-enforcement with consultation not only has a legal aspect—of the inefficacy, not acting in accordance with the mandatory control of conventionality, the Brazilian Constitution, neither the binding international treaty—but also that the non-application of the norm entails severe economic damages. The data and literature show that the government is the one on the hook to pay-off involved parties in case the projects are prematurely shut down. This occurred in *Belo Monte* case,[66] the *Tapajós* case,[67] the *Polo Naval de Manaus* case,[68] and more recently, the *Ferrogão* case.[69]

Consequently, the economic damages of an improper application of the requirement of consultation are paid by the states using taxpayers' money. In the case of the Belo Monte, for instance, the construction work was budgeted at R$19 billion. Up to 80% of this amount was financed by the BNDES, although this still did not cover the total cost of the investment.[70]

In the Tapajós case, the results showed that the monetary value of socio-environmental damage amounts to R$334.49 million for the 100-year flow and R$439.34 million for an infinite flow of environmental capital exploitation. The payment in annual flow was estimated at R$28.18 million and the rest in a fixed amount. These resources might have enabled the implementation of a receivables fund to finance development projects for the local population.[71]

Most of the international financial institutions and transnational companies are far from being held liable for any of the damages.[72] The debate has been ongoing since the 1970s, as there have been numerous examples of events where companies have

[65] Farjado (2008).

[66] See e.g. Atkins (2017), Fearnside (2006), Hurwitz et al. (2011), and Hall and Branford (2012).

[67] Alarcon et al. (2016).

[68] Amazonas Atual (2018).

[69] Harari and Zanchetta (2018).

[70] Hall and Branford (2012).

[71] Santana et al. (2015).

[72] See e.g. Baxi (2016), Gilbert et al. (2009), Gedicks (2015), and Independent Evaluation Group World Bank (2016).

been accused of putting the local communities' cultural rights, self-determination and development rights at risk.[73] It is what has happened in Brazil where companies like Belo Sun, JBS, Cargil, Cosan S.A, Forbes & Manhattan, among others, have been found as non-compliant with the requirement of consultation with indigenous peoples when there were natural resource exploitation activities being undertaken in their territories.[74] While there is still a long way towards their legal prosecution, the United Nations have developed a new discursivity on the subject. The first draft of the documents was not binding, as in the Global Compact to the Draft Norms on the Responsibilities of Transnational Corporations and Other Business Enterprises with Regard to Human Rights; and the Guiding Principles on Business and Human Rights. Nowadays, there have been increasing discussions towards the elaboration of a legally binding international instrument framework.[75] Thus, the advancement of those legal instruments is essential, taking into account the fatal implications of these companies' activities as regards indigenous peoples' matters as revealed in the discussion of cases in Chaps. 3–5 of this book.

Relevant lessons can be taken from constitutional courts in other countries as analyzed in Chap. 5. Some courts have sought to strengthen the meaning of the right to consultation, such as the Plurinational Constitutional Court of Bolivia, which in addition recognized that 'the relationship between the state and indigenous communities must be on a level of equality, that is, it must be horizontal, between equals, and not vertical, where one party unilaterally orders and disposes of what is to be consulted'.[76]

The main goal of this chapter was to offer a possibility of presenting a theoretical alternative, amplifying the indigenous peoples' right to consultation grounded by the control of conventionality to guarantee efficacy of the right under Brazilian law.

References

Alarcon DF, Brent M, Mauricio T (eds) (2016) Ocekadi: hidrelétricas, conflitos socioambientais e resistência na bacia Tapajós. International Rivers/Universidade Federal do Oeste do Pará, Santarém/Brasília, DF

Alter KJ (2014) The new terrain of international law: courts, politics, rights. Princeton University Press, Princeton

Alter KJ, Helfer LR, Madsen MR (2015) How context shapes the authority of international courts. SSRN Electron J. https://doi.org/10.2139/ssrn.2574233

[73] High Commissioner for Human Rights (2008) Report of the Special Representative of the Secretary General on the Issue of Human Rights and Transnational Corporations and Other Business Enterprises.

[74] Association of Brazil's Indigenous Peoples (2020).

[75] Söderlund (2018).

[76] Constitutional Court of Bolivia, *Constitutional decision 0300*, 00157-2021-01-AIA, Judgment of 18 June 2012.

Alter KJ, Helfer LR, Madsen MR (eds) (2018) International court authority, 1st edn. Oxford University Press, Oxford

Amazonas Atual (2018) Justiça decide que polo naval em Manaus precisa de apoio de povos tradicionais

Anaya JS (2004) Indigenous peoples in international law, 2nd edn. Oxford University Press, New York

Antkowiak TM (2013) Rights, resources, and rhetoric: indigenous peoples and the Inter-American Court. Univ Pa J Int Law 2

Association of Brazil's Indigenous Peoples (2020) Complicity in destruction III: how global corporations enable violations of indigenous people's rights in the Brazilian Amazon

Atkins E (2017) The multi-dimensional framing of Brazil's Belo Monte dam: dammed and diversionary. Singap J Trop Geogr 38:276–292. https://doi.org/10.1111/sjtg.12206

Barroso R (2020) Curso de Direito Constitucional Contemporâneo. Saraivajur

Basta PC (2016) Avaliação da exposição ambiental ao mercúrio proveniente de atividade garimpeira de ouro na terra indígena Yanomami

Baxi U (2016) Human rights responsibility of multinational corporations, political ecology of injustice: learning from Bhopal thirty plus? Bus Hum Rights J 1:21–40. https://doi.org/10.1017/bhj.2015.7

Cabrera MV (2017) The requirement of consultation with indigenous peoples in the ILO between normative flexibility and institutional rigidity. Brill Nijhoff, Leiden

Canineu ML, Cavalho A (2020) A proposta de Bolsonaro para legalizar crimes contra povos indígenas. Hum Rights Watch

CIMI O (2017) Congresso anti-indígena: 33 propostas, reunindo mais de 100 projetos, ameaçam direitos indígenas

Davis SH (2002) Indigenous peoples, poverty and participatory development: the experience of the World Bank in Latin America. In: Sieder R (ed) Multiculturalism in Latin America. Palgrave Macmillan UK, London, pp 227–251

de Area Leão Pereira EJ, de Santana Ribeiro LC, da Silva Freitas LF, de Barros Pereira HB (2020) Brazilian policy and agribusiness damage the Amazon rainforest. Land Use Policy 92:104491. https://doi.org/10.1016/j.landusepol.2020.104491

Devereux A (1995) Should 'Duties' play a larger role in human rights? - A critique of western liberal and African human rights jurisprudence. Univ New South Wales Law J 18

Donoso G (2010) Inter-American Court of Human Rights' reparation judgments. Strengths and challenges for a comprehensive approach. Rev IIDH 49

Doyle CM (2016) Indigenous peoples, title to territory, rights and resources - the transformative role of the free prior and informed consent. Routledge, New York

Duprat D (ed) (2015) Audiência pública, oitiva constitucional e consulta prévia: limites e aproximações. In: Convenção n. 169 da OIT e os Estados Nacionais. ESMPU, Brasília, DF

Farjado RY (2008) Tomando en serio y superando el derecho de consulta previa: el consentimiento y la participación. V Congr Red Latinoam Antropol Juríd

Fearnside PM (2006) Dams in the Amazon: Belo Monte and Brazil's hydroelectric development of the Xingu River Basin. Environ Manage 38:16–27. https://doi.org/10.1007/s00267-005-0113-6

Garavito CR (2012). Etnicidad.gov: Los recursos naturales, los pueblos indígenas y derecho a la consulta previa en los campos minados. Centro de Estudos de Derecho, Justicia y Sociedad, Bogotá

Gedicks A (2015) Transnational mining corporations, the environment, and indigenous communities. Brown J World Aff 22

Gilbert J, Tugendhat H, Couillard V, Doyle C (2009) Business, human rights and indigenous peoples: the right to free, prior and informed consent. SSRN Electron J. https://doi.org/10.2139/ssrn.1403985

Hall A, Branford S (2012) Development, dams and Dilma: the Saga of Belo Monte. Crit Sociol 38: 851–862. https://doi.org/10.1177/0896920512440712

Harari I, Zanchetta I (2018) Governo admite que custos socioambientais da Ferrogrão vão sobrar para os brasileiros. Inst Socioambiental

Hurwitz Z, Millikan B, Monteiro T, Widmer R (eds) (2011) Mega Projeto, mega riscos: Análise de Riscos para Investidores no Complexo Hidrelétrico Belo Monte, 1ª. International Rivers-Amigos da Terra - Amazônia Brasileira

Independent Evaluation Group World Bank (2016) Lessons from environmental policy lending

Instituto Socioambiental (2018) Povos indígenas isolados são ameaçados por 123 obras na Amazônia. ISA

Ioca L (2019) Conhecimentos tradicionais, patrimônio imaterial e repartição justa dos benefícios: uma análise dos sistemas de proteção no contexto Latino-Americano. Insur Rev Direitos E Mov Sociais. https://doi.org/10.26512/insurgencia.v5i1.28893

Jaichand V, Sampaio AA (2013) Dam and be damned: the adverse impacts of Belo Monte on indigenous peoples in Brazil. Hum Rights Q 35:408–447. https://doi.org/10.1353/hrq.2013.0023

Kirmser JRT (2014) Diálogo Jurisprudencial entre la Justicia Nacional y las Cortes Internacionales. Rev Juríd Fac Derecho Cienc Soc Univ Nac Asunción

Koivurova T (2011) Jurisprudence of the European Court of Human Rights regarding indigenous peoples: retrospect and prospects. Int J Minor Group Rights 18

Liebenthal A, Michelitsch R, Tarazona EI (2005) Extractive industries and sustainable development: an evaluation of the World Bank Group experience. World Bank/International Finance Corp./Multilateral Investment Guarantee Agency, Washington, DC

Luís Castilho A et al (2020) Candidatos acumulam terras públicas e práticas violentas no campo. El País

Lupion B (2020) Número de indígenas eleitos para cargos municipais cresce 28%. Dtsch. Welle

Mac-Gregor EF (2013) Eficacia de la sentencia interamericana y la cosa juzgada internacional: vinculación directa hacia las partes (res judicata) e indirecta hacia los Estados parte de la Convención Americana (res interpretata). Estud Const 11

Mac-Gregor EF (2015) Conventionality control the new doctrine of the Inter-American Court of Human Rights. AJIL Unbound 109:93–99. https://doi.org/10.1017/S2398772300001240

Mazzuoli VO (2011) The Inter-American Human Rights protection system: structure, functioning and effectiveness in Brazilian law. Afr Hum Rights J 11

Mendes Junior J (1912) Os indigenas do Brasil: seus direitos, individuais e politicos. Hennies Irmãos, São Paulo

Mera MEG (2015) Judicialização da discriminação estrutural contra povos indígenas e afrodescendentes na América Latina: conceptualização e tipologia de um diálogo interamericano/Juridicalization of structural discrimination against indigenous peoples and afro... Rev QUAESTIO IURIS 8. https://doi.org/10.12957/rqi.2015.16908

Monteiro de Matos M (2018) Individual and collective aspects of property rights in the Inter-American System for the protection of Human Rights: tribal and indigenous lands. Doctor in Law, Göttingen University

Morris M, Rodríguez Garavito C, Salinas NO, Buriticá P (2010) La consulta previa a pueblos indígenas: los estándares del derecho internacional. Programa de Justiça Global y Derechos Humanos, Colombia

Navarro GCB (2021) Measuring the effectiveness of the Inter-American System of Human Rights: the case of indigenous territorial rights. Dissertation, Goethe-Universität Frankfurt, Frankfurt am Main

Piovesan F (2018) Direitos humanos e o direito constitucional internacional

Rangel LH (2018) Violência contra os Povos Indígenas no Brasil – Dados de 2018

Rech D (ed) (2007) Direitos humanos no Brasil 2: diagnóstico e perspectivas, 1a. ed. CERIS/Mauad/Misereor, Rio de Janeiro

Ribotta S (2012) Reglas de Brasilia sobre Acceso a la Justicia de las Personas en Condición de Vulnerabilidad. Vulnerabilidad, pobreza y acceso a la justicia. Rev Electrónica Iberoam 6

Rombouts SJ (2014) Having a say: indigenous peoples, international law and free, prior and informed consent. Wolf Legal Publishers, Oisterwijk

Santana A, Santana A, Santana A et al (2015) Valoração dos danos ambientais causados por hidrelétricas para a produção de energia na bacia do Tapajós. Reflexões Econômicas 1

Sauer S (2019) Rural Brazil during the Lula administrations: agreements with agribusiness and disputes in agrarian policies. Lat Am Perspect 46:103–121. https://doi.org/10.1177/0094582X16685176

Scherer G (2020) Catastrophic Amazon tipping point less than 30 years away: study. Mongabay

Simionatto I, Costa CR (2012) Como os dominantes dominam: o caso da bancada ruralista. Rev Temporalis 12

Söderlund E (2018) Transnational corporations and human rights: assessing the position of TNCs within international human rights law, and the appropriateness of an international treaty on business and human rights. Dissertation, Uppsala University

Souza O et al (2020) Urnas demarcadas: Brasil elege maior número de candidatos indígenas na história da democracia. Inst. Socioambiental

The Guardian (2020) Brazil's Bolsonaro unveils bill to allow commercial mining on indigenous land

Tribunal Superior Eleitoral (2019) Candidatos indígenas aumentam participação em eleições nacionais. TSE

von Bogdandy A, Venzke I (2016) In whose name? A public law theory of international adjudication, First published in paperback. Oxford University Press, Oxford

Walker RT, Simmons C, Arima E et al (2019) Avoiding Amazonian catastrophes: prospects for conservation in the 21st century. One Earth 1:202–215. https://doi.org/10.1016/j.oneear.2019.09.009

Yamada EM (2011) Quem ganha com conflitos não resolvidos? In: Ricardo CA (ed) Povos Indígenas no Brasil 2006-2010. Instituto Socioambiental, São Paulo

Young S (2020) Indigenous peoples, consent and rights: troubling subjects. Routledge, an imprint of the Taylor & Francis Group, Abingdon

Chapter 7
Conclusion

The present research conducted a reappraisal of the efficacy of consultation with indigenous peoples living in rural and urban areas, as set out by the Inter-American System of Human Rights and international law, and its application in Brazil.

The relevant international treaties are characterized by a dispersed definition, interpretation and applicability of consultation, which often provoke legal uncertainty over the adequate application of the requirement of consultation. The analysis encourages appropriate solutions for Brazil to overcome these legal problems. In order to build an adequate consultation aimed at redressing processes in which indigenous peoples have been marginalized, the administrative and legislative measures directed at them must consider the multi-dimensional perspective of self-determination and cultural rights.

Efficacy in this work is understood as the degree to which the jurisprudence of the Inter-American Court of Human Rights is applied and enforced in the national legal system, taking into account the judicial rulings, legislation and the indigenous peoples' Protocols. It is thereby closely related to control of conventionality, which is defined as the requirement for ratifying states to interpret domestic law in accordance with an internationally agreed obligation.

The inquiry aimed to examine the following overarching research question: What constitutes the efficacy of consultation with indigenous peoples in Brazil? In order to derive pointed responses, the main question was separated into three specific sub-questions: (1) Has Brazil applied consultation with indigenous peoples as required by the Inter-American Court of Human Rights? (2) Has the framework of international law contributed to the efficacy of consultation with indigenous peoples in Brazil? (3) Has the implementation of self-determination and cultural rights strengthened the efficacy of consultation with indigenous peoples in Brazil?

To address these questions, the study analyzed a large set of literature, jurisprudence, international treaties, official data and online interviews of chosen experts. As most of the documents were only available in Spanish and Portuguese, they were translated into English by the author for the purposes of this original analysis.

C. Woyames Dreher, *A Legal Assessment of the Efficacy of Consultation with Indigenous Peoples*, https://doi.org/10.1007/978-3-031-50539-3_7

For responding to the research questions, this study assessed the efficacy of consultation in Brazil against the international treaties of the Indigenous and Tribal Peoples Convention No. 169, the American Convention, the United Nations Declaration of Rights of Indigenous Peoples, the Vienna Convention of Law of Treaties and the American Declaration of Indigenous Peoples together with the control of conventionality and the *pro personae* principle, as well as the Brazilian Constitution of 1988, mentioned in all chapters of this work.

As previously addressed in Chap. 2 and Chap. 4 of the work, the Brazilian judiciary interprets the human rights standards in accordance with the Federal Constitution of 1988 and international treaties. The interpretation of the Constitution provides the indigenous peoples, in theory, with the most comprehensive protection as entailed in the jurisprudential understanding of collective rights. The control of conventionality understands national legal systems and international human rights law as interconnected and interdependent systems that enable the use of legal instruments existing in Brazilian law to ensure respect for and the application of the decisions of the Inter-American Court of Human Rights, the international treaties, and at the domestic level the Brazilian Constitution of 1988.

Therefore, part of the Brazilian Federal Courts and the Prosecutor's Office contributed to the leading interpretation. At the same time, the higher courts and the members of the Brazilian legislature have indeed proven far from aligned with the prerequisites of consultation as laid out in international standards in their congressional activities.

So far, the evidence of the research indicates a multi-speed process: there are national courts that are at the forefront in producing normative standards beyond the internationally established minimum and participate more fluidly in dialogue with the Inter-American Court. In notable contrast, there are other national courts that have refrained from citing decisions from foreign courts, or when they do, they are usually monologues with a merely rhetorical purpose (for example, to reinforce an argument with a foreign judgment that employed similar reasoning, ignoring other alternatives in comparative law) and with very limited impact on the final resolution. There are also national constitutional courts that rarely cite the Inter-American Court of Human Rights and maintain antiquated judicial practices, focused on national positive law and impervious to the dynamics of international law.

Furthermore, as also indicated in the research, the indigenous peoples' normative standards were achieved despite continuous attacks against the Inter-American System of Human Rights, the budgetary limitations of the organs of the system, the weaknesses of Latin American judicial systems and the difficult socio-political conditions under which the law operates in the region. The difficulties encountered are an indicator of the discursive authority that the Inter-American Court of Human Rights has gained since its implementation until nowadays as is the potential for dialogue among the national courts of the members of the Inter-American system as a collective search for solutions to the enormous challenges and specific needs of societies marked by exclusion and inequality.

Against the possible backlash of not being aligned with American and extra-American implementations, in Brazil the Federal Courts assume a relevant role in reviewing the legality and to ensure the rule of law. In this scenario, the control of conventionality appears as mandatory according to the international law in general, as the best possibility to deal with technicalities of application and enforcement with the treaties as well as regarding the efficacy of decisions.

Due to the plurality of the society and the delay of the higher courts of the Brazilian judiciary to incorporate the mandatory control of conventionality, the efficacy of consultation is in question. However, the analyses of the legal claims provided evidence for the continuous efforts of federal judges, indigenous peoples themselves, non-profit organizations and the Federal Prosecutors' Office to fight against the non-enforcement of the norm. The efficacy of the norm has been detected in all cases explored in this work; not by the acceptance of the state or the transnational companies to conduct the consultation, but by attesting that Brazil, composed by different spheres of checks and balances, had proven to still pursue the legal solution.

Thus, following question 1, has Brazil applied consultation with indigenous peoples as required by the Inter-American Court of Human Rights?

In accordance with the Inter-American Court of Human Rights, consultation must be carried out while taking into account good faith, adequate and accessible consultation and conducting the environmental impact study. Bringing these three concepts together reveals the architecture of execution of the requirement of consultation. Nevertheless, the analyses in Chaps. 3 and 5 showed that the right to consultation originated from the expanded interpretation of Article 21 of the American Convention on property rights. The limited protection given by this interpretation was mentioned in Chaps. 3 and 4. In Chap. 3, it was shown that the jurisprudence of the Inter-American Court of Human Rights missed the opportunity to join the interpretations of the United Nations Declaration of Indigenous Peoples Rights and the American Declaration of Indigenous Peoples Rights. The result is an interpretation of consultation lacking the inclusion of the aspect of consent. Chapter 4 however revealed, in the analysis of legal claims in Brazilian courts and legislative measures, that the promotion of a lower level of protection was still possible.

In conclusion, Brazil has only partially applied the requirement of consultation. Despite certain setbacks examined, a sensible approach has been adopted by the Prosecutor's Office and the Federal Courts which balance those institutions that constantly violate the requirement. In a nutshell, as mentioned in Chap. 3, the Inter-American Court of Human Rights is bound by its mandate and cases must thus be tried accordingly to this format. In Chap. 4 it was discussed that Brazil has a range of implementation issues, which have been translated into efforts by the Federal Courts based on the Prosecutor's Office claims to comply with the control of conventionality. And those have indeed proved responsible for offering opportunities for indigenous peoples to participate in order to address violations.

As shown in Chap. 6, however, there is still the need that the Inter-American Court of Human Rights amplifies the right to consultation to become the core of indigenous peoples' means to participation, providing tools for their self-determination and cultural rights according to binding international treaties.

As regards question 2, has the framework of international law contributed to the efficacy of consultation with indigenous peoples in Brazil?

As seen in Chap. 2, in the international arena, the debate advanced not only on the efficacy of consultation, but also on the aspects that it should entail free, prior and informed consent, based on self-determination, which shall lead to a mutual agreement among stakeholders and a possible veto for indigenous peoples.

Hence, the Brazilian enforcement with the requirement of consultation faces severe hindrances to its forthcoming application. The detailed data analysis shows the constant lack of enforcement with consultation, undermining the efficacy of consultation by leading to systemic forms of restrictive interpretations of the obligation for the Brazilian judiciary and legislature.

As discussed in Chaps. 3 and 6, the appropriate institutional arrangement for the right to consultation to achieve its potential relies on the obligation of the Inter-American Court to adopt a more complete interpretation of consultation, providing the definition in accordance with international standards. The interpretation of self-determination and cultural rights as a way to achieve consultation offers the corpus iures of international law that was once provided by the Inter-American Court of Human Rights.

In sum, the interpretation of the international legal treaties has changed the jurisprudence of part of the federal jurisprudence, however, in order to have the enforcement of the higher courts, there is the need for the expressed accordance—and not to only omit the debate—with international treaties and United Nations official data.

Finally, on question 3, has the implementation of self-determination and cultural rights strengthened the efficacy of consultation with indigenous peoples in Brazil?

As noted in the chapters regarding the application of consultation, self-determination and cultural rights were only achievable after the discussion of territorial rights. The meaningful application of those rights is the reason why there was consideration of the definitions and the jurisprudence of the Inter-American Court of Human Rights.

The book has argued that the requirement of consultation has reached a tipping point, as there is an increasing contestation of its legitimacy in view of continued inefficacy. Due to the recent developments of the interpretation of Article 21 of the American Convention considering the advance of the Inter-American Court of Human Rights and the Free, Prior and Informed Consent discussions, the efficacy of the norm has been more starkly compromised.

The efficacy of the norm can only be ensured when there is comprehensive application. As noted in the comparisons in Chap. 4, as regards the Brazilian legal claims and draft legislative acts, and Chap. 5, considering the application in some countries of the region and the African Human Rights System, consultation processes that have been established under the national regulatory regime have the capacity to accommodate all indigenous peoples.

As pointed out in Chap. 3, it would benefit indigenous peoples the most if consultation would have been recognized as a derivation of consent. The Inter-American Court of Human Rights still may take the lead and redefine consultation as it was once decided in the Saramaka case. The consent was an elaboration of the definition in cases of projects of great impact, in matters that affect all indigenous peoples involved. However, the Inter-American Court of Human Rights took a step back and interpreted consultation as relevant in projects that affect the property only. The position that the Inter-American Court of Human Rights has taken is contrary to international standards and weakened the Inter-American System of Human Rights a whole, having an impact on the Brazilian state as well.

As was learned in Chaps. 2, 5 and 6, this flawed reasoning led to the application of lenient procedural elements in which the Inter-American Court of Human Rights has yet to pronounce any requirements towards self-determination and cultural rights as a means to guarantee the application of the right. Cultural rights are a way for the indigenous to explore their natural resources and self-determination as the freedom to dispose of their resources, a possible means to ensure the efficacy of the international standard of consultation. The interpretation proposed guarantees that the indigenous peoples' Protocols, an aspect of their self-determination, can become a matter in future judicial cases to provide legitimacy to the expectation of the role of consultation. Furthermore, the American Declaration on Indigenous Peoples Rights is also a relevant international treaty and must be implemented in the decisions of the Inter-American Court of Human Rights in order to strengthen the realization of the requirement of consultation.

MIX
Papier aus verantwortungsvollen Quellen
Paper from responsible sources
FSC® C105338

If you have any concerns about our products,
you can contact us on
ProductSafety@springernature.com

In case Publisher is established outside the EU,
the EU authorized representative is:
Springer Nature Customer Service Center GmbH
Europaplatz 3, 69115 Heidelberg, Germany

Printed by Libri Plureos GmbH
in Hamburg, Germany